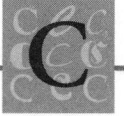

Advanced C

Advanced C

Peter D. Hipson

A Division of Prentice Hall Computer Publishing
11711 North College, Carmel, Indiana 46032 USA

Trademarks

All terms mentioned in this book that are known to be trademarks or service marks have been appropriately capitalized. Sams Publishing cannot attest to the accuracy of this information. Use of a term in this book should not be regarded as affecting the validity of any trademark or service mark.

About the Author

Peter Hipson and his wife live and work in New Hampshire. He has worked with computers since 1972, in hardware design and software development. He has developed numerous software programs for both PCs and larger systems. He holds patents in the field of CPU design and has been involved with microcomputers since their inception. Peter is the developer of the Windows applications STARmanager and STARmanager A/E.

You can contact Peter Hipson at P.O. Box 28, West Peterborough, NH, 03468. Enclosing an SASE greatly enhances the likelihood of a reply.

To Bianca, who has shown me what great fun it is having a granddaughter.

Overview

Contents

Acknowledgments

I would like to offer my thanks to the following organizations and people for their support, help, guidance, and enthusiasm.

The Sams editorial and production staff, especially Gregory Croy, Stacy Hiquet, Susan Pink, Mary Corder, and Rebecca Whitney, all who put enormous effort into making this a good book. I would also like to thank Timothy C. Moore, who did the technical editing.

Borland International Inc., Microsoft Corporation, and Watcom Products, Inc., have provided valuable support and assistance.

Thanks to William Colley, III, and the C User's Group, for the Highly Portable Utilities (CUG-236) files that are included on the sample source diskette.

Eric Jackson ("Eric in the Evening") and public radio station WGBH for providing all the jazz.

Thank you all.

Introduction

C has become one of the most frequently used computer languages. The first C language was developed by Dennis Ritchie at Bell Laboratories in 1972 and ran on a DEC PDP-11. The ANSI standard for C, which replaced the standard written by Kernighan and Ritchie in 1978, is only a few years old.

C's structure is similar to PL/I (a popular language used on IBM's mainframe computers), FORTRAN, Pascal, and BASIC. C is a simple language. It has only a small group of keywords and no support for I/O or advanced math. The power of C comes from its simplicity and its use of a standard library of functions.

Who Should Read This Book?

Advanced C is for the programmer who has some experience writing applications in C or a similar language, such as PL/I or Pascal. Regardless of whether you are an intermediate or experienced programmer, this book is intended to improve your skills as easily as possible.

What Is in This Book?

This book has several purposes. First, it introduces advanced parts of the C language. It also describes changes in the ANSI standard, which is the only true definition of the C language. In addition, the book contains much of what I have learned (often the hard way) about C programming.

Advanced C is divided into five parts, and each part can be used by itself. Part I gets you started and lays the groundwork for the rest of the book. In Part II, you learn how to manage data and files when programming in C. Part III introduces integrating C with other languages and interfacing with other environments such as database programs. Part IV is a reference section that covers the header files, the intrinsic functions, the preprocessor, and some performance and debugging techniques. Part V (the appendixes) contains an ASCII table, information about different compilers, an introduction to C++, and a cross-reference of functions and their header files.

Many chapters contain example programs. In some chapters, a single example program is used to demonstrate several topics in the chapter.

For a platform to develop C software, I recommend at least a 386/25, and preferably a 386/33 or 486. A 286 will do, but most linkers and some compilers are noticeably slower when you do not have a fast CPU. I suggest that you have at least a 100M hard disk. The compiler I use most frequently is QuickC for Windows. It is powerful and easy to use (because it has an integrated debugging environment), and supports both ANSI C and Microsoft's extensions.

Conventions Used in This Book

I used the following conventions in the book:

- All program listings and code fragments are in monospace.

- All function names are in monospace.

- ANSI C keywords are in monospace.

- All function names appearing in text (not in the code) are followed by an empty set of parentheses, for example, sprintf().

- Something that must be substituted (such as a filename or a value) is in *monospace italic*.

- When a listing title shows a filename in uppercase, that file is usually found on the sample diskette. If a filename is not given or it is in lowercase, then it is not a separate source file on the diskette, but probably part of another file on the sample diskette. The text usually indicates which file the code fragment is from.

A Note on Practicing C

You can read, attend lectures, or discuss a subject, but as the saying goes, "practice makes perfect."

Do not be afraid to practice with the programs in this book. But practice does not mean copying a program from the diskette, compiling it, and running it. Change the example programs. Make them do things they weren't intended to do and learn from your mistakes. Make backups often and program away. Because C is a powerful language and many of us are programming on PCs using DOS (which has very poor memory protection), be careful; it is easy to trash the disk.

Good luck improving your C programming skills, have fun writing your software, and remember Peter's rule: Back up your disk frequently!

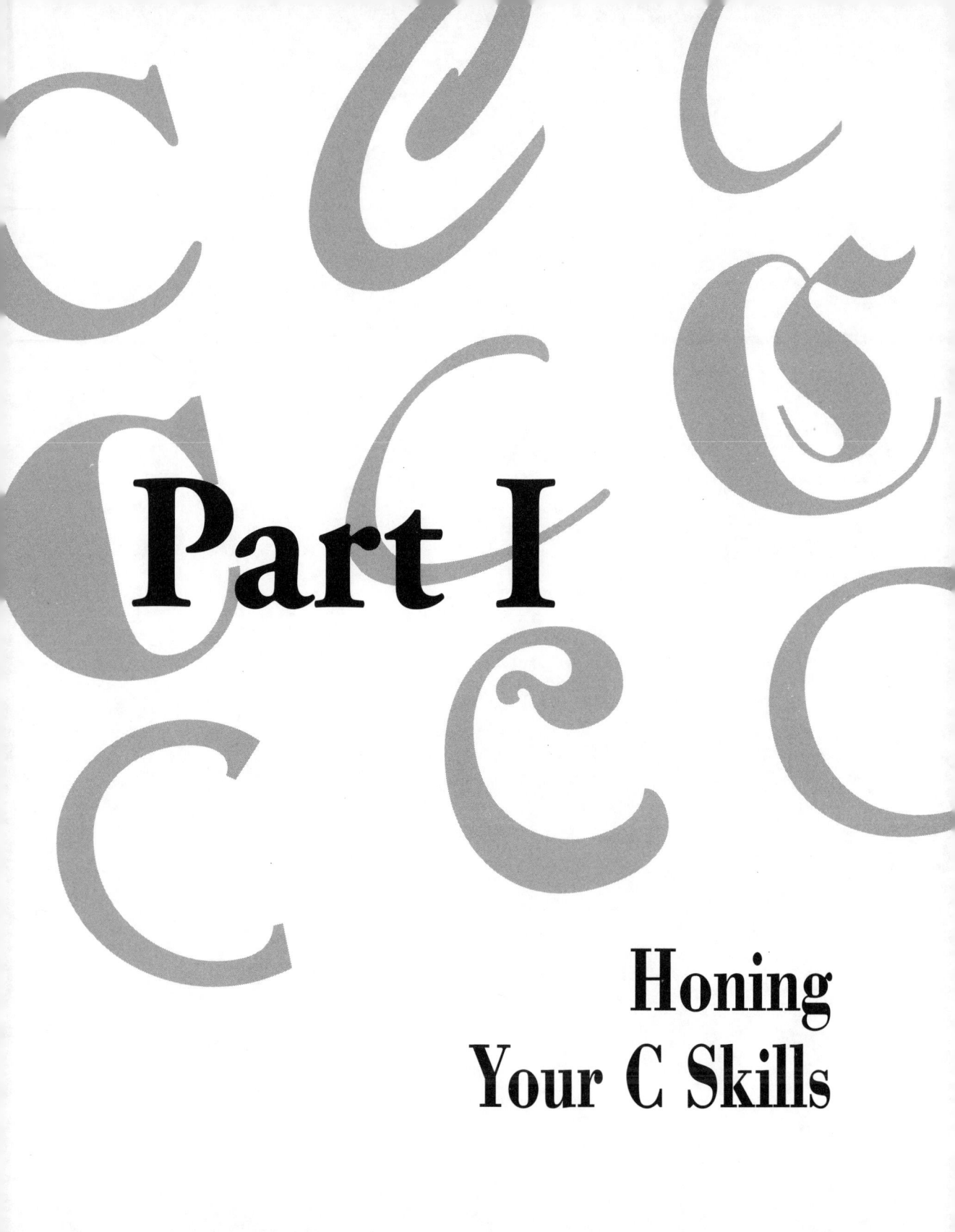

Part I

Honing
Your C Skills

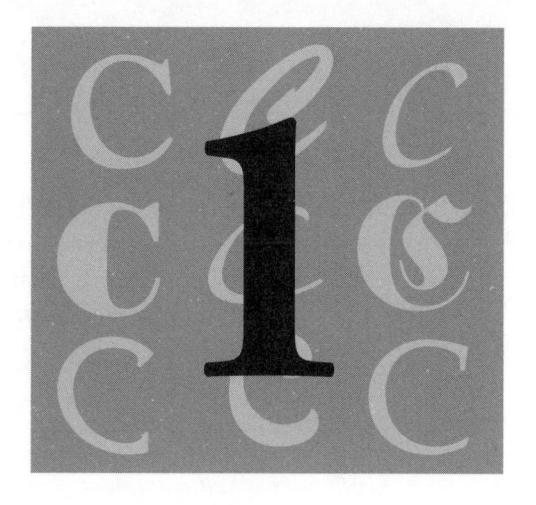

The C Philosophy

C probably wasn't your first computer language. Mine was FORTRAN, and many other people began their study of computer language with either BASIC or PASCAL. No matter which language was your first, you probably will spend much time programming in C from now on. This chapter covers a number of introductory topics.

A Brief History of C and the Standard

Until the past few years, no absolute standard for the C language existed. *The C Programming Language*, by Kernighan and Ritchie, served as a standard, but most compiler manufacturers added extensions and did not follow all the specifications presented by Kernighan and Ritchie. As C became one of the most popular computer languages for programming small computers, the need for a true standard became apparent.

The American National Standards Institute (ANSI) produced standards that help keep each of the compilers working in the same manner. These standards, which are very exacting, spell out exactly what the language should do and what should not happen. Specified limits and definitions exist also.

C is an interesting language. Because its syntax is simple, it's not the most powerful language, and it has only a few operations. Most of C's power comes from these attributes:

- *C can address and manipulate memory by direct address.* A program can obtain the memory address of any object (both data objects and functions) and manipulate without restriction the contents of the memory specified by the address. This capability is good to have because it allows flexibility. However, you have no protection from the program overwriting critical parts of the operating system when you are programming a PC using DOS.

- *C has a powerful library of functions.* This library of functions enables program-mers to perform I/O, work with strings (which are arrays of characters), and perform many other tasks.

There is a lot of talk (much I consider to be blown out of proportion) about portability. Generally, for each program, you should consider whether it is likely to be needed on a different system, and how much effort must be dedicated to planning the move to a future system. Some C programming is never portable. Programs written for Microsoft Windows, for example, don't move well to the Apple Macintosh or IBM's OS/2 Presentation Manager (a system much like Windows). The decision to maintain portability is one that you must make—sometimes the effort to maintain portability far exceeds what is required if later parts of the program must be rewritten.

The ANSI standard specified a number of language limits (see Table 1.1). Many of these limits are really compiler limits; however, because they affect the language, you sometimes must take them into consideration. These limits are not usually a problem; in the ten years that I've been writing C programs, I've run into problems with these limits only once or twice.

Table 1.1. ANSI compiler minimums.

Minimum	Item
6	Significant characters in an external name
8	`#include` nesting
8	`#if`, `#ifndef`, `#ifdef` and `#elif`
1	`()`, `[]`, or `*` in a declaration
15	Nested compound statements
15	Levels of `struct` or `union` nesting
31	`()` declarators within a declaration
31	Significant characters in a macro or identifier
31	Parameters passed to a function or macro (important for `printf()`, `scanf()`, and so on)
32	Levels of nested parentheses
127	Local identifiers in a block
127	Members in a single `struct`, `union` or `enum`
257	`case` statements in a `switch()` statement
509	Characters in a literal string (after any concatenation)
511	External identifiers in a single source file
1024	Simultaneously defined macros
32767	Bytes in a single data object

Of course, nothing prevents a compiler producer from extending these limits; however, you should review the documentation supplied with your compiler to see whether any (or all) limits are different from the ANSI standard. If your compiler does extend these limits and you use the extensions, you can be sure that when your program is compiled with another compiler, it will either not compile correctly or not execute correctly.

Some of these limits will change (soon, I hope) with future revisions of the ANSI specification. One of the most bothersome limits, six significant characters in an external name, was issued because some linkers cannot use more than the first six characters in an external name. As noted by the ANSI standards committee, this limit is a rather poor one and probably will change soon. If your compiler doesn't have a published limit on the number of significant characters in an external name, you can test it. Compile and link the programs shown in Listing 1.1 (it has two source files). As noted in the listing, changing the names of the functions called (and the missing one) can be used to indicate the number of characters that are significant (13 in this example) in an external name.

Listing 1.1. External name lengths for FILEONE.C and FILETWO.C.

```
FILEONE.C

void    sixchr1234567(void);
void    sixchr1234567(void);

int    main()
{
    sixchr1234567();
    sixchr12345678();   /* Will be unresolved external if more than */
                        /* 13 characters are significant. */
}

FILETWO.C

void    sixchr1234567()
{
    return;
}
```

Another significant factor in external names is that most linkers *ignore* case. You should be very careful, therefore, not to have two functions that differ only in the case of their names, such as in the following example (in which both functions are external):

```
OurPrinter();  /* Print, using initial caps. */
OURPRINTER();  /* Print, using all caps. */
ourprinter();  /* Print, using only lowercase. */
```

In this fragment, the three different names will be linked to the same function by the linker. Some linkers have the option to retain case, which solves this problem, but many don't. Be careful: I got burned by this one once, and it took a long time to determine why the wrong function was being called. (I didn't know about the other, different-case function).

A number of keywords are reserved in ANSI C (see Table 1.2). You must be careful not to use these names (all of the ANSI keywords are in lowercase) as identifiers in your program. Generally, the compiler "complains" when you incorrectly use any reserved keyword.

Table 1.2. ANSI C reserved identifiers.

Keyword	Usage
asm	Begins assembly code and is not part of the ANSI standard.
FORTRAN	The entry follows FORTRAN calling conventions; FORTRAN may be in lowercase for some implementations and is not part of the ANSI standard.
PASCAL	The entry follows PASCAL calling conventions; PASCAL may be in lowercase for some implementations and is not part of the ANSI standard. Generally, the PASCAL conventions are identical to FORTRAN's.
const	The variable will be used as a constant and will not be modified.
volatile	The compiler may make no assumptions about whether the variable's value is current. This keyword limits optimization, and possibly slows program execution.
signed	The variable is a signed integer (with the actual size unspecified).
auto	The variable is created when the function is called, and is discarded when the function exits. An auto variable is not initialized by the compiler.

continues

Table 1.2. continued

Keyword	Usage
break	Ends the enclosing do(), for(), switch()/case or while() statement and is used most often to end a case statement. Using break outside of a switch()/case block may be considered to be unstructured programming, in the same way that embedded return statements are considered by some programmers.
case	Used with the switch() statement to mark the beginning of a group of statements that are executed when the case's value matches the switch() statement's value. Execution continues until a break statement is encountered or no more statements are in the switch() statements.
char	A character variable that may be either signed or unsigned.
continue	Passes control to the next iteration of a do(), for(), or while() statement.
default	Used with a switch() statement, the statements following the default statement are executed until the first break statement if no case statement value matches the switch() statement's expression.
do	Used with the while() statement, the statement or statements between the do and the closing while() are executed until the while() condition evaluates to false. The statements between are executed at least one time.
double	An eight-byte floating point variable.
else	Used with the if() statement, the statement or statements within the else block are executed if the if() expression evaluates to false.
enum	An integer defining a range of values. The actual internal representation of the value is not significant.
extern	The object is defined in a different source file.
float	A four-byte floating point variable.

Keyword	Usage
for	The iterative loop statement for C. Enables one (or more) identifiers to be initialized, tested, and modified.
goto	Causes an unconditional branch (change flow of execution). (Many programmers consider using goto to be one step short of sacrilege).
if	Causes execution of a block of statements depending on the logical evaluation of the if() statement's expression.
int	The object is defined as an integer (with a default size dependent on the CPU's default integer size.
long	The object is defined as a long (four-byte) integer.
register	The object (usually an integer) is retained in one of the CPU's registers whenever possible. The compiler often is forced to remove the variable from the register to perform various other tasks, however. This keyword can help speed program execution when a variable must be accessed frequently.
return	Causes a function to return to its caller. Most programmers insist that there be only one return statement at the end of a function. The return statement may specify a value to be returned to the caller if the called function was defined as returning a value.
short	A two-byte integer.
sizeof	Returns the size of a specified data object, which can be a simple data type, structure, union, or other complex data object.
static	A data object created when the program is linked and initialized (to zero), and retains its value throughout the program's execution. The opposite of an auto variable.
struct	Used to define or declare a complex data type, which can consist of a number of different data types.

continues

Table 1.2. continued

Keyword	Usage
switch	Used with an expression (that must yield either a long or short integer), which used with the case statement, allows for conditional execution of code based on the current value of the expression.
typedef	Allows creation of a specific data type that is not part of C's provided data types. Usually (but not always) used with either struct or union to create complex data types.
union	Creates a complex data type in which two or more variables occupy the same data memory at the same time. Often used to enable the reading of different types of records into a common buffer, which then can be referred to with the correct type variables.
unsigned	An unsigned integer (either long or short) always can contain only positive values.
void	Defines a function that either doesn't return a value or has no parameters, or defines a pointer to a variable of an unspecified type. An object pointed to by a void pointer cannot be directly modified.
while	Used either alone or with the do statement to conditionally execute statements until the while()'s conditional statement evaluates as false.

Even with the ANSI set of reserved keywords, you can generally expect that a specific compiler may reserve, as necessary, other words as well. A number of keywords are reserved also for library names, for example. Table 1.3 lists these reserved names.

Table 1.3. ANSI C reserved names.

Name	Usage
%	Used in a printf()/scanf() format string; to create a literal percent sign, use %%

Name	Usage
is... or to...	Lowercase function names beginning with either is or to, where the next character also is a lowercase letter
str..., mem..., or wcs...	Lowercase function names beginning with either str, mem, or wcs, where the next character also is a lowercase letter
E	Macros that begin with an uppercase E
SIG... or SIG_...	Macros that begin with either an uppercase SIG or SIG_
...f or ...l	Existing math library names with a trailing f or l
LC_	Macros that begin with an uppercase LC_

As you can see from Table 1.3, there are a number of reserved prefixes and postfixes; it isn't difficult, however, to find a suitable name, because all these reserved names are either all uppercase or all lowercase—just using mixed-case names should enable you to avoid conflicts with the reserved names in ANSI C (remember that some linkers ignore case).

A Programming Style

I know that at least half of all C programmers use a formatting style different from the one I'm going to propose. I can't resist, however—I've used this style for years (longer even than I've programmed in C), and I can (and will) justify why you should consider using it.

Let's look at the style in which all the example code in this book is presented. The following list shows a few simple rules.

1. Each tab stop is indented four characters.

2. Lines should be a maximum of 80 characters if at all possible.

3. Comments can use either the ANSI standard /* comment */ or the newer // single line comment (supported by many compilers even though it's not part of the ANSI standard).

4. When variables are defined or declared, only one variable is allowed per definition or declaration.

5. All functions are prototyped, either in the header include file, or if there is none, at the top of the file.

6. All data objects (variables) use Hungarian notation (see Table 1.4) and are mixed case.

7. All function names are mixed case and should be descriptive of what the function does. If the return is not clear, use Hungarian notation for the function name.

8. Opening and closing braces are on their own lines, aligned in the same column. In either case, a comment (one or more lines) may be used to describe what the particular block of code is doing.

9. Document *why*, not what, you are doing. For example, you always can see that you are incrementing the variable, but you can't always see why you had to increment it. Comments are just notes to yourself (and perhaps others) reminding you of what you did. It's almost painful to go back to a complex piece of code and find that you no longer understand it. It's easier to rewrite poorly documented code than to try to figure it out.

10. Use blank lines wherever necessary to make the code readable.

11. Use the variables i, j, k, l, m, and n as for() loop indexes, and use them in order. Using this rule saves many hours of trying to figure out which index is changing faster. *Avoid using these variables for scratch variables.*

12. Avoid "cute" code. You may think that it makes you look like you're the world's greatest programmer; however, you will have unreadable source code that is difficult to maintain. If you must create a relatively strange piece of code, don't forget to document what it's doing and why you needed to create it. Don't make yourself have to go back and ask, "Why did I do that?" when you might realize that there was an easier way to get the job done.

13. Use parentheses liberally. When in doubt, use them. Then you can be sure in what order things will be done.

14. Use the "new"-style function headers. This style, as shown in the code fragment later in this section, is much easier to read because the variables and their types and order are clearly defined. The fact that you can't assume that the old style will remain in future releases of the standard is a good incentive to switch.

Hungarian notation prefixes a variable name with a letter or letters to tell the programmer what data type the variable contains (see Table 1.4). This type of notation is very helpful when you must maintain the program later. Hungarian notation helps to prevent assigning the wrong data type to a variable, and helps you understand why you are using a particular data object.

Table 1.4. Hungarian notation prefixes.

Prefix	Description
c	char
by	BYTE (unsigned char)
n	short int
x	Usually a short int, used for x coordinate in graphics
y	Usually a short int, used for y coordinate in graphics
i	int
b	BOOL (int)
w	WORD (unsigned int)
h	HANDLE (WORD)
dw	DWORD (unsigned long int)
fn	Function, usually used with function pointers
s	Character array (not necessarily NULL terminated)
sz	Character string (must be NULL terminated)

Modifier	Description
p	Pointer
lp	long (or far) pointer
np	short (or near) pointer

Although it often is recommended that programmers use these same prefixes for functions, I do so only if the function's return type is not obvious and it does not return an int.

When you are writing a function, you must have a function declaration. The new-style function declaration (the *header*, as it sometimes is called) looks like the following example, when it is formatted as I have suggested:

```
int     MyFunction(
    int     nFirstParameter,
    char    szString[],
    char    chMode)


{ // Function's opening brace
```

The preceding example is basically the new ANSI C style, with each of the function's parameters coded on a separate line for readability. The same example in the old style (I do *not* recommend this method) looks like this:

```
int     MyFunction(nFirstParameter, szString[], chMode)
    int     nFirstParameter;
    char    szString[];
    char    chMode;


{ // Function's opening brace
```

If for no other reason, you should use the new style because it requires less typing.

Let's look at a piece of well-formatted code. Listing 1.2 is a simple program that prints on the screen a message that is an implementation of the standard HELLO.C. Comments about the formatting are in italic type to highlight them, but these comments are not necessary in the program.

Listing 1.2. HELLO.C.

```
/* HELLO, written 12 May 1992 by Peter D. Hipson */
/* A source formatting example. */

#include <stdio.h> // Make includes first part of file

int main(void); // Declare main() and the fact that this program doesn't
                // use any passed parameters
int main()

{  // First opening brace for each function is at the left margin
    int     i;                  // Used as a for loop index
```

```
int     nCount = 0;          // Always initialize your auto variables
char    szString[] = "We want to impress you %d\n";

    for (i = 0; i < 5; i++) // Spaces around operators
    {                       // Brace on its own line
        nCount += printf(szString, i + 1);
    } /* for (i...) */

    return (nCount);        // Brackets around all return values

} // Closing brace for a function is at left margin also.
```

Notice in Listing 1.2 that if you draw a vertical line from any opening brace, you eventually can connect with its closing brace. Therefore, you can easily see the various blocks that are part of the code. When you place the opening brace at the end of the preceding line (`for()` in the example), it's difficult to move up from a closing brace and find its opening counterpart.

All the variables declared in the function, except for the loop counter, are initialized. Neglecting to initialize a variable is perhaps the most problematic error that C programmers make. It seems that, at some point, we make an assumption that the contents of a variable are valid, we use it, and the program crashes.

I recommend that you order your C source files in this order:

1. Use a one-line file description with the filename (it can be handy when it is printed), the entire project's name, and perhaps the initial date written and the programmer's name.

2. Add #include statements. Remember to comment `include` files that are not part of ANSI C and tell what is in the file. It's not unusual for a large project to have five or more `include` files. I usually have an include file with `typedefs`, one with prototypes, one (or more) with `defines`, and an `include` file with external definitions.

3. Following the #include statements, I recommend a full program header block. In the example I use (see Listing 1.2), you can see what information usually is included with a typical source file.

4. After the program header, put the definitions and declarations used in this file (and that are not found in the header files).

5. List the file's functions. The order of functions in a source file is generally not critical. I often reorder the files and place at the top (or end, if I am working on two functions at one time) the function on which I am working. This ordering makes the function easy to find. I don't recommend that you have each 20- or 30-line function in its own source file or that your project consist of two or three source files of 10,000 (or more) lines. When a source file is more than about 1,000 lines, I break it into two files, if possible. You can load the source file into the editor faster, and compile faster most of the time.

Listing 1.3 shows a typical header block comment used in creating a C source file. Using a header such as this one is helpful when you work on the program again later (perhaps years later). The more comments you have, the easier it is to fix the program. Remember that no one will have sympathy for you if you don't understand your own programming, even if it's been a while since you worked on it.

Listing 1.3. A typical source file header block.

```
/
***********************************************************************
**
**    PROJECT: The project's name goes here.
**
**      TITLE: The FILE'S title (not the project title).
**
**   FUNCTION: What the function(s) in this file does.
**             More than one line if necessary.
**
**     INPUTS: What generally is passed to the functions.
**
**    OUTPUTS: What the functions return.
**
**    RETURNS: Some functions don't return normally; say so if necessary.
**
**    WRITTEN: When the file was created.
**
**      CALLS: Significant calls to other parts of program.
**
**  CALLED BY: Who (generally) calls these functions.
```

```
**
**      AUTHOR: Your name.
**
**       NOTES: Modifications, special considerations, and so on.
**
**      COPYRIGHT 1992: By whomever. All rights reserved. All wrongs
**                      deserved.
**
***************************************************************************/
```

Here's a final comment about programming style. Always correct all the problems that create compiler warning messages. Doing so may seem to be a bother; the messages wouldn't be there, however, if they were not important. Make it a goal to have your program (no matter how large) compile with no warnings or errors. Make sure that the error-message level is set as high as possible. In Microsoft compilers, use either /W3 or /W4; with other compilers, use the equivalent. It *can* be done—I've written programs with hundreds of thousands of lines and no compiler messages.

Memory Models

If you're not programming on an IBM PC (or other computer that uses the Intel segmented architecture), skip this part of this chapter. You have enough to fill your head without having to add the information in this section.

The PC, when running in real mode, is able to address only 64K at any time using 16-bit addresses, referred to as *near pointers*. This limitation is a problem because many programs and their data are larger than 64K. To address more than 64K, it is necessary to use segments and offsets, which are forms of 24-bit addresses. If the compiler is told to use segments, it generally creates two problems: Segment arithmetic will cause your application to be slightly slower, and the size of the program will be larger. Using segments and offsets is referred to as far pointers. Because you can choose to use far pointers for function calls, or for data references or both, there are four combinations of models, as shown in Table 1.5.

Table 1.5. PC segmented architecture models.

Model	Addressing Used
Small	Near addresses for both data and function calls, where functions and data each have one segment allocated to them.
Compact	Near pointers for the function calls and far pointers for data; used for small programs that use large amounts of data memory.
Medium	Far pointers for the function calls and near pointers for data; for larger programs that don't have more than 64K of data allocated.
Large	Far pointers for the function calls and far pointers for data; for larger programs that have more than 64K of data allocated.

On the positive side, using a memory model larger than necessary isn't always a serious problem. The size of the program often isn't increased much (less than 10 percent), and the differences in execution speed may be slight. It is possible to benchmark your compiler and determine the execution times and executable program size differences.

> **NOTE** When in doubt, use the large model when you are writing your applications. Using this model enables you to develop any size program. If you find later that the program wasn't as large as you expected, you can change to one of the other models and not have to change compiler memory models in the middle of the project.

Summary

In this chapter, you learned about subjects that will assist you in writing better C programs:

- The history of the C language, and the ANSI standard.

- Programming style, and commenting and formatting your source code.

- The use of the PC's memory models; how and why to select a specific memory model.

Data Types, Constants, Variables, and Arrays

The C language offers a number of data types, which can be used for constants, variables, and arrays. This chapter helps you become more familiar with data objects and how to use them.

Data Types

The C language supports a number of data types, all of which are necessary in writing programs. Because most CPUs generally support these data types directly, it is unnecessary for the compiler to convert the data types into the types the CPU understands. In addition to the standard types, new data types are needed, which are often unique to a given application, and C provides the mechanisms to create and use types of data created by the programmer.

The basic data types as they are defined by the ANSI standard are listed in Table 2.1. They are all that are needed when simpler applications are created (and are generally adequate for many of the more complex programs).

Table 2.1. C's data types.

Type	Size	Description
char	1 byte	Used for characters or integer variables.
int	2 or 4 bytes	Used for integer values.
float	4 bytes	Floating-point numbers.
double	8 bytes	Floating-point numbers.

In addition to these data types, some of them may be used with a modifier that affects the characteristics of the data object. These modifiers are listed in Table 2.2.

Table 2.2. C's data type modifiers.

Modifier	Description
long	Forces a type int to be 4 bytes (32 bits) long and forces a type double to be larger than a double (but the actual size is implementation defined). Cannot be used with short.
short	Forces a type int to be 2 bytes (16 bits) long. Cannot be used with long.
unsigned	Causes the compiler (and CPU) to treat the number as containing only positive values. Because a 16-bit signed integer can hold values between −32,768 and 32,767, an unsigned integer can hold values between 0 and 65,535. The unsigned modifier can be used with char, long, and short (integer) types.

Each of the data types (and their modifiers) has a minimum and maximum value (see Table 2.3). Check your compiler documentation because some compilers extend

these values. Be careful not to assume that a variable created as int is either 16 bits or 32 bits. Different compilers, on different computers, may default the size of an int variable to either size, depending on the CPU's default integer size. If you must know the size of the variable, be sure you specify either long or short when you create it.

When you are entering constants, determining the value to use can be difficult. For instance, if the following line is in your program, the results probably are not going to be what you expected:

```
#define INT_MAX 0x8000 /* Really not a good idea! */
```

In this example, you expect INT_MAX to contain the value (–32768); the compiler promotes the constant to unsigned, however, and the value of INT_MAX, 32,768, is probably not what you expect.

A much easier solution exists. A number of useful identifiers are defined in the limits.h header file in ANSI C (see Table 2.3). Use limits.h so that predefined identifiers can define the limits for the integer data types. The values shown in Tables 2.3 through 2.5 represent the ANSI limits, although many compilers exceed the values shown.

Table 2.3. C's int limits identifiers, from limits.h.

Identifier	Value	Description
	char types	
CHAR_BIT	8	Number of bits in a char type
SCHAR_MIN	–127	Minimum signed char type
SCHAR_MAX	127	Maximum signed char type
UCHAR_MAX	255	Maximum unsigned char type
CHAR_MIN	SCHAR_MIN	Minimum char value, if characters are unsigned
CHAR_MAX	SCHAR_MAX	Maximum char value, if characters are unsigned
CHAR_MIN	0	If characters are signed

continues

Table 2.3. continued

Identifier	Value	Description
CHAR_MAX	UCHAR_MAX	If characters are signed
MB_LEN_MAX	1	Maximum number of bytes in multibyte char
short int types		
SHRT_MIN	–32767	Minimum (signed) short type
SHRT_MAX	32767	Maximum (signed) short type
USHRT_MAX	65535	Maximum unsigned short type
INT_MIN	–32767	Minimum (signed) int type
INT_MAX	32767	Maximum (signed) int type
UINT_MAX	65535	Maximum unsigned int type
long int types		
LONG_MIN	–2147483647	Minimum (signed) long type
LONG_MAX	2147483647	Maximum (signed) long type
ULONG_MAX	4294967295	Maximum unsigned long type

Three different-size variables can be defined for floating-point variables (see Table 2.4). The identifiers for floating-point numbers are subdivided into three parts. The first three letters indicate the size of the floating-point object: DBL_ for a double, FLT_ for a float, and LDBL_ for a long double.

Table 2.4. C's floating-point limits identifiers, from float.h.

Identifier	Value	Description
DBL_DIG	15	Number of decimal digits of precision

Identifier	Value	Description
DBL_EPSILON	2.2204460492503131e-016	Smallest value that, added to 1.0, makes the result no longer equal to 1.0
DBL_MANT_DIG	53	Number of bits in mantissa
DBL_MAX	1.7976931348623158e+308	Maximum value
DBL_MAX_10_EXP	308	Maximum decimal exponent
DBL_MAX_EXP	1024	Maximum binary exponent
DBL_MIN	2.2250738585072014e-308	Minimum positive value
DBL_MIN_10_EXP	(-307)	Minimum decimal exponent
DBL_MIN_EXP	(-1021)	Minimum binary exponent
DBL_RADIX	2	Exponent radix
DBL_ROUNDS	1	Addition rounding: near
FLT_DIG	7	Number of decimal digits of precision
FLT_EPSILON	1.192092896e-07F	Smallest value that, added to 1.0, makes the result no longer equal to 1.0

continues

23

Table 2.4. continued

Identifier	Value	Description
FLT_MANT_DIG	24	Number of bits in mantissa
FLT_MAX	3.402823466e+38F	Maximum value
FLT_MAX_10_EXP	38	Maximum decimal exponent
FLT_MAX_EXP	128	Maximum binary exponent
FLT_MIN	1.175494351e-38F	Minimum positive value
FLT_MIN_10_EXP	(-37)	Minimum decimal exponent
FLT_MIN_EXP	(-125)	Minimum binary exponent
FLT_RADIX	2	Exponent radix
FLT_ROUNDS	1	Addition rounding: near
LDBL_DIG	19	Number of decimal digits of precision
LDBL_EPSILON	5.4210108624275221706e-020	Smallest value that, added to 1.0, makes the result no longer equal to 1.0
LDBL_MANT_DIG	64	Number of bits in mantissa
LDBL_MAX	1.189731495357231765e+4932L	Maximum value

Identifier	Value	Description
LDBL_MAX_10_EXP	4932	Maximum decimal exponent
LDBL_MAX_EXP	16384	Maximum binary exponent
LDBL_MIN	3.3621031431120935063e-4932L	Minimum positive value
LDBL_MIN_10_EXP	(-4931)	Minimum decimal exponent
LDBL_MIN_EXP	(-16381)	Minimum binary exponent
LDBL_RADIX	2	Exponent radix
LDBL_ROUNDS	1	Addition rounding: near

Other identifiers generally are defined in float.h; however, they usually are either CPU- or compiler-dependent. Refer to your compiler manual for a description of these other identifiers, or print float.h to see whether comments in the file help you understand the purpose of the identifiers.

Rather than code constants for these values into your program, you should use one of the predefined identifiers shown in Tables 2.3 and 2.4. These identifiers allow for better portability and make the meaning of your program clear.

Constants

All homes are buildings, but not all buildings are homes. All literals are constants, but not all constants are literals. Maybe this example is not clear, but with the const modifier applied to a variable, it becomes nonmodifiable—a constant. Let's look at a few constants. Constants can come in any data type that the C compiler supports. A special constant, the string, can be used to either initialize a character array or be substituted for one. Table 2.5 shows a number of constants.

Table 2.5. Constants in C.

Constant	Description	Comments
123	`int`, in the smallest size and type that will hold the value specified	Never a decimal point; a unary is allowed if the value is negative. Be careful not to specify a value too large for the data type for which it is being used. The C compiler may change the size (or to an unsigned integer) if necessary to fit the value into the specified data type.
123U	unsigned `int`, in the smallest size and type that will hold the value specified	Never a decimal point; a unary is not allowed because the value must be positive. Be careful not to specify a value too large for the data type for which it is being used. The C compiler may change the size if necessary to fit the value into the specified data type.
123L	`long int`, signed	Never a decimal point; a unary is allowed if the value is negative.
123UL	`long int`, unsigned	Never a decimal point; a unary is not allowed because the value must be positive.
'A'	Character constant	A single character, enclosed within single quotes. For nonprintable characters, you can use \xNN, where NN are valid hex digits.
"ABCDE"	Character string constant	One or more characters (to the limit of 509) enclosed in double quotes. For nonprintable characters, you can use \xNN, where NN are valid hex digits.

Constant	Description	Comments
1.23	double—floating-point constant	Always a decimal point; both leading and trailing zeros are optional, but for readability, at least one digit should precede and follow the decimal point.
1.23F	float—floating-point constant	Always a decimal point; both leading and trailing zeros are optional, but for readability, at least one digit should precede and follow the decimal point.
1.23L	long double—floating-point constant	Always a decimal point; both leading and trailing zeros are optional, but for readability, at least one digit should precede and follow the decimal point.

The suffixes shown in Table 2.5 can be in either upper- or lowercase. I prefer uppercase because a lowercase *l* is difficult to distinguish from the number 1. If a number that does not fit in the default size is presented to the compiler, it either is changed to an unsigned type or its size is increased. As an example, when the value 45000 is encountered, the compiler assumes that is an unsigned value; 500000, which is too large for either a signed or unsigned 16-bit value, is promoted to a 32-bit `long` value.

String constants present several unique situations. First, unlike numeric constants, it's possible to obtain the address of a string constant. This capability is necessary because string functions use addresses (see Listing 2.1).

Listing 2.1. BADSTR.C.

```
/* BADSTR, written 12 May 1992 by Peter D. Hipson */
/* An example of changing a string constant. */

#include <stdio.h> // Make includes first part of file
#include <string.h>

int main(void); // Declare main() and the fact that this program doesn't
                // use any passed parameters.
```

continues

Listing 2.1. continued

```c
int main()

{
char    szMyName[] = "John Q. Public";
char    szYourName[50];

    szYourName[0] = '\0';

    strcpy(szYourName, szMyName);  // szYourName is now the same as
                                   // szMyName.

    printf("MyName '%s' YourName '%s' \n",
        szMyName,
        szYourName);

    strcpy(szMyName, "My New Name"); // strcpy() actually receives the
                                     // address of the constant
                                     // "My New Name"

    printf("MyName '%s' YourName '%s' \n",
        szMyName,
        szYourName);

    printf("Before: MyName '%s' Constant '%s' \n",
        szMyName,
        "My New Name");

    strcpy("My New Name",   // strcpy() actually receives the address
        szYourName);        // of the constant "My New Name"
                            // This will fail and destroy the constant!

    printf("After: MyName '%s' Constant '%s' \n",
        szMyName,
        "My New Name"); // The result can be seen because QuickC
                        // for Windows keeps identical strings
                        // constants with only a single copy in
                        // memory, and they are not read-only.
```

```
    return (0);


}
```

In Listing 2.1, strcpy() receives two addresses—a destination string and a source string. When the prototype for strcpy() is examined by the compiler, it sees that the second parameter is a constant and that it will not be modified. The first parameter, however—the destination—is not a constant and can be modified. Compiling the example in the listing enables you to determine whether your compiler keeps separate copies of strings that are identical or keeps only one copy (in an attempt to conserve memory). You cannot depend on the compiler to store identical strings either once in memory or separately for each occurrence. Nor can you depend on the compiler (or the CPU) to make a string constant read-only. On some systems, this attempt causes an error (at execution time); on others, the program generally fails.

Except for string constants, obtaining the address of a constant or modifying the constant is not possible. Using the address of operator (&) on a constant isn't allowed.

Because a string literal can be more than 500 characters long, and because it is difficult (or even impossible) to edit source lines that are that long, you can concatenate string literals. The process is easy because no operator is used—you simply follow one string literal with a second (or third):

```
char    szMyAddress[] =
    "John Q. Public\n"
    "123 Main Street\n"
    "Our Town, NH 03458\n";
```

In this code fragment, the variable szMyAddress prints as three lines (because of the embedded \n newline character). The initialization is easier to read because it's not spread out on a single line; rather, it is formatted the way it should look.

Definitions versus Declarations

There is a difference between defining an object and declaring it. This section looks at the differences and the information that should be provided to the compiler in defining and declaring objects.

Both data objects (variables) and functions are defined or declared. This chapter discusses only variables; however, the concepts are the same for a function also.

The difference between defining and declaring a data object is that, when a data object is declared, only its attributes are made known to the compiler. When an object is defined, not only are its attributes made known, but also the object is created. For a variable, memory is allocated to hold it; for a function, its code is compiled into an object module.

Because this chapter deals with data objects, this section looks at both declarations and definitions.

Declarations

The simplest declaration of a variable is shown in the following code fragment:

```
void OurFunction(
    int    nType)

{

int    nTest;

    nTest = nType;

}
```

In the fragment, an integer variable is defined. That is, both its attributes (the variable is an integer) were made known to the compiler, and storage was allocated. Because the variable is located in a function, its scope is limited and its life is auto (by default, you can change it). This means that each time OurFunction() is called, the storage for the variable nTest is reallocated automatically (using C's stack). Notice that nTest wasn't initialized when it was declared. This isn't good programming style. To prevent your using an uninitialized variable, I recommend that you initialize all auto variables.

The following fragment shows a declaration for a static variable. The difference is that the static variable's storage space is allocated by the compiler when the program is compiled; and because the storage space is never reallocated, it remembers its previous value.

```
void OurFunction(
    int    nType)

{

static  int    nTest;

    nTest += nType;

}
```

You do not initialize this declaration either. Fortunately, however, because the compiler initializes static variables (to zero), the preceding function works and adds nType to nTest every time the function is called. If the function were called enough times, it is likely that nTest would not be capable of holding the constantly increasing sum, and that an integer overflow would occur.

A fatal error? Perhaps, but on most implementations, integer overflow isn't caught as an error, and on these systems (and compilers), this error doesn't cause any warning messages to be displayed to the user. The only solution is to make sure that nType, when added to nTest, doesn't overflow.

Whenever a variable is defined within a function, it has *local scope*. Whenever a variable is defined outside any functions, it is said to have *global scope*.

In each of the preceding examples, you have created a variable that is known within the function and that cannot be referenced by any other function. Many programmers (almost all of whom are very good programmers) will argue that a variable should be known within a single function, and for any external data objects to be known, the objects should be passed as parameters.

Experience has shown, however, that this viewpoint can be idealistic. You often will want to share variables between a number of functions, and these variables may be unknown to the caller. Common uses include common buffers, storage areas, flags, indexes, tables, and so on.

To enable a variable to be used by more than one function, it must be declared outside any function—usually very near the top of the source file (see Chapter 1, "The C Philosophy"). An example is shown in Listing 2.2.

Listing 2.2. An example of a global variable, in a single source file.

```
long   int    lSum;    // Using 'int' is optional.
long   int    lCount;

void SumInt(
    int     nItem)

{

    lSum += (long)nItem;
    ++lCount;
}

void SubInt(
    int     nItem)

{

    lSum -= (long)nItem;
    —lCount;
}

int Average()

{
int  nReturn = 0;

    nReturn = (int)(lSum / lCount);

    return (nReturn);
}
```

The preceding code fragment has a set of two functions that add to a sum and count (used to create an average), and return an average.

If you look at the Average() function, you may wonder why I thought that I could divide two long (32-bit) integers and be sure that I would get a returned value that fit in a short (16-bit) integer. The answer is easy because I know that I've never added to the sum a value that was larger than would fit into a short integer, and that

when the sum was divided by the count, the result had to be smaller than (or equal to) the largest value added. Or, will it? No. I made a bad assumption because SumInt() can add a large number, and SubInt() then could remove a smaller number.

Again, in the preceding example, all three of the functions are located in a single source file. What if each of these functions is large and you need to have three source files? For that, you must use both declarations and definitions.

Definitions

Assume that your three functions are larger than they really are, and that each one therefore has its own source file. In this case, you must declare the variables (but in *only* one file) and then define them in the other files. Let's look at what this declaration would look like. Listing 2.3 shows each of the files.

Listing 2.3. An example of a global variable, in three source files.

```
-------------------FILE-SUMINT.C-------------------------------

/* SUMINT.C routines to sum integers and increment a counter. */

/* Declare the variables that will be shared between these functions. */

long  int   lSum;    // Using 'int' is optional.
long  int   lCount;

void SumInt(
    int    nItem)

{

    lSum += (long)nItem;
    ++lCount;
}

-------------------FILE-SUBINT.C-------------------------------

/* Declare the variables that will be shared between these functions. */
```

continues

Listing 2.3. continued

```
extern long  int   lSum;   // Using 'int' is optional.
extern long  int   lCount;

/* SUBINT.C routines to de-sum integers and decrement a counter. */

void SubInt(
    int     nItem)

{

    lSum -= (long)nItem;
    --lCount;
}

- - - - - - - - - - - - - - - - - - - - FILE-AVERAGE.C - - - - - - - - - - - - - - - - - - - - - - - - - - - - - - -
/* AVERAGE.C routines to return the average. */

/* Declare the variables that will be shared between these functions. */

extern long  int   lSum;   // Using 'int' is optional.
extern long  int   lCount;

int Average()

{
int  nReturn = 0;

    nReturn = (int)(lSum / lCount);

    return (nReturn);
}
```

Notice that the two variables lSum and lCount in the SUBINT.C and AVERAGE.C files are defined—using the extern attribute. This definition tells the compiler what the variables' attributes are (long int), and tells the compiler *not* to allocate any memory for these variables. Instead, the compiler writes special information into the object module to tell the linker that these variables are declared in a different module.

In both files, this information constitutes a definition of the variable, but not a declaration (which would have allocated the storage for the variable three times—once for each file).

You might ask what would happen if the variables never were declared in any module. The linker (not the compiler) usually is the one to complain, by displaying an error message. The typical error message is that an object was undefined (the message provides the name of the object). Don't confuse the linker's use of the word *defined* with the C compiler's use of it: The linker doesn't use the word *defined* in exactly the same way as the compiler uses it.

When ANSI C uses the modifier `static`, its meaning changes depending on the context of how it is used. To help you understand the differences, the following section describes variables and their scope and life span.

Variables

Variables make it all happen. Unlike constants, a *variable* data object can be modified. C's use of variables can be rather complex when you consider its capability to modify any variable either directly or by using its address. Any data object that can be defined as a singular variable can be defined also as an array. The definition (and use) of arrays is discussed later in this chapter.

Variable Types and Initializing Variables

A variable can be of any type that C supports: an integer or character, or composed of compound data objects—structures or unions. This section discusses some examples.

In the following declaration, nCount is an integer:

```
int     nCount; /* An integer of default size, uninitialized */
```

On most PCs, it is a `short int`; when it is compiled with one of the 32-bit compilers (or under a different operating system), however, it can be a 32-bit `long` integer.

```
long    lCount = 0; /* An integer of long size, initialized */
```

This declaration leaves no doubt about the size of the object. First, because `long` and `short` are defaulted to integer types (to create a `long double`, you must specify `long` double in your declaration), the keyword int is optional. It might be better style to include it (I usually try to). The variable lCount is initialized explicitly; if it were a static variable, this initialization would be optional, but by including it, you can be sure of its value.

```
char    cKeyPressed = '\0';
```

This declaration is interesting: Because the data type is character, it must be initialized with the correct type. Because character constants are enclosed in single quotes, this initialization works well. I don't recommend it, but you can use

```
char    cKeyPressed = (char)NULL;
```

Because the NULL identifier is intended for use as a pointer value, the cast to type char isn't a smart idea. This hasn't prevented much C code from being written in exactly this way.

Look at the following floating-point number:

```
float    fTimeUsed = 0.0F;
```

If this code had been written before the ANSI C standard was written, the initialization probably would look like this:

```
float    fTimeUsed = (float)0.0;
```

It was necessary to cast the double to a float because there was no other way to specify a float value.

Because the default floating-point constant size is double, the following initialization is fine.

```
double    dTimeUsed = 0.0;
```

ANSI introduced the long double, a data type that was not often found in various C implementations:

```
long double    fTimeUsed = 0.0L;
```

Again, because the default floating-point constant is a double, the size is specified in the initializer. This specification definitely is much easier than specifying a cast of (long double), unless you like to type.

This chapter discusses character string declaration later, in the "Arrays" section. In all cases, C creates strings using arrays of type char because there is no distinct data type for strings.

Scope (Or I Can See You)

The scope of a variable is often one of the things programmers don't understand at first. Depending on where they are declared, variables can be either visible or not visible.

Let's look at an example of scope that shows some poor programming practices. SCOPE.C is created in Listing 2.4. Because the program has two variables with the same name, it can be difficult to know which variable is being referred to.

Listing 2.4. SCOPE.C.

```c
/* SCOPE, written 15 May 1992 by Peter D. Hipson */
/* An example of variable scope. */

#include <stdio.h> /* Make includes first part of file */
#include <string.h>

int main(void); /* Declare main() and the fact that this program doesn't
                   use any passed parameters. */
int main()

{

int nCounter = 0;

    do
    {
    int nCounter = 0;   /* This nCounter is unique to the loop. */

        nCounter += 3; /* Increments (and prints) the loop's nCounter */
        printf("Which nCounter is = %d?\n", nCounter);
    }
    while (++nCounter < 10); /* Increments the function's nCounter */

    printf("Ended, which nCounter is = %d?\n", nCounter);

    return (0);

}
```

This is the result of running SCOPE.C:

```
Which nCounter is = 3?
Which nCounter is = 3?
Which nCounter is = 3?
Which nCounter is = 3?
Which nCounter is = 3?
Which nCounter is = 3?
Which nCounter is = 3?
Which nCounter is = 3?
Which nCounter is = 3?
Which nCounter is = 3?
Ended, which nCounter is = 10?
```

Notice that nCounter was never greater than three inside the loop. The reason is that the variable is being reallocated from *within* the do{} block, and, because it is initialized, it is set to zero when it is reallocated. To create a variable that can be used in the loop and still not have scope outside the loop, you have to create a dummy block:

```
{
int nCounter = 0;   /* This nCounter is unique to the loop */

    do
    {
        nCounter += 3; /* Increments (and prints) the loop's nCounter */
        printf("Which nCounter is = %d?\n", nCounter);
    }
    while (++nCounter < 10); /* Increments the function's nCounter */
}
```

This example doesn't work, however, because the while()'s use of nCounter then uses the wrong nCounter. Only one solution exists: Use unique names for variables when you are declaring them from within a block in a function. Resist the urge, if you are using the style shown in Chapter 1, "The C Philosophy," to redefine the for() loop index variables—i, j, and so on. Listing 2.5 shows the successful implementation of SCOPE.C.

Listing 2.5. SCOPE1.C.

```
/* SCOPE1, written 15 May 1992 by Peter D. Hipson */
/* An example of variable scope that works. */
```

```
#include <stdio.h> /* Make includes first part of file */
#include <string.h>

int main(void); /* Declare main() and the fact that this program doesn't
                   use any passed parameters. */
int main()

{

int nCounter = 0;

    {
    int nCountLoop = 0;   /* This nCounter is unique to the loop */

        do
        {
            nCountLoop += 3; /* Increments (and prints) the loop's
nCounter */
            printf("nCountLoop is = %d?\n", nCountLoop);
        }
        while (++nCounter < 10); /* Increments the function's nCounter */
    }

    printf("Ended, nCounter is = %d?\n", nCounter);

    return (0);

}
```

Using unique variable names is the only way to guarantee that there will be no confusion over which variable is being used. This is a good case of "the language lets you do something, but you really don't want to."

Life Span (Or How Long Is It Going To Be Here?)

Determining how long a variable will be kept is another problem that perplexes aspiring programmers. Let's look at the keyword modifier static. This modifier has several purposes that, unfortunately, are related.

When static is used on a variable found within a function or block, it tells the compiler never to discard or reallocate the variable. The variable is created at compile time and is initialized to zero. The opposite of static in this situation is auto (the default). That variable, found inside a function or block, is reallocated every time the function or block is entered.

When static is used on a variable that is defined outside any functions or blocks, its meaning is that the variable is known to only those functions contained in the specified source file, and are not known outside the source file. When a variable is known outside the source file, it is called an *external variable*. (Don't confuse this with the keyword extern.) The extern keyword tells the compiler that the variable is being defined (and not declared). Because extern and static conflict, they cannot be used together. The program LIFETIME.C, in Listing 2.6, shows a variable's lifetime.

Listing 2.6. LIFETIME.C.

```c
/* LIFETIME, written 15 May 1992 by Peter D. Hipson */
/* An example of variable lifetime. */

#include <stdio.h> // Make includes first part of file
#include <string.h>

int  nLife = {5};  // Initialize to 5, default is 0.

int main(void); // Define main() and the fact that this program doesn't
                // use any passed parameters.

void    DisplayLife(void); // Define DisplayLife()

int main()

{

int nCounter = 0;

    do
    {
    int nCountLoop = 0;   /* This nCounter is unique to the loop */

        nCountLoop += 3; /* Increments (and prints) the loop's
                            nCounter */
```

```
        nLife += nCounter;
        printf("nCountLoop is = %d\n", nCountLoop);
    }
    while (++nCounter < 10); /* Increments the function's nCounter */

    DisplayLife();

    printf("Ended, nCounter is = %d\n", nCounter);

    return (0);

}

void DisplayLife()

{

    printf("DisplayLife(), nLife = %d?\n", nLife);

}
```

In LIFETIME.C, the variable nLife is known to both main() and DisplayLife(). This sharing of the variable is an acceptable programming practice and is commonly used as outlined previously.

In the preceding example, if the declaration of nLife had been the following:

```
static int  nLife = {5};  // Initialize to 5, default is zero.
```

the result would have been the same. The reason is that only one source file is in this program; therefore, nLife had to be visible in only one file. Whenever possible, remember to make your external variables static: If they are known in only one source file, they are much less likely to be modified unintentionally by another function in a different source file.

Type Casting

This chapter has referred to type casting, but what is a cast? A *cast* is C's way of converting a variable of one type to another type. This topic is very important when errors and misuse of a variable's types occur. Nothing is more disastrous in a C program than inadvertently assigning a pointer to an integer using a cast and not catching the error.

Won't the compiler give a message? No. If you cast one type of variable to a different type, the compiler assumes that you know what you are doing, and it says nothing. There *is* a time and a place for a cast. Before using one, however, be sure to look carefully at your code and determine that the effect of the cast (or the lack of the cast) is what you want and expect.

Listing 2.7 shows the CASTS.C program. A number of variables, all initialized, are in this program. First, the initialized values of each variable are printed, a few assignments are made, and then the result of these assignments is printed.

Listing 2.7. CASTS.C.

```
/* CASTS, written 15 May 1992 by Peter D. Hipson */
/* Using casts to change a data type. */

#include <stdio.h> // Make includes first part of file
#include <string.h>

int main(void); // Define main() and the fact that this program doesn't
                // use any passed parameters.

int main()

{
float      fValue  = 123.0F;
double     dValue  = 987.0;
long double ddValue = 123123123123.0L;

int        nInteger     = 12345;
int        nIntegerAgain  = 12345;
long       lLong    = 987;
unsigned long ulLong = 987;
char       cChar    = 'A';

    printf(" fValue %f \n dValue %lf \n ddValue %Lf \n "
        "nInteger %d \n lLong %ld \n ulLong %lu \n cChar %c\n",
        fValue,
```

```
            dValue,
            ddValue,
            nInteger,
            lLong,
            ulLong,
            cChar);

/*  These assignment statements generate a warning message
    about type conversion. */

    nInteger = dValue;
    lLong    = ddValue;
    ulLong   = ddValue;
    cChar    = nIntegerAgain;

    printf("\n fValue %f \n dValue %lf \n ddValue %Lf \n "
        "nInteger %d \n lLong %ld \n ulLong %lu \n cChar %c\n",
        fValue,
        dValue,
        ddValue,
        nInteger,
        lLong,
        ulLong,
        cChar);

/*  With a cast, there is no warning message;
    however, the conversion is the same */

    nInteger = (int)dValue;
    lLong    = (long)ddValue;
    ulLong   = (unsigned long)ddValue;
    cChar    = (char)nIntegerAgain;

    printf("\n fValue %f \n dValue %lf \n ddValue %Lf \n "
        "nInteger %d \n lLong %ld \n ulLong %lu \n cChar %c\n",
        fValue,
        dValue,
        ddValue,
        nInteger,
        lLong,
        ulLong,
```

continues

Listing 2.7. continued

```
            cChar);

    printf("\nNotice that 'lLong' and 'ulLong'"
        "both have the wrong value.\n");

    return (0);
}
```

After compiling and running CASTS.C, you get the following result:

```
fValue 123.000000
dValue 987.000000
ddValue 123123123123.000000
nInteger 12345
lLong 987
ulLong 987
cChar A

fValue 123.000000
dValue 987.000000
ddValue 123123123123.000000
nInteger 987
lLong -1430928461
ulLong 2864038835
cChar 9

fValue 123.000000
dValue 987.000000
ddValue 123123123123.000000
nInteger 987
lLong -1430928461
ulLong 2864038835
cChar 9

Notice that 'lLong' and 'ulLong' both have the wrong value.
```

You may want to know how ulLong managed to get such a strange value. Your first guess probably is that it should have received the least-significant digits from ddValue; there seems to be no relationship, however, between the value 123123123123

and the result held in ulLong of 2864038835. The difference is easy to explain, though, when you look at the hex values of the converted number. The value 123123123123 is too large to store in a single 32-bit unsigned (or signed) integer. The hex representation of 123123123123 is 1C AA B5 C3 B3, a value that requires five bytes to store. Because ulLong has only four bytes, the leading digits, 1C, are truncated, leaving the result that is assigned to ulLong: AA B5 C3 B3 (2864038835 in decimal).

This same type of truncation happens when a short int is assigned a value that was stored in a long int that was too large. For example, if the value 123123123 is stored in ulLong, when it is assigned to an unsigned integer the result is 46515 (see Table 2.6).

Table 2.6. Examples of conversions of C data types.

Original data type	Original in decimal	Original in hex	Conversion	Result in hex	Result in decimal
long int	123123123	0x756B5B3	To short int, by truncating (the leading 0x756 is dropped).	0xB5B3	46515
short int	12345	0x3039	To char by truncating and type change (the leading 0x30 is dropped).	0x39	'9'
long double	123123123123	0x1CAAB5C3B3	Convert to integer, and truncate (the leading 0x1C is dropped).	0xAAB5C3B3	2864038835

As shown in Table 2.6, it's important to remember that truncation occurs using the internal format of the number, not the number you see and use. It is easy to lose the number you had, and if you are changing types (such as from integer to char), the result can be difficult to predict.

Casts have their place in C programming. Because your goal should be to have your program compile with no warning messages, a cast can sometimes be the only way to suppress a warning.

When a cast is used on a parameter used in a function call, the effect is predictable: First, the variable is converted to the correct type, and then it is passed. If you have prototyped the function correctly, the compiler knows the data types of the parameters and ensures that the conversions are completed, giving whatever warnings are appropriate. If no parameter types are provided with the prototype or the prototype is missing, the compiler doesn't know the correct types, makes no conversions for you, and issues only a missing prototype message.

Arrays

Arrays are collections of identical data objects, known by a common name and addressable either as a group or as a single object. Any data object that can be defined can be defined as an array.

Declaration of Arrays

Like a single data object, arrays have to be declared. The process of declaring an array is not difficult. You must, however, provide the compiler with some more information. You must tell how many of the desired data objects will be found in the array. For example, an array of int may be defined as

```
int    nArray[15];
```

In this declaration, an array of integers has been created (remember that a declaration allocates memory). The first member in the array is addressed as nArray[0], and the final member is addressed as nArray[14]. Here's an example of one of the most common coding errors:

```
#define  MAX_SIZE    20

int    nArray[MAX_SIZE];
int    i;

/* Other lines of code */
```

```
for (i = 1; i <= MAX_SIZE; i++)
{
    nArray[i] = i;
}
```

In the preceding fragment, the array element `nArray[15]` is initialized. Your program crashes because *there is no element 15*. The probable result is that some part of the program (often much later past the loop) that probably is not related to the failed part either produces incorrect results or simply crashes and dies. Also, the array element `nArray[0]` is never initialized because the loop starts with the second element in the array.

When a `for()` loop is used to initialize an array, always make sure that the following two statements are true:

1. The initial value is zero (unless there is a valid reason for some other starting value).

2. When the array is being tested to the end, the test does not exceed the number of elements defined.

An example of the preceding loop being written correctly shows that the first element is initialized correctly and that the loop ends with the last element, `nArray[14]`:

```
for (i = 0; i < MAX_SIZE; i++)
{
    nArray[i] = i;
}
```

Working with arrays can be difficult, especially when their bounds are exceeded. Many C implementations have little or no array bound checking. Generally, you should be sure that you have not exceeded the bounds of any arrays in your program.

Definition of an Array

An array can be declared with the following line:

```
int    nArray[15];
```

When an array is external (defined in a different source file), it must be defined in any other source files that may need to access it. Because you don't want the compiler to reallocate the storage for an array, you must tell the compiler that the array is allocated externally and that you want only to access the array. To do this, you use an array definition, which might look like this:

```
extern int    nArray[];
```

This statement tells the compiler two important things:

1. The array has been declared (and storage allocated) in a different source file.

2. The size of the array is unknown.

Because the compiler knows only what you tell it (the compiler doesn't search your source files to find where nArray[] was declared), it needs at least the name of the array and its type (so that the array can be indexed properly). Although it's not necessary, especially in dealing with single-dimensional arrays, to tell the compiler the number of elements in an array, the compiler has *no* way of knowing where the end of the array is. You must make sure the array is used properly and you don't exceed the bounds of the array.

If you choose to use the following definition:

```
extern int    nArray[MAX_SIZE];
```

you will tell the compiler at least the number of elements in the array. This is a good start in being able to ensure that you have not exceeded the bounds of the array. Again, note that the majority of C compilers (whether ANSI or not) do not check array (or string) bounds.

Array Indexing

When C stores an array in memory, it uses a rather complex set of pointers. Generally, you have to consider only that a block of memory has been allocated for the array. Then you can work with this memory and let C do the address computations for you.

At times, however, it's necessary to work with the array as a single object. The most common time is when the array must be passed to a function. The most common occurrence of arrays passing to functions is when you pass a string to a character function, such as C's strlen() function.

Let's look at a simple program that creates one-, two-, and three-dimensional strings. ARRAY1, in Listing 2.8, creates three arrays, initializes them using the standard C array-subscripting techniques, and then accesses the members in the string using an alternative array indexing method. (I'm not saying that you should use this method.)

Listing 2.8. ARRAY1.C.

```c
/* ARRAY1, written 18 May 1992 by Peter D. Hipson */
/* A program that demonstrates multidimensional arrays. */

#include <stdio.h> // Make includes first part of file

#define MAX_COMPANIES  3
#define MAX_CARS       10
#define MAX_MODELS     5

// This is a 10-element array.
int   nArray1[MAX_CARS];

// This is a 10-by-5 array.
int   nArray2[MAX_CARS][MAX_MODELS];

// This is a 10-by-5-by-3 array.
int   nArray3[MAX_CARS][MAX_MODELS][MAX_COMPANIES];

int main(void); // Define main() and the fact that this program doesn't
                // use any passed parameters.

int main()

{
int     i;
int     j;
int     k;

    for (i = 0; i < MAX_CARS; i++)
    {
        nArray1[i] = i;          i = 0 → 9

        for (j = 0; j < MAX_MODELS; j++)
        {
            nArray2[i][j] = (j * 10) + i;   j = 0 → 4

            for (k = 0; k < MAX_COMPANIES; k++)   k = 0 → 2
            {
```

continues

Listing 2.8. continued

```
                nArray3[i][j][k] = (i * 100) + (j * 10) + k;
            }
        }
    }

    for (i = 0; i < MAX_CARS; i++)
    {
        printf("%3.3d ", *(nArray1 + i));
    }

    printf("\n");

    for (i = 0; i < (MAX_CARS * MAX_MODELS); i++)
    {
        if ((i % MAX_MODELS) == 0)
        {
            printf("\n");
        }

        printf("%3.3d ", *(*(nArray2) + i));
    }

    printf("\n");

    for (i = 0; i < (MAX_COMPANIES * MAX_CARS * MAX_MODELS); i++)
    {
        if ((i % MAX_COMPANIES) == 0)
        {
            printf("\n");
        }

        printf("%3.3d ", *(*(*(nArray3)) + i));
    }

    printf("\n");

// Notice that string concatenation makes the printf() format
// string more readable. Also note the blank line between the
// format string and the other arguments to printf().
```

```
    printf(
        "&nArray3 %4.4X \n"
        "&nArray3[0][0][0] %4.4X \n"
        "nArray3 %4.4X \n"
        "*(nArray3) %4.4X \n"
        "*(*(nArray3)) %4.4X \n"
        "*(*(*(nArray3))) %d \n",

        &nArray3,
        &nArray3[0][0][0],
        nArray3,
        *(nArray3),
        *(*(nArray3)),
        *(*(*(nArray3))));

    printf("\n");

    printf(
        "&nArray3 %4.4X \n"
        "&nArray3[0][0][0] %4.4X \n"
        "nArray3 + 1 %4.4X \n"
        "*(nArray3 + 1) %4.4X    "
        "*(*(nArray3 + 1) + 1) %4.4X \n"
        "*(*(*(nArray3 + 1) + 1) + 1) %d \n"
        "*(*(*(nArray3)) + ((1 * (10 * 3)) + (1 * 3) + (1))) %d \n"
        "nArray3[1][1][1] %d\n",

        &nArray3,
        &nArray3[0][0][0],
        nArray3 + 1,
        *(nArray3 + 1),
        *(*(nArray3 + 1) + 1),
        *(*(*(nArray3 + 1) + 1) + 1),
        *(*(*(nArray3)) + ((1 * (10 * 3)) + (1 * 3) + (1))),
        nArray3[1][1][1]
        );

    printf("\n");

    return (0);
}
```

In ARRAY1, notice the three `printf()` statements. Each of the three arrays is accessed in a slightly different manner. This difference, due to the different number of dimensions in each array, dictates how you access them.

The single-dimensional array is the simplest type of array in C. To initialize the single-dimensional array, `nArray1[]`, you use a simple loop, which sets each element equal to its index:

```
for (i = 0; i < MAX_CARS; i++)
{
    nArray1[i] = i;
}
```

Next, to initialize the two-dimensional array, `nArray2[]`, you use a pair of loops, one for each index. To initialize the elements, you add a simple math statement that computes the initializer value based on the indexes:

```
for (i = 0; i < MAX_CARS; i++)
{
    for (j = 0; j < MAX_MODELS; j++)
    {
        nArray2[i][j] = (j * 10) + i;
    }
}
```

This array, which is more complex than a single-dimensional array, is still easy to use because it has only two indexes.

Next, to initialize the three-dimensional array, `nArray3[]`, you use three loops, one for each index. To initialize the elements, you use a simple math statement that computes the initializer value based on the indexes:

```
for (i = 0; i < MAX_CARS; i++)
{
    for (j = 0; j < MAX_MODELS; j++)
    {
        for (k = 0; k < MAX_COMPANIES; k++)
        {
            nArray3[i][j][k] = (i * 100) + (j * 10) + k;
        }
    }
}
```

This array, still more complex than either a single- or two-dimensional array, is still easy to use, even with its three indexes. When you are using arrays with a large number of dimensions, you must make sure that the correct values are being applied to each of the indexes. Errors, which usually occur in transposing an array index position, can lead to innumerable problems and can be very difficult to find and correct.

This discussion leads to how an array is stored in memory. The methods of accessing an array, if you simply use C's array indexing, are of no great importance. If you are writing a program, however, that needs to access the array in ways other than the simple index method that C supports, you can benefit from an understanding of how C accesses the array.

First, let's look at a single-dimensional array. In memory, the array's name is a pointer to the first element in the array. If this pointer is incremented, you can point to successive elements in the array. Figure 2.1 is an example of a single-dimensional array and how it is accessed.

```
int   nArray[11]; /* Define nArray[] with 11 members, 0 through 10 */
```

nArray

nArray contains a pointer to the first element in the array. This first element can be addressed using *(nArray). Each successive element may be accessed by incrementing nArray, as in *(nArray) + n, which will access the nth element in nArray. To obtain the address of the first element in the array, use &nArray[0].

```
*(nArray) *(nArray) *(nArray) *(nArray) *(nArray)        *(nArray) *(nArray)
  + 0       + 1       + 2       + 3       + 4              + 9       + 10
```

```
   0      1      2      3      4     ...    9      10
```

Figure 2.1. A single-dimensional array in memory.

Figure 2.1 shows that a single-dimensional array is simply a pointer that points to the first element in the array. Each successive array element is accessed by incrementing the pointer by the size of the array's elements.

In Figure 2.2, you can see that a two-dimensional array is a set of pointers that, when unmodified by the array index values, point to the first element in the array. Each successive array element is accessed by incrementing the pointers by the size of the array and the array elements.

int nArray[5][10]; /* define a two dimensional array, 5 by 10 elements in size */

nArray contains a pointer to the first element in the array, which is
incremented by the index values.

nArray

*(*(nArray + (desired row)) + (desired column))

Address:	0	2	4	6	8		18
+ 00	[0][0]	[0][1]	[0][2]	[0][3]	[0][4]		[0][9]
+ 20	[1][0]	[1][1]	[1][2]	[1][3]	[1][4]		[1][9]
+ 40	[2][0]	[2][1]	[2][2]	[2][3]	[2][4]		[2][9]
+ 60	[3][0]	[3][1]	[3][2]	[3][3]	[3][4]		[3][9]
+ 80	[4][0]	[4][1]	[4][2]	[4][3]	[4][4]		[4][9]

Figure 2.2. A two-dimensional array in memory.

Figure 2.2 shows that a three-dimensional array is a set of pointers that, when unmodified by the array index values, point to the first element in the array. This situation is exactly the same as in a two-dimensional array, except that this array has an additional address pointer. Each successive array element is accessed by incrementing the pointers by the size of the array and the array elements.

Most array accesses are either for the entire array (usually to pass it as a parameter) or for an individual array element. You can treat a multidimensional array as an array of arrays.

Seeing is believing. Compile the program ARRAY1, and run it. Print the results if you cannot see all of the program's output on the screen at one time. Notice how the final two printf() calls reference the array nArray3. This addressing is important to understand if you must access an array using indirection.

Why use indirection? I really can't answer that. With ANSI C, I suspect that there are few reasons for using this technique. Because programming is an art, however, I have no doubt that someone will come up with a good reason to use indirection addressing for array elements.

Using Array Names as Pointers

In the ARRAY1 program in Listing 2.8, you used indirection to index an array. This indirection tells you that the array name nArray1 is in fact a pointer. One of the nice things about ANSI C is it improved the accessing of arrays. Part of the change is that now you can obtain a pointer to an array, and you can specify to C the dimension of an array, which enables you to declare a dynamically allocated array and use simple array indexing on that array.

An example of a dynamically allocated multidimensional array is shown in Listing 2.9, ARRAY2.C. In this program, an array is created that has more than one dimension, using malloc().

Listing 2.9. ARRAY2.C.

```
/* ARRAY2, written 18 May 1992 by Peter D. Hipson */
/* A program that demonstrates multidimensional arrays. */

#include <stdio.h>  // Make includes first part of file
#include <malloc.h> // For memory allocation.

#define MAX_COMPANIES  3
#define MAX_CARS       5
#define MAX_MODELS     10

int main(void); // Define main() and the fact that this program doesn't
                // use any passed parameters.

int main()

{

int     (*nPointer)[MAX_MODELS];

int     i;
int     j;
int     k;

    nPointer = (int (*) [MAX_MODELS])
```

continues

Listing 2.9. continued

```
        malloc(MAX_CARS * sizeof(*nPointer));

    for (i = 0; i < MAX_CARS; i++)
    {
        for (j = 0; j < MAX_MODELS; j++)
        {
            nPointer[i][j] = (i * 100) + j;
        }
    }

    for (i = 0; i < MAX_CARS; i++)
    {
        for (j = 0; j < MAX_MODELS; j++)
        {
            printf("nPointer[%d][%d] = %4d\n",
                i,
                j,
                nPointer[i][j]);
        }
    }

    free(nPointer);

    return (0);
}
```

The technique shown in ARRAY2 is not limited to two-dimensional arrays, nor do you have to "preallocate" the nPointer variable. The variable could have been allocated using other techniques also. In ARRAY2, it was allocated using a standard declaration statement.

Strings: Character Arrays

You should be aware by now that C doesn't support strings. Many people consider this shortcoming to be serious; because so much of C's power is in the library functions, however, the lack of basic string functionality is not a serious shortcoming.

The definition of a string is an array of type char. This definition can be modified, however; because the library string functions assume that strings are arrays of type char, it is best to use the default definition.

A string constant such as "This is a string" can be considered a pointer to a character array.

Because the C compiler cannot generate code that knows how long a string is (a string's length is never saved), the end of the string must be marked with a special character. The character used to mark the end of a string is NULL (0x00). Don't confuse this use of NULL with the keyword of the same name. In a character string, the NULL character is the first character of the 256 ASCII character set. It has a numeric value of 0 (the lowercase *a* has a numeric value of 98, which means that it is the 98th character in the ASCII character set).

Note that ANSI C doesn't assume any specific character set. Most of the time, on the IBM PC family of computers, you use the IBM PC character set, and on most other computers you access one of the ANSI character sets. Both the PC character set and the ANSI character set are shown in Appendix A, "The ASCII Character Set."

If you look at character string declarations, you can see that they may be sized (and initialized) in several different ways.

The following declaration creates an uninitialized string with space to hold 19 characters plus the terminating NULL. Remember that this string is uninitialized, and can contain any characters, many of which might be unprintable.

```
char    szString[20];
```

In the following example, the string initializes with the characters This is the time., and the C compiler adds the NULL automatically.

```
char    szString[20] = "This is the time.";
```

Whenever a double quoted string constant is specified, the compiler always provides a terminating NULL. It is unnecessary to provide this NULL explicitly, as in

```
char    szString[20] = "This is the time.\0";
```

In this string, the string is terminated with two NULLs. This error is not serious, but it is not necessary, either. Because the initializing string is less than 20 characters long, the remaining characters in the string are undefined with most C implementations. You should not assume the string will be padded with NULLs or any other character.

In the following example, the length of the string is determined by the length of the initializing string.

```
char    szString[] = "This is the time.";
```

This determination can be tricky because, if you change the contents of the string, you must be careful not to exceed the length, which you either must know in advance or compute. This type of string declaration generally is used only for string constants. Therefore, I recommend that you use the const type modifier:

```
const  char  szString[] = "This is the time.";
```

Using const helps retain the string's integrity because you can modify it only by creating a new pointer to the string or by passing the string as a parameter to a function that modifies the string. Using const is helpful in preventing unintended modification of a string; it is *not* absolute insurance, however, that the string's contents will not be changed.

The following example doesn't work.

```
char    szString[30] = {'T'"his is the time"'.'};
```

I can think of no reason to try to mix char and string constants in an initializer, because you can simply write the following:

```
char    szString[30] = {"T""his is the time""."};
```

The example is "pushing it" a little, but as shown in Listing 2.9, sometimes you can format strings using concatenation to make their final printed format more obvious. Notice that when you are concatenating strings, you don't use commas or any other nonwhitespace separator (to the compiler, a comment is a whitespace separator).

We all know that the most serious weakness of strings under C is that they cannot be manipulated directly. You cannot assign, test, or compare strings without using one of the library functions, such as strcpy() or strcmp().

Using Arrays of Pointers

Just as you can have arrays of type int, you can have arrays of pointers. The use of arrays of pointers is a handy C feature. This section does not discuss pointers themselves, but they are described in Chapter 3, "Pointers and Indirection."

Let's look at an example of a program called REPEAT.C that reads in strings, places them in an array, and prints them to a terminal. This program, shown in Listing 2.10, forms the basis for the sort program you write in a later chapter.

Listing 2.10. REPEAT.C.

```
/* REPEAT, written 19 May 1992 by Peter D. Hipson */
/* Prints, in the same order, the strings that are entered. */

/* On PCs with memory models, you can compile with LARGE model */

#include <stdio.h>  // Make includes first part of file
#include <string.h> // For string functions

int main(void); // Define main() and the fact that this program doesn't
                 // use any passed parameters.


#define MAX_CHARACTERS 32767 /* Total maximum characters */
#define MAX_LINES       1000  /* Total maximum lines */
#define BIGEST_LINE      128   /* The longest line readable from keyboard
*/

/* Although these variables are defined as external, they can
 *     be defined inside the function or be allocated dynamically,
 *     depending on the program's needs and memory available.
 */


char    szInput[BIGEST_LINE];
char    szBuffer[MAX_CHARACTERS];
char    *pBuffer[MAX_LINES];
int     nBufferPointer = {0};
int     nLine = 0;

int main()

{
int     i;
```

continues

Listing 2.10. continued

```c
        printf(
            "Enter lines, when last one is entered\n"
            "provide a End-Of-File (ctrl-Z on most systems)\n"
            "to print the entered text\n\n");

        while (gets(szInput))
        {
            if ((nBufferPointer + strlen(szInput)) > MAX_CHARACTERS)
            { // The line won't fit! End input loop.
                break;
            }

            pBuffer[nLine] = &szBuffer[nBufferPointer];

//          The strcpy() could have been written as:
//            strcpy(&szBuffer[nBufferPointer], szInput);

            strcpy(pBuffer[nLine], szInput);

//          the + 1 skips over the terminating NULL in each string.
            nBufferPointer += strlen(szInput) + 1;

            if (++nLine >= MAX_LINES)
            { // Too many lines! End input loop.
                break;
            }
        }

//
//  Later, you add a sort to provide sorted output.
//

        for (i = 0; i < nLine; i++)
        {
            printf("String %d '%s'\n", i, pBuffer[i]);
        }

        printf("\n");

        return (0);
}
```

This program allocates space for as much as 32,767 bytes of strings, and a maximum of 1,000 strings. These limits may not be reasonable for a program that will be used. Also, when either limit is exceeded, REPEAT.C simply assumes that the end of the input file has been reached. In reality, a (meaningful) message to the user is in order.

Following the #define statements that define your limiting parameters, you allocate storage for the necessary variables. As the comments in the C program indicate, these variables can be defined inside the main() function; because an external (or static) variable is automatically initialized to zero (or zeroes), however, you don't have to initialize the variables. Again, the way your program (or function) is used dictates how or where you allocate the storage.

In allocating storage, you create first a character array called szBuffer that is used to hold the strings as they are read in. The next variable, pBuffer, an array of pointers to type char, is declared. The first member in this array points to the first string stored in szBuffer, the second member in pBuffer points to the second string stored, and so on.

A count of the number of strings entered by the user is kept in nLine. This variable is initialized to zero (the first string) and is incremented until the user finishes entering strings. It then is used in the for() loop that is used to print the user's strings.

An index pointing to the character position in szBuffer in which the next string will be placed is kept in nBufferPointer. This variable is initialized to zero (the first character position in szBuffer) and is incremented by the number of characters in each of the user's strings until the user finishes entering strings.

The program's input is handled using a while() loop, which calls gets(), a C library function that reads a line from stdin (the keyboard).

```
    while (gets(szInput))
    {
        if ((nBufferPointer + strlen(szInput)) > MAX_CHARACTERS)
        { // The line won't fit! End input loop.
            break;
        }

        pBuffer[nLine] = &szBuffer[nBufferPointer];

//      The strcpy() could have been written as:
//          strcpy(&szBuffer[nBufferPointer], szInput);
```

61

```
        strcpy(pBuffer[nLine], szInput);

//      The + 1 skips over the terminating NULL in each string.
        nBufferPointer += strlen(szInput) + 1;

        if (++nLine >= MAX_LINES)
        { // Too many lines! End input loop.
            break;
        }
    }
}
```

In the input `while()` loop, first you check to see whether `szBuffer` has enough room for this line, and then abort the input if there is no more room. Then you add the line to `szBuffer` and update the pointers. If no more input line pointers remain in `pBuffer`, you end the input phase as well. This error checking is not the best, but this program is intended to show a usage for an array of pointers—not to show error checking.

When the user signals the end of input, the program then can process the lines. This program alludes only to the fact that perhaps you sort the lines, or count characters, lines, and words, or justify the text or change its case. Who knows, and for now, who cares? You have a program that reads lines in and writes them out.

To write the lines out, a simple `for()` loop has been used. This loop simply uses `printf()` to print the user's inputted lines:

```
for (i = 0; i < nLine; i++)
{
    printf("String %d '%s'\n", i, pBuffer[i]);
}
```

In the call to `printf()`, you use the pointer to the string in the buffer rather than try to use an array index—again, to show the use of an array of pointers.

Summary

C provides the basic data types necessary to create most programs. C's flexibility is due in part to its capability to create new data types as they are needed. The limits of each type of variable were described in this chapter.

Using constants in C is much like using a constant in any other computer language. The only different situation is that in C you can modify a character constant (even though it's an error).

There is a difference between a variable's declaration (which allocates storage and defines the variable's attributes) and a variable's definition (which only defines the variable's attributes and does not allocate storage).

The use and initialization of variables were discussed, along with arrays, including using indirection as a method to access an array's members. The chapter discussed multidimensional arrays and how they are stored in memory, with a demonstration of one-, two-, and three-dimensional arrays provided by an example program.

The last part of the chapter described arrays of pointers and a simple program demonstrated their use.

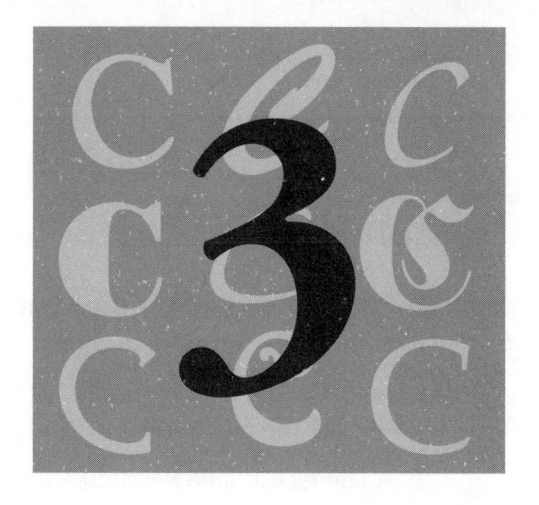

Pointers and Indirection

You probably couldn't write anything except the simplest program without arrays. Having worked with programming languages that don't support arrays, I know how difficult it can be to create meaningful applications using only singular variables.

The C language provides programmers with an additional tool to access memory, for both arrays and singular variables. This method, using pointers, seldom is found in higher-level languages, which often "protect" the programmer from direct memory manipulation.

With pointers, you use the technique of *indirection*, which is the method of obtaining the value of the memory object to which the pointer is pointing.

Pointers, Indirection, and Arrays

The concept of pointers, indirection, and arrays is an advanced idea. You can write programs (very good programs) without using pointers or indirection, and you can write good programs using only direct array accessing, without using pointers or indirection. Let's look at each—pointers, indirection, and arrays.

Pointers

A *pointer* is a variable (or constant) that contains the address (in memory) of a specific object. It has the following qualities:

1. A pointer can hold the address of any valid data object, including an array, a singular variable, a structure, and a union.

2. A pointer can hold the address of a function.

3. A pointer *cannot* hold the address of a constant, with one possible exception: A string constant has an address, which can be stored in a pointer variable indirectly (usually as the result of being passed as a function call parameter).

Pointers enable you to access any block of memory you want, but there are restrictions, of course:

- You must have the operating system's permission to access the memory (the memory accessed must have been allocated to your program).

- You must know where the block of memory you want to access is located. For many applications, knowing this information is easy because the memory will have been allocated for the program, and the program will have been given the address of the memory. If the memory is a common block, such as a video buffer, either the memory will be found in a fixed location or a pointer to the memory will be found in a known location.

Let's review the C address of operator &. To obtain the address of a singular variable and an array, or the element in an array, simply prefix the variable's name with the & operator. This section has several examples of using the & operator.

When you use pointers, you must tell the compiler the size of the object the pointer will be used with. What does size have to do with it? If a pointer variable can point to only one thing at a time, why do you have to tell the compiler that the variable is a pointer to type char, or type int? If you remember that a pointer variable can be modified, you begin to get the idea that there is nothing wrong with incrementing a pointer, adding to its value, or decrementing it. Because a char is an 8-bit-wide value (1 byte), an int is a 16-bit-wide value (2 bytes), and a long is a 32-bit-wide value (4 bytes), the compiler must know how many bytes are between the data objects to which the pointer will point.

Figure 3.1 shows how the memory for both the integer array and a pointer to a variable of type int typically is allocated. The figure shows also the memory allocated to szString and the pointer to a variable of type char.

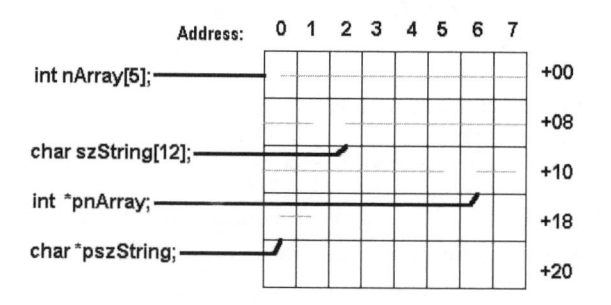

Note: This example assumes that the size of an int is 2 bytes, and that the size of a pointer is 2 bytes.

Figure 3.1. char and int pointers to arrays.

Always remember that when a pointer is incremented, its value is increased by the sizeof() the pointer's type. When a pointer is decremented, its value is decreased by the sizeof() the pointer's type.

You use the pointer declaration type modifier to tell the compiler that a variable will be a pointer to a variable type rather than being that variable type. Let's look at some identifiers, both variables that hold data and pointer variables:

```
int     nCounter = 0;
int     *pnCounter;

    pnCounter = &nCounter;
```

Two variables have been created in this code fragment. The first, an int called nCounter, holds a simple counter that your program may use. The second variable, pnCounter, has the address of nCounter assigned to it. This assignment could have been done as an initialization also.

Notice that both the pointer and the variable whose address will be stored in it have similar names. This naming is important when you need some way to know the purpose of the pointer. If you had named the pointer pPointer, you wouldn't know its purpose.

Two variables are allocated again in the following lines of code. First, a character string called szString is created (and initialized) and then a pointer to that string is created.

```
char    szString[20] = {"This is a string."};
char    *pszString;

    pszString = szString;
    pszString = &szString;
    pszString = &szString[0];
```

In all three of the following assignment statements, pszString contains the same value and always contains a pointer to the first character in szString. Subtle differences exist in these assignments, however.

```
    pszString = szString;

    pszString = &szString;

    pszString = &szString[0];
```

The first assignment assigns the address of the array to pszString. This yields the address of the first element in the array.

In the second statement, the compiler assigns the address of the array to pszString. Generally, this also yields the address of the first element in the array. The primary difference is that, with an array of more than one dimension, you can have the C compiler take care of indexing.

The third statement has a pointer to the specified element in the array (or string). Some compilers (*not* all of them) check to see whether the element specified is within the bounds of the array; you should not count on the compiler to catch this error, however.

Here's a difficult issue: An array name is not a pointer, but an array name can be assigned to a pointer variable to create a pointer to the array, it can be passed to a function as though it is a pointer to the array, and so on. I've had few problems considering the name of an array as a pointer to the first element in the array; however, only experience (and the compiler, I hope) can tell when this is not true.

Indirection

Now that you have a pointer, what do you do with it? Because it's part of your program, you can't write your address on it or nail it to a tree so that your friends can find your home. You can, however, assign to a pointer the address of a variable and pass it to a function, and then the function can find and use the variable (just as some of your friends might find and use your home).

The C operator * is called the *indirection operator*. It tells C to use whatever the pointer variable is pointing to and use the value contained in the memory that the pointer is pointing to.

An Example of Pointers, Indirection, and Arrays

It took a while for me to understand the relationship between pointers and indirection (and arrays), but tables, pictures, and example programs can help you understand it too. The program in Listing 3.1 is a useless program. It does nothing except assign values to variables and test the values and addresses of the variables.

Listing 3.1. POINTERS.C.

```
/* POINTERS, written 20 May 1992 by Peter D. Hipson */
/* Demonstration of pointers and indirection. */

#include <stdio.h>  // Make includes first part of file
#include <string.h> // For string functions.

int main(void); // Define main() and the fact that this program doesn't
                // use any passed parameters.

int main()

{
```

continues

Listing 3.1. continued

```
int     nCounter   = 33;
int     *pnCounter = (int *)NULL;

char    szSaying[] = {
    "Firestone's Law of Forecasting:\n"
    "  Chicken Little only has to be right once.\n\n"};

char    *pszSaying = (char *)NULL;

    printf(
        "nCounter ¦ pnCounter ¦ *(pnCounter) ¦ pszSaying ¦ "
        "szSaying[0] ¦ szSaying[0-20]\n");

    printf("%8d ¦ %8p ¦   %8d  ¦ %8p ¦   %c       ¦ %20.20s\n",
        nCounter,
        pnCounter,
        *(pnCounter),
        pszSaying,
        *(pszSaying),
        szSaying);

    printf("pnCounter = &nCounter; \n");
    pnCounter = &nCounter;

    printf("%8d ¦   %8p ¦   %8d  ¦ %8p ¦   %c       ¦ %20.20s\n",
        nCounter,
        pnCounter,
        *(pnCounter),
        pszSaying,
        *(pszSaying),
        szSaying);

    printf("pszSaying = szSaying; \n");
    pszSaying = szSaying;

    printf("%8d ¦   %8p ¦   %8d  ¦ %8p ¦   %c       ¦ %20.20s\n",
        nCounter,
        pnCounter,
        *(pnCounter),
```

```
        pszSaying,
        *(pszSaying),
        szSaying);

    printf("pszSaying = &szSaying; \n");
    pszSaying = &szSaying;  // Different levels of indirection!
                            // A cast (char *) will work here.

    printf("%8d ¦ %8p ¦  %8d   ¦ %8p ¦    %c         ¦ %20.20s\n",
        nCounter,
        pnCounter,
        *(pnCounter),
        pszSaying,
        *(pszSaying),
        szSaying);

    printf("pszSaying = &szSaying[0]; \n");
    pszSaying = &szSaying[0];

    printf("%8d ¦ %8p ¦  %8d   ¦ %8p ¦    %c         ¦ %20.20s\n",
        nCounter,
        pnCounter,
        *(pnCounter),
        pszSaying,
        *(pszSaying),
        szSaying);

    printf("*(pnCounter) = 1234; \n");
    *(pnCounter) = 1234;

    printf("%8d ¦ %8p ¦  %8d   ¦ %8p ¦    %c         ¦ %20.20s\n",
        nCounter,
        pnCounter,
        *(pnCounter),
        pszSaying,
        *(pszSaying),
        szSaying);

    return (0);
}
```

Running POINTERS.C in Listing 3.1 produces the output shown in Listing 3.2. This output shows what happens when each of the pointer variables is modified and as the value pointed to by pnCounter is changed using the pointer.

Listing 3.2. The output from POINTERS.C.

```
nCounter ¦ pnCounter ¦ *(pnCounter) ¦ pszSaying ¦ szSaying[0] ¦
szSaying[0-20]
      33 ¦     0000 ¦        0  ¦     0000 ¦             ¦
Firestone's Law of F
pnCounter = &nCounter;
      33 ¦     24F6 ¦       33  ¦     0000 ¦             ¦
Firestone's Law of F
pszSaying = szSaying;
      33 ¦     24F6 ¦       33  ¦     24A6 ¦     F       ¦
Firestone's Law of F
pszSaying = &szSaying;
      33 ¦     24F6 ¦       33  ¦     24A6 ¦     F       ¦
Firestone's Law of F
pszSaying = &szSaying[0];
      33 ¦     24F6 ¦       33  ¦     24A6 ¦     F       ¦
Firestone's Law of F
*(pnCounter) = 1234;
    1234 ¦     24F6 ¦     1234  ¦     24A6 ¦     F       ¦
Firestone's Law of F
```

Pointers are most commonly used when a called function must modify a variable. This process usually happens when a function returns two different values and therefore cannot use normal function-value returning mechanisms. A pointer is passed to a variable, and the called function changes the contents of the variables as required (see Listing 3.3). In Listing 3.3, ADDER.C, a function is called to add two numbers, and the result is placed in the third. This function then returns TRUE if the two numbers fit in the sum, or false if overflow occurs.

Listing 3.3. ADDER.C.

```
/* ADDER, written 20 May 1992 by Peter D. Hipson */
/* Calling functions with passed pointers. */
```

```
#include <stdio.h>  // Make includes first part of file
#include <string.h> // For string functions.
#include <limits.h> // For integer value limits.

#define     TRUE    1
#define     FALSE   0

int main(void); // Define main() and the fact that this program doesn't
                // use any passed parameters.

int DoAdd(int * nResult, int nFirstValue, int nSecondValue);

int main()

{

int     nFirst  = 3000;
int     nSecond = 700;
int     nSum    =   0;

    printf("BEFORE: nSum = %4d nFirst = %4d nSecond = %4d\n",
        nSum,
        nFirst,
        nSecond);

    if (!DoAdd(&nSum, nFirst, nSecond))
    {
        printf("%d + %d don't fit in an int\n",
            nFirst,
            nSecond);
    }


    printf("AFTER:  nSum = %4d nFirst = %4d nSecond = %4d\n",
        nSum,
        nFirst,
        nSecond);

    return (0);
}
```

continues

Listing 3.3. continued

```c
int DoAdd(
    int * nResult,
    int nFirstValue,
    int nSecondValue)

{
    if ((long)nFirstValue + (long)nSecondValue > (long)INT_MAX)
    {
        return(FALSE);
    }
    else
    {
        *nResult = nFirstValue + nSecondValue;
    }

    return(TRUE);
}
```

You should notice two interesting things about ADDER.C:

1. The function is called with a pointer to an integer that will receive the results of the addition. Also, before the numbers are summed, the program checks to make sure that the results will fit in an int without overflow. If the result doesn't fit, the numbers are not summed and the function returns FALSE, if the result fits, the sum is saved at the address pointed to by nResult, and the function returns TRUE.

2. The test is made using casts to type long because the result of adding two shorts can never be larger than a long. You cannot use int types here because the test isn't meaningful if an overflow occurs.

Running ADDER.C with both nFirst and nSecond set to a large value (30,000, for example) shows how the test for overflow works.

Character Arrays and Strings

C stores strings as arrays of type char. Note that *no* operators work on strings directly. You cannot copy a string using the assignment (equal sign) operator, nor can you compare two strings using logical operators.

To make up for the shortcomings in C's character handling, a large number of string functions are in the standard library (see Chapter 14, "ANSI C Library Functions"). Because the particular functionality your application requires might not be present in one of the C library functions, you can write a function to do whatever you want.

This section doesn't show you how to count words in a string (the demo program does that), but it does show you how easy it is to work with strings and manipulate pointers to strings.

By now, you should not still be writing programs that compare strings using logical operators, as in the following example:

```
char szFirst[] = {"This is a string"};
char szNext[]  = {"Before this one");

if (szFirst > szNext)
{
    /* the test was meaningless! */
}
```

This comparison simply evaluates the addresses of the two strings, not their contents. The result of the test is undefined because you cannot predict where in memory the strings will be located, nor are their contents related to their memory address.

The correct way to compare two strings is to call the library function strcmp(), which returns a value based on the logical relationship between the two strings:

```
char szFirst[] = {"This is a string"};
char szNext[]  = {"Before this one");

if (strcmp(szFirst, szNext) > 0)
{
    /* szFirst is before szNext! */
}
```

This relationship is much more useful to your programs than are the string's addresses. NUMWORD.C counts the number of words in a sentence that are entered from the keyboard (see Listing 3.4).

Listing 3.4. NUMWORD.C.

```
/* NUMWORD, written 20 May 1992 by Peter D. Hipson */
/* Program to count words in sentences. */

#include <stdio.h>  // Make includes first part of file
#include <string.h> // For string functions

#define    TRUE    1
#define    FALSE   0

int main(void); // Define main() and the fact that this program doesn't
                // use any passed parameters.


int    NumberWords(char    * pString);

#define BIGEST_LINE    256    /* The biggest line readable from keyboard */

/* Though these variables are defined as external, they can be
 *     defined inside the function or be allocated dynamically,
 *     depending on the program's needs and the amount of memory available */


char    szInput[BIGEST_LINE];

int main()

{

int    i;

    printf(
        "Enter lines, when last one is entered\n"
        "provide a End-Of-File (ctrl-Z on most systems)\n"
        "to end the program.\n\n");

    while (gets(szInput))
    {
```

```
        printf("Words = %2d '%.50s'\n",
            NumberWords(szInput),
            szInput);
    }

    printf("\n");

    return (0);
}

int     NumberWords(
    char    szString[])

{

int     i;
int     nBlank = TRUE;
int     nCount = 0;

for (i = 0; szString[i]; i++)
    {
        if (szString[i] != ' ')
        {
            if (nBlank)
            {
                ++nCount;
            }

            nBlank = FALSE;
        }
        else
        {
            nBlank = TRUE;
        }
    }

    return(nCount);
}
```

NUMWORD has a very simple loop that calls gets() until the end-of-file is reached. After gets() returns, the loop itself calls printf(), which has as one of its parameters a call to the NumberWords() function.

```c
printf("Words = %2d '%.50s'\n",
    NumberWords(szInput),
    szInput);
```

C first calls NumberWords() and then passes to printf() the returned value, along with the other parameters.

```c
for (i = 0; szString[i]; i++)
    {
        if (szString[i] != ' ')
        {
            if (nBlank)
            {
                ++nCount;
            }

            nBlank = FALSE;
        }
        else
        {
            nBlank = TRUE;
        }
    }
```

NumberWords() has a loop that looks at the passed string and parses out the words. The format for this loop is a for() loop; while() can be used, however. This loop moves through the character string and increments an index to the passed string. When the loop starts, it is assumed that a blank has been encountered already. This assumption is made by setting the blank flag (nBlank) on so that you can count the first word regardless of whether it's preceded by blanks. Also, the word count (nCount) is set to zero, which indicates that no words have been counted.

When the first nonblank character is found, the word counter is incremented (a word has been found), and the blank flag is turned off. The loop continues searching for the next blank; when it is found, the blank flag is set to on and the process continues until the end of the string is found.

Indirection to Access Character Strings

To change NUMWORD to use indirection to access the string, the loop in
NumberWords() must change slightly (see Listing 3.5).

Listing 3.5. NUMWORD1.C.

```c
/* NUMWORD1, written 21 May 1992 by Peter D. Hipson */
/* Program to count words in sentences. */

#include <stdio.h>  // Make includes first part of file
#include <string.h> // For string functions

#define     TRUE    1
#define     FALSE   0

int main(void); // Define main() and the fact that this program doesn't
                // use any passed parameters.


int     NumberWords(char    * pString);

#define BIGEST_LINE     256    /* The biggest line readable from keyboard */

/* Although these variables are defined as external, they can be
 *    defined inside the function or be allocated dynamically,
 *    depending on the program's needs and memory available. */


char    szInput[BIGEST_LINE];

int main()

{

int     i;

    printf(
```

continues

Listing 3.5. continued

```
                "Enter lines, when last one is entered\n"
                "provide a End-Of-File (ctrl-Z on most systems)\n"
                "to end the program.\n\n");

        while (gets(szInput))
        {
            printf("Words = %2d '%.50s'\n",
                NumberWords(szInput),
                szInput);
        }

        printf("\n");

        return (0);
    }

int     NumberWords(
        char    * pString)

    {

int     nBlank = TRUE;
int     nCount = 0;

        do
        {
            if (*(pString) && *(pString) != ' ')
            {
                if (nBlank)
                {
                    ++nCount;
                }

                nBlank = FALSE;
            }
            else
            {
                nBlank = TRUE;
            }
```

```
    } while(*(pString++));

    return(nCount);
}
```

NumberWords() again has a loop that looks at the passed string and parses out the words. The format for this loop is do()...while(). A straight while() or even a for() loop, however, can be used:

```
do
{
    if (*(pString) && *(pString) != ' ')
    {
        if (nBlank)
        {
            ++nCount;
        }

        nBlank = FALSE;
    }
    else
    {
        nBlank = TRUE;
    }

} while(*(pString++));
```

You no longer need to use an index variable, because you are using the pointer that was passed to keep track of where you are in the string. One possible advantage to this method is that by incrementing the pointer rather than an index to a string, the function generally is both faster and smaller.

This loop moves through the character string and increments the passed pointer. Remember that this passed pointer is a private copy for this function and can be modified. It is assumed that a blank has been encountered already, by setting the blank flag on so that you can count the first word regardless of whether it is preceded by blanks. Also, the word count is set to zero so that no words are counted. When the first nonblank character is found, the word counter is incremented (a word has been found) and the blank flag is turned off. The loop continues searching for the next blank; when it is found, the blank flag is set to on and the process continues until the end of the string is found.

Listing 3.6 shows the assembly listing for the version of NumberWords() that uses pointer indexing. The compiler produces this machine code, commented with the original source lines, when the function is compiled.

Listing 3.6. NUMWORD3.COD, the assembly listing for the pointer version of NumberWords().

```
; Edited for size.
;     Static Name Aliases
;
    TITLE    numword3.c
    NAME     numword3


    .8087
_TEXT     SEGMENT  WORD PUBLIC 'CODE'
_TEXT     ENDS
_DATA     SEGMENT  WORD PUBLIC 'DATA'
_DATA     ENDS
CONST     SEGMENT  WORD PUBLIC 'CONST'
CONST     ENDS
_BSS      SEGMENT  WORD PUBLIC 'BSS'
_BSS      ENDS
DGROUP    GROUP    CONST, _BSS, _DATA
    ASSUME  CS: _TEXT, DS: DGROUP, SS: DGROUP
EXTRN       --acrtused:ABS
EXTRN       --chkstk:NEAR
_TEXT        SEGMENT
    ASSUME     CS: _TEXT
;¦*** /* NUMWORD3, written 21 May 1992 by Peter D. Hipson */
;¦***
;¦*** #include <stdio.h>  // Make includes first part of file
;¦*** #include <string.h> // For string functions
;¦***
;¦*** #define    TRUE    1
;¦*** #define    FALSE    0
;¦***
;¦***
;¦*** int    NumberWords(char    * pString);
;¦***
;¦*** int    NumberWords(
```

```
;|***    char    * pString)
;|***
;|*** {
; Line 15
    PUBLIC    _NumberWords
_NumberWords    PROC NEAR
    *** 000000    55              push    bp
    *** 000001    8b ec           mov     bp,sp
    *** 000003    b8 06 00        mov     ax,6
    *** 000006    e8 00 00        call    __chkstk
;    pString = 4
;    nBlank = -2
;    nCount = -4
;|***
;|*** int    nBlank = TRUE;
; Line 17
    *** 000009    c7 46 fe 01 00          mov    WORD PTR [bp-2],1
;nBlank
;|*** int    nCount = 0;
; Line 18
    *** 00000e    c7 46 fc 00 00          mov    WORD PTR [bp-4],0
;nCount
;|***
;|***    do
; Line 20
                $D239:
;|***    {
; Line 21
;|***        if (*(pString) && *(pString) != ' ')
; Line 22
    *** 000013    8b 5e 04        mov     bx,WORD PTR [bp+4]       ;pString
    *** 000016    8a 07           mov     al,BYTE PTR [bx]
    *** 000018    88 46 fa        mov     BYTE PTR [bp-6],al
    *** 00001b    0a c0           or      al,al
    *** 00001d    74 15           je      $I242
    *** 00001f    3c 20           cmp     al,32
    *** 000021    74 11           je      $I242
;|***        {
; Line 23
;|***            if (nBlank)
```

continues

Listing 3.6. continued

```
; Line 24
    *** 000023    83 7e fe 00           cmp    WORD PTR [bp-2],0    ;nBlank
    *** 000027    74 03           je     $I243
;|***               {
; Line 25
;|***                   ++nCount;
; Line 26
    *** 000029    ff 46 fc           inc    WORD PTR [bp-4]    ;nCount
;|***               }
; Line 27
;|***
;|***               nBlank = FALSE;
; Line 29
                $I243:
    *** 00002c    c7 46 fe 00 00           mov    WORD PTR [bp-2],0
;nBlank
;|***           }
; Line 30
;|***           else
; Line 31
    *** 000031    eb 06           jmp    SHORT $I244
    *** 000033    90           nop
                $I242:
;|***           {
; Line 32
;|***               nBlank = TRUE;
; Line 33
    *** 000034    c7 46 fe 01 00           mov    WORD PTR [bp-2],1
;nBlank
;|***           }
; Line 34
                $I244:
;|***
;|***       } while(*(pString++));
; Line 36
    *** 000039    8b 5e 04           mov    bx,WORD PTR [bp+4]    ;pString
    *** 00003c    ff 46 04           inc    WORD PTR [bp+4]    ;pString
    *** 00003f    80 3f 00           cmp    BYTE PTR [bx],0
    *** 000042    75 cf           jne    $D239
```

```
;¦***
;¦
;¦***      return(nCount);
; Line 38
    *** 000044    8b 46 fc          mov    ax,WORD PTR [bp-4]      ;nCount
    *** 000047    8b e5              mov    sp,bp
    *** 000049    5d             pop    bp
    *** 00004a    c3             ret
    *** 00004b    90             nop


_NumberWords    ENDP
_TEXT    ENDS
END
;¦*** }
```

Listing 3.7 is the assembly listing for the version of NumberWords() that uses an index to the passed array. As in the preceding example, the compiler produces this machine code, commented with the original source lines, when the function is compiled.

Listing 3.7. NUMWORD4.COD, the assembly listing for the array indexed version of NumberWords().

```
; Edited for size.
;    Static Name Aliases
;
    TITLE    numword4.c
    NAME     numword4

    .8087
_TEXT    SEGMENT  WORD PUBLIC 'CODE'
_TEXT    ENDS
_DATA    SEGMENT  WORD PUBLIC 'DATA'
_DATA    ENDS
CONST    SEGMENT  WORD PUBLIC 'CONST'
CONST    ENDS
_BSS     SEGMENT  WORD PUBLIC 'BSS'
_BSS     ENDS
DGROUP   GROUP    CONST, _BSS, _DATA
    ASSUME  CS: _TEXT, DS: DGROUP, SS: DGROUP
```

continues

Listing 3.7. continued

```
EXTRN     --acrtused:ABS
EXTRN     --chkstk:NEAR
_TEXT        SEGMENT
    ASSUME     CS: _TEXT
;|*** /* NUMWORD, written 20 May 1992 by Peter D. Hipson */
;|***
;|*** #include <stdio.h>  // Make includes first part of file
;|*** #include <string.h> // For string functions
;|***
;|*** #define    TRUE    1
;|*** #define    FALSE   0
;|***
;|***
;|*** int     NumberWords(char    * pString);
;|***
;|***
;|*** int     NumberWords(
;|***     char    szString[])
;|***
;|*** {
; Line 16
    PUBLIC    _NumberWords
_NumberWords    PROC NEAR
    *** 000000    55            push    bp
    *** 000001    8b ec             mov    bp,sp
    *** 000003    b8 08 00          mov    ax,8
    *** 000006    e8 00 00          call   --chkstk
    *** 000009    56            push    si
;   szString = 4
;   i = -6
;   nBlank = -2
;   nCount = -4
;|***
;|*** int     i;
;|*** int     nBlank = TRUE;
; Line 19
    *** 00000a   c7 46 fe 01 00          mov    WORD PTR [bp-2],1
;nBlank
;|*** int     nCount = 0;
```

```
; Line 20
    *** 00000f   c7 46 fc 00 00        mov    WORD PTR [bp-4],0
;nCount
;|***
;|***       for (i = 0; szString[i]; i++)
; Line 22
    *** 000014   c7 46 fa 00 00        mov    WORD PTR [bp-6],0    ;i
    *** 000019   eb 09                 jmp    SHORT $F240
    *** 00001b   90             nop
                 $I243:
;|***       {
;|***           if (szString[i] != ' ')
;|***           {
;|***               if (nBlank)
;|***               {
;|***                   ++nCount;
;|***               }
;|
;|***               nBlank = FALSE;
;|***           }
;|***           else
;|***           {
; Line 34
;|***               nBlank = TRUE;
; Line 35
    *** 00001c   c7 46 fe 01 00        mov    WORD PTR [bp-2],1
;nBlank
;|***           }
; Line 36
;|***       }
; Line 37
                 $FC241:
    *** 000021   ff 46 fa              inc    WORD PTR [bp-6]     ;i
                 $F240:
    *** 000024   8b 5e fa              mov    bx,WORD PTR [bp-6]     ;i
    *** 000027   8b 76 04              mov    si,WORD PTR [bp+4]      ;szString
    *** 00002a   8a 00                 mov    al,[bx][si]
    *** 00002c   88 46 f8              mov    BYTE PTR [bp-8],al
    *** 00002f   0a c0                 or     al,al
    *** 000031   74 15                 je     $FB242
```

continues

87

Listing 3.7. continued

```
;|***     {
; Line 23
;|***         if (szString[i] != ' ')
; Line 24
    *** 000033   3c 20             cmp    al,32
    *** 000035   74 e5             je     $I243
;|***     {
; Line 25
;|***         if (nBlank)
; Line 26
    *** 000037   83 7e fe 00       cmp    WORD PTR [bp-2],0    ;nBlank
    *** 00003b   74 03             je     $I244
;|***         {
; Line 27
;|***             ++nCount;
; Line 28
    *** 00003d   ff 46 fc          inc    WORD PTR [bp-4]     ;nCount
;|***         }
; Line 29
;|***
;|***         nBlank = FALSE;
; Line 31
             $I244:
    *** 000040   c7 46 fe 00 00         mov    WORD PTR [bp-2],0
;nBlank
;|***     }
; Line 32
;|***         else
; Line 33
    *** 000045   eb da             jmp    SHORT $FC241
    *** 000047   90                nop
             $FB242:
;|***     {
;|***         nBlank = TRUE;
;|***     }
;|***     }
;|***
```

```
;¦***        return(nCount);
; Line 39
    *** 000048    8b 46 fc          mov    ax,WORD PTR [bp-4]    ;nCount
    *** 00004b    5e                pop    si
    *** 00004c    8b e5               mov    sp,bp
    *** 00004e    5d                pop    bp
    *** 00004f    c3                ret

_NumberWords    ENDP
_TEXT    ENDS
END
;¦*** }
```

The assembly listings show the major differences from what the original C version shows; you should consider several factors, however, when you are deciding whether to use indexing or to modify pointers:

- Functions that use indexing often are easier to read and understand.

- Functions that use indexing often generate more machine code than functions that use pointer modification. This situation is more prevalent in functions that have many references to the variable (or variables) accessed with pointers.

- Functions that use indexing often are slower than functions that use pointer modification. This situation is more prevalent in functions that have many references to the variable (or variables) accessed with pointers, and occurs because the functions usually must add the index to the array base for each access.

- Functions with array indexing require local variables that require stack space. This consideration usually is a minor one, but it may be a factor when stack usage must be either minimized or eliminated.

You should note that even though the example program used a string (which is a character array), the concepts are the same in other arrays, such as int, long, or float. The important thing with nonstring arrays is that the function the string is being passed to *must* know how many elements are found in the array, because only strings have a meaningful end marker, NULL.

Protecting Strings in Memory

If I could find a way to protect strings in memory, I would be rich. Seriously, the only thing that protects strings in memory is careful programming. Although many operating environments offer some forms of memory protection and some compilers offer bounds checking, this protection is limited and easily circumvented—often unknowingly by programmers.

A number of dangerous functions in the C language's library don't know how long a string is and easily can overwrite a string's memory allocation without notifying the programmer. Even functions that tell you how much of the string they used have possibly already destroyed valuable memory when they write past the end of the string.

Two of the worst offenders are input/output functions and the various string functions. The input/output functions are often given a buffer in order to read in the desired information. The problem is that they don't know how long the buffer is. In the following example fragment, the programmer made the assumption that a user never would enter a line longer than 80 characters:

```
char    szBuffer[80]; // You'll never read more than 80 characters
                      // (ha-ha).


    if (gets(szBuffer))
    {
//        Process the buffer inputted.
    }
```

The programmer might have thought, for example, that the terminal to be used allowed only 80 characters per line. The user first used I/O redirection to provide input to the program, though, and the lines in the user's file were about 200 characters long. Of course, the program crashed.

This problem doesn't really have a fix that always works. The fix most often consists of putting a realistic maximum on the buffer size, which means that the buffer must be capable of holding a very large string. In the preceding example, it would not be unreasonable to define the input buffer to be several thousand bytes long. I usually create in my programs a generic buffer (called szTempBuffer), which is used for places where I don't want to experience buffer overflow.

In the following example, a set of two strings has been defined and then concatenated, when necessary.

```
char    szMyName[] = {"Peter D. Hipson");
char    szMyAddress[]= {"New Hampshire");

// bFullAddress says that the user wants my full address:

    if (bFullAddress)
    {
        strcat(szMyName, szMyAddress);
    }
```

The only problem is that szMyName is not large enough to hold both strings. Crash—it's over! Again, the fix is to be sure that the destination for the library string functions is large enough. One possible fix is to use szTempBuffer to hold the result of the concatenation and then test to see whether it fits into the final destination, as in this example:

```
strcpy(szTempBuffer, szMyName);
strcat(szTempBuffer, szMyAddress);

if (strlen(szTempBuffer) > sizeof(szMyName))
{   // Truncate the result to fit.
    szTempBuffer[sizeof(szMyName) - 1] = '\0';
    printf("String '%s' won't fit into buffer\n", szTempBuffer);
}

strcpy(szMyName, szTempBuffer);
```

Or if the preceding example doesn't require that the operation take place if the number of characters being assigned to a string doesn't fit, you can simply test and perform the operation if it fits:

```
if (strlen(szMyName) + strlen(szMyAddress) < sizeof(szMyName))
{
    strcat(szMyName, szMyAddress);
}
else
{
    printf("String '%s%s' won't fit into buffer\n",
        szMyName,
        szMyAddress);
}
```

The primary difference is that the first example copies as many characters as will fit, and the second does not. For either example to work, the compiler must know how large the strings are. It knows how large when the strings are declared in the source file, or when they are defined *with sizes*. Because you often define arrays by specifying their size, you can get into trouble when an error message tells you that the size of the object is unknown.

When you are using sprint() to print to a string, the function can cause innumerable problems because most format specifiers for floating-point numbers, when given an invalid value, print some rather strange results. Often, you assume that your numbers are always correct; that assumption is a weak one, however, because the majority of the numbers the program works with are provided by the user. In this case also, I try to use a large buffer, such as my szTempBuffer, to hold the results of sprintf() until I can be sure that the resulting string is not too large for the intended destination.

Ragged-Right String Arrays

There is a problem with using strings. Suppose that you have a program with a large number of strings, such as list of common sayings. Each line of the sayings is placed in a string buffer. If these strings are used as constants (they won't be modified), you may well want to pack the strings together, with no wasted space.

A more common way of storing strings is shown in the program FIXSTR.C. It allocates an array of 25 lines, each of which is 80 characters long. The total storage required for this array is 2,000 bytes (see Listing 3.8).

Listing 3.8. FIXSTR.C.

```
/* FIXSTR, written 20 May 1992 by Peter D. Hipson */
/* Fixed-length strings in a program. */

#include <stdio.h>  // Make includes first part of file
#include <string.h> // For string functions.

#define MAX_LINES   25
#define MAX_LENGTH  80

int main(void); // Define main() and the fact that this program doesn't
                // use any passed parameters.
```

```
int main()

{

int     i;

char    szSaying[MAX_LINES][MAX_LENGTH] =
    {
        "Firestone's Law of Forecasting:",
        "  Chicken Little only has to be right once.",
        "",
        "",
        "Manly's Maxim:",
        "  Logic is a systematic method of coming to",
        "  the wrong conclusion with confidence.",
        "",
        "",
        "Moer's truism:",
        "  The trouble with most jobs is the job holder's",
        "  resemblance to being one of a sled dog team. No one",
        "  gets a change of scenery except the lead dog.",
        "",
        "",
        "Cannon's Comment:",
        "  If you tell the boss you were late for work because you",
        "  had a flat tire, the next morning you will have a flat tire."
    };

printf(
    "Number of lines is %d\n"
    "size of item is %d\n"
    "size of (char) is %d\n",
    sizeof(szSaying) / sizeof(szSaying[0]), // Number of elements.
    sizeof(szSaying[0]),                    // Size of char *
    sizeof(szSaying[0][0]));                // Size of char

switch (sizeof(char *))
{
    case 2: // Near pointers
        printf("Addr len saying\n");
        break;
```

continues

Listing 3.8. continued

```c
        case 4: // Far pointers, 808x segmented pointers.
            printf("Address    len saying\n");
            break;
    }

    for (i = 0; i < sizeof(szSaying) / sizeof(szSaying[0]); i++)
    {
        printf("%p %3d '%s'\n",
            szSaying[i],
            strlen(szSaying[i]),
            szSaying[i]);
    }

    return (0);
}
```

Figure 3.2 shows an example of how the memory for FIXSTR.C's szSaying is allocated and used. In this program, szSaying is a single, two-dimensional character array.

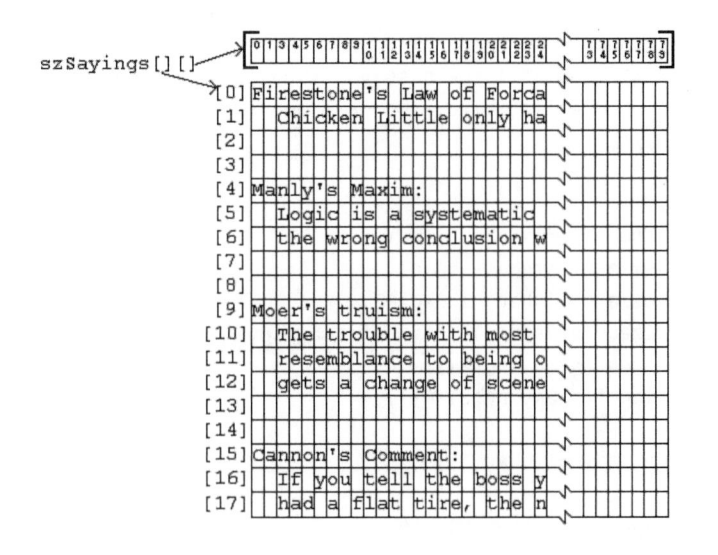

Note: Columns 25 through 72 are not shown.

Figure 3.2. szSaying in FIXSTR.C.

In Listing 3.9, RAGSTR.C shows a different way of allocating the strings. In this program, C has been told to allocate an array of *string pointers*, and then give constants as initializers. This technique wastes no space, and with two allocated arrays (one is the pointer to a string array, and the other is the string array that's being pointed to), only 521 bytes of storage are required.

Listing 3.9. RAGSTR.C.

```c
/* RAGSTR, written 20 May 1992 by Peter D. Hipson */
/* Non-fixed-length strings in a program. */

#include <stdio.h>  // Make includes first part of file
#include <string.h> // For string functions.

int main(void); // Define main() and the fact that this program doesn't
                // use any passed parameters.


int main()

{

int     i;

char    *szSaying[] =
    {
        "Firestone's Law of Forecasting:",
        "  Chicken Little only has to be right once.",
        "",
        "",
        "Manly's Maxim:",
        "  Logic is a systematic method of coming to",
        "  the wrong conclusion with confidence.",
        "",
        "",
        "Moer's truism:",
        "  The trouble with most jobs is the job holder's",
        "  resemblance to being one of a sled dog team. No one",
        "  gets a change of scenery except the lead dog.",
        "",
```

continues

Listing 3.9. continued

```
                    "",
                    "Cannon's Comment:",
                    "  If you tell the boss you were late for work because you",
                    "  had a flat tire, the next morning you will have a flat tire."
                };

                printf(
                    "Number of lines is %d\n"
                    "size of item is %d\n"
                    "size of (char) is %d\n",
                    sizeof(szSaying) / sizeof(szSaying[0]), // Number of elements.
                    sizeof(szSaying[0]),                    // Size of char *
                    sizeof(szSaying[0][0]));                // Size of char

                switch (sizeof(char *))
                {
                    case 2: // Near pointers
                        printf("Addr len saying\n");
                        break;

                    case 4: // Far pointers, 808x segmented pointers.
                        printf("Address   len saying\n");
                        break;
                }

                for (i = 0; i < (sizeof(szSaying) / sizeof(szSaying[0])); i++)
                {
                    printf("%p %3d '%s'\n",
                        szSaying[i],
                        strlen(szSaying[i]),
                        szSaying[i]);
                }

                return (0);
            }
```

Notice that the main body of the program, especially the for() loop used to print the strings, is identical in each program, despite the fact that each program has two different types of array addressing.

Figure 3.3 shows an example of how the memory for RAGSTR.C's szSaying is allocated and used. In this program, szSaying is a single-dimensional array of character pointers. Each pointer then is initialized to point to the correct initializing character string.

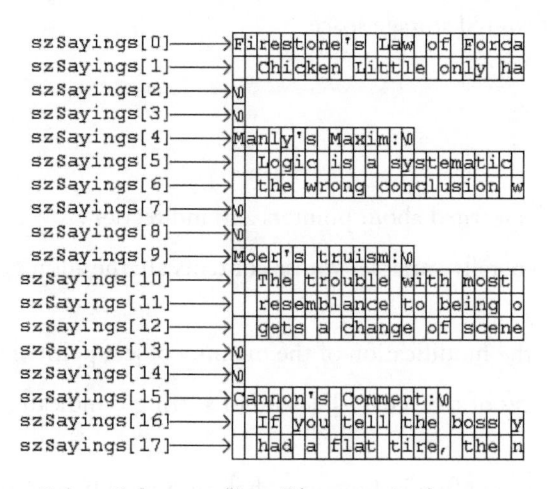

Note: Columns after 24 are not shown.
Each element in szSayings points to a string
constant.

Figure 3.3. szSaying in RAGSTR.C.

Don't be concerned if this discussion leaves you confused—certain parts of the C language, and the way it is used, can confuse anyone. The important factors in the preceding two programs include the following:

1. A two-dimensional array of type char, accessed with only one subscript, effectively returns a pointer to a character string.

2. A single-dimensional array of type char * can be initialized with a set of string constants.

3. If a single-dimensional array of type char * is initialized with a set of string constants, you should be careful about modifying them. The process of modifying a string constant is undefined under ANSI C, and many compilers keep only one copy of a set of identical strings (also legitimate under ANSI C).

4. A single-dimensional array of type char *, initialized with a set of string constants, uses less memory than a two-dimensional array of type char.

5. A two-dimensional array of type char can be initialized and effectively modified by a program.

When you are working under the constraint that character strings stored in a ragged-right format are difficult—if not impossible—to modify, this format can save a large amount of wasted storage space.

Summary

In this chapter, you learned about pointers and indirection.

- Pointers are generally variables whose contents are the address of a memory object.

- Indirection is the modification of the memory object pointed to by a pointer.

- Strings are arrays of type char. The end of a string is indicated by the NULL character.

- Indirection is used often in functions that must modify one (or more) of the parameters that was passed to the function.

- Strings are best protected by good programming style: Be sure all buffers and string variables can hold the objects placed in them.

- Strings can be stored in a ragged-right format that saves memory. Generally, such strings are difficult to modify.

Special Pointers and Their Use

Chapters 2 and 3 described pointers as they pertain to data objects. This chapter discusses pointers that point to objects other than data. Just as you can have a pointer that points to a data object, you can also have a pointer that points to a function. Pointers have several special uses in programming, too. One such use is to obtain the program's name and any parameters that have been entered by the user and passed to the program by the operating system.

Command Line Arguments

Command line arguments are vital to many programs you create. Command line arguments are used for options, input and output data sources, and to enable the user to pass parameters to the program.

The operating system processes the arguments the user enters, and places each one in a string that is pointed to by a pointer that you can access. Suppose that the user enters the following command line:

```
WONDER /Why Ask.dat
```

The program can access not only the program's name, but also the command line arguments. These are passed to the main() function as parameters. Until now, the main() function has taken no parameters; in reality, however, three parameters are passed to main() when it is called. The function prototype for the main() function is

```
int main(
    int     argc,
    char    *argv[],
    char    *envp[]
    )
```

The argc parameter, an integer, contains the number of elements in the passed array of argv[]. Because the first member of argv[] is the program's name (usually this is a fully qualified name, complete with the drive and directory information), the value of argc is always at least 1. Some compilers and operating systems don't provide the program name, but have argv[0] point instead to some predefined string constant, such as "C".

The * argv[] parameter is an array of char pointers. The first element in argv[] always points to the program's name, and each subsequent member points to a parameter. Each parameter is separated by the operating system's default parameter separator, usually a blank or comma. Under the PC's DOS operating system, only a blank is used as a separator. The end of this list of parameters can be determined by either using argc or testing the pointer, which is NULL to signify the end of the list.

The * envp[] parameter is an array of char pointers. The first element in argv[] points to the first environment string (when you are using DOS on the PC). Each subsequent member points to a succeeding environment string. Each environment string looks just like it does when you enter the DOS command SET, where you have an environment variable, an equal sign, and a string. The end of this list of environment strings can be determined by testing each envp[] pointer, when NULL is encountered, signifying the end of the environment list.

Listing 4.1 is a simple program that prints both the passed parameters and the environment strings to the screen. This program's output depends somewhat on which operating system it runs; however, it shouldn't fail when it is run under different operating systems.

Listing 4.1. MAINARGS.C.

```c
/* MAINARGS, written 22 May 1999 by Peter D. Hipson */
/* This program prints a program's arguments. */

#include <stdio.h>  // Make includes first part of file
#include <string.h> // For string functions.

int main(            // Define main() and the fact that this program uses
    int     argc,    // the passed parameters.
    char    *argv[],
    char    *envp[]
    );

int main(
    int     argc,
    char    *argv[],
    char    *envp[]
    )

{

int     i;

    printf("\n");

    printf("Program name is '%s'\n\n",
        argv[0]);

//  argc includes the program name, so decrement for actual
//  passed parameters.

    printf("Number of parameters %d \n\n",
        argc - 1);

//  It's just as valid is to use:
//  for (i = 1; i < argc; i++)

    for (i = 1; argv[i]; i++)
```

continues

Listing 4.1. continued

```
    {
        printf("Passed   parameter   %2d is '%.50s'\n",
            i,
            argv[i]);
    }

    printf("\n");

//  Environment variables may not be meaningful for all
//  operating systems. Check the compiler's documentation.
//  If this information is not available on your system,
//  delete the below for() loop.

    for (i = 0; envp[i]; i++)
    {
        printf("Environment string %2d is '%.50s'\n",
            i,
            envp[i]);
    }

    return (0);
}
```

As the MAINARGS program shows, the command line parameters are easy to access—the operating system does all the work for you. *Almost* all the work, at least. You still have to process the arguments and do whatever is required of your program.

Programs generally accepts three types of information:

1. Input or output filenames

2. Options, generally preceded by either a hyphen (-) or a slash (/)

3. Parameters, which may or may not be in any given format

Let's write a program that expects two filenames (both input and output), several options, and a parameter. This program reformats the lines of the input to the number of characters specified by the parameter. Possible options are to justify the lines or make them flush left or flush right. For simplicity, you don't write the program to actually do this work; however, you process the program's command line, and set flags, filenames, and the line width. Listing 4.2, JUSTIFY.C, is the basis for this program.

Listing 4.2. JUSTIFY.C.

```c
/* JUSTIFY, written 22 May 1999 by Peter D. Hipson */
/* This program justifies text files (shell only). It assumes
 * and uses Microsoft's extensions to C. Readers with other
 * compilers may have to change the program to use the calls
 * that their compiler supplies to perform the same functions. */

/* This program assumes the command line syntax shown in
 * the GiveHelp() function. */

#include <stdio.h>   // Make includes first part of file
#include <string.h>  // For string functions.
#include <stdlib.h>  // Standard include items.
#include <process.h> // For exit() etc.

#define  LEFT     1
#define  RIGHT    2
#define  JUSTIFY  3

#define  INNAME    1
#define  OUTNAME   2
#define  WIDTH     3
#define  LAST_THING 4

#define  ARG_LEFT    'l'
#define  ARG_RIGHT   'r'
#define  ARG_JUSTIFY 'j'
#define  ARG_SLASH   '/'
#define  ARG_DASH    '-'
#define  ARG_HELP    '?'

#define  NOINNAME     1
#define  NOOUTNAME    2
#define  BAD_WIDTH    3
#define  BAD_PARM     4
#define  BAD_OPTION   5
#define  NAME_MISSING 6
```

continues

Listing 4.2. continued

```
int main(            // Define main() and the fact that this program uses
    int    argc,     // the passed parameters.
    char   *argv[],
    char   *envp[]
    );

void   GiveHelp(
    int    nLevel,
    char   *psItem);

int main(
    int    argc,
    char   *argv[],
    char   *envp[]
    )

{

char   *pszTemp;
char   szBuffer[129];     // Temporary work buffer.
char   szProgram[30];
char   szInputFile[132];  // Make large enough for your OS.
char   szOutputFile[132]; // Make large enough for your OS.

/* strings for _splitpath() (which parses a filename) */
char   szDrive[_MAX_DRIVE];
char   szDir[_MAX_DIR];
char   szFname[_MAX_FNAME];
char   szExt[_MAX_EXT];

int    i;
int    j;
int    nCurrentParameter = INNAME;
int    nTempWidth = 0;
int    nLineWidth = 80;
int    nJustification = LEFT;
```

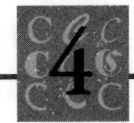
```
if (argc <= 2)
{
    GiveHelp(argc, NULL);
    return(16);
}

_splitpath(argv[0],
    szDrive,
    szDir,
    szFname,
    szExt);

strncpy(szProgram, szFname, sizeof(szProgram) - 1);

for (i = 1; argv[i]; i++)
{
    if (argv[i][0] == '/' ¦¦ argv[i][0] == '-')
    {   /* You have an argument, convert to lowercase, and test. */
        pszTemp = strlwr(argv[i]);

        for (j = 1; j < strlen(pszTemp); j++)
        {
            switch(pszTemp[j])
            {
                case ARG_LEFT:
                    nJustification = LEFT;
                    break;

                case ARG_RIGHT:
                    nJustification = RIGHT;
                    break;

                case ARG_JUSTIFY:
                    nJustification = JUSTIFY;
                    break;

                case ARG_HELP:
                    GiveHelp(NOINNAME, NULL);
                    exit(4);
                    break;
```

continues

Listing 4.2. continued

```
                    case ARG_SLASH:
                    case ARG_DASH:
                        break;

                    default:
                        GiveHelp(BAD_OPTION, &pszTemp[j]);
                        break;
                }
            }
        }
        else
        {   /* Either a filename or width. */
            switch(nCurrentParameter)
            {
                case INNAME:
                    strcpy(szInputFile, argv[i]);
                    nCurrentParameter = OUTNAME;
                    break;

                case OUTNAME:
                    strcpy(szOutputFile, argv[i]);
                    nCurrentParameter = WIDTH;
                    break;

                case WIDTH:
                    sscanf(argv[i], "%d", &nTempWidth);

                    if (nTempWidth < 20 ¦¦ nTempWidth > 128)
                    {
                        GiveHelp(BAD_WIDTH, NULL);
                    }
                    else
                    {
                        nLineWidth = nTempWidth;
                    }

                    nCurrentParameter = LAST_THING;

                    break;
```

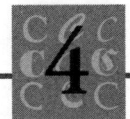
```
            default:
                GiveHelp(BAD_PARM, NULL);
                break;
        }
    }
}

if (nCurrentParameter < WIDTH)
{   /* Didn't get two filenames! */
    GiveHelp(NAME_MISSING, NULL);
    return(16);
}


printf("\n");

printf(
    "%s would read the file '%s' and write the file '%s'\n\n",
    szProgram,
    szInputFile,
    szOutputFile);

switch(nJustification)
{
    case LEFT:
        printf("The lines would be %d characters long, left \
                aligned\n",
            nLineWidth);
        break;

    case RIGHT:
        printf("The lines would be %d characters long, right \
                aligned\n",
            nLineWidth);
        break;

    case JUSTIFY:
        printf("The lines would be %d characters long, justified\n",
            nLineWidth);
        break;
}
```

continues

Listing 4.2. continued

```c
/* In the final version of this program, the files would
 * be opened next and the input file would be read into a buffer,
 * formatted according to the wishes of the user, and written
 * to the output file. At the end, the files would be closed,
 * and perhaps some statistical information could be
 * presented to the user.
 */


    return (0);
}


void    GiveHelp(
    int     nLevel,
    char    *psItem)

{
    printf("\n");

    switch(nLevel)
    {
        case NOINNAME:
        case NOOUTNAME: // Not enough parameters!
            printf(
                "FORMAT [-r¦-l¦-j] inputfile outputfile width\n"
                "    where \n"
                " Options - -r (or /r) to right align \n"
                "          -l (or /l) to left align \n"
                "          -j (or /j) to justify\n"
                "\n"
                " inputfile - is the input file name \n"
                " outputfile - is the output file name \n"
                "\n"
                " width is the desired output width (20 to 128)\n"
                " (default is 80 characters).\n"
                "\n"
                " Note: lines are concatenated, paragraph breaks are\n"
                "       signaled with a blank line\n\n");
            break;
```

```
            case BAD_WIDTH:
                printf(
                    "The width parameter must be between 20 and 128!\n"
                    "the width is ignored\n");
                break;

            case BAD_PARM:
                printf("Excessive parameters have been entered\n");

                /* Force a display of full help! */

                GiveHelp(NOINNAME, NULL);
                break;

            case BAD_OPTION:
                printf("'%c' is an invalid option! (Use only -l, -r or -j)\n",
                    *psItem);

                break;

            case NAME_MISSING:
                printf("One or both of the required file names is missing!\n");

                /* Force a display of full help! */

                GiveHelp(NOINNAME, NULL);
                break;

            default:
                printf(
                    "An unspecified error occurred! FORMAT has ended!\n"
                    );

                exit(16);

                break;
    }
}
```

This isn't so hard, is it? You have three possible options in JUSTIFY. You don't check to see whether one of these options has been entered—you just accept the last one entered. You can set a flag, and if too many options are entered or there are conflicting options, warn the user. The syntax of JUSTIFY shows the following:

1. The filenames (input and then output) and the width must be entered in that order.

2. The options must be preceded by either a slash (/) or a dash (-) option flag. One or more options can follow the option flag.

3. The options can be entered anywhere in the command line, before, after, or interspersed with other parameters.

4. The filenames must be entered; the width, however, is optional.

5. The GiveHelp() function is recursive—it calls itself to give the command syntax for some errors.

You can use JUSTIFY as a shell to create almost any simple utility program by changing what it expects for files, parameters, and options.

So that you have a better understanding of what JUSTIFY does with the command line arguments, let's look at several parts of the program in detail. First, you check to see that there are at least two command line arguments. Because both an input and an output filename are required, if there are not two arguments, one (or both) of these is missing. This test isn't exhaustive—you must test again later to make sure that you have received two filenames and not just a lot of options. The test for the number of arguments is simply:

```
if (argc <= 2)
{
    GiveHelp(argc, NULL);
    return(16);
}
```

The return's value is passed back to the operating system, and if this program was run under DOS, the value can be tested using the DOS BATCH command if errorlevel *command*.

After you have checked to see that you have the minimum number of command line arguments, rather than hard-code the name of the program, you then extract the program's name. You do this extraction so that, if the user has renamed your program, you present the user with the correct program name. It's confusing to rename a

command and have the error messages continue to give the old name. You then loop through the list of command line arguments, using a simple `for()` loop:

```
for (i = 1; argv[i]; i++)
{
```

You test for the terminating NULL command line argument pointer that signifies the end of the list. For each parameter, you look at the first character. If it is either a slash or a dash, the command line argument is an option:

```
if (argv[i][0] == '/' || argv[i][0] == '-')
{   /* You have an argument, convert to lowercase, and test. */
    pszTemp = strlwr(argv[i]);
```

You convert options to lowercase (to minimize the testing) because you don't have case-sensitive options in this program. Because in some programs the options -p and -P have different meanings, it's unlikely that users will remember the difference between the two. Make your program user-friendly by ignoring case if possible.

After changing the case, you simply loop through the option's string. Start with the second character because you know that the first character is the slash or dash. Using a switch, you check each valid letter option, and when there is a match, you set that option as required. Some programs have used the slash as the option prefix flag, and a dash to turn the option off; however, I suggest that you turn an option on with one letter, and off with another. Two-letter options (common with compilers and other complex programs) can be processed by looking at the first letter, and then the second, simply by adding a second nested `switch()` statement where needed:

```
for (j = 1; j < strlen(pszTemp); j++)
{
    switch(pszTemp[j])
    {
        case ARG_LEFT:
            nJustification = LEFT;
            break;

        case ARG_RIGHT:
            nJustification = RIGHT;
            break;

        case ARG_JUSTIFY:
            nJustification = JUSTIFY;
            break;
```

111

```
        case ARG_HELP:
            GiveHelp(NOINNAME, NULL);
            exit(4);
            break;

        case ARG_SLASH:
        case ARG_DASH:
            break;

        default:
            GiveHelp(BAD_OPTION, &pszTemp[j]);
            break;
    }
  }
}
```

In the preceding `switch()` block, you ignore imbedded slashes and dashes. Users commonly enter a set of options with a slash or dash before each option and with no intervening spaces.

You also process correctly the `/?` option, the relatively standard syntax for help. You can also process `/h` for help.

Notice the `default:` in this block: If the user has entered an unrecognized option letter, you provide a message that indicates the invalid option letter.

In the following block, you have either one of the filenames or the width specifier.

```
        else
{   /* Either a filename or width. */
```

These three items are positional; that is, the input filename is always the first of the three, the output filename is the second, and the width (which is optional) is always the third. There are numerous reasons for this order: One reason is that a filename can be a number (and therefore, width cannot be first if it is to be optional); another reason is that the two filenames must be provided in a known order because they are indistinguishable to the program.

You keep track of which of these three items you are processing by using the variable `nCurrentParameter`. This variable works as a state machine (see the "State Machines" section, later in this chapter), and changes its state every time a parameter is encountered:

```
switch(nCurrentParameter)
{
    case INNAME:
        strcpy(szInputFile, argv[i]);
        nCurrentParameter = OUTNAME;
        break;

    case OUTNAME:
        strcpy(szOutputFile, argv[i]);
        nCurrentParameter = WIDTH;
        break;

    case WIDTH:
        sscanf(argv[i], "%d", &nTempWidth);

        if (nTempWidth < 20 || nTempWidth > 128)
        {
            GiveHelp(BAD_WIDTH, NULL);
        }
        else
        {
            nLineWidth = nTempWidth;
        }

        nCurrentParameter = LAST_THING;

        break;

    default:
        GiveHelp(BAD_PARM, NULL);
        break;
    }
  }
}
```

The width parameter is tested, and the variable nLineWidth is updated only if the width is within the program's bounds of 20 to 128. (I'm not saying that these bounds are realistic—just that they can be.) You know that the user entered at least two parameters, but you don't know whether two of them were filenames. A confused user might have entered the command name, with no filenames, and with all three option letters as separate command line parameters:

```
JUSTIFY /j /l -r
```

This command line syntax has the minimum number of command line parameters; however, you don't have any filenames. You test for this with the following code:

```
if (nCurrentParameter < WIDTH)
{   /* Didn't get two filenames! */
    GiveHelp(NAME_MISSING, NULL);
    return(16);
}
```

Again, the state machine variable, nCurrentParameter, lets you know how many filenames the user entered. If the state machine variable isn't at least to the WIDTH state, you didn't get the required filenames.

The remainder of the program is simple because I didn't write the text-formatting part of this program. It has minimal error checking and a simple error-message function that receives an error message code and an optional character pointer. The character pointer can point to either a single character or a string. You must make sure that the message's printf() statements know what the pointer is pointing to.

One of the interesting things about the error message processor is that it is recursive: It calls itself when the user needs to have the full command syntax. The following syntax is accepted: /lr. That is, more than one option can follow the slash or dash option flag. If the user has entered a number of options following the slash or dash, and one of the options is invalid, do you stop processing this command line parameter? Probably not, but you must consider all possible situations and program accordingly.

Function Pointers

Function pointers can be used to do almost anything you can do with a function name. You can still pass parameters to a function that is being called with a pointer.

Sometimes, using pointers to functions is the only way to do something. A classic example is the library function qsort(), which takes a pointer to a function. This pointer often is coded as a constant; you might, however, want to code it as a function pointer variable that gets assigned the correct function to do qsort()'s compare.

The program FUNPTR.C, in Listing 4.3, has an example of one use of function pointers. This program calls a different function for each character in an input string. Although initializing the array of function pointers may take some time (and effort) in most programs, this time factor is not as significant as the effort to program separate calls, even if the separate calls are in a function by themselves.

Listing 4.3. FUNPTR.C.

```
/* FUNPTR, written 22 May 1999 by Peter D. Hipson */
/* An array of function pointers. */

#include <stdio.h>    // Make includes first part of file
#include <string.h>   // For string functions.
#include <stdlib.h>   // Standard include items.
#include <process.h>  // For exit() etc.

int main(          // Define main() and the fact that this program uses
    int     argc,   // the passed parameters.
    char    *argv[],
    char    *envp[]
    );

void NonPrint(const char    chChar);
void Letter(const char    chChar);
void Number(const char    chChar);
void Space(const char    chChar);


int main(
    int     argc,
    char    *argv[],
    char    *envp[]
    )

{

void    (*function[256])(const char);

char    *pszTemp;
char    szBuffer[512];   // Your input buffer.
```

continues

Listing 4.3. continued

```
int     i;

/*  First initialize your array of function pointers. Notice that,
 *  because you have specified what the function pointed to by this
 *  pointer requires for a parameter, all the functions assigned to
 *  this array require the same number and types of parameters.
 *  The parameters could have been omitted, but then you don't
 *  benefit from type checking on parameters. */

    for (i = 0; i < 256; i++)
    {
        if ((unsigned char)i < ' ')
        {
            function[i] = NonPrint;
        }
        else
        {
            if ((unsigned char)i >= '0' &&
                (unsigned char)i <= '9')
            {
                function[i] = Number;
            }
            else
            {
                if ((unsigned char)i == ' ')
                {
                    function[i] = Space;
                }
                else
                {
                    function[i] = Letter;
                }
            }
        }
    }

    while (gets(szBuffer))
    {
        for (i = 0; szBuffer[i]; i++)
```

```c
        {
/*          Now, this is nice syntax:                    */
            function[(int)szBuffer[i]] (szBuffer[i]);
        }
    }

    return(0);
}

void NonPrint(
    const char    chChar)

{
/*  Make it printable by adding a '@' to it.*/

    printf("CTRL -    '%c'\n", chChar + '@');
}


void Space(
    const char    chChar)

{
    printf("Space     '%c'\n", chChar);
}

void Letter(
    const char    chChar)

{
    printf("Letter    '%c'\n", chChar);
}


void Number(
    const char    chChar)

{
    printf("Number    '%c'\n", chChar);
}
```

(Remember, I didn't promise that FUNPTR does anything significant.)

I've shown that function prototypes are important, but, in a program that is using function pointers, they are vital. Notice that each of the functions that will be assigned to the function pointer has identical prototypes—their return types are the same and their parameters match equally.

Let's look at some of the fun parts of FUNPTR. The declaration of the array of function pointers has a number of critical parts:

```c
void    (*function[256])(const char);
```

The `void` tells C that these functions don't return anything. If the functions return a value, use that value's type. Because the order and positioning of the parentheses are critical, the name of the function pointer is next. If this were not an array declaration, the declaration would be

```c
void    (*function)(const char);
```

Following the function pointer name are the function's parameters (again, the parentheses are important). Keep it simple—try to avoid having functions assigned that take different types or counts of parameters. Having functions with different parameters weakens the compiler's capability to check for errors, although it is possible.

After declaring the function pointer array, you initialize it. When you assign a function's address to a function pointer, *do not use the function's parentheses.*

```c
for (i = 0; i < 256; i++)
{
    if ((unsigned char)i < ' ')
    {
        function[i] = NonPrint; /* NOTICE: No (), just the name */
    }
    else
    {
        if ((unsigned char)i >= '0' &&
            (unsigned char)i <= '9')
        {
            function[i] = Number; /* NOTICE: No (), just the name */
        }
        else
        {
            if ((unsigned char)i == ' ')
```

```
      {
           function[i] = Space; /* NOTICE: No (), just the name */
      }
      else
      {
           function[i] = Letter; /* NOTICE: No (), just the name */
      }
    }
  }
}
```

Because FUNPTR has an array of 256 possible functions to call, you initialize all of them. Because you potentially call a different function for each of the possible 256 characters in the character set and because (with a few exceptions) the user can enter any character, you must make sure that all the members of the function pointer array are initialized.

After you have initialized the function pointer array, you can continue with the rest of the program. Use a simple loop to get a line from the keyboard, and then for each character in the line, call the appropriate function:

```
    while (gets(szBuffer))
    {
        for (i = 0; szBuffer[i]; i++)
        {
/*          Now, this is nice syntax:                 */
            function[(int)szBuffer[i]] (szBuffer[i]);
        }
    }
```

Notice the strange call function[]() (using an array of function pointers doesn't always look good). It eliminates a large if()...else block that saves valuable programming time if this letter-by-letter parsing of the string is done often (more than once) in a program. A second important factor is that the while() loop runs faster because many if() statements are eliminated.

Using a function pointer as a parameter in a function call is not unusual. As mentioned, the library function qsort() does this.

Look at the following prototype for qsort(). The prototype is in the standard header file stdlib.h and in search.h, if your compiler has such a header file.

```
void _FAR_ __cdecl qsort(
    void _FAR_ *,     /* array to be sorted */
    size_t,           /* number of elements in the array */
    size_t,           /* size of each array element */
    int (_FAR_ __cdecl *)(const void _FAR_ *, const void _FAR_ *));
```

qsort()'s first three parameters are as expected: an array pointer, two integers showing the number of elements in the array, and the size of the elements.

The final parameter in the call to qsort() is the most interesting one. It specifies that the parameter is the address of a function that returns an int value and takes two far pointers. Both of these pointers are declared as type void so that any type of pointer can be passed; the function being called, however, *must know the pointer's type*. Because each call to qsort() is generally for a specific type of array, the function being called will know about the array's types. qsort() is discussed in detail in Chapter 10, "Data Management: Sorts, Lists, and Indexes."

Menus and Pointers

Peter's programming rule number 6: Don't reinvent the wheel. OK, it's not an original rule, but even with Peter's rules, I didn't want to reinvent the rule.

There are several easy ways to put menus in a program without writing them all yourself. The first and by far the best is to use Windows. No kidding, Windows is an effective way to create slick user interfaces. Don't be put off by the learning curve of Window's programming—it is much less than writing the user interface yourself.

If you are determined not to use Windows, systems are available that enable almost any type of program to have extensive menu support, such as pull-down menus, pop-up dialog menus, and so on.

It's well beyond the scope of this book to write an entire pull-down menu system. One simple text-only system requires many thousands of lines of code. This book can, however, cover many of the basics.

A pull-down menu might, for example, call a different function for each of the menu items. The function call to the menu system might include such parameters as an array for each menu item's text and an array of function pointers to call for each menu item.

You can look at the top bar menu separately and use a rather simple call to a function such as getch() to process the keystrokes entered. Part of MENU1.C assumes that the program is running under DOS on a PC, that the ANSI.SYS device driver (used for screen control) is installed, and that the compiler supports the functions this program calls.

In Listing 4.4, the program MENU1.C implements a simple pull-down menu that has a simple dialog box to enable the user to enter a filename.

Listing 4.4. MENU1.C.

```
/* MENU1, written 23 May 1992 by Peter D. Hipson */
/* A simple menu program. */

/* This program assumes and uses Microsoft's extensions to C.
 * Readers with other compilers may have to change the program
 * to use the calls that their compiler supplies to perform
 * the same functions. */

#include <stdio.h>    // Make includes first part of file
#include <string.h>   // For string functions.
#include <stdlib.h>   // Standard include items.
#include <process.h>  // For exit(), etc.
#include <conio.h>    // For getch() and other console I/O.
#include <ctype.h>    // For char functions (_toupper()...)

/* ANSI.SYS screen control #define's below:
*/

#define BOLD        "\x1B[1m"
#define NORMAL      "\x1B[0m"
#define RED         "\x1B[31m"
#define BLACK       "\x1B[30m"
#define GREEN       "\x1B[32m"

#define CLEAR_SCREEN "\x1B[2J"
#define CLEAR_EOL    "\x1B[K"

#define MOVE_CURSOR  "\x1B[%d;%df"
```

continues

Listing 4.4. continued

```c
char   szTopBar[] = {/* Must be 80 characters long MAX. */
    CLEAR_SCREEN
    BOLD"F"NORMAL"iles    "
    BOLD"E"NORMAL"dit     "
    BOLD"V"NORMAL"iew     "
    BOLD"P"NORMAL"roject  "
    BOLD"R"NORMAL"un      "
    BOLD"D"NORMAL"ebug    "
    CLEAR_EOL
    };

/* Line-drawing characters for the PC = " ³ ´ ¿ À Á Â Ã Ä Å Ú Ù"*/

void    MenuBar(); /* Never called! Make the array look good. */

char    *szFiles[] = {
    "ÚÄÄÄÄÄÄÄÄÄÄÄÄÄÄ¿",
    "³"BOLD"N"NORMAL"ew           ³",
    "³"BOLD"O"NORMAL"pen          ³",
    "³"BOLD"C"NORMAL"lose         ³",
    "³"BOLD"S"NORMAL"ave          ³",
    "³save "BOLD"A"NORMAL"s       ³",
    "ÃÄÄÄÄÄÄÄÄÄÄÄÄÄÄ´",
    "³"BOLD"P"NORMAL"rint         ³",
    "ÃÄÄÄÄÄÄÄÄÄÄÄÄÄÄ´",
    "³e"BOLD"X"NORMAL"it          ³",
    "ÀÄÄÄÄÄÄÄÄÄÄÄÄÄÄÙ",
    NULL};


void    DoFilesNew();
void    DoFilesOpen();
void    DoFilesClose();
void    DoFilesSave();
void    DoFilesSaveAs();
void    DoFilesPrint();
void    DoFilesEXit();
```

```
void    (*FilesFunctions[])(void) = {
    MenuBar,
    DoFilesNew,
    DoFilesOpen,
    DoFilesClose,
    DoFilesSave,
    DoFilesSaveAs,
    MenuBar,
    DoFilesPrint,
    MenuBar,
    DoFilesEXit,
    MenuBar,
    NULL
    };


int main(           // Define main() and the fact that this program uses
    int     argc,   // the passed parameters.
    char    *argv[],
    char    *envp[]
    );

void PullDown(char **, int, void (__cdecl **)(void));

int main(
    int     argc,
    char    *argv[],
    char    *envp[]
    )

{

char    chEntered;

    while (1)
    {
        printf(szTopBar);

        chEntered = (char)getch();
```

continues

123

Listing 4.4. continued

```c
if (chEntered == '\0' || chEntered == '\xE0')
{   // PC Extended character (function key etc.)
    chEntered = (char)getch();
}

printf(MOVE_CURSOR, 10, 10); /* Using printf() fully here! */

switch (_toupper((int)chEntered))
{
    case 'F':
        PullDown(szFiles, 1, FilesFunctions);
        break;

    case 'E':
        printf("Edit submenu called" CLEAR_EOL);
        break;

    case 'V':
        printf("View submenu called" CLEAR_EOL);
        break;

    case 'P':
        printf("Project submenu called" CLEAR_EOL);
        break;

    case 'R':
        printf("Run submenu called" CLEAR_EOL);
        break;

    case 'D':
        printf("Debug submenu called" CLEAR_EOL);
        break;

    default:
        printf("Invalid key!" CLEAR_EOL);
        break;
}

}
```

```
    return(0);
}

void PullDown(
    char *  szMenu[],
    int     nColumn,
    void (__cdecl *pFunctions[])(void))


{

int     i;
int     nMenuItem = -1;

char    chEntered;

    for (i = 0; szMenu[i]; i++)
    {
        printf(MOVE_CURSOR, i + 1, nColumn);
        printf(szMenu[i]);
    }

    while (nMenuItem < 0)
    {
        chEntered = (char)getch();

        if (chEntered == '\0' || chEntered == '\xE0')
        {   // PC Extended character (function key etc.)
            chEntered = (char)getch();
        }

        chEntered = (char)_toupper((int)chEntered);

/* find the correct menu item index */

        if (isalnum((int)chEntered))
        {
            for (i = 0; szMenu[i]; i++)
            {
```

continues

Listing 4.4. continued

```
                if (strchr(szMenu[i], chEntered))
                {
                    nMenuItem = i;
                    break;
                }
            }
        }

        if (nMenuItem >= 0)
        {
            pFunctions[nMenuItem]();
        }
    }
}

void    DoFilesNew()

{
    printf(MOVE_CURSOR, 20, 10);

    printf("Files, new");

    printf(MOVE_CURSOR, 24, 10);

    printf("Any key to continue");

    (void)getch();
}

void    DoFilesOpen()

{
/*  Presents to the user a simple get a filename dialog box,
 *  enabling character string to be entered. Basic editing supported.
 */

int     i;
/*  These hard-coded constants, for placement of dialog box,
 *  normally would be passed.
```

```
    */
int     nColumn = 15;
int     nRow = 15;
int     nInputColumn = 2;
int     nInputRow = 4;

char    szFileName[132];
char    *szFilesOpen[] = {
    "ÚÄÄÄÄÄÄÄÄÄÄÄÄÄÄÄÄÄÄÄÄÄÄÄÄÄÄÄÄÄÄÄÄÄÄÄÄÄÄÄÄÄÄÄÄ¿",
    "³                                           ³",
    "³Enter the name of the file to open:        ³",
    "³                                           ³",
    "³ .........................................  ³",
    "³                                           ³",
    "ÀÄÄÄÄÄÄÄÄÄÄÄÄÄÄÄÄÄÄÄÄÄÄÄÄÄÄÄÄÄÄÄÄÄÄÄÄÄÄÄÄÄÄÄÄÙ",
    NULL};

    for (i = 0; szFilesOpen[i]; i++)
    {
        printf(MOVE_CURSOR, i + nRow, nColumn);
        printf(szFilesOpen[i]);
    }

    printf(MOVE_CURSOR,
        nInputRow + nRow,
        nInputColumn + nColumn);

    scanf("%s", szFileName);

    printf(MOVE_CURSOR, 24, 10);

    printf("NAME: '%s' Any key to continue", szFileName);

    (void)getch();
}

void    DoFilesClose()

{
    printf(MOVE_CURSOR, 20, 10);

    printf("Files, close selected");
```

continues

Listing 4.4. continued

```c
        printf(MOVE_CURSOR, 24, 10);

        printf("Any key to continue");

        (void)getch();
}

void    DoFilesSave()

{
    printf(MOVE_CURSOR, 20, 10);

    printf("Files, save selected");

    printf(MOVE_CURSOR, 24, 10);

    printf("Any key to continue");

    (void)getch();
}

void    DoFilesSaveAs()

{
    printf(MOVE_CURSOR, 20, 10);

    printf("Files, save as selected");

    printf(MOVE_CURSOR, 24, 10);

    printf("Any key to continue");

    (void)getch();
}

void    DoFilesPrint()

{
    printf(MOVE_CURSOR, 20, 10);
```

```
    printf("Files, print selected");

    printf(MOVE_CURSOR, 24, 10);

    printf("Any key to continue");

    (void)getch();
}

void    DoFilesEXit()

{
    printf(MOVE_CURSOR, 20, 10);

    printf("Files, exit selected");

    exit(0);
}

void    MenuBar()

{
/* This function is never called! */
}
```

MENU1.C is the most complex program this book has discussed. It shows several important features, including passing an array of function pointers and using screen control and—of course—menus.

One of the first things you do in MENU1 is define some string identifiers. These identifiers are used to format the menu items, position the cursor, and perform other screen-management functions:

```
/* ANSI.SYS screen control #define's below: */

#define BOLD        "\x1B[1m"
#define NORMAL      "\x1B[0m"
#define RED         "\x1B[31m"
#define BLACK       "\x1B[30m"
```

```
#define GREEN        "\x1B[32m"

#define CLEAR_SCREEN "\x1B[2J"
#define CLEAR_EOL     "\x1B[K"

#define MOVE_CURSOR  "\x1B[%d;%df"
```

Notice the identifier MOVE_CURSOR. Used with printf() and a set of integer parameters specifying cursor row and column, you can position the cursor using the following statement:

```
printf(MOVE_CURSOR, 10, 20);
```

The definition of the program's top menu bar makes heavy use of string constant concatenation and ANSI screen control.

```
char  szTopBar[] = {/* Must be 80 characters long MAX. */
    CLEAR_SCREEN
    BOLD"F"NORMAL"iles    "
    BOLD"E"NORMAL"dit     "
    BOLD"V"NORMAL"iew     "
    BOLD"P"NORMAL"roject  "
    BOLD"R"NORMAL"un      "
    BOLD"D"NORMAL"ebug    "
    CLEAR_EOL
    };
```

The maximum true length of the screen's title bar is equal to the screen's width. Counting these characters can be difficult; if you remove the ANSI screen-control identifiers and the string concatenation quotes, however, you can see the length of the menu bar more easily.

After the top menu-bar string definition, you define for the Files menu a pull-down that offers a number of common operations:

```
char   *szFiles[] = {
    "ÚÄÄÄÄÄÄÄÄÄÄÄÄÄÄÄ¿",
    "³"BOLD"N"NORMAL"ew          ³",
    "³"BOLD"O"NORMAL"pen         ³",
    "³"BOLD"C"NORMAL"lose        ³",
    "³"BOLD"S"NORMAL"ave         ³",
    "³save "BOLD"A"NORMAL"s      ³",
    "ÀÄÄÄÄÄÄÄÄÄÄÄÄÄÄÄÙ",
```

```
"³"BOLD"P"NORMAL"rint        ³",
"ĀÄÄÄÄÄÄÄÄÄÄÄÄÄÄÄ´",
"³e"BOLD"X"NORMAL"it         ³",
"ÀÄÄÄÄÄÄÄÄÄÄÄÄÄÄÄÄÙ",
NULL};
```

After you know what the `Files` pull-down menu will contain, you then build the function pointer array. You first define the functions, and then the array, and then initialize it with the functions that perform each task.

```
void      DoFilesNew();
void      DoFilesOpen();
void      DoFilesClose();
void      DoFilesSave();
void      DoFilesSaveAs();
void      DoFilesPrint();
void      DoFilesEXit();

void      (*FilesFunctions[])(void) = {
    MenuBar,
    DoFilesNew,
    DoFilesOpen,
    DoFilesClose,
    DoFilesSave,
    DoFilesSaveAs,
    MenuBar,
    DoFilesPrint,
    MenuBar,
    DoFilesEXit,
    MenuBar,
    NULL
    };
```

Notice that you have allowed the number of initializers to define how many elements are found in this array, and that you have set the final member to NULL so that you can test for the end of the array if necessary. Setting the last element of an array of pointers to NULL is a good idea because you don't have to pass the length of the array to functions that use it.

Finally, just before you start the `main()` function, you define the function that controls the pull-down menus. This function's prototype is

```
void PullDown(char **, int, void (__cdecl **)(void));
```

Notice how an array of pointers (usually written as *array[]) is described as an array of pointers to pointers (type **). This description is necessary because you don't specify the name of the actual array in this prototype. The array of function pointers must be specified with both the return values and parameters. In this program, both are simply void.

The main program has just a large loop that reads the keyboard and processes the characters. This program uses getch() to get a character (without echoing it to the screen); because this program runs on a PC, you test (and process) special keypresses, such as the function keys. Other computers with different keyboards may require some other changes to this part of the program.

```c
while (1)
{
    printf(szTopBar);

    chEntered = (char)getch();

    if (chEntered == '\0' || chEntered == '\xE0')
    {   // PC Extended character (function key etc.)
        chEntered = (char)getch();
    }
```

After a character is read in, it is converted to uppercase (so that it can be tested), and then you use a case statement to find which of the top bar menu items has been selected.

```c
switch (_toupper((int)chEntered))
{
    case 'F':
        PullDown(szFiles, 1, FilesFunctions);
        break;

    case 'E':
        printf("Edit submenu called" CLEAR_EOL);
        break;

    case 'V':
        printf("View submenu called" CLEAR_EOL);
        break;
```

```
    case 'P':
        printf("Project submenu called" CLEAR_EOL);
        break;

    case 'R':
        printf("Run submenu called" CLEAR_EOL);
        break;

    case 'D':
        printf("Debug submenu called" CLEAR_EOL);
        break;

    default:
        printf("Invalid key!" CLEAR_EOL);
        break;
}
```

When a top bar menu item is selected (Files in this example), the PullDown() function is called. This generic function is provided with the starting column for the pull-down menu (the starting row is always 2), an array of char pointers pointing to each menu item, and an array of function pointers pointing to the functions that will be called when a specific menu item is called. Except for Files, none of the top menu items are implemented.

PullDown() has the code to display the pull-down menu. A better program would save the screen at the location where the pull-down menu is displayed and restore it when the function returns; this simple program, however, doesn't "clean up" after itself well:

```
for (i = 0; szMenu[i]; i++)
{
    printf(MOVE_CURSOR, i + 2, nColumn);
    printf(szMenu[i]);
}
```

The menu items are printed, one to a line, until the end of the list (signified by the NULL pointer) is encountered. After the pull-down menu is displayed, you read the keyboard until a valid key is pressed, and then perform the requested action. Because this is a simple program, you again require the user to select a menu item before you let the user return to the main menu.

```
    while (nMenuItem < 0)
    {
        chEntered = (char)getch();

        if (chEntered == '\0' || chEntered == '\xE0')
        {   // PC Extended character (function key etc.)
            chEntered = (char)getch();
        }

        chEntered = (char)_toupper((int)chEntered);

/* find the correct menu item index */

        if (isalnum((int)chEntered))
        {
            for (i = 0; szMenu[i]; i++)
            {
                if (strchr(szMenu[i], chEntered))
                {
                    nMenuItem = i;
                    break;
                }
            }
        }
    }
```

To check the keys pressed by the user, you get the character pressed, convert it to uppercase, and then scan each menu item for the key character. Because each menu item is allowed only one capitalized character (the desired character for this action), you can use strchr() to look at each of the menu lines. If no match is found, you wait for the user to press a new key; if a match is found, you call the appropriate function:

```
    if (nMenuItem >= 0)
    {
        pFunctions[nMenuItem]();
    }
}
```

Calling the correct function is as easy as indexing the array of function pointers.

MENU1 is a relatively crude program, yet it exceeds 300 lines of source code and doesn't do anything. Remember my comments about reinventing the wheel at the beginning of the chapter? Now you can see why. I could write this program (and make

it work properly) under Windows in less time than it took to write the entire thing myself. I had to write it, though, to provide the example of both menus and the use of arrays of pointers. Now you can decide what you want to do.

State Machines

You might think that state machines are part of your state government, but not for the purposes of this book. The example program JUSTIFY is a state machine (refer to Listing 4.1). Most state machines consist of a controlling variable (the state variable), whose value indicates the current operating status of the function (or program). The state variable generally is an integer value, and depending on its current state, can be changed to another state.

Generally, in most state machines the state of the controlling variable does not need to be incremented (or decremented) in single steps. For example, it may change directly from one state to another. States generally can be considered to be unique but equal. When you are writing a state machine, you must consider the process and what needs to be done (see Figure 4.1).

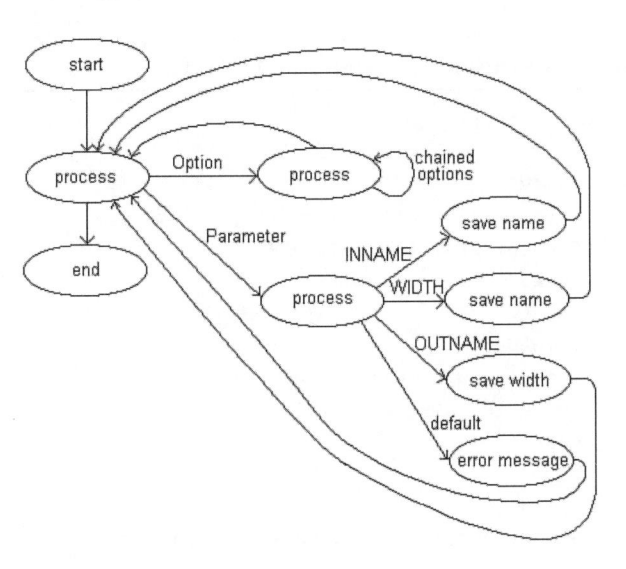

Figure 4.1. An example of a state machine's state transitions.

Figure 4.1 shows that the program has a number of "states." The state machine part of JUSTIFY is the processing of the three parameters: the input filename, the output filename, and the output width you want.

Listing 4.5 shows the way the state machine works. The major part of this machine is a simple switch() loop, with a case to handle each state. At the end of each state's case statement is the code necessary to update the status of the state variable, nCurrentParameter. The next time the switch() statement is executed, this new state of nCurrentParameter controls which case: statement is executed. As usual with a switch() statement, only one case statement block is executed (you don't allow case statements to fall through, into the following case statement, in this state machine).

One important factor limits JUSTIFY's state machine: You allow the state variable to change to only the next state, and you don't allow states to be skipped. The only way to get to the WIDTH state, therefore, is from the OUTNAME state, and the only way to get to the OUTNAME state is from the INNAME state. After the WIDTH state has been achieved, any further changes in the state are errors because you have nothing else to get. The result is that the next state from the WIDTH state is the error state, LAST_THING, which, if processed, gives the user an error message. Listing 4.5 is the parameter processor from the JUSTIFY program.

Listing 4.5. State machine from JUSTIFY.C.

```
switch(nCurrentParameter)
{
    case INNAME:
        strcpy(szInputFile, argv[i]);
        nCurrentParameter = OUTNAME;
        break;

    case OUTNAME:
        strcpy(szOutputFile, argv[i]);
        nCurrentParameter = WIDTH;
        break;

    case WIDTH:
        sscanf(argv[i], "%d", &nTempWidth);

        if (nTempWidth < 20 || nTempWidth > 128)
        {
            GiveHelp(BAD_WIDTH, NULL);
        }
```

136

```
        else
        {
            nLineWidth = nTempWidth;
        }

        nCurrentParameter = LAST_THING;

        break;

    default:
        GiveHelp(BAD_PARM, NULL);
        break;
}
```

State machines can prove valuable in helping to organize your programs. The use of a state variable was a logical choice as a method to keep track of where I was in the program's command line and to track which parts of the required command parameters had been processed.

Summary

In this chapter, you learned about command line arguments, pointer arrays, function pointers, and state machines.

- Each program is passed, as parameters to the main() function, the command line parameters.

- Command line parameters are processed by the operating system, by being parsed into separate tokens.

- You can obtain the name of your program (the executable file's name) using the parameters passed to main().

- Like data objects, functions can have pointers to them.

- Like any other pointer, a function pointer can be placed in an array and indexed using an index variable.

- Function pointers can be passed as parameters to other functions, which then can call these functions.

- Properly designed menu-driven programs can offer an excellent user interface.

- It generally is not worth the effort to design your own menu system. Using Windows, OS/2, the Macintosh, XWindows, or some other commercially available menuing system is a much better choice.

- Using state machines enables you to efficiently design a program that must process data in either a fixed or random format.

Decimal, Binary, Hex, and Octal

By now, you probably have realized that computers don't save numbers in memory in the same format as humans do. The CPU converts a number that the computer's user provides to a format that the CPU better understands. This conversion, transparent to both the user and the programmer, enables the computer to work efficiently.

Decimal

We work with decimal (base 10) numbers. Decimal numbers have become popular primarily because we, as humans, usually have ten fingers. Yes, it's true, our number system is based on counting on our fingers. Why, then, don't we use base 5, (the fingers on one hand), or base 20 (both hands and feet)?

Decimal numbers have become so natural to use that we no longer stop to think about the concept of what we are doing. We add, carry, subtract, multiply, and divide with ease (most of us do, anyway) and don't stop to consider any other based number systems; when we are asked whether we use any of these other systems, most people reply "No." The next most common system, however, is base 60—time, where 60 seconds make a minute, and 60 minutes make an hour. We don't get shaken when we are presented with time computations; when we have to convert to or work in number systems other than decimal, however, our palms sweat and we get the shakes.

Let's review the decimal number system. First, decimal numbers have the characters to represent items. Figure 5.1 shows the first ten digits and what they represent.

Character	Value
0	
1	
2	
3	
4	
5	
6	
7	
8	
9	

Figure 5.1. Decimal numbers 0 through 9.

The first use of numbers was probably to count food stocks, livestock, and other objects encountered daily. As shown in Figure 5.1, a problem begins when you have more than nine objects. Things get difficult then: Should new digits be created, or a new system?

When the decimal system was developed, someone decided that ten characters (or digits) were sufficient and that a system had to be created to indicate how many hands there were to represent the object being counted—the tens column was created. It then was possible to write, using two digits, numbers that were ten times as large as before. No one realized that there would ever be a need for a number larger than 99. (After all, the greatest number of fish ever caught at a single time probably was only 18). The decimal number system was born, capable of representing as many as 99 objects.

Then Joe came along. Brighter than most, he invented the fishing net. He forgot to patent the fishing net, and soon a number of cheap but usable clone fishing nets were available. Bob, who bought one of the better clones, managed one day to catch much more than 99 fish. He went home and proudly announced that his catch was "99 and many more," to which his loving wife wanted to know how many more. The hundreds column then was created. Bob's wife simply carried the concept of the tens column out to a new column. And so it went—soon thousands, millions, and (when government was created) billions were only a short way off.

All of this math, using the decimal number system, could be done with the help of the oldest digital computer, the hand.

Binary

Digital computers, invented later, didn't have hands. They used memory to store numbers. This memory, which lacked fingers, could hold only a zero (nothing) or a one (something). Any number greater than one couldn't be represented within a single computer memory location. (I'm ignoring the analog computer, which could store more than zero and one in a single memory location—they never became popular and are not widely available today).

After the first few hours of working with zero and one, it was apparent that a way to represent numbers larger than one had to be developed. This task wasn't difficult because designers and engineers are bright folks, and a scheme of using consecutive locations in memory was quickly developed.

Because only two states existed in a single memory location, the representation of numbers with computers was called *binary*. The use of this word is common with computers: Computers sometimes are referred to today as *binary computers*. To a computer, binary is as natural as decimal is to humans. Computers have no problems counting, doing math, storing, and performing I/O using binary numbers. The representation of binary numbers, however, left much to be desired. For instance, the year 1992 can be represented using only four digits with the decimal number system; in binary, it is represented as 11111001000 (11 digits). This number is not nearly as easy for humans to work with, write, or understand.

Look at Figure 5.2 to see how the binary value for 1992 is determined. This figure shows the binary value, the value of each bit, and the decimal result.

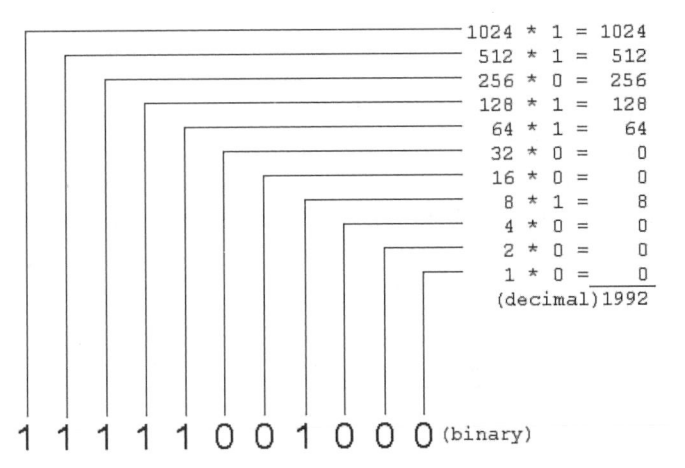

```
                              1024 * 1 = 1024
                               512 * 1 =  512
                               256 * 0 =  256
                               128 * 1 =  128
                                64 * 1 =   64
                                32 * 0 =    0
                                16 * 0 =    0
                                 8 * 1 =    8
                                 4 * 0 =    0
                                 2 * 0 =    0
                                 1 * 0 =    0
                              (decimal)1992

1 1 1 1 1 0 0 1 0 0 0 (binary)
```

Figure 5.2 The year 1992 in decimal and binary.

Hex

Computers did not always have an 8-bit block of memory defined. Early computers used 10, 11, and 16 bits, and other computers probably were developed that had every other possible number of bits.

Hex is the compromise that enables both computers and people to understand number representation. The hex number system is based on 16. My guess is that the word *hex* was adopted because the base was 6 greater than base 10. Hex adds a new wrinkle: Binary uses only 2 digits, 0 and 1; decimal uses 10, 0 to 9; hex, however, uses 16 numeric digits. Because you don't have 16 digits, either 6 new characters must be created to represent the new numbers, or you must use 6 existing characters. Introducing 6 new characters into the currently used character set isn't easy, but reusing 6 other characters *is* easy.

The developers of hex notation chose to use the characters *A* through *F* for the new digits (see Figure 5.3). No standard exists for whether the digits are represented in upper- or lowercase; I prefer uppercase, however, because numeric characters give the appearance of being uppercase (or larger) characters.

Character	Bit positions	Value
0	0000	
1	0001	
2	0010	
3	0011	
4	0100	
5	0101	
6	0110	
7	0111	
8	1000	
9	1001	
A	1010	
B	1011	
C	1100	
D	1101	
E	1110	
F	1111	

Figure 5.3. Hex numbers 0 through F.

Because most of the development of computers was done in countries that used the Roman alphabet, the choice of the number of bits in a computer's word generally was determined by the number of characters the computer could recognize. As the computer was being developed, a number of systems to organize the characters and assign each to a numeric value already were in existence. The minimum number of characters was fairly large: It was necessary to have letters—both upper- and lowercase (52), numbers (10), punctuation and symbols (about 20), which brought the total to between 80 and 90 characters.

In binary number systems, the number of bits increases in the following progression: 1, 2, 4, 8, 16, 32, 64, 128, 256, and so on. Most people quickly realized that 64 (a 6-bit word) was too small, 128 (a 7-bit word) was much better, and that 256 (an 8-bit word) was all that would ever be needed. Obviously, this artificial limit was based on current needs, with no consideration of the future. Sixteen bits now are used to represent characters in some applications.

Eight bits generally was accepted for the size of the basic block of computer memory. This amount was referred to as a *byte*; the origins of this word, however, escape me.

Hex might have been developed as a compromise between binary, required for the computer, and decimal, required for programmers. Two hex digits can be held in the standard-size computer memory, which is eight bits.

The example of 1992 becomes 7C8 when it is represented in hex. This number, which is not as long as its decimal equivalent (it has only three digits), is almost as indecipherable as the binary. It isn't necessary to be able to read hex numbers to be a good programmer, but it helps.

To see how the hex value for 1992 is determined, look at Figure 5.4. It shows the hex value, the value of each digit, and the decimal result.

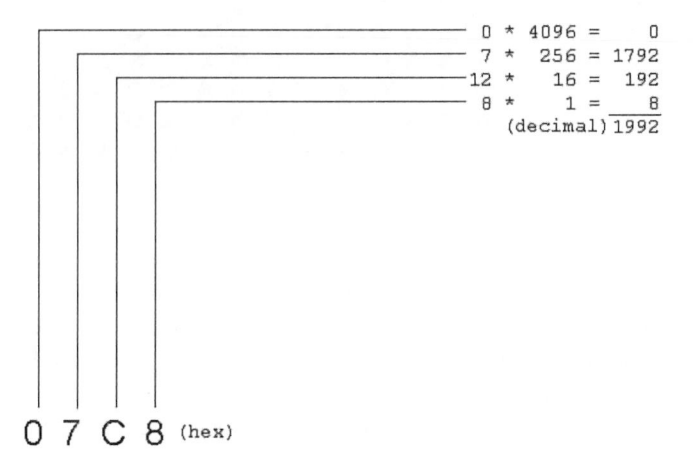

```
                                        0 *  4096 =     0
                                        7 *   256 =  1792
                                       12 *    16 =   192
                                        8 *     1 =     8
                                          (decimal) 1992


  0 7 C 8 (hex)
```

Figure 5.4. The year 1992 in decimal and hex.

Octal

Octal, the base 8 number system, enjoyed great popularity on a number of DEC computers, primarily the PDP-8. Trust me, though, octal is dead. Don't use it, because no one else uses it anymore. Some computers used word lengths that were not 8 bits (a byte) long. Rather, they used a 12-bit word that easily was divided into 4 octal digits of 3 bits each. Unlike hex, which has more than 10 characters, octal has only 8, which

makes the decimal-number characters fully usable. Octal is used for DEC minicomputers, and C was developed on DEC minicomputers—therefore, the support for octal. Figure 5.5 shows a representation of the octal numbers, which are similar to the ones in the decimal-based systems; octal, however, doesn't have numbers 8 or 9.

Character	Bit pattern	Value
0	000	
1	001	
2	010	
3	011	
4	100	
5	101	
6	110	
7	111	

Figure 5.5. Octal numbers 0 through 7.

When the 1992 example is represented in octal, it becomes 3710. This rather misleading number is as long as its decimal equivalent (and could have been longer). Without some form of prefix (or postfix) notation, you have no way to determine whether any number is octal- or decimal-based (3710 is a legitimate number).

Look at Figure 5.6 to see how that octal value for 1992 is determined. This figure shows the octal value, the value of each digit, and the decimal result.

```
                                    3 *  512 = 1536
                                    7 *   64 =  448
                                    1 *    8 =    8
                                    0 *    1 =    0
                                       (decimal)1992


   3  7  1  0  (octal)
```

Figure 5.6. The year 1992 in decimal and octal.

Looking at a File

In any program that writes a file that is not pure text, you must able to look at the file and determine whether the program has written the file properly. When you run the DEBUG utility, a crude debugger, on the PC, it enables you to dump programs and data files. Because the program is difficult to use, however, it is not used often.

One solution is to have a program that dumps files and provides both a hex and ASCII listing of the file's contents (see Listing 5.1,). DUMP is a simple program that reads files of any length and lists their contents in an easy-to-use format.

Listing 5.1. DUMP.C.

```
/* DUMP, written 23 May 1992 by Peter D. Hipson */
/* A program that dumps files in hex and ASCII. */

#include <stdio.h>   // Make includes first part of file
#include <string.h>  // For string functions.
#include <stdlib.h>  // Standard include items.
#include <process.h> // For exit(), etc.
#include <time.h>    // For time information.

#define  ARG_HELP    '?'
#define  ARG_SLASH   '/'
#define  ARG_DASH    '-'

int main(          // Define main() and the fact that
    int     argc,  // this program uses the passed parameters.
    char    *argv[],
    char    *envp[]
    );

int main(
    int argc,
    char *argv[],
    char *envp[])

{

FILE    *fpFilePointer;
```

```
long      lPosition;

int       i;
int       j;
int       nNumberBytesRead;

unsigned     int nHexNumber;

char      *pszTemp;

/* strings for _splitpath() (which parses a file name) */
char      szDrive[_MAX_DRIVE];
char      szDir[_MAX_DIR];
char      szFname[_MAX_FNAME];
char      szExt[_MAX_EXT];
char      szInputFile[128];
char      szProgram[132];
char      szBuffer[132];
char      sBuffer[257];

time_t   tTime;
struct   tm  *pTM;


    _splitpath(argv[0],
        szDrive,
        szDir,
        szFname,
        szExt);

    strncpy(szProgram, szFname, sizeof(szProgram) - 1);

    if (argc <= 1)
    {
        printf("%s: - No file name given.\n", szProgram);
        exit(4);
    }

    for (i = 1; argv[i]; i++)
    {
```

continues

147

Listing 5.1. continued

```
        if (argv[i][0] == '/' || argv[i][0] == '-')
        {   /* You have an argument, convert to lowercase, and test. */
            pszTemp = strlwr(argv[i]);

            for (j = 1; j < strlen(pszTemp); j++)
            {
                switch(pszTemp[j])
                {
                    case ARG_HELP:
                        printf("Usage: %s filename.ext \n",
                            szProgram);
                        exit(4);
                        break;

                    case ARG_SLASH:
                    case ARG_DASH:
                        break;

                    default:
                        printf("%s: - Invalid option '%c'.\n",
                            pszTemp[j],
                            szProgram);
                        break;
                }
            }
        }
        else
        {   /* Either a filename or width. */
            strcpy(szInputFile, argv[i]);
        }
    }


    if ((fpFilePointer = fopen(szInputFile, "r+b")) == NULL)
    {
        printf("%s: Unable to open file: %s\n",
            szProgram,
            szInputFile);
```

```c
        exit(16);
    }

    lPosition = 0l;

    printf("\n");

    time(&tTime);

    pTM = localtime(&tTime);

/*  format a time string, using strftime() (new with ANSI C) */

    strftime(szBuffer,
        sizeof(szBuffer),
        "%A %B %d, %Y at %H:%M:%S",
        pTM);

    printf("Dump of %s, %s\n\n",
        szInputFile,
        szBuffer);

    while((nNumberBytesRead = fread((char *)sBuffer,
        sizeof(char), 16, fpFilePointer)) > 0)
    {
        printf(" %8.8X -", lPosition);

        for (i = 0; i < 16; i++)
        {
            if (i == 8)
            {
                printf("  -  ");
            }
            else
            {
                if (i == 0 ||
                    i == 4 ||
                    i == 12)
                {
```

continues

Listing 5.1. continued

```
                    printf("  ");
                }
            }

            if (i < nNumberBytesRead)
            {
                nHexNumber =  (unsigned char)sBuffer[i];

                printf("%2.2X", (unsigned int)nHexNumber);
            }
            else
            {
                printf("  ");
            }

        }

        for (i = 0; i < nNumberBytesRead; i++)
        {
            if (sBuffer[i] < ' ' ||
                sBuffer[i] == '\xFF')
            {
                sBuffer[i] = '.';
            }
        }

        sBuffer[nNumberBytesRead] = '\0';

        printf(" : %s", sBuffer);

        printf(" \n");
        lPosition += 16;
    }

    return(0);

}
```

DUMP.C has few unusual parts. The first part of the program is the same command line arguments parser from Chapter 4, "Special Pointers and Their Use," with a test for the help option (standardized as /? under DOS on the PC). DUMP has no other options and simply requires the name of the file to dump.

The file is opened and read in 16 bytes at a time (or less, if fewer than 16 bytes remain in the file). The buffer, with 16 bytes, is written out, first in hex format and then in ASCII format (with control characters, and a . character substituted for DEL.

DUMP enables you to look at a file's output; you still must understand what the output means, however.

There are two ways to store integers in memory. The first method, in which the high-order bits are stored in the low byte or bytes, makes dumps easy to read; in the second method, the low-order bits are stored in the low byte or bytes. One method makes it easier for you to look at a dump and determine an integer's value, and the other method makes you work a little harder. The PC, of course, makes you work harder; supposedly, it makes the CPU faster, but we'll never know. Figure 5.7 shows both a 16-bit integer and a 32-bit integer, as they are stored in the PC's format.

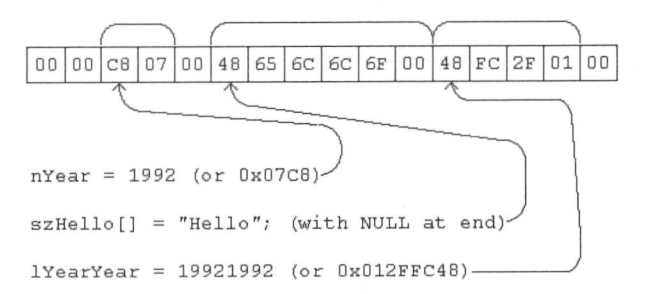

```
nYear = 1992 (or 0x07C8)

szHello[] = "Hello"; (with NULL at end)

lYearYear = 19921992 (or 0x012FFC48)
```

Notice that the text strings are not byte swapped,
even if integers are.

Figure 5.7. Integers in memory (16 and 32 bits).

The method your CPU uses to store integers must always be considered whenever you are viewing memory directly. If you do not know the order of the bits in storage, the simple program in Listing 5.2 tells you which method is being used.

Listing 5.2. WCHBYTE.C.

```c
/* Program WCHBYTE, written 25 May 1992 by Peter D. Hipson */
/* Program that shows byte swapping (if present) by the CPU. */

#include <stdio.h>   // Make includes first part of file
#include <string.h>  // For string functions.
#include <stdlib.h>  // Standard include items.
#include <process.h> // For exit() etc.

int main(            // Define main() and the fact that this program uses
    int     argc,    // the passed parameters.
    char    *argv[],
    char    *envp[]
    );

void NonPrint(const char    chChar);
void Letter(const char    chChar);
void Number(const char    chChar);
void Space(const char    chChar);


int main(
    int     argc,
    char    *argv[],
    char    *envp[]
    )

{

unsigned char    cTemp[10];
unsigned char    *pcTemp;

int       nYear = 1992;

long int lYearYear = 19921992;

char         szHello[] = "Hello";

    pcTemp = (unsigned char *)&nYear;
    cTemp[0] = *(pcTemp++);
    cTemp[1] = *(pcTemp);
```

```c
    printf("nYear = %d decimal, %4.4X hex, in memory %2.2X %2.2X\n",
        nYear,
        nYear,
        cTemp[0],
        cTemp[1]);

    pcTemp = (unsigned char *)&lYearYear;
    cTemp[0] = *(pcTemp++);
    cTemp[1] = *(pcTemp++);
    cTemp[2] = *(pcTemp++);
    cTemp[3] = *(pcTemp);

    printf("lYearYear = %ld decimal %8.8lX hex, in memory %2.2X %2.2X \
            %2.2X %2.2X\n",
        lYearYear,
        lYearYear,
        cTemp[0],
        cTemp[1],
        cTemp[2],
        cTemp[3]);

    pcTemp = (unsigned char *)&szHello[0];
    cTemp[0] = *(pcTemp++); // H
    cTemp[1] = *(pcTemp++); // e
    cTemp[2] = *(pcTemp++); // l
    cTemp[3] = *(pcTemp++); // l
    cTemp[4] = *(pcTemp++); // o
    cTemp[5] = *(pcTemp++); // \0 (NULL)

    printf("szHello = '%s' (string), in memory '%c' '%c' '%c' '%c' '%c' \
            '%c' \n",
        szHello,
        cTemp[0],
        cTemp[1],
        cTemp[2],
        cTemp[3],
        cTemp[4],
        cTemp[5]);

    return(0);
}
```

If the hex representation and the memory view of the variables are the same when you run WCHBYTE, dumps made using DUMP will be correct. If they are different, however (which is the case for *all* PCs), you have to swap the bytes manually when you are using a DUMP listing.

Bit Operators

Bit operators form the basis for C's powerful bit-manipulation capabilities. Never confuse these operators with their logical counterparts, which work on different principles. In Table 5.1, the keyword TRUE signifies a true bit (or bits) that is set to one, and FALSE signifies a bit (or bits) that is set to zero.

Table 5.1. Bitwise operators.

Operator	Description
&	Performs a bitwise AND operation. If both operands are TRUE, the result is TRUE; otherwise, the result is FALSE.
¦	Performs a bitwise OR operation. If either operand is TRUE, the result is TRUE; otherwise, the result is FALSE.
^	Performs a bitwise exclusive OR operation. If both operands are TRUE or both operands are FALSE, the result is FALSE. The result is TRUE if one operand is TRUE and the other is FALSE. Exclusive OR is used to test to see that two operands are *different*.
<<	Shifts the X operand, Y operand bits to the left. For example, (1 << 4) returns a value of 8. In bits, (0001 << 4) results in 1000. New positions to the left are filled with zeroes. This is a quick way to multiply by 2, 4, 8, and so on.
>>	Shifts the X operand, Y operand bits to the right. For example, (8 >> 4) returns a value of 1. In bits, (1000 >> 4) results in 0001. New positions to the right are filled with ones or zeroes, depending on the value and whether the operand being shifted is signed. This is a quick way to divide by 2, 4, 8, and so on.
~	Returns the 1's complement of the value. The 1's complement is defined as setting all bits that are 1 to 0, and all bits that are 0 to 1.

Do not confuse the bitwise operators with the logical operators. The misuse of these operators can cause problems that are difficult to repair, such as those in the following program fragment:

```
int     x = 1;
int     y = 2;

//  Using a logical AND:

    if(x && y)
    {
//      With x == 1, and y == 2, this will ALWAYS be TRUE.
    }

// Using a bitwise AND:

    if (x & y)
    {
//      With x == 1, and y == 2, this will NEVER be TRUE.
    }
```

Why does the bitwise test fail in this fragment? The answer is easy, but only if you look at the bits themselves. The bit pattern for x is `0000 0001`, and the bit pattern for y is `0000 00010`. Doing a bitwise AND shows the following:

```
0000 0001 & 0000 0010 = 0000 0000
```

Practice is one of the best teachers—practice using these operators to get a better feel for how they work. The following section discusses the use of these operators, including some example code fragments.

Bit Fields

A bit field is a data object being accessed at the bit level. These fields, which may be only one bit long, have for each bit a defined meaning that may or may not be related. A good programming practice is to make all the bits in a single bit field variable-related so that management of the bit field is easier. When you are using ANSI C, you generally can have a maximum of 16 bits in a bit-mapped variable. There are two ways to use bit fields:

1. Assign a meaning to each of the bits of any integer variable.

2. With a structure, you may create a bit field that is any length (to a maximum of 16 bits).

Let's look first at user-defined bit fields. When you declare an integer variable, such as the following:

```
unsigned short int  nFlag = 0;
```

the compiler allocates a 16-bit short integer and initializes it to zero. This example is less than meaningful for bit flags. To harness the power of a bit flag, you have to define each bit position and be able to test, set, and reset each bit without regard to the other bits. You know that you have 16 bits to work with, but you don't know how to address them. This process isn't as difficult as it might seem, because each bit has a logical value, and working with these values is easy.

Figure 5.8 shows the bits in the variable. You can easily determine (and assign) a meaningful flag for each of these bits, such as shown.

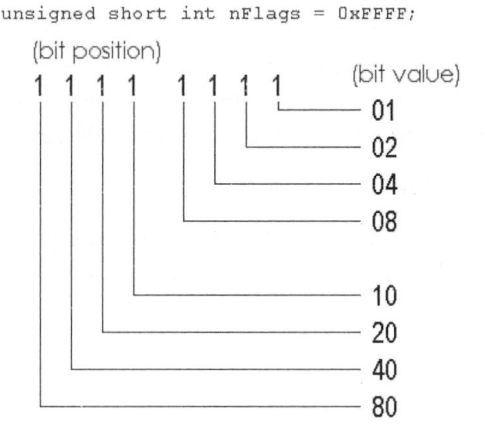

Figure 5.8. Bit values in a 16-bit integer.

Figure 5.8 shows that you use the value 4 to access the third bit from the right. Assume that if this bit is set, it tells you the user has a middle name, and if it is not set, the user doesn't have a middle name. You first make a defined identifier so that your program is manageable:

```
#define  MIDDLE_NAME    0x04
```

You use the hex value because it's easiest to remember and use. The decimal equivalents are not that usable. Assign the first bit from the left to tell you that the user's middle name is just an initial:

```
#define  MIDDLE_INITIAL    0x80
```

Now that you have some defines, let's look at how to use them. First, you can clear all flags in the flag variable `nFlag` by simply assigning a zero to it:

```
nFlag = 0;
```

To set the flag so that you know that the user has a middle name, you can use the following line:

```
nFlag |= MIDDLE_NAME;
```

This statement uses one of C's bit operators. These operators seldom are used by most programmers, primarily because they are not well understood. This is a shame because they make management of logical information much easier.

Next, suppose that the person's middle name is only an initial. You set both the `MIDDLE_NAME` flag and the `MIDDLE_INITIAL` flag. You can use one assignment or combine both:

```
nFlag |= (MIDDLE_NAME | MIDDLE_INITIAL);
```

This statement could have been written as

```
nFlag = (MIDDLE_NAME | MIDDLE_INITIAL | nFlag);
```

If the flag bits were already set for some reason, they don't change. After they are set, performing a bitwise OR on them doesn't change their state.

Now assume that you set the middle-name flag, but later you must change it to indicate that there is no middle name (or initial). Because the OR only sets (and doesn't reset), you have to do something different:

```
nFlag &= (~MIDDLE_NAME & ~MIDDLE_INITIAL);
```

This statement introduces both the *one's complement* operator ~ and the bitwise AND operator &. You have used the ONES COMPLEMENT operator to invert the identifier's bits. For example, if the identifier's bit pattern (as MIDDLE_NAME's) is

```
0000 0100
```

the result of the ~ is

```
1111 1011
```

This bit flag, when it is combined using the bitwise &, enables you to turn off a bit in the nFlags variable. This effect is important because setting and resetting the bits is a common operation.

Finally, you must test bits. You want to test only those bits that are significant for whatever we are testing. For example, to see whether there is a middle name (the MIDDLE_NAME flag is set), you can use the following test:

```
if ((nFlag & MIDDLE_NAME))
```

In this test, several things are important. You must be careful not to use the logical AND operator (&&) when you intend to use the bitwise one. Also, you should use parentheses around each bitwise operation so that the order of precedence is clear. In the preceding test, the expression yields a nonzero value if the bit is set, or a zero if it is not. You can test two bits at one time using either

```
if ((nFlag & (MIDDLE_NAME ¦ MIDDLE_INITIAL))
```

or

```
if ((nFlag & MIDDLE_NAME) &&
    (nFlag & MIDDLE_INITIAL))
```

Because either expression is correct, which one you use is probably more a matter of programming style rather than efficiency. Just make sure that you are clear about the order in which the expression is evaluated; when in doubt, use parentheses.

Summary

In this chapter, you learned about decimal, hex, binary, and octal notation. You learned also about bit field usage.

- Decimal (base 10) is the number base we use in everyday life.

- Hex (base 16) most commonly is used by programmers in writing software. Some programmers can do hex addition and subtraction without the aid of a calculator.

- Binary (base 2) is the only base the CPU understands directly. All other number systems must be converted to binary for the CPU's use.

- Octal, originally developed for DEC's PDP-8 computers, seldom is used by today's programmers, primarily because octal worked best with 12-bit-word computers.

- C supports six bitwise operators, enabling direct manipulation of bits by the programmer.

- Using bit fields, programmers can store much information by using individual bits.

Separate Compilation and Linking

Not all programs are as simple as the examples in this book. Rarely do you write a significant program that has only a single source file; if you do, it usually is too large to be maintained easily. Whether your program is huge, with hundreds of thousands of lines, or is a smaller one, with only a few thousand lines of code, you can benefit from using separate source files.

Some of the information in this chapter is based on Microsoft's tools, such as its MAKE utility and the LIB program. If you are not using Microsoft's products or are not even using a PC, much of the discussion in this chapter will be very helpful because it is information that is new to you.

Compiling and Linking Multiple Source Files

There are a number of reasons to have more than one source file. The most important reason is to help keep your program's source organized. Without this organization, as the program grows larger, it becomes increasingly more difficult to maintain.

Because there are few rules regarding the subdivision of source code between files, how do you determine what to put in each file? First and foremost, the majority of the programs written don't start out large. Most software developers create a shell for their programs (using the main() function) and then build the user interface and the program's functionality using calls from main(). This process allows the developer to test and debug small parts of the program with the hope of not creating new problems for other parts of the program.

Prototyping is a technique for writing larger (and smaller) programs. Don't confuse this use of prototyping with C's use of it. Prototyping a program requires that you do (and have) a number of things, including the following:

1. Establish the program's basic functionality. You must do this by working with the program's final users.

2. Select an operating environment—whether it's a standard character-based application (becoming increasingly rare) or a graphical user interface (GUI) Windows-based program such as Microsoft Windows or IBM Presentation Manager. Pay particular attention to whether the program will use graphics (a GUI interface is a necessity), whether it will be mass marketed (or is intended for a very small vertical market), and whether the users with whom you are working will be the same users that use the program later.

3. After the program's basic functionality and operating environment have been selected, the user interface then is developed. The user interface is the *most important* part of the program. In a GUI program, follow standards that already have been established, including Microsoft's guidelines and IBM's book *Systems Application Architecture Common User Access Advanced Interface Design Guide.* Resist the urge (and pressure from others) to do your own thing when you are writing GUI Windows applications. A prime example is a program for Microsoft Windows that, although it's a good application, has a nonstandard user interface that makes using it nearly impossible if you are an experienced Windows user.

4. After the basics of the user interface are developed (at this point there probably won't be much functionality), potential users should review the interface and suggest additional functionality.

5. Create and implement the standard parts of the user interface, such as the capability to open, close, and save files. Create the help access. Create the look and feel of the application's screen. You probably won't ever face a "look and feel" lawsuit, and the standards make it easier for users to become familiar with your program. The fewer unique things the user must learn, the less support you have to provide.

6. Add each of the functionalities, one at a time, that the program requires. Each can have its own source file and should be fully self-contained. Don't use too many shared supporting functions: Wanting to change a supporting function is common, but problems occur when some calls to these functions then fail. Utility functions—the building blocks of your programs—should be as simple as possible.

Suppose that you have a large program, which therefore is divided into several source files. How do you put the pieces of the program together and create a single program that runs? The process of creating a large, multisource file program is shown in Figure 6.1. It shows generically what you must do (at a minimum) to create a multisource file program. You first compile all of your source files and then link them.

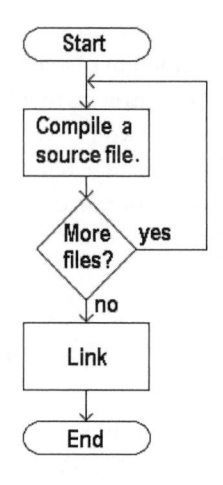

Figure 6.1. A multisource file program.

Compiling Multifile Programs

Compiling a multifile program isn't much more difficult than compiling a single-file program. Many compilers can perform the compile and link using a single command, usually either CC or CL; other variations exist, however. You must tell the compiler that it should not link the program when it does the compiling. You tell it (with the Microsoft compilers) by using the /c option, which simply specifies that you want only a compile.

A couple of things are necessary in creating a functioning multisource file program:

- Be sure that you have properly defined each variable that will be shared between different parts of the program, using the extern keyword.

- Be sure that all functions have a single sharable prototype the compiler can use. *Never* create more than one copy of the prototypes: Make a single copy and place it in a shared header file (this subject is discussed in this section).

Because function parameters and shared variables (to a lesser extent) are the primary methods of passing information among different functions in the program, by defining them properly you increase the likelihood that the program will run properly.

Because you don't yet have an automated system to control which of the source files is compiled (don't try to remember "I changed this one, but not that one"), you must compile each source file. For projects that have only a few source files, compiling each one isn't as bad as it seems; if you have several hundred source files, however, compiling all of them every time a change is made is a little excessive. Later, the "Using MAKE Files" section discusses automated project systems and how to make your program creation more efficient.

Linking Multifile Programs

When you are linking a program, the linker requires a minimum (other than options) of the name of the compiler output .OBJ file. This name then is used for the executable program's name (which has an EXE extension under DOS on the PC). If more than one object file is specified, the first file's name is used if no executable filename is specified.

The linker, whose command line can be lengthy, accepts a multiline command line. You type the first line and end it with a plus sign (+) and a return. The linker then prompts for the next part of the command line. This process of continuing the command line can continue for as long as necessary.

The following short code fragment shows a typical larger multisource file program's link command. (You shouldn't have multiple lines with comments in a real command).

```
link /linenumbers /al:16 /nod /map      + /* Linker options */
   mainprog.obj file2.obj  file3.obj,   + /* Compiler output obj */
   mainprog,                            + /* Executable file's name */
   ,                                    + /* No map file specified */
   MLIBCEW LIBW STARBOTH STARAE         + /* Libraries */
```

The link command has a number of options (all of which probably will be different for other linkers). These options tell the linker to include line number information for the debugger (/linenumbers), align objects on 16-byte boundaries (/al:16), not use the default libraries (/nod) that the compiler inserts in the OBJ files, and create a load map used for debugging (/map).

After the options are the input OBJ files. You can generally omit the OBJ extension. You can specify as many OBJ files, separated by blanks, as you want. If several OBJ files are needed, you may have to use the multiline command format.

Then the name of the output file is specified. This filename receives the EXE extension if no extension is specified. If no output filename is provided, the executable filename is derived from the name of the first OBJ file.

The next parameter is the name of the linker map file. This file (see Chapter 16, "Debugging and Efficiency," for an example) is useful for debugging your program and for certain performance considerations. If you don't specify a filename and the /map option is specified, the map filename is derived from the executable file's name.

The final parameters are the libraries. This parameter (like the input OBJ files) can have more than one name, separated by blanks. If you have specified the /nod option, you *must* specify all the necessary libraries; otherwise, it is necessary to specify only the libraries that are special to this program. It is not an error to specify a library that is not needed, and the linker does not load extra code if an unneeded library is specified.

Using #include

The preprocessor's #include statement is a powerful part of creating a C program. You cannot create a program that compiles without warnings if you do not use at least one #include statement. A set of include files is supplied with every C compiler. These files always have the .h extension, which is shorthand for headers. The ANSI C definitions, prototypes, and other necessary information the compiler needs to function properly are contained in these files (see Chapter 13, "All About Header Files").

The #include statement can be coded in two formats. Each is slightly different; the differences, however, are easy to understand. The first format is

```
#include "stdio.h"
```

In this format, the file to be included is delimited by the " character. The delimiter in this #include statement means: "When the compiler searches for the file to be included, the search starts with the current directory of the file that has the #include; if the file is not found and the file containing the #include is also an included file, then it's a parent." This process continues recursively until all directories in the chain of included files have been searched. If the file still has not been found, the search continues as though the second format has been specified. The second format is

```
#include <stdio.h>
```

In this format, the file to be included is delimited by the < and > characters. When the compiler searches for the file to be included, the search starts with the directories specified on the compile command line (using the /I option) and then the directories specified using the environment variable include. The current directory is not searched unless it has been specified in one of these two places. If the file cannot be found, the compiler issues an error message and the compile ends.

You know that you must include C's header files because they have the function prototypes and other defined identifiers needed to write your program. What else can be included? An include file can contain anything that could have been put in a source file. You can have preprocessor statements, C source code, and so on, and the compiler treats the information as though it all were in the same file. The only difference is that when an error is in an include file, the compiler's error message provides the necessary name and line number of the include file.

For large projects, I generally recommend that you have the following custom include files. Although some projects do not need all these files, you can create and include them at any time.

- The first file is named with the same name as the program. This file has *only* include statements and looks like Listing 6.1. It contains only #include statements to include the other include files.

- The second file, defines.h, contains all common #define statements. Using a single, included file for a define helps prevent the use of the same identifier being defined for two purposes.

- The next file, typedef.h, contains the program's typedef statements. By placing all typedef statements in a single include file, all parts of the program can access them. There is no possibility of the same name being used for two different types if a single include file is used.

- The vars.h file contains all the variable definitions (and declarations). To see how a single file can contain both, see Listing 6.4, later in this chapter.

- The final file, prototyp.h, contains the function prototypes for each of the program's functions. Always keep prototypes in a single file, using the format shown in Listing 6.5, later in this chapter.

Listing 6.1 shows the main include file for a multisource file program.

Listing 6.1. An example of a main include file for a large project.

```
#include "defines.h"
#include "typedef.h"
#include "vars.h"
#include "prototyp.h"
```

Listing 6.2 shows the defines.h file. You should document each #define's use as shown in this example.

Listing 6.2. An example of the defines.h include file.

```
#ifndef DEFINES_H
#define DEFINES_H
```

continues

Listing 6.2. continued

```
#define   MAX_SIZE    123 /* Maximum size of array */
#define   USER        "I AM USER" /* The user's name */
#define   MAXFONT     50  /* Maximum number of fonts available */

#ifndef MIN
#define   MIN(a, b)   (((a) < (b)) ? (a) : (b))
#endif /* MIN */

#ifndef MAX
#define   MAX(a, b)   (((a) > (b)) ? (a) : (b))
#endif /* MAX */

#ifndef TRUE
#define   TRUE        1   /* LOGICAL TRUE */
#endif /* TRUE */

#ifndef FALSE
#define   FALSE       0   /* if not TRUE, must be FALSE */
#endif /* FALSE */

#endif /* DEFINES_H */
```

Listing 6.3 shows the typedef.h file. As in other include files, you should document each typedef's use as the example shows.

Listing 6.3. An example of the typedef.h include file.

```
#ifndef TYPEDEF_H
#define TYPEDEF_H

typedef struct
{
    char    FontList[MAXFONT][LF_FACESIZE]; // MAXFONT is 50. LF_FACESIZE
                                            // is in windows.h file.
    BYTE    CharSet[MAXFONT];               // The font's character set
    BYTE    PitchAndFamily[MAXFONT];        // The font's pitch and
                                            // family
    BYTE    VectorOrRaster[MAXFONT];        // The font's type
```

```
BYTE      FontType[MAXFONT];                    // RASTER_FONTTYPE,
                                                // DEVICE_FONTTYPE, or
                                                // TRUETYPE_FONTTYPE
                                                // (windows.h)
    int    nSizeIndex;                          // Index to the font size.
    int    nFontIndex;                          // Index to the font.

    int    nSizeList[MAX_SIZE];                 // List of font's sizes.

} FONTSPECS;

typedef FONTSPECS       *PFONTSPECS;
typedef FONTSPECS NEAR *NPFONTSPECS;
typedef FONTSPECS FAR  *LPFONTSPECS;


#endif /* TYPEDEF_H */
```

The typedef.h file includes not only a typedef for the structure, but also typedefs for various pointers that may point to this structure. This inclusion makes it easy to create prototypes and to define the necessary structures and pointers later in the program.

Listing 6.4, the vars.h file, includes all the global variables. It does *not* contain any of the static variables because they are known in only the current source file. Notice the use of the defined identifier EXTERN. This identifier is defined to the C keyword extern if the file that is including the vars.h file is not the main file. The variables then can be either declarations (done only once) or definitions (done in each file). For any initialized variable, you must check the EXTERN identifier and process each one as necessary. As in the other include files, you should document each variable's use as the example shows.

Listing 6.4. An example of the vars.h include file.

```
#ifndef VARS_H
#define VARS_H

#ifndef EXTERN
#define EXTERN /*NULL, do variable declarations */
```

continues

Listing 6.4. continued

```
#define INITIALIZE_EXTERN
#endif /* EXTERN */


EXTERN   char szBuffer[257];  /* Scratch buffer, contents undefined */
EXTERN   char szFileName[129]; /* Input filename */

EXTERN   int nErrorCount;      /* How many errors so far? */

EXTERN   int nErrorValue
#if defined(INITIALIZE_EXTERN) /* Do the initialization */
    = {NO_ERROR} /* Initialized */
#endif
;


#if defined (INITIALIZE_EXTERN)
#undef   INITIALIZE_EXTERN
#endif
#endif /* VARS_H */
```

Notice that vars.h uses the identifier EXTERN and defines a new identifier called INITIALIZE_EXTERN. Whenever you are declaring a variable that you want to initialize, you can use this example to make sure that the variable is not declared twice.

Listing 6.5, the prototyp.h file, includes all the function prototypes for the various functions in the program. This file should be the last of the group of included files because it uses the typedefs created in typedef.h. As with the other include files, you should document each function's use and the file in which it is found, as the example shows.

Listing 6.5. An example of the prototyp.h include file.

```
#ifndef PROTOTYP_H
#define PROTOTYP_H

/* source file   return   name(parameters); */

/* ADDARRAY.C */ int     ArrayAdd(LPARRAY, LPARRAY);
/* SUBARRAY.C */ int     ArraySubtract(LPARRAY, LPARRAY);
```

```
/* UTILITY.C */ void    ErrorMessage(LPSTR szSubString, WORD wError,
                            long  lSomething);



#endif /* PROTOYTP_H */
```

The prototyp.h file has enough information for you to know each function's parameters, what the function returns, and where it is located (so that you can fix it when it breaks).

By using these `include` files for your project, you can be confident that you have much of the project under control. You will not have duplicate external variables with the same name and different usage, and you won't have functions defined with one set of parameters and declared with another. You must work at keeping the `include` files in order; however, in the long run, the result is worth the effort.

External Variables

This chapter has discussed using a set of standard `include` files. These files enable you to control the way objects are defined in your programs, preventing duplicate identifiers with different meanings. Chapter 2, "Data Types, Constants, Variables, and Arrays," discussed variables, including external variables, and this chapter has discussed using a single `include` file to create both a definition and a declaration for an external variable. Now let's look at a "real" program that shows how external variables work for you.

The TWOFILE program, shown in Listings 6.6 through 6.14, is a simple program with two source C files and a full set of `include` files that uses shared external (global) variables to share data. TWOFILE doesn't do much; however, it has the framework to enable you to build a more meaningful application.

Listing 6.6. TWOFILE1.C.

```
/* Program TWOFILE, written 22 May 1992 by Peter D. Hipson
 * A multisource file program.
 * This is the first source file for TWOFILE.
 */
```

continues

171

Listing 6.6. continued

```
/* This program assumes and uses Microsoft's extensions to C.
 * Readers with other compilers may need to change the program
 * to use the calls their compiler supplies to perform the
 * same functions.
 */

#include "twofile.h" /* TWOFILE's include has all other #includes. */

int main(
    int     argc,
    char    *argv[],
    char    *envp[]
    )

{

char    *pszTemp;
char    szBuffer[129];      /* Temporary work buffer. */
char    szProgram[30];
char    szInputFile[132];   /* Make large enough for your OS. */
char    szOutputFile[132];  /* Make large enough for your OS. */

/* strings for _splitpath() (which parses a file name) */
char    szDrive[_MAX_DRIVE];
char    szDir[_MAX_DIR];
char    szFname[_MAX_FNAME];
char    szExt[_MAX_EXT];

int     i;
int     j;
int     nCurrentParameter = INNAME;
int     nTempWidth = 0;
int     nLineWidth = 80;
int     nJustification = LEFT;

    if (argc <= 2)
    {
        GiveHelp(argc, NULL);
        return(16);
    }
```

```
_splitpath(argv[0],
    szDrive,
    szDir,
    szFname,
    szExt);

strncpy(szProgram, szFname, sizeof(szProgram) - 1);

for (i = 1; argv[i]; i++)
{
    if (argv[i][0] == '/' || argv[i][0] == '-')
    {   /* You have an argument, convert to lowercase, and test. */
        pszTemp = strlwr(argv[i]);

        for (j = 1; j < (int)strlen(pszTemp); j++)
        {
            switch(pszTemp[j])
            {
                case ARG_LEFT:
                    nJustification = LEFT;
                    break;

                case ARG_RIGHT:
                    nJustification = RIGHT;
                    break;

                case ARG_JUSTIFY:
                    nJustification = JUSTIFY;
                    break;

                case ARG_SLASH:
                case ARG_DASH:
                    break;

                default:
                    GiveHelp(BAD_OPTION, &pszTemp[j]);
                    break;
            }
        }
    }
    else
```

continues

Listing 6.6. continued

```
        {   /* Either a filename or width. */
        switch(nCurrentParameter)
        {
            case INNAME:
                strcpy(szInputFile, argv[i]);
                nCurrentParameter = OUTNAME;
                break;

            case OUTNAME:
                strcpy(szOutputFile, argv[i]);
                nCurrentParameter = WIDTH;
                break;

            case WIDTH:
                sscanf(argv[i], "%d", &nTempWidth);

                if (nTempWidth < 20 || nTempWidth > 128)
                {
                    GiveHelp(BAD_WIDTH, NULL);
                }
                else
                {
                    nLineWidth = nTempWidth;
                }

                nCurrentParameter = LAST_THING;

                break;

            default:
                GiveHelp(BAD_PARM, NULL);
                break;
        }
    }
}

if (nCurrentParameter < WIDTH)
{   /* Didn't get two file names! */
    GiveHelp(NAME_MISSING, NULL);
    return(16);
```

```
    }


    printf("\n");

    printf(
        "%s would read the file '%s' and write the file '%s'\n\n",
        szProgram,
        szInputFile,
        szOutputFile);

    switch(nJustification)
    {
        case LEFT:
            printf("The lines would be %d characters long, left \
                    aligned\n",
                nLineWidth);
            break;

        case RIGHT:
            printf("The lines would be %d characters long, right \
                    aligned\n",
                nLineWidth);
            break;

        case JUSTIFY:
            printf("The lines would be %d characters long, justified\n",
                nLineWidth);
            break;
    }

/*  In the final version of this program, the files next
 *  are opened, and the input file is read into a buffer,
 *  formatted according to what the user wants, and written
 *  out to the output file. At the end, the files are closed,
 *  and perhaps some statistical information can be presented
 *  to the user.
 */


    return (0);
}
```

Listing 6.7 is TWOFILE2.C, the second source file. It contains the help function.

Listing 6.7. TWOFILE2.C.

```
/* Program TWOFILE, written 22 May 1992 by Peter D. Hipson
 * A multisource file program.
 * This is the second source file for TWOFILE: TWOFILE2.C.
 */

/* This program assumes and uses Microsoft's extensions to C.
 * Readers with other compilers may need to change the program
 * to use the calls their compiler supplies to perform the
 * same functions.
 */

#include "twofile.h" // TWOFILE's include has all other #includes.

void    GiveHelp(
    int     nLevel,
    char    *psItem)

{
    printf("\n");

    switch(nLevel)
    {
        case NOINNAME:
        case NOOUTNAME: // Not enough parameters!
            printf(
                "FORMAT [-r¦-l¦-j] inputfile outputfile width\n"
                "    where \n"
                "  Options - -r (or /r) to right align \n"
                "            -l (or /l) to left align \n"
                "            -j (or /j) to justify\n"
                "\n"
                "  inputfile - is the input file name \n"
                "  outputfile - is the output file name \n"
                "\n"
                "  width is the desired output width (20 to 128)\n"
```

```
            "  (default is 80 characters).\n"
            "\n"
            "  Note: lines are concatenated, paragraph breaks are\n"
            "        signaled with a blank line\n\n");
        break;

    case BAD_WIDTH:
        printf(
            "The width parameter must be between 20 and 128!\n"
            "the width is ignored\n");
        break;

    case BAD_PARM:
        printf("Excessive parameters have been entered\n");

        /* Force a display of full help! */

        GiveHelp(NOINNAME, NULL);
        break;

    case BAD_OPTION:
        printf("'%c' is an invalid option! (Use only -l, -r or \
                -j)\n",
            *psItem);

        break;

    case NAME_MISSING:
        printf("One or both of the required file names is \
                missing!\n");

        /* Force a display of full help! */

        GiveHelp(NOINNAME, NULL);
        break;

    default:
        printf(
            "An unspecified error occured! FORMAT has ended!\n"
            );
```

continues

Listing 6.7. continued

```
        exit(16);

        break;
    }
}
```

Listing 6.8 is TWOFILE.H, the main include file for TWOFILE.

Listing 6.8. TWOFILE.H.

```
/* Program TWOFILE, written 22 May 1992 by Peter D. Hipson
 * A multisource file program's main include file.
 * This is TWOFILE's include file.
 */

/* This program assumes and uses Microsoft's extensions to C.
 * Readers with other compilers may need to change the program
 * to use the calls their compiler supplies to perform the
 * same functions.
 */

/* First include the C language's include files: */

#include <stdio.h>    // Make includes first part of file
#include <string.h>   // For string functions.
#include <stdlib.h>   // Standard include items.
#include <process.h>  // For exit(), etc.

/* Next, include TWOFILE's include files */

#include "define.h"
#include "typedef.h"
#include "vars.h"
#include "prototyp.h"

/* End of this include file; put nothing but #include statements
 * in this header!
 */
```

Listing 6.9 is DEFINE.H, the identifier identification include file for TWOFILE.

Listing 6.9. DEFINE.H.

```
/* Program TWOFILE, written 22 May 1992 by Peter D. Hipson
 * A multisource file program's #define include file.
 * This is TWOFILE's DEFINE.H include file.
 */

/* This program assumes and uses Microsoft's extensions to C.
 * Readers with other compilers may need to change the program
 * to use the calls their compiler supplies to perform the
 * same functions.
 */


#define  LEFT    1
#define  RIGHT   2
#define  JUSTIFY 3

#define  INNAME  1
#define  OUTNAME 2
#define  WIDTH   3
#define  LAST_THING 4

#define  ARG_LEFT    'l'
#define  ARG_RIGHT   'r'
#define  ARG_JUSTIFY 'j'
#define  ARG_SLASH   '/'
#define  ARG_DASH    '-'

#define  NOINNAME     1
#define  NOOUTNAME    2
#define  BAD_WIDTH    3
#define  BAD_PARM     4
#define  BAD_OPTION   5
#define  NAME_MISSING 6
```

Listing 6.10 is TYPEDEF.H, the identifier identification include file for TWOFILE.

Listing 6.10. TYPEDEF.H.

```
/* Program TWOFILE, written 22 May 1992 by Peter D. Hipson */
 * A multisource file program's #define include file.
/* This is TWOFILE's TYPEDEF.H include file. */

/* This program assumes and uses Microsoft's extensions to C.
 * Readers with other compilers may need to change the program
 * to use the calls their compiler supplies to perform the
 * same functions.
 */

/* This program uses no typedefs. */
```

Listing 6.11 is VARS.H, the external variables include file for TWOFILE.

Listing 6.11. VARS.H.

```
/* Program TWOFILE, written 22 May 1992 by Peter D. Hipson */
 * A multisource file program's external variables include file.
/* This is TWOFILE's VARS.H include file. */

/* This program assumes and uses Microsoft's extensions to C.
 * Readers with other compilers may need to change the program
 * to use the calls their compiler supplies to perform the
 * same functions.
 */

/* This program uses no external variables. */
```

Listing 6.12 is PROTOTYP.H, the function prototypes' include file for TWOFILE.

Listing 6.12. PROTOTYP.H.

```
/* Program TWOFILE, written 22 May 1992 by Peter D. Hipson
 * A multisource file program's prototypes' include file.
 * This is TWOFILE's PROTOTYP.H include file.
 */
```

```
/* This program assumes and uses Microsoft's extensions to C.
 * Readers with other compilers may need to change the program
 * to use the calls their compiler supplies to perform the
 * same functions.
 */


/* TWOFILE1.C */ int    main(int argc, char *argv[], char *envp[]);

/* TWOFILE1.C */ void   GiveHelp(int nLevel, char *psItem);
```

For a simple project that has only one source file, having five `include` files may seem like overkill. Perhaps it is, but for larger projects (with two or more source files), it isn't long before you thank yourself for the organization these files offer.

One of the keys to success is organization. Another is planning. Plan your program, and be sure it is organized. Disarray and chaos have no place in programming. Let's look at how you can keep your compiler output files better organized.

Using an Object Library Manager

When a large program is created with many source files, the process of creating the program is called *building*. This process consists of the following steps (refer to Figure 6.1):

1. Compile each of the source files. The compiler's output usually is referred to as an *object module* and often has an *.obj* extension.

2. Combine all the object modules the compiler has produced with the C language's libraries to create an executable program.

3. In this optional step, you create symbol files that your debugger uses. Because each debugger is different, program creation is not discussed here.

Everything's OK so far, but problems lurk. First, if your program is large, the linker's command-line input can get huge, even if the linker is driven by a file containing the necessary filenames. I have seen linker command lines that are several hundred lines long, but they're not pretty.

You can have a group of object modules in which your project isn't a program, but is just a collection of functions that perform a specific purpose and that (usually) is used with more than one program. The various C library functions are an example.

Grouping a number of functions together is called *creating a library*. Utility programs (supplied with your compiler and usually called LIB) perform various tasks with libraries. Let's look at Microsoft's LIB utility. This program enables you to maintain your object code libraries and performs the following functions:

- Adds an object module to the library

- Deletes an existing object module from the library

- Replaces an existing object module in the library by performing a delete followed by an add

- Extracts an object module from the library

- Maps a library and provides a listing of the library's contents, the sizes of the library's members, and the member's entry points and other external names

In all cases, if the library doesn't exist, you have the option of creating it. An empty library can exist; however, it doesn't have much value. When Microsoft's LIB program runs, it creates a backup copy of the library and enables you to recover easily from errors.

You can group functions in an object library by what they do. This capability is handy because you can, for example, create a library of functions that read database files and a library of special math functions and keep them separate.

Using MAKE Files

Suppose that you have a program that consists of 35 source files. As you are editing them, you note on paper which ones you have changed so that you can recompile them. How long before you forget to compile one of the changed source files, and what are the effects? The answer is "not long and the problems are difficult to find."

Now suppose that you compile the entire program every time. How long until you finish your program, and do you have any friends when you finish? The answer is "forever, and your friends have left you long ago."

There has to be a better way—that's why we have computers. Many programmers are faced with the dilemma of whether it is faster to do it by hand or to figure out how to make the computer do it. In this case, it's always preferable to let the computer do the work. This is where MAKE (also known by other names, such as NMAKE) comes in handy.

The MAKE utility has one purpose: It looks at the date on which one file was created or last modified and compares it to the date of another file. If the first file is older than the second, the MAKE performs some specified action, such as compiling, linking, or another command that can be called from the command prompt.

Some of the more advanced compilers have a utility that creates the MAKE files for you. If your compiler has one, use it. (Creating a MAKE file by hand involves some work, but it can be done.) Listing 6.13 is a simple MAKE file that compiles TWOFILE, the example program discussed earlier.

Listing 6.13. TWOFILE.MAK, a MAKE file to compile TWOFILE.

```
includes = twofile.h define.h typedef.h vars.h prototyp.h

twofile1.obj: twofile1.c $(includes)
    cl -c -u -as -gsw -os -zpe twofile1.c

twofile2.obj: twofile2.c $(includes)
    cl -c -u -as -gsw -os -zpe twofile1.c

twofile.exe: twofile1.obj twofile2.obj
    link clockdat;
```

In Listing 6.13, the variable `includes` is defined first (yes, MAKE has variables). It contains the following string:

```
twofile.h define.h typedef.h vars.h prototyp.h
```

You use this technique to reference the `include` files in a MAKE file to save typing and make it easy to update the list (if you need to add a new `include` file later). A defined variable in a MAKE file can be referenced by enclosing it within parentheses and preceding the opening parenthesis with a dollar sign. If the variable is undefined, the result is a blank, and no error is generated. This capability can come in handy because you can define variables on the MAKE command line to change compiler options, linker options, or almost anything else.

Not listing the include file prototyp.h in the MAKE file is not uncommon; however, I recommend that you reference every file that makes up part of your project.

The following line is called a *dependency line*:

```
twofile1.obj: twofile1.c $(includes)
```

It tells MAKE that the file twofile1.obj might change if any of the files following the : change. In this case, twofile1.obj may change if twofile.c or any of the include files changes. There is a limit to what MAKE can see: It looks only at the files' time stamp. If twofile1.c or any of the include files is newer than twofile1.obj, the dependency is true, and MAKE performs whatever commands immediately follow the dependency line:

```
cl -c -u -as -gsw -os -zpe twofile1.c
```

These commands, however, must start in a column other than the first one (I recommend that you indent them four spaces).

In a MAKE file, the # character is the comment delimiter. If you want to comment your MAKE file (I recommend it), simply use the comment delimiter (see Listing 6.14). MAKE continues to process the MAKE file until one of the commands returns a nonzero return code or until the MAKE file ends. Rarely do you want to continue to run MAKE after an error has been detected. Listing 6.13 is a simple MAKE file. Listing 6.14 is a more advanced MAKE file, again written for TWOFILE.

Listing 6.14. TWOFILE, an advanced MAKE file for the TWOFILE program.

```
##### Module Macro #####
NAME    = twofile
SRCS    = twofile1.c twofile2.c
OBJS    =


##### C7 Macro (if you have Microsoft C-7) #####
C7    = 1


##### Library Macros (if programming under Windows) #####
LIBS    = libw mlibcew
MOD     = -AM


##### Include Macro #####
INCLS    = $(NAME).h define.h typedef.h vars.h prototyp.h
```

```
#### DEBUG Defined #####
DEBUG   = 1


##### Build Option Macros #####
!if $(DEBUG)
DDEF    = -DDEBUG
CLOPT   = -Zid -Od
MOPT    = -Zi
LOPT    = /CO /LI /MAP
!else
DDEF    =
CLOPT   = -Os
LOPT    =
!endif


##### General Macro #####
DEF     =


##### Tool Macros #####
ASM     = masm -Mx $(MOPT) $(DDEF) $(DEF)
CC      = cl -nologo -c $(MOD) -G2sw -Zp -W3 $(CLOPT) $(DDEF) $(DEF)
LINK    = link /NOD /NOE $(LOPT)
RC      = rc $(DDEF) $(DEF)
HC      = hc


##### Inference Rules #####
.c.obj:
    $(CC) $*.c

.asm.obj:
    $(ASM) $*.asm;

.rc.res:
    $(RC) -r $*.rc


##### Main (default) Target #####
goal: $(NAME).exe


##### Dependents For Goal and Command Lines #####
$(NAME).exe: $(SRCS:.c=.obj)
```

continues

Listing 6.14. continued

```
        $(LINK) @<<
        $(SRCS:.c=.obj) $(OBJS),
        $(NAME).exe,
        $(NAME).map,
        $(LIBS),
        $(NAME).def
<<
!if $(DEBUG)
!if !$(C7)
        cvpack -p $(NAME).exe
!endif
        mapsym $(NAME).map
!endif

##### Dependents #####
$(SRCS:.c=.obj): $(INCLS)

##### Clean Directory #####
clean:
        -del *.obj
        -del *.exe
```

This example of a MAKE file does little more than the first, simpler example, but it does have the capability to quickly add new source (.C) files, to switch between debug mode and a final production version, and to handle Microsoft C 7's differences.

In all, MAKE is one of the most important tools you have to help you produce your program. Without it, you have to do most of the work in creating your program, such as calling the compiler and linker.

Summary

This chapter described programs made up of more than one source file and how to manage larger, multisource file projects.

- The compiler is used to compile each source file.

- When all the source files are compiled (successfully), they are combined, using a linker, to produce the final executable program.

- The #include statement causes the C compiler to read in the named file as though it were part of the original file.

- When the included file ends, the compiler continues with the original file.

- External variables, identified with the extern keyword, can be used to share information between functions, even when the functions reside in different source files.

- The object library utility (LIB) is used to maintain library files.

- MAKE files are used to help automate the process of creating a large program that has more than one source file.

Part II

Managing Data in C

C Structures

A computer language would be ineffective if it did not offer a way to create complex data objects. C structures are objects that contain more than one item. A structure often contains data objects grouped according to their usage, but a structure can contain unrelated data objects as well.

Using the struct Keyword

You use the struct keyword to define a structure. A structure definition consists of several parts, as the following shows:

```
struct tag_name {
       type member_name;
       type member_name;
       type member_name;
    } structure_name =
       {initializer_values};
```

Although the formatting is up to the programmer, I suggest that you use the preceding format for easy readability.

The first line contains the `struct` keyword, then the optional *tag_name*:

```
struct tag_name {
```

The *tag_name* can be used to create a copy of the structure (as shown in STRUCT4.C, one of the example programs in this chapter). An opening brace follows the *tag_name* (or the `struct` keyword, if the *tag_name* is not used). This brace signals to the compiler that the next lines are member definitions. Each member definition consists of a variable type and a name. The members can be any valid variable type, including arrays, structures, and unions, as follows:

```
type member_name;
type member_name;
type member_name;
```

Following the last member name is a closing brace and the optional *structure_name*, as follows:

```
} structure_name =
```

When using the *structure_name* and the *tag_name*, you can choose any of the following:

- If a *structure_name* is not specified and a *tag_name* is specified, the structure is being defined but not declared.

- If a *structure_name* is specified and a *tag_name* is not specified, the structure is being declared but not defined.

- If a *structure_name* and a *tag_name* are provided, the structure is being both defined and declared.

- If neither a *structure_name* nor a *tag_name* is provided, a compile-time error will result.

If you want to initialize the structure, you must have a *structure_name* because it signals the compiler that this is a declaration. The *structure_name* is also necessary if you want to refer to the structure.

After the *structure_name* are optional initializers:

```
{initializer_values};
```

The following is a simple structure:

```
struct
    {
    char        szSaying[129];
    int         nLength;
    } MySaying;
```

This structure definition provides a data object that can be referenced with a single name, `MySaying`. Each member of `MySaying` provides different information.

Structures offer us a number of important advantages, including the following:

You can refer to the entire data object using a single name.

You can use the structure name as a parameter to a function. For example, you could pass the address and the length of the structure name to `read()` to read the structure's contents to a disk file.

Structures can be assigned directly. You cannot assign strings (you must use the `strcpy()` library function), but you can assign two structures simply by using an assignment statement.

A function can return a structure.

A simple program that allocates and initializes a structure is shown in Listing 7.1.

Listing 7.1. STRUCT1.C.

```
/* STRUCT1, written 1992 by Peter D. Hipson
 * This is a simple structure program.
 */

#include <stdio.h>  // Make includes first part of file
#include <string.h> // For string functions

int main(void); // Define main() and the fact that this
                // program doesn't use any passed parameters


int main()

{
```

continues

Listing 7.1. continued

```
int     i;

struct
    {
      char      szSaying[129];
      int       nLength;
    } MySaying =
        {"Firestone's Law of Forecasting:",
        strlen(MySaying.szSaying)};

    printf("sizeof(MYSaying)  = %d\n", sizeof(MySaying));

    printf("MySaying  %p %3d '%s'\n",
        &MySaying.szSaying,
        MySaying.nLength,
        MySaying.szSaying);

    printf("\n\n");

    return (0);
}
```

In STRUCT1, you can see the definition of the MySaying structure. This structure has two members: a character string (with a length of 129) called szSaying and an integer variable called nLength. The structure is initialized with a line of text and a number. The program then initializes the nLength member to the length of the string in the szSaying member. (Using a function call to initialize a data object is permitted but uncommon.)

Notice how the program refers to each member in the structure. The shorthand for a structure reference is the structure name followed by a period and the member name:

structure.member

If the member is also a structure (more on this later), the member name is followed by a period and its member name:

structure.memberstructure.member

Arrays of Structures

As mentioned, an array can consist of any data type. In this section, you look at an example of a program that uses an array of type `struct`. Listing 7.2, STRUCT2, creates a structure, makes it an array, and initializes it.

 Some compilers will not compile Listing 7.2 correctly, even though it is legitimate ANSI code.

Listing 7.2. STRUCT2.C.

```
/*  STRUCT2, written 1992 by Peter D. Hipson
 *  This program creates an array of type struct
 */

#include <stdio.h>  // Make includes first part of file
#include <string.h> // For string functions

int main(void); // Define main() and the fact that this
                // program doesn't use any passed parameters


int main()

{

int     i;


struct
    {
      char    szSaying[129];
      int     nLength;
    } MySaying[] = {
      "Firestone's Law of Forecasting:", 0,
```

continues

Listing 7.2. continued

```
            "  Chicken Little has to be right only once.", 0,
            "", 0,
            "", 0,
            "Manly's Maxim:", 0,
            "  Logic is a systematic method of coming to", 0,
            "  the wrong conclusion with confidence.", 0,
            "", 0,
            "", 0,
            "Moer's truism:", 0,
            "  The trouble with most jobs is the job holder's", 0,
            "  resemblance to being one of a sled dog team. No one", 0,
            "  gets a change of scenery except the lead dog.", 0,
            "", 0,
            "", 0,
            "Cannon's Comment:", 0,
            "  If you tell the boss you were late for work because you", 0,
            "  had a flat tire, the next morning you will have a flat tire.",
            0,
            };

    for (i = 0;
        i < (sizeof(MySaying) / sizeof(MySaying[0]));
        i++)
    {
        MySaying[i].nLength = strlen(MySaying[i].szSaying);
    }

    printf("sizeof(MySaying)   = %d\n", sizeof(MySaying));

    printf("Number of elements = %d\n",
        (sizeof(MySaying) / sizeof(MySaying[0])));

    for (i = 0;
        i < (sizeof(MySaying) / sizeof(MySaying[0]));
        i++)
    {
        printf("MySaying[%2d]  %p %3d '%s'\n",
            i,
            &MySaying[i].szSaying,
            MySaying[i].nLength,
```

```
        MySaying[i].szSaying);
    }

    printf("\n\n");

    return (0);
}
```

Let's look at how the structure is declared. In the first few lines, the structure members and the structure's name are established:

```
struct
    {
    char      szSaying[129];
    int       nLength;
    } MySaying[] = {
```

In the last line of this code fragment, brackets indicate that an array is being defined. (A nonstructure array is declared in this way also.) Following are the array brackets, which do not have a size. This tells the compiler to compute the number of elements in MySaying from the initializers.

I have not specified the number of elements; instead, the compiler computes this number. While the program is executing, it calculates the number of members using a simple formula:

```
nNumberOfMembers = (sizeof(MySaying) / sizeof(MySaying[0]))
```

The total size of the structure is divided by the size of the first member. (Remember that all members must be the same size.) This gives us the number of elements in the structure array. Computing the number of elements in this way is handy. If you want to change the initializers to add a new saying, for example, you won't have to change the program.

You can write a macro to compute the number of elements as follows:

```
#define NUMBER_ELEMENTS(array) (sizeof(array) / sizeof(array[0]))
```

If you give this macro the name of an array (of any type), it returns the number of elements in the array. An example is shown in Listing 7.3, the STRUCTA program. The macro makes it easy to use loops to index an array whose number of elements has been determined by the initializers (or by any other means).

Listing 7.3. STRUCTA.C.

```c
/*  STRUCTA, written 1992 by Peter D. Hipson
 *  A program showing a macro to determine the
 *  number of elements in an array.
 */

#include <stdio.h>  // Make includes first part of file
#include <string.h> // For string functions

/*  The NUMBER_ELEMENTS(array) macro returns the number of
 *  elements found in array. Array can be any array, including
 *  an array of type struct.
 */

#define NUMBER_ELEMENTS(array) (sizeof(array) / sizeof(array[0]))

int main(void); // define main(), and the fact that this program doesn't
                // use any passed parameters.

int main()

{

int     i;

struct
    {
        char    szSaying[129];
        int     nLength;
    } MySaying[] = {
        "Firestone's Law of Forecasting:", 0,
        "  Chicken Little has to be right only once.", 0,
        "", 0,
        "", 0,
        "Manly's Maxim:", 0,
        "  Logic is a systematic method of coming to", 0,
        "  the wrong conclusion with confidence.", 0,
        "", 0,
        "", 0,
        "Moer's truism:", 0,
```

```
            "  The trouble with most jobs is the job holder's", 0,
            "  resemblance to being one of a sled dog team. No one", 0,
            "  gets a change of scenery except the lead dog.", 0,
            "", 0,
            "", 0,
            "Cannon's Comment:", 0,
            "  If you tell the boss you were late for work because you", 0,
            "  had a flat tire, the next morning you will have a flat tire.",
            0,
            };

    for (i = 0; i < NUMBER_ELEMENTS(MySaying); i++)
    {
        MySaying[i].nLength = strlen(MySaying[i].szSaying);
    }

    printf( /* String literal concatenation makes formatting lists easy
             */
        "sizeof(MySaying)              = %d\n"
        "Number of MySaying elements  = %d\n"
        "sizeof(MySaying[0].szSaying) = %d\n",
        sizeof(MySaying),
        NUMBER_ELEMENTS(MySaying),
        NUMBER_ELEMENTS(MySaying[0].szSaying));

    for (i = 0;
        i < NUMBER_ELEMENTS(MySaying);
        i++)
    {
        printf("MySaying[%2d]  %p %3d '%s'\n",
            i,
            &MySaying[i].szSaying,
            MySaying[i].nLength,
            MySaying[i].szSaying);
    }

    printf("\n\n");

    return (0);
}
```

As Listing 7.3 shows, creating arrays of structures is simple and straightforward. Under ANSI C, you can initialize an auto structure as both a singular entity and an array, which makes it easier to use structures.

Listing 7.3 has some problems, however. Note the size of the structure when you run the program. It is huge! Because the size of the largest initializing string cannot be determined easily, I made the szString member large enough for all (or almost all) strings, 129 characters. The compiler adds a byte to pad this length to a word boundary, making the length 130. The total length of the structure—including the integer length member, nLength—is 132 bytes. There are 18 members in the array of structures. When I compiled and executed the program, the total length was 2376 bytes. Perhaps there is a better way.

Structures of Arrays

If you can make an array from a structure, can a structure contain an array? Of course! The process of defining an array in a structure was demonstrated in Listing 7.3, in which the szString variable is a string variable, and string variables are made up of arrays of type char.

An advanced version of STRUCTA is shown in STRUCT3.C, Listing 7.4. This program stores pointers to a ragged-right array of character initializers. Because the program does not allocate additional space, this version is useful when the saved strings will not be modified. If you have to modify the saved strings, STRUCTA is a better choice.

Listing 7.4. STRUCT3.C.

```
/*  STRUCT3, written 1992 by Peter D. Hipson
 *  A structure containing an array (or two).
 */

#include <stdio.h>  // Make includes first part of file
#include <string.h> // For string functions

#define NUMBER_ELEMENTS 35

int main(void); // define main(), and the fact that this program doesn't
                // use any passed parameters.
```

```
int main()

{

int    i;

struct
    {
        char     *szSaying[NUMBER_ELEMENTS];
        int      nLength[NUMBER_ELEMENTS];
    } OurSaying = {
        "Firestone's Law of Forecasting:",
        "  Chicken Little has to be right only once.",
        "",
        "",
        "Manly's Maxim:",
        "  Logic is a systematic method of coming to",
        "  the wrong conclusion with confidence.",
        "",
        "",
        "Moer's truism:",
        "  The trouble with most jobs is the job holder's",
        "  resemblance to being one of a sled dog team. No one",
        "  gets a change of scenery except the lead dog.",
        "",
        "",
        "Cannon's Comment:",
        "  If you tell the boss you were late for work because you",
        "  had a flat tire, the next morning you will have a flat tire.",
        NULL /* Flag to mark the last saying */
        };

    for (i = 0; OurSaying.szSaying[i]; i++)
    {
        OurSaying.nLength[i] = strlen(OurSaying.szSaying[i]);
    }

    printf("sizeof(OurSaying) = %d\n", sizeof(OurSaying));

    for (i = 0; OurSaying.szSaying[i]; i++)
```

continues

201

Listing 7.4. continued

```
    {
        printf("OurSaying %p %3d '%s'\n",
            &OurSaying.szSaying[i],
            OurSaying.nLength[i],
            OurSaying.szSaying[i]);
    }

    printf("\n\n");

    return (0);
}
```

Because I do not want to count by hand how many strings will be used to initialize the structure and cannot (in this context) let the compiler compute the number, I have a problem. I must specify the number explicitly. I chose a value of 35 (the identifier is called NUMBER_ELEMENTS) because I knew that there would not be more than 35 lines of sayings.

Although the number of elements is fixed at 35, all of them are not initialized. Therefore, the program needs a way to know when the end of the list has been reached. This is accomplished by adding a pointer with the NULL value as the last initializer. The program can test for the end of the array using a conditional test, such as

```
for (i = 0; OurSaying.szSaying[i]; i++)
```

Because ANSI C has defined NULL as a pointer that is never used, and because the value of NULL is usually zero when programming under DOS, this test always works.

If you are unwilling to assume that NULL is always defined as a zero value, the test could be rewritten as

```
for (i = 0; OurSaying.szSaying[i] != NULL; i++)
```

This conditional comparison of the pointer and NULL makes the test more explicit. I did not test for a zero-length string because the blank lines between sayings have a length of zero.

Structures of Structures

It is common to have members of a structure be structures themselves. The maximum level of nesting is 15 according to the ANSI C standard. (You are unlikely to reach this limit.)

Listing 7.5, STRUCT4, has nested structure definitions. This program (built from STRUCT) has Murphy's sayings and a few others I have collected over the years.

Listing 7.5. STRUCT4.C.

```
/*  STRUCT4, written 1992 by Peter D. Hipson
 *  A program with nested structures.
 */

#include <stdio.h>  // Make includes first part of file
#include <string.h> // For string functions

int main(void); // Define main(), and the fact that this program doesn't
                // use any passed parameters.

int main()

{

int     i;

struct SAYING
    {
        char    *szSaying[35];
        int     nLength[35];
    };

struct
    {
        struct SAYING   Murphy;
        struct SAYING   Peter;
    } OurSaying = {{
        "Firestone's Law of Forecasting:",
```

continues

Listing 7.5. continued

```
                "  Chicken Little has to be right only once.",
                "",
                "",
                "Manly's Maxim:",
                "  Logic is a systematic method of coming to",
                "  the wrong conclusion with confidence.",
                "",
                "",
                "Moer's truism:",
                "  The trouble with most jobs is the job holder's",
                "  resemblance to being one of a sled dog team. No one",
                "  gets a change of scenery except the lead dog.",
                "",
                "",
                "Cannon's Comment:",
                "  If you tell the boss you were late for work because you",
                "  had a flat tire, the next morning you will have a flat tire.",
                NULL /* Flag to mark the last saying */
                }, {
                "David's rule:",
                "  Software should be as easy to use as a Coke machine.",
                "",
                "",
                "Peter's Maxim:",
                "  To be successful, you must work hard, but",
                "  Hard work doesn't guarantee success.",
                "",
                "",
                "Teacher's truism:",
                "  Successful people learn.",
                "",
                "",
                "Player's Comment:",
                "  If you don't play to win,",
                "  you don't win.",
                NULL /* Flag to mark the last saying */
                }};

        for (i = 0; OurSaying.Murphy.szSaying[i]; i++)
        {
```

```
    OurSaying.Murphy.nLength[i] =
    strlen(OurSaying.Murphy.szSaying[i]);
}

printf("sizeof(OurSaying.Murphy) = %d\n", sizeof(OurSaying.Murphy));

for (i = 0; OurSaying.Murphy.szSaying[i]; i++)
{
    printf("OurSaying.Murphy %p %3d '%s'\n",
        &OurSaying.Murphy.szSaying[i],
        OurSaying.Murphy.nLength[i],
        OurSaying.Murphy.szSaying[i]);
}

printf("\n\n");

for (i = 0; OurSaying.Peter.szSaying[i]; i++)
{
    OurSaying.Peter.nLength[i] = strlen(OurSaying.Peter.szSaying[i]);
}

printf("sizeof(OurSaying.Peter) = %d\n", sizeof(OurSaying.Peter));

for (i = 0; OurSaying.Peter.szSaying[i]; i++)
{
    printf("OurSaying.Peter %p %3d '%s'\n",
        &OurSaying.Peter.szSaying[i],
        OurSaying.Peter.nLength[i],
        OurSaying.Peter.szSaying[i]);
}

printf("\n\n");

return (0);
}
```

STRUCT4 is the first program in this book that has used the structure tag. The definition of the structure is

```
struct SAYING
    {
```

```
        char     *szSaying[35];
        int      nLength[35];
    };
```

I create a definition of a structure, but I do not declare the structure (that is, I do not allocate storage). I assign the name SAYING to the optional tag position. This name can be referred to in future declarations of structures of the same type.

Next, I declare the structure, which has two members: Murphy and Peter. The structure is then initialized:

```
struct
    {
        struct SAYING   Murphy;
        struct SAYING   Peter;
    } OurSaying = {{...},{...}};
```

Note the use of initialization braces: the entire initializer is enclosed with a set of braces, then each of the nested structure's initializers is enclosed in a set of braces. By grouping the initializers into two blocks, these braces tell the compiler which initializer goes with which nested structure.

Then the structure is accessed using the same syntax shown in the previous examples, except a name (either Murphy or Peter) is added to tell the compiler which member to use:

```
for (i = 0; OurSaying.Murphy.szSaying[i]; i++)
{
    OurSaying.Murphy.nLength[i] = strlen(OurSaying.Murphy.szSaying[i]);
}
```

A saying or length in the Murphy part of the structure is accessed with

OurSaying.Murphy.

and a saying or length in the Peter part of the structure is accessed with

OurSaying.Peter.

Bit Fields in Structures

In a scalar data object, the smallest object that can be addressed directly is usually a byte. In a structure, you can define data objects from 1 to 16 bits long.

Suppose your program contains a number of TRUE/FALSE variables grouped in a structure called `Status`, as follows:

```
struct {
    unsigned int    bIsValid;
    unsigned int    bIsFullSize;
    unsigned int    bIsColor;
    unsigned int    bIsOpen;
    unsigned int    bIsSquare;
    unsigned int    bIsSoft;
    unsigned int    bIsLong;
    unsigned int    bIsWide;
    unsigned int    bIsBoxed;
    unsigned int    bIsWindowed;
} Status;
```

This structure requires 20 bytes of storage, which is a lot of memory for saving a few TRUE/FALSE variables. It would be better to save each variable using only one bit. Perhaps you could use a single, bit-mapped variable (described in Chapter 5, "Decimal, Binary, Hex, and Octal"). Sometimes, however, your flags must keep the identity that a unique name offers.

C offers the capability to define the width of a variable, but only when the variable is in a structure called a *bit field*. For example, you could rewrite the definition of `Status` as follows:

```
struct {
    unsigned int    bIsValid:1;
    unsigned int    bIsFullSize:1;
    unsigned int    bIsColor:1;
    unsigned int    bIsOpen:1;
    unsigned int    bIsSquare:1;
    unsigned int    bIsSoft:1;
    unsigned int    bIsLong:1;
    unsigned int    bIsWide:1;
    unsigned int    bIsBoxed:1;
    unsigned int    bIsWindowed:1;
} Status;
```

The `:1` that appears after each variable's name tells the compiler to allocate one bit to the variable. Thus, the variable can hold only a 0 or a 1. This is exactly what is needed, however, because the variables are TRUE/FALSE variables. The structure is only two bytes long (one tenth the size of the previous example).

A bit field can hold more than a single bit. For example, it can hold a definition of a structure member, such as

```
unsigned int   nThreeBits:3;
```

In this example, nThreeBits can hold any value from 0 to 7.

The most critical limitation to using bit fields is that you cannot determine the address of a bit field variable. If you use the address of operator, a compile-time error results. This means that you cannot pass a bit-field's address as a parameter to a function.

When the compiler stores bit fields, it packs them into storage without regard to alignment. Therefore, storage is used most efficiently when all your bit fields are grouped together in the structure. You can force the compiler to pad the current word so that the next bit field starts on a word boundary. To do so, specify a dummy bit field with a width of 0, for example:

```
struct {
    unsigned int    bIsValid:1;
    unsigned int    bIsFullSize:1;
    unsigned int    bReserved1:0;
    unsigned int    bIsBoxed:1;
    unsigned int    bIsWindowed:1;
} Status;
```

The bReserved1 bit field tells the compiler to pad to the next word boundary, which results in the bIsBoxed bit field starting on a known boundary. This technique is useful when the compiler is packing structures and you need to know that the alignment is as optimal as possible. (Some computers access objects faster when the objects are aligned on word or double word boundaries.)

Using the typedef Keyword

I think that the typedef keyword is one of the best parts of the C language. It enables you to create any data type from simple variables, arrays, structures, or unions.

The typedef keyword is used to define a type of variable, just as its name implies. You can define any type from any other type. A variable created with typedef can be used just like any other variable. Listing 7.6, CREATEDB.C, is a simple example of using typedef with structures.

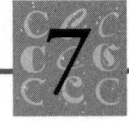

Listing 7.6. CREATEDB.C.

```c
/*  CREATEDB, written 1992 by Peter D. Hipson
 *  This program demonstrates typedef. The program
 *  has minimal error checking; it will fail if
 *  you enter a field value that is too long for
 *  the structure member that holds the value.
 *  Use with caution!
 */


#include <string.h>
#include <ctype.h>
#include <stdio.h>
#include <process.h>
#include <stdlib.h>


#define CUSTOMER_RECORD 1
#define SUPPLIER_RECORD 2

/* Define the structure for the customer database */

typedef struct  _CUSTNAME {
    int     nRecordType;    // 1 == Customer record
    char    szName[61];     // 60 chars for name; 1 for null at end
    char    szAddr1[61];    // 60 chars for address; 1 for null at end
    char    szAddr2[61];    // 60 chars for address; 1 for null at end
    char    szCity[26];     // 25 characters for city; 1 for null at end
    char    szState[3];     // 2-character state abbrev. plus null
    int     nZip;           // Use integer. Print as %5.5d for leading 0
    int     nRecordNumber;  // Which record number?
    double  dSalesTotal;    // Amount customer has purchased
    } CUSTNAME;


typedef CUSTNAME   near *NPCUSTNAME;
typedef CUSTNAME   *PCUSTNAME;

void    main()
```

continues

Listing 7.6. continued

```c
{

FILE      *DataFile;

CUSTNAME    Customer;

char      szFileName[25];
char      szBuffer[129];

int       i;
int       nResult;

double    dSales = 0.0;  // Forces loading of floating-point support

    printf("Please enter customer database name: ");

    gets(szFileName);

    DataFile = fopen(szFileName, "wb");

    if (DataFile == NULL)
    {
        printf("ERROR: File '%s' couldn't be opened.\n", szFileName);

        exit(4);
    }

    Customer.szName[0] = 'A';  // To get past while() the first time

    i = 0;
    Customer.nRecordNumber = 0;

    while (strlen(Customer.szName) > 0)
    {
        memset(&Customer, 0, sizeof(CUSTNAME));

        printf("Enter the Customer's name: ");
        gets(Customer.szName);
```

```
if (strlen(Customer.szName) > 0)
{
    Customer.nRecordNumber = i;

    do
    {
        printf("Enter 1 for customer, 2 for supplier ");
        gets(szBuffer);
        sscanf(szBuffer, "%d",   &Customer.nRecordType);
    }
    while (Customer.nRecordType != CUSTOMER_RECORD &&
        Customer.nRecordType != SUPPLIER_RECORD);

    printf("Enter address line 1: ");
    gets(Customer.szAddr1);
    printf("Enter address line 2: ");
    gets(Customer.szAddr2);
    printf("Enter City: ");
    gets(Customer.szCity);
    printf("Enter state postal abbreviation: ");
    gets(Customer.szState);
    printf("Enter ZIP   Je: ");
    gets(szBuffer);
    sscanf(szBuffer, "%d",   &Customer.nZip);
    printf("Enter total sales: ");
    gets(szBuffer);
    sscanf(szBuffer  "%f",   &Customer.dSalesTotal);

    nResult = fwrite((char *)&Customer, sizeof(CUSTNAME), 1,
    DataFile);

    if (nResult != 1)
    {
        printf("ERROR: File '%s', write error.\n",
            szFileName);

        fclose(DataFile);

        exit(4);
    }
```

continues

Listing 7.6. continued

```
            ++i;
        }
    }

    fclose(DataFile);
}
```

In Listing 7.6, the lines that define the structure that holds the customer's name and address use the `typedef` keyword. This enables us to define the data object using only one line of code:

```
CUSTNAME    Customer;
```

This line creates a structure named `Customer`. As many different structures as needed could have been created using the name `CUSTNAME`.

You access a structure created by a `typedef` in the same way as you access a structure created by any other method. However, now the compiler has a data type that it can work with, so you can obtain the size of the structure type by referring to its name. This is valuable when you must allocate memory for the structure—you cannot get the size from the object because it doesn't exist yet!

The program clears the structure's contents to 0 by using `sizeof()` with the name:

```
memset(&Customer, 0, sizeof(CUSTNAME));
```

In the call to `memset()`, you must pass the address of the structure (`&Customer`), the value that you are setting all the bytes to (`0`), and the size of the structure (`sizeof(CUSTNAME)`). The `memset()` C library function then stores the specified value in all the bytes in `Customer`.

The rest of CREATEDB is straightforward. The program reads from the keyboard each field in the structure. Fields that are not character fields (such as `.dSalesTotal`) are converted to the correct type for the field before being saved in the structure.

 Listing 7.6 does not check the size of the input, so the program may fail if an input line is too long.

Using the offsetof() Macro

ANSI C introduced a new macro, called offsetof(), that you use to determine the offset of a member in a structure. There are many reasons for wanting to know the location of a member in a structure. You might want to write part of a structure to a disk file or read part of a structure in from the file.

Using the offsetof() macro and simple math, it is easy to compute the amount of storage used by individual members of a structure. An example use of the offsetof() macro is shown in Listing 7.7.

Listing 7.7. OFFSETOF.C.

```
/*  OFFSETOF, written 1992 by Peter D. Hipson
 *  This program illustrates the use of the
 *  offsetof() macro.
 */

#include <stdio.h>  // Make includes first part of file
#include <string.h> // For string functions
#include <stddef.h> // For offsetof()

#define MAX_SIZE  35

int main(void); // Define main(), and the fact that this program doesn't
                // use any passed parameters

int main()

{

int     i;
```

continues

Listing 7.7. continued

```
typedef struct
    {
        char     *szSaying[MAX_SIZE];
        int      nLength[MAX_SIZE];
    } SAYING;

typedef struct
    {
        SAYING   Murphy;
        SAYING   Peter;
        SAYING   Peter1;
        SAYING   Peter2;
        SAYING   Peter3;
        SAYING   Peter4;
    } OURSAYING;

OURSAYING  OurSaying = {{
        "Firestone's Law of Forecasting:",
        "  Chicken Little has to be right only once.",
        "",
        "",
        "Manly's Maxim:",
        "  Logic is a systematic method of coming to",
        "  the wrong conclusion with confidence.",
        "",
        "",
        "Moer's truism:",
        "  The trouble with most jobs is the job holder's",
        "  resemblance to being one of a sled dog team. No one",
        "  gets a change of scenery except the lead dog.",
        "",
        "",
        "Cannon's Comment:",
        "  If you tell the boss you were late for work because you",
        "  had a flat tire, the next morning you will have a flat tire.",
        NULL /* Flag to mark the last saying */
        }, {
        "David's rule:",
        "  Software should be as easy to use as a Coke machine.",
        "",
```

```
            "",
        "Peter's Maxim:",
        "  To be successful, you must work hard, but",
        "  Hard work doesn't guarantee success.",
            "",
            "",
        "Teacher's truism:",
        "  Successful people learn.",
            "",
            "",
        "Player's Comment:",
        "  If you don't play to win,",
        "  you don't win.",
        NULL /* Flag to mark the last saying */
        }};

    printf(
        "sizeof(SAYING)               = %d (each member's size)\n"
        "offsetof(OURSAYING, Peter)   = %d (the second member)\n"
        "offsetof(OURSAYING, Peter3)  = %d (the fifth member)\n",
        sizeof(SAYING),
        offsetof(OURSAYING, Peter),
        offsetof(OURSAYING, Peter3));

    return (0);
}
```

To use the offsetof() macro, you supply both the structure and the member name. In addition, the structure name must be created using typedef because the offsetof() macro must create the pointer type with a value of 0, and an identifier—not a variable name—is required.

Here is another use of the offsetof() macro. Suppose that a structure has 75 members that consist of strings, structures, and scalar variables. You want to save the middle 30 members in a file. You have to know the starting address and how many bytes to write to the file.

You could use the sizeof() keyword to compute the size of the block of memory to write, but this would be difficult and complex. You would have to get the size of each member that you want to save to the file, then add the results. Also, serious problems would result if members contained packing bytes (to align them on word boundaries).

A better solution is to take the `offsetof()` of the first member to write and the `offsetof()` of the member just after the last member to write. Subtract one from the other, and you have the number of bytes to save. As you can see, this method is quick and easy.

Pointers to Structures

A pointer to a structure is handled in the same way as a pointer to any other data type, except the syntax of the structure pointer operator differs. You can have a pointer to a structure, and use the pointer to access any member in the structure.

When calling functions that have structures as parameters, it is more efficient to pass a pointer to a structure rather than pass the entire structure. See Listing 7.8, STRUPTR.C.

Listing 7.8. STRUPTR.C.

```
/*  STRUPTR, written 1992 by Peter D. Hipson
 *  Pointers and structures
 */

#include <stdio.h>  // Make includes first part of file
#include <string.h> // For string functions

#define MAX_SIZE  35

int main(void); // Define main(), and the fact that this program doesn't
                // use any passed parameters.

int main()

{

int     i;

typedef struct
    {
        char     *szSaying[MAX_SIZE];
```

```
         int        nLength[MAX_SIZE];
     } SAYING;


typedef struct
     {
         SAYING     Murphy;
         SAYING     Peter;
     } OURSAYING;


OURSAYING  OurSaying = {{
         "Firestone's Law of Forecasting:",
         "  Chicken Little has to be right only once.",
         "",
         "",
         "Manly's Maxim:",
         "  Logic is a systematic method of coming to",
         "  the wrong conclusion with confidence.",
         "",
         "",
         "Moer's truism:",
         "  The trouble with most jobs is the job holder's",
         "  resemblance to being one of a sled dog team. No one",
         "  gets a change of scenery except the lead dog.",
         "",
         "",
         "Cannon's Comment:",
         "  If you tell the boss you were late for work because you",
         "  had a flat tire, the next morning you will have a flat tire.",
         NULL /* Flag to mark the last saying */
         }, {
         "David's rule:",
         "  Software should be as easy to use as a Coke machine.",
         "",
         "",
         "Peter's Maxim:",
         "  To be successful, you must work hard, but",
         "  Hard work doesn't guarantee success.",
         "",
         "",
         "Teacher's truism:",
```

continues

Listing 7.8. continued

```
            "  Successful people learn.",
            "",
            "",
            "Player's Comment:",
            "  If you don't play to win,",
            "  you don't win.",
            NULL /* Flag to mark the last saying */
            }};

    OURSAYING * pOurSaying;
    SAYING    * pSaying;

        pOurSaying = &OurSaying;
        pSaying    = &OurSaying.Peter;

        printf(
            "sizeof(OURSAYING)          = %d\n"
            "sizeof(OurSaying)          = %d\n"
            "sizeof(SAYING)             = %d\n"
            "sizeof(pOurSaying->Murphy) = %d\n"
            "sizeof(pOurSaying->Peter)  = %d\n"
            "sizeof(pSaying)            = %d\n"
            "sizeof(*(pSaying))         = %d\n",
            sizeof(OURSAYING),
            sizeof(OurSaying),
            sizeof(SAYING),
            sizeof(pOurSaying->Murphy),
            sizeof(pOurSaying->Peter),
            sizeof(pSaying),
            sizeof(*(pSaying)));

        for (i = 0; pOurSaying->Murphy.szSaying[i]; i++)
        {
            pOurSaying->Murphy.nLength[i] = strlen(pOurSaying-
            >Murphy.szSaying[i]);
        }

        for (i = 0; pOurSaying->Murphy.szSaying[i]; i++)
        {
```

```
        printf("pOurSaying->Murphy %p %3d '%s'\n",
            &pOurSaying->Murphy.szSaying[i],
            pOurSaying->Murphy.nLength[i],
            pOurSaying->Murphy.szSaying[i]);
    }

    printf("\n\n");

    for (i = 0; pSaying->szSaying[i]; i++)
    {
        pSaying->nLength[i] = strlen(pSaying->szSaying[i]);
    }

    for (i = 0; pSaying->szSaying[i]; i++)
    {
        printf("pOurSaying->Peter %p %3d '%s'\n",
            &pSaying->szSaying[i],
            pSaying->nLength[i],
            pSaying->szSaying[i]);
    }

    printf("\n\n");

    return (0);
}
```

When a structure is accessed with a pointer, the usual method of obtaining a value from memory (using the * operator) is unsatisfactory. To access a member of a structure pointed to by a pointer, you use the -> structure pointer operator rather than the . structure member operator. The -> operator is used as shown in Listing 7.8. You use the address of operator to assign the address of the structure to the pointer.

Understanding unions

If a structure is a group of related data objects, what is a union?

In a structure, each member is stored separately. Modifying one member of a structure does not change the contents of any other member.

219

In a union, all the members share the same block of storage. The block of storage is large enough to hold the largest member; smaller members use only as much storage as necessary. If you change what is stored in one member of a union, all other members are changed too.

Figure 7.1 shows the relationship between a structure and a union in memory. This figure shows the relationship between allocated memory and the members that are part of the data object.

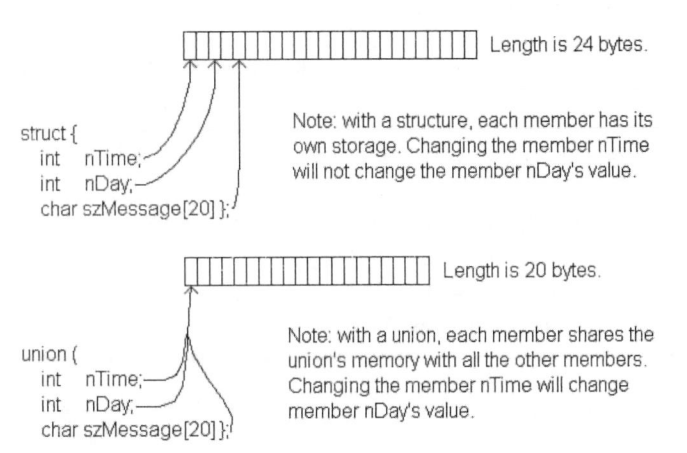

Figure 7.1. A structure and a union in memory.

The UNION.C program in Listing 7.9 reads the database file created with the CREATEDB.C program (Listing 7.6). UNION.C places the result of the read into a union. It then checks what type of record was read and calls the correct function to process the record.

Listing 7.9. UNION.C.

```
/*  UNION, written 1992 by Peter D. Hipson
 *  This program reads the CREATEDB.C database. The
 *  program has minimal error checking; it will fail
 *  if you provide a field value that is too long for the
 *  structure member that holds it. Use with caution!
 */
```

```c
#include <string.h>
#include <ctype.h>
#include <stdio.h>
#include <process.h>
#include <stdlib.h>


#define CUSTOMER_RECORD 1
#define SUPPLIER_RECORD 2

// Define the structure for the customer database.

typedef struct  _CUSTNAME {
    int     nRecordType;
    char    szName[61];      // 60 chars for name; 1 for null at end
    char    szAddr1[61];     // 60 chars for address; 1 for null at end
    char    szAddr2[61];     // 60 chars for address; 1 for null at end
    char    szCity[26];      // 25 characters for city; 1 for null at end
    char    szState[3];      // 2-character state abbreviation + null
    int     nZip;            // Use integer; print as %5.5d for leading 0
    int     nRecordNumber;   // Which record number?
    double  dSalesTotal;     // Amount the customer has purchased
    } CUSTNAME;

typedef CUSTNAME near *NPCUSTNAME;
typedef CUSTNAME  *PCUSTNAME;

typedef struct  _SUPPLIERNAME {
    int     nRecordType;
    char    szName[61];      // 60 chars for name; 1 for null at end
    char    szAddr1[61];     // 60 chars for address; 1 for null at end
    char    szAddr2[61];     // 60 chars for address; 1 for null at end
    char    szCity[26];      // 25 characters for city; 1 for null at end
    char    szState[3];      // 2-character state abbreviation + null
    int     nZip;            // Use integer. Print as %5.5d for leading 0
    int     nRecordNumber;   // Which record number?
    double  dSalesTotal;     // Amount the customer has purchased

    } SUPPLIERNAME;
```

continues

Listing 7.9. continued

```
typedef SUPPLIERNAME near *NPSUPPLIERNAME;
typedef SUPPLIERNAME  *PSUPPLIERNAME;

typedef union _DBRECORD {
    CUSTNAME        Customer;
    SUPPLIERNAME    Supplier;
    } DBRECORD;


/*  Local prototypes (use the typedef'ed names,
 *  so must follow typedefs):
 */

SUPPLIERNAME    ProcessSupplier(NPSUPPLIERNAME);
CUSTNAME        ProcessCustomer(NPCUSTNAME);

// main() function, the called functions

void    main()

{

DBRECORD    dbRecord;

FILE    *DataFile;

char    szFileName[25];
char    szBuffer[129];

int     i;
int     nResult[3];

double  dSales = 0.0; // Forces loading of floating-point support

    printf("Please enter customer database name: ");

    gets(szFileName);

    DataFile = fopen(szFileName, "rb");
```

```
if (DataFile == NULL)
{
    printf("ERROR: File '%s' couldn't be opened.\n", szFileName);

    exit(4);
}

nResult[0] = 1;

while (nResult[0] == 1)
{
    nResult[0] = fread((char *)&dbRecord, sizeof(DBRECORD), 1,
    DataFile);

    if (nResult[0] != 1)
    {
        if (!feof(DataFile))
        {
            printf("ERROR: File '%s', read error.\n", szFileName);

            fclose(DataFile);

            exit(4);
        }
        else
        {
            printf("End of database file '%s'.\n", szFileName);
        }
    }
    else
    {
// You could test dbRecord.Supplier.nRecordType, or
    switch(dbRecord.Customer.nRecordType)
        {
            case CUSTOMER_RECORD:

                ProcessCustomer(&dbRecord.Customer);

                break;

            case SUPPLIER_RECORD:
```

continues

Listing 7.9. continued

```
                        ProcessSupplier(&dbRecord.Supplier);

                    break;

            default:

                    printf("ERROR: Invalid record type read from \
                            database \n");

                    break;
            }
        }
    }

    fclose(DataFile);
}


SUPPLIERNAME    ProcessSupplier(
    NPSUPPLIERNAME          npSupplier)

{

SUPPLIERNAME    WorkSupplier;

    WorkSupplier = *npSupplier;

    printf("Supplier name: %s\n", npSupplier->szName);

//   Do other processing for Supplier...
//   .
//   .
//   .
//   Return WorkSupplier to caller.

    return(WorkSupplier);
}

CUSTNAME    ProcessCustomer(
    NPCUSTNAME          npCustomer)
```

```
{

CUSTNAME    WorkCustomer;

    WorkCustomer = *npCustomer;

    printf("Customer name: %s\n", npCustomer->szName);

//    Do other processing for customer...
//    .
//    .
//    .
//    Return WorkCustomer to caller.

    return(WorkCustomer);
}
```

An integer that determines the record type is the first field of each of the two structures that make up the union. Another common way to refer to a field like this is to code the definitions as

```
typedef union _DBRECORD {
    int             nRecordType;
    CUSTNAME        Customer;
    SUPPLIERNAME    Supplier;
    } DBRECORD;
```

In this definition, you also have a record type variable as part of the union. You can check the value of the record type variable by simply using the following format, rather than Customer or Supplier:

```
DBRECORD    dbRecord;

/*  Read a database record into dbRecord */

    switch(dbRecord.nRecordType) // Rather than
dbRecord.Customer.nRecordType
    {
```

With this format, the first field of each structure must still be an integer that will hold the record type. However, you can refer to the first field directly, which makes the code easier to read.

Summary

In this chapter, you learned about structures and unions.

- A structure is a group of related data objects that are stored in a contiguous block of memory and can be referred to collectively by a given name.

- A union is a group of (related) data objects that share a single block of memory and can be referred to collectively by a given name.

- In a union, usually only one member at a time contains valid data.

- The `typedef` keyword enables the programmer to define new data types. These new data types can be simple variables, arrays, structures, or unions.

- A bit field is defined as part of a structure. It consists of a named variable whose length is defined as a specific number of bits.

- The `offsetof()` macro returns the offset of a structure's member, from the beginning of the structure.

Dynamic Memory Allocation

Allocating large data objects at compile time is seldom practical—especially if the data objects are used infrequently and for a short time. Instead, you usually allocate these data objects at runtime.

To make more memory available to the programmer, ANSI C offers a number of memory allocation functions, including `malloc()`, `realloc()`, `calloc()`, and `free()`. Many compiler suppliers complement these functions with similar functions that optimize the allocation of memory based on the specifics of your computer's architecture. In this chapter, you look at these four functions and Microsoft's enhanced versions of them.

Using the malloc() Function

The memory allocation functions in Table 8.1 include both the ANSI C standard malloc() functions and Microsoft's extensions.

Table 8.1. Microsoft C malloc() functions.

Function	Description
void * malloc(size_t size);	The ANSI C standard memory allocation function.
void __based(void) *_bmalloc (__segment seg, size_t size);	Does based memory allocation. The memory is allocated from the segment you specify.
void __far *_fmalloc(size_tsize);	Allocates a block of memory outside the default data segment, returning a far pointer. This function is called by malloc() when the large or compact memory model is specified.
void __near *_nmalloc (size_t size);	Allocates a block of memory inside the default data segment, returning a near pointer. This function is called by malloc() when the small or medium memory model is specified.

The malloc() library function allocates a block of memory up to the size allowed by size_t. To use malloc(), you must follow a few simple rules:

- The malloc() function returns a pointer to the allocated memory or NULL if the memory could not be allocated. You should always check the returned pointer for NULL.

- The pointer returned by malloc() should be saved in a static variable, unless you are sure that the memory block will be freed before the pointer variable is discarded at the end of the block or the function.

- You should always free a block of memory that has been allocated by malloc() when you are finished with it. If you rely on the operating system to free the block when your program ends, there may be insufficient memory to satisfy additional requests for memory allocation during the rest of the program's run.

- Avoid allocating small blocks (that is, less than 25 or 50 bytes) of memory. There is always some overhead when malloc() allocates memory—16 or more bytes are allocated in addition to the requested memory.

The malloc() function requires only one parameter: the size of the block of memory to allocate. As mentioned, the length of this parameter is size_t, which on many systems is a short int (16 bits).

You could assume that you cannot allocate a block of memory larger than the ANSI C maximum of 32,767 bytes. Another method is to check the defined identifier (usually in malloc.h) for the maximum for the particular system. With Microsoft C compilers, for example, the maximum is approximately 65,500 bytes. If you assume the worst case (the ANSI C value), however, your program has a better chance of working if the limit changes.

The constraint on the size of a data object may seem unreasonable, but you will rarely reach the 32K limit imposed by ANSI C. If you have large data objects, it is always possible (and desirable) to break them into smaller, more manageable pieces.

If you are determined to define a data object larger than the allowed size (something I do not recommend) and are using a Microsoft C compiler, you can use the halloc() function. This function allocates an array that can be any size (up to the amount of available free memory). You must define the array element size as a power of two, which is not an issue if the array is type char, int, or long. If the array is a structure, type union, or a floating-point long double, this constraint may need to be addressed with padding. If you use the halloc() function, your code will not be portable, but you could probably create a workaround if necessary.

When you use the malloc() function, remember that the block of allocated memory is not initialized. If you want initialized memory, use memset() after the memory is allocated or use calloc() (discussed in the next section). I recommend that you always initialize any memory allocated with the malloc() function.

Listing 8.1, MALLOC2.C, allocates blocks of memory. There is no way to determine the size of the largest available block, so the program begins with the largest size (32,767). If malloc() fails, the program reduces this size by 50 percent; this continues until the requested size is less than 2 bytes. The program stops when there is no more memory, or a total of 2M has been allocated.

Listing 8.1. MALLOC2.C.

```
/* MALLOC2, written 1992 by Peter D. Hipson
 * This program allocates memory.
 */

#include  <io.h>      // I/O functions
#include <stdio.h>  // Make includes first in program
#include <string.h> // For string functions
#include <malloc.h> // For memory allocation functions

int main(void); // Define main() and the fact that this
                // program doesn't use any passed parameters

int main()

{

int     i = 0;
int     j = 0;
int     *nPointer[100] = {NULL};
int     nSize = 32767;

long    lTotalBytes = 0;

    while(nSize > 0 &&          // Make nSize valid
        nSize <= 32767 &&
        lTotalBytes < 2000000) // Not more than 2M will be allocated
    {
        nPointer[i] = (int *)malloc(nSize);

        if (nPointer[i] != NULL)
        {
            ++i;

            lTotalBytes += nSize;
```

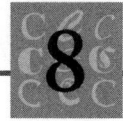
```
        printf("Allocated        %5u bytes, total %10ld\n",
            nSize,
            lTotalBytes);
    }
    else
    {
        printf("Couldn't allocate %5u bytes, total %10ld\n",
            nSize,
            lTotalBytes);

        nSize /= 2;
    }
}

for (j = 0; j < i; j++)
{
    free(nPointer[j]);
    nPointer[j] = NULL;
}

return (0);
}
```

Listing 8.1 is system dependent. If you are using a PC under DOS in real mode, for example, about 400,000 bytes of memory might be allocated. Under a protected-mode environment such as OS/2 or Windows, you can allocate much more memory. For example, on a system running in protected mode with 10M of free memory, 2M of memory might be allocated, as follows:

```
Allocated        32767 bytes, total        32767
Allocated        32767 bytes, total        65534
Allocated        32767 bytes, total        98301
and so on...
Allocated        32767 bytes, total      1966020
Allocated        32767 bytes, total      1998787
Allocated        32767 bytes, total      2031554
```

If you are not sure of the environment in which your application will be running, assume the worst case—less than 32K of free memory.

231

Notice that a loop at the end of the program frees the memory that `malloc()` has allocated. This loop is performing housekeeping—something that every well-written program should do.

Using the calloc() Function

Because `malloc()` does not initialize memory and `calloc()` does, programmers often prefer `calloc()`. When using Microsoft's C compilers, the array memory allocation functions in Table 8.2 are used with `calloc()`.

Table 8.2. Microsoft C calloc() Functions.

Function	Description
`void *calloc( size_t num, size_t size );`	The ANSI C standard array memory allocation function.
`void __based( void ) *_bcalloc( __segment seg, size_t num, size_t size );`	Does based memory allocation. You provide the segment that the data will be allocated from.
`void __far *_fcalloc ( size_t num, size_t size );`	Allocates a block of memory outside the default data segment, returning a `far` pointer. This function is called by `calloc()` when the `large` or `compact` memory model is specified.
`void __near *_ncalloc ( size_t num, size_t size );`	Allocates a block of memory inside the default data segment, returning a `near` pointer. This function is called by `calloc()` when the `small` or `medium` memory model is specified.

The `calloc()` library function allocates memory much like the `malloc()` function, with two main differences. With the `calloc()` function, you specify two parameters, not one: the number of elements and the size of each element. The product of these parameters determines the size of the memory block to allocate, and must fit in type `size_t`, which on many systems is a short int (16 bits). If you specify an element

size of 1, the `calloc()` num parameter functions similarly to the `malloc()` size parameter.

The second difference is that the `calloc()` function initializes the memory it allocates to zero. The value used to initialize the memory is an absolute zero, which usually—but not always—evaluates to a floating-point zero or a `NULL` pointer value. This is fine if the memory will be used for string storage or integers. If the memory will be used for floating-point values, you should explicitly initialize the block of memory after `calloc()` returns. I recommend that you always initialize memory allocated with `calloc` if you do not know the format of the data that you will be storing in it.

To use `calloc()`, you follow the same rules for using `malloc()`. These rules are outlined in the first section, "Using the malloc() Function."

Listing 8.2, CALLOC1.C, allocates blocks of memory. The size of the largest available block cannot be determined, so the program begins with the largest size possible (using the size of `int`) and tries to allocate an array of 32,767 members. If `calloc()` fails, the program reduces the size by 50 percent; this continues until the requested size is less than 2 bytes. The program allocates buffers, each containing 32,767 2-byte integers. When an allocation request fails, the program decreases the size of the array until more memory can be allocated. It stops when there is no more memory or 2M have been allocated. The only major difference between MALLOC2.C and CALLOC1.C is the call to the memory allocation function.

Listing 8.2. CALLOC1.C.

```
/* CALLOC1, written 1992 by Peter D. Hipson
 * This program allocates arrays of memory.
 */

#include <stdio.h>  // Make includes first part of file
#include <string.h> // For string functions
#include <malloc.h> // For memory allocation functions

int main(void); // Define main() and establish that this
                // program does not use any passed parameters


int main()
```

continues

Listing 8.2. continued

```c
{

int     i = 0;
int     j = 0;
int     *nPointer[100] = {NULL};
int     nSize = 32767;

long    lTotalBytes = 0;

    while(nSize > 0 &&          // Make nSize valid
        nSize <= 32767 &&
        lTotalBytes < 2000000) // No more than 2M will be allocated

    {
        nPointer[i] = (int *)calloc(nSize, sizeof(int));

        if (nPointer[i] != NULL)
        {
            ++i;

            lTotalBytes += (nSize * sizeof(int));

            printf("Allocated        %5u short int, total %10ld\n",
                nSize,
                lTotalBytes);
        }
        else
        {
            printf("Couldn't allocate %5u short int, total %10ld\n",
                nSize,
                lTotalBytes);

            nSize /= 2;
        }
    }

    for (j = 0; j < i; j++)
    {
```

```
        free(nPointer[j]);
        nPointer[j] = NULL;
    }

    return (0);
}
```

When CALLOC1 was run, it could not allocate an integer array of 32,767 members, as the following output shows:

```
Couldn't Allocate 32767 bytes, total            0
Allocated          16383 bytes, total        32766
Allocated          16383 bytes, total        65532
Allocated          16383 bytes, total        98298
and so on...
Allocated          16383 bytes, total      1965960
Allocated          16383 bytes, total      1998726
Allocated          16383 bytes, total      2031492
```

The reason for this is not the ANSI C limit of 32,767 bytes in a data object—my C compiler does not enforce this limit. The limit in my compiler is that a data object created by calloc() or malloc() cannot be larger than 65,510 bytes. The array of integers consisted of 32,767 members (each 2 bytes long), for a total of 65,534 bytes, which is too large.

CALLOC1 then attempted to allocate the next size, 16,383, and was successful.

Using the free() Function

The free() functions in Table 8.3 can be used with a Microsoft C compiler.

Table 8.3. Microsoft C free( ) Functions.

Function	Description
void free(void *memblock);	The ANSI C standard array memory deallocation function.

continues

Table 8.3. continued

Function	Description
`void _bfree( __segment seg,` `void __based( void ) *memblock );`	Based memory deallocation.
`void _ffree( void __far` `*memblock );`	Frees a block of memory outside the default data segment.
`void _nfree( void __near` `*memblock );`	Frees a block of memory inside the default data segment.

The `free()` memory allocation function was shown in Listings 8.1 and 8.2. Its function is to return to the operating system memory that you have allocated. (You could think of the memory as borrowed.) Memory is usually a limited resource—even when you are running a system with virtual memory—so you must give memory back when you are finished with it.

The `free()` function is almost foolproof. Errors could occur, however, when you try to free memory that

Was not allocated with one of the memory allocation functions;

Has been released through a prior call to `free()` or a call to `realloc()`;

Is currently in use by another thread in a multithreaded operating system;

Is not yours to free.

When `free()` is called, be sure you are passing a valid pointer to it. To make sure that the pointer is valid, check that it contains NULL or points to a properly allocated block of memory. Note that `free()` considers a NULL pointer to be always valid, and treats a call with a NULL pointer as a no-operation, which means `free()` simply returns without freeing any memory.

Look at the following variable declarations in the CALLOC1 program:

```
int    j = 0;
int    *nPointer[100] = {NULL};
int    nSize = 32767;
```

The pointer array is initialized to NULL, which is a safe value for initialization because it will not cause an error if it is passed to free(). In addition, because the loop that allocates the memory uses an index into the array of memory pointers (nPointer[]), only valid pointers to allocated blocks of memory will be stored in nPointer[].

In the final cleanup, the memory pointed to by nPointer[] is freed. The following loop resets each pointer to NULL after the block of memory is freed:

```
for (j = 0; j < i; j++)
{
    free(nPointer[j]);
    nPointer[j] = NULL;
}
```

If the program tries to free one of the already freed nPointer[]s later (because of a programming error), the NULL pointer prevents an error that would be caused by trying to free a block of memory twice.

Using the realloc() Function

When using Microsoft's C compilers, the array memory allocation functions in Table 8.4 are used with realloc().

Table 8.4. Microsoft C realloc() functions.

Function	Description
void *realloc(void *memblock,size_t size);	The ANSI C standard array memory reallocation function.
void __based(void) *_brealloc(__segment seg, void __based(void) *memblock, size_t size);	Does based memory reallocation. You must provide the segment that the data will be allocated from.
void __far *_frealloc (void __far *memblock, size_t size);	Reallocates a block of memory outside the default data segment, returning a far pointer. This function is called by realloc() when the large or compact memory model is specified.

continues

Table 8.4. continued

Function	Description
`void __near *_nrealloc` `( void __near *memblock,` `size_t size );`	Reallocates a block of memory inside the default data segment, returning a near pointer. This function is called by `realloc()` when the `small` or `medium` memory model is specified.

Assume that you have a program that reads customer records from the keyboard and stores each in a structure. When the user is finished entering the names, the program saves them to disk. You want to be sure that there is enough memory (within reason) to hold the entered names, but you do not want to allocate more memory than necessary.

You could call `calloc()` and allocate all available free memory for the structures. This might work, but it wastes a lot of memory. Another method is to call `calloc()` and allocate a small block, but the program would have to pause to save the information, something that might irritate the user. Or you could call `calloc()`, allocate a small block, call `calloc()` again when the block was filled and get a bigger block of memory, copy the small block of memory to the larger one, then free the small block. As you can see, that would require a lot of work.

The best solution is to call `calloc()` to allocate the initial array, then call `realloc()` to make the block larger. The `realloc()` function copies the contents of the original block of memory to the new block, then frees the original block, so your work is minimized.

Listing 8.3 is the CDB program. Like the CREATEDB program in Chapter 7, "C Structures", CDB reads in customer records. Unlike CREATEDB, CDB writes the records entered by the user to the file only after the user has finished entering the names.

Listing 8.3. CDB.C.

```
/* CDB, written 1992 by Peter D. Hipson
 * This program uses calloc() and realloc(). It has
 * better error checking than the CREATEDB program,
 * which was presented in Chapter 7.
 */
```

```
#include <string.h>
#include <ctype.h>
#include <stdio.h>
#include <process.h>
#include <stdlib.h>

#define INCREMENT_AMOUNT  2

#define CUSTOMER_RECORD   1
#define SUPPLIER_RECORD   2

/* Define our structure for the customer database. */

typedef struct  _CUSTNAME {
    int     nRecordType;    // 1 == Customer record
    char    szName[61];     // 60 chars for name, 1 for null at end
    char    szAddr1[61];    // 60 chars for address, 1 for null at end
    char    szAddr2[61];    // 60 chars for address, 1 for null at end
    char    szCity[26];     // 25 chars for city, 1 for null at end
    char    szState[3];     // 2-char state abbreviation, plus null
    long    lZip;           // Use integer, print as %5.5ld for leading 0
    int     nRecordNumber;  // Which record number?
    double  dSalesTotal;    // How much customer has purchased
    } CUSTNAME;

typedef CUSTNAME  near *NPCUSTNAME;
typedef CUSTNAME  *PCUSTNAME;

void    main()

{

FILE    *DataFile;

PCUSTNAME   Customer = NULL;
PCUSTNAME   TempCustomer = NULL;

char    szFileName[25];
char    szBuffer[257];
```

continues

239

Listing 8.3. continued

```c
int     i;
int     nNumberRecords = 0;
int     nRecord = 0;
int     nResult = 0;

double  dSales = 0.0; // Forces loading of floating-point support

    Customer = (PCUSTNAME)calloc(sizeof(CUSTNAME),
        INCREMENT_AMOUNT);

    nNumberRecords += INCREMENT_AMOUNT;

    printf("Please enter customer database name: ");

    gets(szFileName);

    DataFile = fopen(szFileName, "wb");

    if (DataFile == NULL)
    {
        printf("ERROR: File '%s' couldn't be opened.\n", szFileName);

        exit(4);
    }

    printf("Demo of calloc() and realloc(). sizeof(CUSTNAME) = %d\n",
        sizeof(CUSTNAME));

    nRecord = 0;

    Customer[nRecord].szName[0] = 'A'; // To get past while() first time

    while (strlen(Customer[nRecord].szName) > 0)
    {
        memset(&Customer[nRecord], 0, sizeof(CUSTNAME));

        printf("Enter name %d: ", nRecord + 1);
        gets(szBuffer);
```

```
szBuffer[sizeof(Customer[nRecord].szName) - 1] = '\0';
strcpy(Customer[nRecord].szName, szBuffer);

if (strlen(Customer[nRecord].szName) > 0)
{
    Customer[nRecord].nRecordNumber = i;

    do
    {
        printf("Enter 1 for customer, 2 for supplier ");
        gets(szBuffer);
        sscanf(szBuffer, "%d",   &Customer[nRecord].nRecordType);
    }
    while (Customer[nRecord].nRecordType != CUSTOMER_RECORD &&
        Customer[nRecord].nRecordType != SUPPLIER_RECORD);

    printf("Enter address line 1: ");
    gets(szBuffer);
    szBuffer[sizeof(Customer[nRecord].szAddr1) - 1] = '\0';
    strcpy(Customer[nRecord].szAddr1, szBuffer);

    printf("Enter address line 2: ");
    gets(szBuffer);
    szBuffer[sizeof(Customer[nRecord].szAddr2) - 1] = '\0';
    strcpy(Customer[nRecord].szAddr2, szBuffer);

    printf("Enter City: ");
    gets(szBuffer);
    szBuffer[sizeof(Customer[nRecord].szCity) - 1] = '\0';
    strcpy(Customer[nRecord].szCity, szBuffer);

    printf("Enter state postal abbreviation: ");
    gets(szBuffer);
    szBuffer[sizeof(Customer[nRecord].szState) - 1] = '\0';
    strcpy(Customer[nRecord].szState, szBuffer);

    printf("Enter ZIP code: ");
    gets(szBuffer);
    sscanf(szBuffer, "%ld",   &Customer[nRecord].lZip);
```

continues

Listing 8.3. continued

```
            printf("Enter total sales: ");
            gets(szBuffer);
            sscanf(szBuffer, "%f",    &Customer[nRecord].dSalesTotal);

            ++nRecord;

            if (nRecord == nNumberRecords)
            {
                TempCustomer = (PCUSTNAME)realloc(Customer,
                    sizeof(CUSTNAME) * (nNumberRecords +
                    INCREMENT_AMOUNT));

                if (TempCustomer)
                {
                    nNumberRecords += INCREMENT_AMOUNT;

                    printf("realloc() added records, now total is %d\n",
                        nNumberRecords);

                    Customer = TempCustomer;

                    Customer[nRecord].szName[0] = 'A'; // To get past
while()
                }
                else
                {
                    printf("ERROR: Couldn't realloc the buffers\n\n\g");
                    --nRecord;
                    Customer[nRecord].szName[0] = '\0';
                }
            }
            else
            {
                Customer[nRecord].szName[0] = 'A'; // To get past while()
            }
        }
    }

    for (i = 0; i < nRecord; i++)
    {
```

```
        printf("Name '%10s' City '%10s' State '%2s' ZIP '%5.5ld'\n",
            Customer[i].szName,
            Customer[i].szCity,
            Customer[i].szState,
            Customer[i].lZip);
    }

    nResult = fwrite((char *)Customer,
        sizeof(CUSTNAME),
        nRecord,
        DataFile);

    if (nResult != nRecord)
    {
        printf("ERROR: File '%s', write error, record %d.\n",
            szFileName,
            i);

        fclose(DataFile);

        exit(4);
    }

    fclose(DataFile);
}
```

By expanding the buffers used for storing data, the data can be saved in memory and written to the disk at one time. In addition, summary information such as totals could be displayed, the user could edit the entered information, and the information could be processed if necessary. The one hitch is that all the user's data that is in RAM and not written to the disk will be lost if the computer fails. With CREATEDB, at most one record would be lost.

When you write a program in which the user will be entering substantial amounts of data from the keyboard, you should plan for events that might cause the loss of information just entered. One solution to retaining this information is to write to the file after the user inputs a record. Summary information can be presented, records can be edited, and so on, and the records the user entered can be rewritten by the program to a master file later as necessary.

The `realloc()` function enables you to have some control over the size of your dynamic data objects. Sometimes, however, the data objects will become too large for available memory. In CDB, for example, each data object is 228 bytes long. If 40,000 bytes of free memory were available, the user could enter about 176 records before using up free memory. Your program must be able to handle the problem of insufficient memory in a way that does not inconvenience the user or lose data.

Allocating Arrays

Allocating an array is an easy process when you use `calloc()`. Its parameters are the size for each element of the array and a count of the number of array elements. To dynamically allocate an array at runtime, you simply make a call.

Refer to Listing 8.4, SORTALOC. The program prompts the user for a number of integers, in the range 10 to 30,000. It then creates a list of integers, sorts them, and prints the result.

Listing 8.4. SORTALOC.C.

```
/* SORTALOC, written 1992 by Peter D. Hipson
 * This program prompts for the number of integers to sort,
 * allocates the array, fills the array with random numbers,
 * sorts the array, then prints it, using 10 columns.
 */

#include <search.h>
#include <stdio.h>
#include <process.h>
#include <stdlib.h>
#include <time.h>

int     compare(const void *, const void *);

int     main()

{

int     i;
int     *nArray = NULL;
```

```c
int     nArraySize = 0;

while(nArraySize < 10 || nArraySize > 30000)
{
    printf("Enter the number of random integers to sort (10 to \
            30,000): ");
    scanf("%d", &nArraySize);

    if(nArraySize < 10 || nArraySize > 30000)
    {
        printf("Error: must be between 10 and 30,000!\n");
    }

    nArray = (int *)calloc(sizeof(int), nArraySize);

    if (nArray == NULL)
    {
        printf("Error: couldn't allocate that much memory!\n");
        nArraySize = 0;
    }
}

srand((unsigned)time(NULL));

for (i = 0; i < nArraySize; i++)
{
    nArray[i] = rand();
}

qsort(nArray, nArraySize, sizeof(int), compare);

for (i = 0; i < nArraySize; i += 10)
{
    printf("%5d %5d %5d %5d %5d %5d %5d %5d %5d %5d\n",
        nArray[i],
        nArray[i + 1],
        nArray[i + 2],
        nArray[i + 3],
        nArray[i + 4],
        nArray[i + 5],
```

continues

Listing 8.4. continued

```
                nArray[i + 6],
                nArray[i + 6],
                nArray[i + 7],
                nArray[i + 8],
                nArray[i + 9]);
    }

    free(nArray);

    return(0);
}

int     compare(
    const void * a,
    const void * b)

{
    return (*(int *)a - *(int *)b);
}
```

SORTALOC illustrates several important points about using the memory allocation functions. First, the array is simply declared as an integer pointer called nArray. This pointer is initialized with NULL to prevent an error when the free() function frees the pointer. Although always initializing variables may seem excessive, using an uninitialized variable is a common programming error.

After calloc() allocates the array, it can be accessed in the same way as any other array. For example, standard array indexing can be used, as shown in the following:

```
for (i = 0; i < nArraySize; i++)
{
    nArray[i] = rand();
}
```

The loop assigns a random number to each element (indexed by i).

After the array is filled, it is passed to the qsort() function like any other array. The qsort() function can sort almost any type of data. You just give qsort() the size of the array's elements, the number of elements, and the compare function. (Note: The compare function in Listing 8.4 is valid for integers but not floating-point values.

This is because the compare must return an integer, and a floating-point value may differ by less than the truncation value of an integer.)

Finally, the array is printed in ten columns. There is nothing tricky about this portion of the code—one print statement prints ten elements, then the index is incremented by ten.

Global Memory versus Local Memory

The discussion of local memory and global memory is applicable to computers with Intel 80x86 CPUs. These CPUs use segmented architecture, in which a data object can be addressed with a full address (consisting of both a segment and an offset from the segment) or as an offset (where the segment used is the default data segment).

Not all operating systems and compilers offer access to both local memory (found in the default data segment) and global memory (located outside the default data segment, usually in its own segment). A compiler that offers memory models, such as small, medium, large, and compact, is generally found on a PC-type of computer. The discussion in this section pertains to compilers used on an 80x86 CPU.

For most compilers, the memory model determines the area from which memory will be allocated. If your program uses the large or compact memory model, the default memory pool is global. If your program is a small or medium model program, the default memory pool is local. You can always override the compiler's default memory allocation area.

When running in real mode, Intel 80x86 CPUs can access a maximum of 64K in each segment. This limitation, and the way the default data segment is allocated (it is often used for the stack, initialized data variables, constants, literals, and the heap, which is where memory is allocated from when using local memory), affects how much data a program can have.

Global memory has its own segment, and thus can have up to 64K in a single data object (or more than 64K by using several contiguous segments). To use global memory, however, your program must use far (4-byte) pointers rather than near (2-byte) pointers, and this can slow program execution. If you need to determine the effect this has on performance, you could create one version of your program with small data blocks and near pointers, and the other with large data blocks and far pointers, then run simple benchmarks.

Summary

In this chapter, you learned about memory allocation, how to change the size of an allocated block of memory, and how to free memory after it is no longer needed.

- The `malloc()` function is the ANSI standard method for allocating memory. It accepts a single parameter that specifies how much memory should be allocated.

- The `calloc()` function allocates memory based on the size of the object and the number of objects. It is typically used to allocate an array.

- When memory allocated with one of the memory allocation functions is no longer needed, the `free()` function returns the memory to the operating system.

- The `realloc()` function changes the size of a block of memory allocated with one of the memory allocation functions. The object's size can be increased or decreased.

- When programming on the PC (and other systems), you can often choose the size of the pointer that accesses the allocated memory. The pointer size affects the size of the executable program and the performance of the program.

Disk Files and Other I/O

Without files, your program could do nothing. It would be without input, unable to provide output, and unable to save the result of any of its computations. Fortunately, ANSI C offers an excellent collection of file I/O functions. You can write to a file in an unformatted (machine readable) manner, or your program can write to a file in a formatted (people readable) manner.

This chapter deals with all types of I/O: to and from files, the console, and other devices. You learn all (at least I hope all) that you will need to develop the I/O portions of your programs. The first part of this chapter deals with disk files. The second part covers console I/O and direct port I/O, including I/O to printer ports and communications ports. Much of the direct port I/O is hardware dependent; the discussion applies to a PC-based system.

File I/O Basics

This section does not discuss how files are arranged, stored, and managed on the disk drive. That is a topic for a book on operating systems, not a book on C programming. This section does cover how to use files.

The most important part of most programs is their capability to save results or the data they use (such as a database) to a disk file. All disk files share things in common. (Again, this discussion is confined to the PC's DOS operating system.)

All files have names. The format for a disk filename is eight characters for the name and three characters for the extension. The selection of a file's name and extension are generally left to the user, except for files that other applications utilize. Many applications suggest an extension (some require it), but few programs place restrictions on the name.

All files have a creation date and time, which is stored in the time stamp. The time stamp is updated each time you save changes to the file, so it serves as a file modification time stamp.

All files have a length. This length is in the operating system's structure saved for each file. When a file consists of only text, it may also contain an EOF (end of file) marker, which under DOS is 0x1A (Ctrl-Z).

All files also have attributes, as follows:

Normal	No special attributes are set for the file.
Directory	The file is a directory. The directory attribute can be used with the hidden attribute.
Hidden	The file's name is not displayed when you issue a DIR command without the /A:H option.
System	The file is used only by the operating system. Generally, only the two files belonging to the operating system have the system attribute.
Read only	The file can be only read, not written or deleted.
Archive	The file has not been backed up since it was last changed. BACKUP and XCOPY can use and change the archive attribute.

You can specify the read-only attribute when you create a file. All other attributes must be set (or cleared) using the DOS ATTRIB command. You use the system() function to call the ATTRIB command from DOS applications.

When a file is opened, the program typically must specify the filename and the mode: read, write, or both read and write. If the file is being created, the program could specify also whether the file will be read only after it is created.

The open functions return an identifier that is a file handle or a pointer to the opened file. You use this identifier when you call the read and write functions. When the program has finished with the file, the file should be closed, or if it is a temporary work file, deleted.

Text Files and Binary Files

If a *text file* is displayed on the screen, it is readable. It shouldn't contain any special characters other than tabs and newlines and is generally formatted so that it presents information to the user in an organized manner. Many text files are used only by programs, however, even though the files are fully readable (and perhaps even understandable). A *binary file* can contain any data, including the internal representation of numbers, special control characters.

A problem arises when you use a text file, the C language, and C's interface to DOS. C specifies a single character (called the *newline* character) to signify the end of a line. DOS uses two characters (a newline character followed by a carriage return character) to signify the end of a line. Each is a control character, and as such, must be specified using the ANSI C escape sequence, which begins with a backslash character.

To specify a newline, you use the \n character sequence. When C encounters the newline character in a string being output to DOS (either to a file or on the screen), C converts it to the two-character sequence that DOS expects (a newline followed by a carriage return). When input is read, C does the opposite, converting the newline and carriage return pair to a single newline character.

This creates a minor problem. When the program reads a specified number of bytes in a text mode file, each time the newline and carriage return pair is encountered, the character count is incremented by only 1 (only one newline character is counted). If your program reads the string from a file, as shown in Figure 9.1, the string is only 29 characters long, not the 31 characters stored in the file.

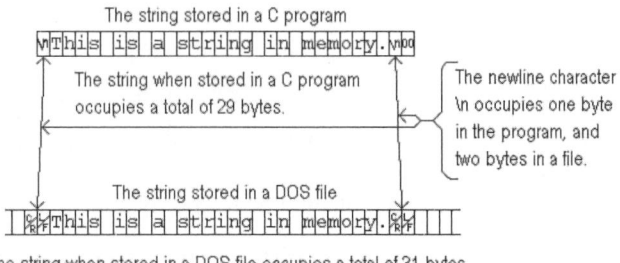

The string stored in a C program

The string when stored in a C program occupies a total of 29 bytes.

The newline character \n occupies one byte in the program, and two bytes in a file.

The string stored in a DOS file

The string when stored in a DOS file occupies a total of 31 bytes, two bytes longer than used when the the string is stored in memory.

Figure 9.1. A string in memory and in a text mode file.

The problem arises when the program must go (seek) to a specific place in the file. You cannot assume how many characters (or bytes) are between a given point and the desired point. If you have written a file containing five different strings that are each 50 characters long (and contain an unknown number of newline characters), you could not get to the beginning of the fourth string, for example, by seeking to character number 150.

To successfully seek in a text file, you must create an index to each string (or record). This index is assigned values by using one of the functions that return the current place in a file, such as `ftell()` or `fgetpos()`. These functions return the correct position of a given data object, taking into consideration the conversion of the newline character to a newline and carriage return pair.

You must save this index to be able to access the strings randomly. The only alternative to saving an index is to read the text file sequentially, which may not be acceptable based on performance considerations.

The TEXTFILE.C program, shown in Listing 9.1, shows the effects of text mode.

Listing 9.1. TEXTFILE.C.

```
/* TEXTFILE, written 1992 by Peter D. Hipson
 * This program demonstrates text file
 * newline conversions.
 */

#include <stdio.h>   // Make includes first part of file
#include <string.h>  // For string functions
```

```
#include <process.h> // For abort(), spawn(), exit(), etc.
#include <malloc.h>  // For memory allocation functions
#include <conio.h>   // For console getch(), getche(), etc.
#include <ctype.h>   // For character-conversion functions

#define MAX_LINES   25
#define MAX_LENGTH  80

char    szSaying[MAX_LINES][MAX_LENGTH] =
    {
        "\nFirestone's Law of Forecasting:                        \n",
        "\n  Chicken Little has to be right only once.            \n",
        "\n                                                     \n\n",
        "\nManly's Maxim:                                         \n",
        "\n  Logic is a systematic method of coming to            \n",
        "\n   the wrong conclusion with confidence.               \n",
        "\n                                                     \n\n",
        "\nMoer's truism:                                         \n",
        "\n  The trouble with most jobs is the job holder's       \n",
        "\n  resemblance to being one of a sled dog team. No one   \n",
        "\n  gets a change of scenery except the lead dog.        \n",
        "\n                                                     \n\n",
        "\nCannon's Comment:                                      \n",
        "\n  If you tell the boss you were late for work because you \n",
        "\n  had a flat tire, the next morning you will have a flat tire.\n",
        "\n                                                     \n\n",
    };


int main(void); // Define main() and the fact that this program
                // does not use any passed parameters

int main()

{

FILE    *DataFile = NULL;

char    szFileName[25];
char    szBuffer[257];
char    szMode[5] = "w\0\0";
```

continues

Listing 9.1. continued

```c
int     i;
int     nNumberRecords = 0;
int     nRecord = 0;
int     nResult = 0;

long    lNewPosition = 0;
long    lOldPosition = 0;

/*  Prompt the user to supply the mode, either lowercase t
 *  for a text file or lowercase b for a binary file.
 */

    while (DataFile == NULL)
    {
        while(szMode[1] != 'b' && szMode[1] != 't')
        {
            printf("\nPlease enter 't' for text file, 'b' for binary: ");

/* For non-Microsoft C systems, use tolower() (no leading underscore) */

            szMode[1] = _tolower(getche());
        }

        printf("\nPlease enter name of file to write: ");

        gets(szFileName);

        DataFile = fopen(szFileName, szMode);

        if (DataFile == NULL)
        {
            printf("ERROR: File '%s' couldn't be opened.\n", szFileName);
        }
    }

    printf("\n");

    switch(szMode[1])
    {
        case 't':
```

```
        printf("Demo of a text file\n\n");
        break;

    case 'b':
        printf("Demo of a binary file\n\n");
        break;
}

for (i = 0; strlen(szSaying[i]); i++)
{
    lOldPosition = ftell(DataFile);

    fwrite(szSaying[i],
        strlen(szSaying[i]),
        1,
        DataFile);

    lNewPosition = ftell(DataFile);

    printf(
        "Start position %5ld "
        "end %5ld, "
        "strlen(...) %d but "
        "wrote %5ld bytes'\n",
        lOldPosition,
        lNewPosition,
        strlen(szSaying[i]),
        (long)lNewPosition - lOldPosition);
}

fclose(DataFile);

printf("\n");

switch(szMode[1])
{
    case 't':
        printf("Note the bytes written don't"
            " equal the string's length\n\n");
        break;
```

continues

255

Listing 9.1. continued

```
        case 'b':
            printf("Note the bytes written always"
                " equal the string's length\n\n");
            break;
    }

    return (0);
}
```

TEXTFILE enables you to open the file in text mode or binary mode so you can see how the modes differ. The `ftell()` function returns the number of bytes in the file, without regard to the file's mode. All strings in TEXTFILE have the same number of characters, according to `strlen()`, but the number of bytes written in the text mode depends on the number of newline characters in the string.

Virtually all files saved by editors and other programs are equivalent to a text file. Many DOS programs cannot read a file that does not have the newline and carriage return combination.

Creating and Using Temporary Work Files

When you create a temporary work file, remember the following simple rules:

- The filename must be unique. This uniqueness can be guaranteed by using `tmpfile()` or `tmpnam()`.

- The file must be deleted when you have finished using it. If you create the file using `tmpfile()`, the operating system deletes the file for you. If you create it with `tmpnam()` and an explicit open, your program must delete the file.

Few programs can store all their data in memory. You cannot be sure of the amount of memory available to your program for data storage, and you therefore won't know if there will be enough memory to load the data the program requires.

Many larger programs with large data objects do not even try to save all their data in memory. They read the data, index the data, then write the data to a temporary work file. Listing 9.2, EDLINE, is a simple editor that reads a text file, provides editing

capabilities, then writes the program's buffers out to the file when the user ends the program. Because this editor is simple, it supports only line-number editing.

Listing 9.2. EDLINE.C.

```c
/* EDLINE, written 1992 by Peter D. Hipson
 * This program is a simple line-oriented editor. If
 * your compiler supports memory models, use the
 * large model.
 */

#include <stdio.h>   // Make includes first part of file
#include <string.h>  // For string functions
#include <process.h> // For abort(), spawn(), exit(), etc.
#include <malloc.h>  // For memory allocation functions
#include <conio.h>   // For console getch(), getche(), etc.
#include <ctype.h>   // For character conversion functions

#define MAX_LINES    15500  /* Allow 64K for indexes      */
#define MAX_LENGTH     513  /* Longest line is 512 + NULL  */
#define DELETED_LINE    -1  /* A line that has been deleted */

long    lLineIndex[MAX_LINES];
char    szInputLine[MAX_LENGTH];


int main(
    int     argc,     /* Count of arguments             */
    char    *argv[],  /* Array of pointers to arguments  */
    char    *envp[]   /* Array of pointers to environment */
    );

int EditLine(char * szInputLine); /* Used to edit a given line */


int main(
    int     argc,
    char    *argv[],
    char    *envp[]
    )
```

continues

Listing 9.2. continued

```c
{

FILE    *DataFile = NULL;
FILE    *WorkFile = NULL;

char    szFileName[25];
char    szBuffer[257];
char    szTempName[L_tmpnam];
char    szNewName[L_tmpnam];
char    szCommand[81];
char    chChar;

int     i;
int     nMaxLines = 0;
int     nStartLine;
int     nEndLine;

/*  First, get the filename to edit */

    if (argc >= 2)
    {
        DataFile = fopen(argv[1], "rt");

        if (DataFile == NULL)
        {
            printf("ERROR: File '%s' couldn't be opened.\n", argv[1]);
        }
        else
        {
            strcpy(szFileName, argv[1]);
        }
    }

    while (DataFile == NULL)
    {
        printf("\nPlease enter name of file to edit: ");

        gets(szFileName);
```

```
        DataFile = fopen(szFileName, "rt");

        if (DataFile == NULL)
        {
            printf("ERROR: File '%s' couldn't be opened.\n", szFileName);
        }
    }

    printf("\n");

/*  Next, get a temporary filename, read the original file, and
 *  write it to the work file. Create a line-number index so that
 *  you can access the records.
 */

    tmpnam(szTempName);

    if (strlen(szTempName) == 0)
    {
        printf("Couldn't get a work file name...\n");
        exit(4);
    }

    WorkFile = fopen(szTempName, "w+t");

    for (i = 0; i < MAX_LINES; i++)
    {
        lLineIndex[i] = DELETED_LINE;
    }

    nMaxLines = 1;
    lLineIndex[nMaxLines] = 0;

    while(fgets(szInputLine, sizeof(szInputLine), DataFile))
    {
        lLineIndex[nMaxLines++] = ftell(WorkFile);
        fputs(szInputLine, WorkFile);
    }

    fclose(DataFile);
```

continues

Listing 9.2. continued

```c
    printf("Total lines in file %d.\n", nMaxLines - 1);

    szCommand[0] = '\0';

    while(szCommand[0] != 'q') // Quit without saving (use w command to
                               // save)
    {
        printf("Command? ");

        gets(szCommand);

        strlwr(szCommand);

        nEndLine = -1;

        sscanf(&szCommand[1], "%d%d",
            &nStartLine,
            &nEndLine);

        if (nEndLine < nStartLine)
        {
            nEndLine = nStartLine;
        }

        if (nEndLine >= nMaxLines)
        {
            nEndLine = (nMaxLines - 1);
        }

        switch(szCommand[0])
        {
            case 'e': /* Edit the specified line */

                if (nStartLine == 0)
                {
                    printf("Line number must be 1 to %d\n", nMaxLines);
                }
                else
                {
```

```
                if (lLineIndex[nStartLine] == DELETED_LINE)
                {
                    printf("Line %d has been deleted, "
                        "and cannot be edited.\n",
                        nStartLine);
                }

                if (nStartLine < nMaxLines &&
                    lLineIndex[nStartLine] != DELETED_LINE)
                {
                    fseek(WorkFile,
                        lLineIndex[nStartLine], SEEK_SET);

                    fgets(szInputLine,
                        sizeof(szInputLine), WorkFile);

                    if (EditLine(szInputLine))
                    {
                        fseek(WorkFile, 0, SEEK_END);

                        lLineIndex[nStartLine] = ftell(WorkFile);

                        fputs(szInputLine, WorkFile);
                    }
                }
            }
            break;

        case 'l': /* List the specified line */

            if (nStartLine == 0)
            {
                nStartLine = 1;

                while(nStartLine < nMaxLines)
                {
                    if (lLineIndex[nStartLine] != DELETED_LINE)
                    {
                        fseek(WorkFile,
                            lLineIndex[nStartLine], SEEK_SET);
```

continues

Listing 9.2. continued

```
                          fgets(szInputLine,
                              sizeof(szInputLine), WorkFile);

                          printf("%4d - %s",
                              nStartLine,
                              szInputLine);
                }
                else
                {
                      printf("%4d ***DELETED LINE***\n",
                          nStartLine);
                }

                ++nStartLine;
        }

        nStartLine = 0;
    }
    else
    {
        while(nStartLine <= nEndLine)
        {
            if (lLineIndex[nStartLine] != DELETED_LINE)
            {
                fseek(WorkFile,
                    lLineIndex[nStartLine], SEEK_SET);

                fgets(szInputLine,
                    sizeof(szInputLine), WorkFile);

                printf("%4d - %s",
                    nStartLine,
                    szInputLine);
            }
            else
            {
                printf("%4d ***DELETED LINE***\n",
                    nStartLine);
            }
```

```
                ++nStartLine;
        }
    }
    break;

case 'd':  /* Delete the specified line */

    if (nStartLine > 0 &&
        nStartLine < nMaxLines)
    {
        printf("Do you really want to delete line %d? (y¦n) ",
            nStartLine);

        chChar = getche();

        printf("\n");

        if (chChar == 'y' ¦¦ chChar == 'Y')
        {
            lLineIndex[nStartLine] = DELETED_LINE;
        }
    }
    break;

case 'w':  /* Write; continue editing? */

    szNewName[0] = '\0';

    tmpnam(szNewName);

    if (strlen(szNewName) == 0)
    {
        printf("Error getting a temporary file name...\n");
    }

    rename(szFileName, szNewName);

    DataFile = fopen(szFileName, "wt");

    nStartLine = 1;
```

continues

263

Listing 9.2. continued

```c
                    while(nStartLine < nMaxLines)
                    {
                        if (lLineIndex[nStartLine] != DELETED_LINE)
                        {
                            fseek(WorkFile,
                                lLineIndex[nStartLine], SEEK_SET);

                            fgets(szInputLine,
                                sizeof(szInputLine), WorkFile);

                            fputs(szInputLine, DataFile);
                        }

                        ++nStartLine;
                    }

                    nStartLine = 0;

                    fclose(DataFile);

/*  In this version, the original file is simply deleted.
 *  A better programming practice is to rename it to .BAK
 *  so the user can recover the original file.
 *
 *  Question:
 *  When renaming to .BAK, does the user recover from the
 *  last save or the original file?
 */

                    remove(szNewName); /* Could be renamed to .BAK */

                    break;

                case 'q': /* Quit, with no save */

                    break;

                default:
                    printf("Error: the command '%c' is not supported!\n",
                        szCommand[0]);
```

```
            break;
        }
    }

    fclose(WorkFile);

    remove(szTempName);

    return (0);
}

int EditLine(
    char * szInputLine)

{

char    chChar = 'A';  // To fool while() the first time!

int     nCurrentChar = 0;

    printf("%s", szInputLine);

    while (chChar)
    {
        chChar = getch();
        if (chChar == '\0')
        {
            chChar = getch();

            switch(chChar)
            {
                case '\x4D':
                    printf("%c", szInputLine[nCurrentChar]);
                    ++nCurrentChar;
                    break;

                default: /* No other keys implemented yet */
                    printf("\a");
                    break;
            }
```

continues

265

Listing 9.2. continued

```
            }
            else
            {
                switch(chChar)
                {
                    case '\n':
                    case '\x0d':
                        chChar = '\0';
                        break;

                    default: /* Change current character to typed character */
                        szInputLine[nCurrentChar] = chChar;
                        printf("%c", szInputLine[nCurrentChar]);
                        ++nCurrentChar;
                        break;
                }
            }
        }

        printf("\n");

        return(1);

}
```

Two parts of EDLINE require closer examination. First, the program declares two character-string buffers to hold temporary file names:

```
char    szTempName[L_tmpnam];
char    szNewName[L_tmpnam];
```

I don't know how long these buffers should be, so I use the L_tmpnam identifier, which is defined in stdio.h. This identifier is system dependent and is large enough to hold any temporary filename returned by tmpnam().

Now that there is a place to save the temporary file names, I can call the ANSI C tmpnam() function, which returns a unique filename. This filename can be used for any purpose (EDLINE, for example, uses it for a work file). In a multitasking environment, the same name might be returned to more than one program. Your application can handle this situation by getting a new temporary name if a file is

opened for writing and an error is returned because another application is using the name. There is no need to signal an error to the user; simply recover by getting a new name.

The following code shows how a temporary filename is obtained and opened:

```
tmpnam(szTempName);

if (strlen(szTempName) == 0)
{
    printf("Couldn't open a work file...\n");
    exit(4);
}
```

The recovery in a multitasking environment could be coded as follows:

```
WorkFile = NULL;

while (WorkFile == NULL)
{
    tmpnam(szTempName);

    if (strlen(szTempName) == 0)
    {
        printf("Couldn't get a work file name...\n");
        exit(4);
    }

/*  fopen() fails if the name has been used by
 *  another application
 */
    WorkFile = fopen(szTempName, "w+t");
}
```

In general, this type of error checking is unnecessary for programs running on the PC under DOS.

When you are finished with your work file, you must delete it. You can do this with the ANSI C remove() function or the unlink() function, which is still found on many C compilers.

ANSI C also supports the tmpfile() function, which creates a temporary file and opens the file. This function does much of the work for the programmer, but it has disadvantages. For example, when the file is closed (whether or not you are finished), it is deleted. This makes it impossible to close the file early in the program's execution and reopen it later. You also cannot specify the mode of the file: it is opened in the binary read/write mode. EDLINE required a temporary work file with the text mode, not the binary mode, so `tmpfile()` could not be used.

The calls to `tmpfile()` are easy to make, as shown in the following lines of code:

```
FILE    *TempFile = tmpfile();

/*  Lines of code to use the file */

    fclose(TempFile);
```

The `tmpfile()` function is handy when the file's attributes (binary read/write) are suitable to your program's needs, and when you want the system to automatically delete the file.

Sometimes you will want the temporary file to stay around. If the program crashes, for example, you may be able to recover the user's data from the temporary work file.

Using a temporary work file is similar to using any other file, except it must be deleted and its name must be unique.

Stream Files and Default File Handles

In C, files can be opened as stream files, which are identified with a pointer to a `FILE` structure, or as low-level files, which are identified with an integer handle. This section covers stream files. Low-level files are described later in the chapter, under "Low-Level I/O and File Handles."

A stream file must be opened with one of the following functions:

`fopen()`	Opens the specified file with the specified mode
`freopen()`	Closes the file specified, then opens a new file as specified
`fdopen()`	Opens a duplicate stream file for an already open low-level file

If a file is opened with `open()` or one of the other file open functions that return an integer handle, the file is a low-level file, not a stream file. Table 9.1 lists the stream functions that C supports.

Table 9.1. Stream file functions (including Microsoft's additions).

Function	Description
_fsopen()	Microsoft's shared file open.
clearerr()	Clears the current error condition flags.
fclose()	Closes the specified file.
fcloseall()	Closes all open stream files.
fdopen()	Opens a low-level file as a stream file.
feof()	Checks for end-of-file in a stream file.
ferror()	Tests for a read or write error.
fflush()	Flushes pending I/O for a file.
fgetc()	Gets a character from a stream file.
fgetchar()	Gets the next character from a file.
fgetpos()	Gets a file's current position, for use by fsetpos().
fgets()	Gets a string from the specified file.
fileno()	Returns the low-level file handle for a stream file.
flushall()	Flushes pending I/O from all opened files.
fopen()	Opens a stream file.
fputc()	Writes a character to the specified file.
fputchar()	Writes a character to the specified file.
fputs()	Writes the buffer to the stream file.
fread()	Reads from the specified stream file.
freopen()	Reopens the file.
fscanf()	Does a formatted read from a stream file.
fseek()	Sets the file's current position as specified.
fsetpos()	Sets the file to the position obtained by fgetpos().
ftell()	Gets the file's current position.

continues

Table 9.1. continued

Function	Description
fwrite()	Writes to a specified file.
getc()	Gets a character.
getchar()	Gets a character from `stdin`.
gets()	Gets a string from `stdin`.
getw()	Gets an integer from the specified file.
printf()	Does a formatted write to `stdout`.
putc()	Writes a character to a stream file.
putchar()	Writes a character to `stdout`.
puts()	Writes a buffer to `stdout`.
putw()	Writes an integer value to a file.
rewind()	Sets the file's current position to the beginning of the file.
rmtmp()	Removes (deletes) temporary files opened with `tmpfile()`.
scanf()	Does a formatted read from `stdin`.
setbuf()	Sets the stream file's buffer.
setvbuf()	Sets the stream file's buffer (variable size buffer).
sprintf()	Does a formatted write to a string.
sscanf()	Reads formatted input from a string.
tempnam()	Gets a temporary filename, allowing the specification of a different directory.
tmpfile()	Opens a uniquely named temporary work file. When the file is closed or the program ends, the file is deleted.
tmpnam()	Returns a unique name for use as a temporary filename.
ungetc()	Puts back a character to a file opened in the read mode. The character put back does not need to be the same as the one read, but only one character can be put back at a time. Two successive calls to `ungetc()` without an intervening read will fail.

270

Function	Description
vfprintf()	Does a formatted write to the specified file. The output is pointed to by a parameter-list pointer.
vprintf()	Does a formatted write to stdout. The output is pointed to by a parameter-list pointer.
vsprintf()	Does a formatted write to the specified string. Output is pointed to by a parameter-list pointer.

The classification of stream files includes a number of standard files. For every C program, five standard files are always open. Programs can use these files to perform basic file I/O to the screen and the keyboard.

Before describing the standard files, remember that most operating systems enable you to redirect files. Usually, a simple redirection symbol automatically allows a file to be used for input or output; the program uses this file as if it were either the keyboard or the screen.

The stdin File

The stdin file is opened by the operating system and is considered to be the keyboard. If the operating system supports I/O redirection, however, stdin could be a file.

If stdin's input comes from an I/I redirected file, several problems can occur when the end of the redirected file is reached. First, the program receives an end-of-file (EOF) error. Many programs do not adequately check for EOF, and the user may have a difficult time ending the program. Second, the operating system does not switch back to the keyboard. You can force your program to use the keyboard by opening a file called con: (under DOS on a PC), but this requires a lot of programming.

The following functions use stdin:

getchar()   Gets a character from stdin

gets()   Gets a string from stdin

scanf()   Performs a formatted read from stdin

These functions make your code easier to read and understand. Each has a counterpart that can be used for any other stream file.

The stdout File

The stdout file is opened by the operating system and is considered to be the screen. If the operating system supports I/O redirection, however, stdout could be a file.

If stdout's output goes to a redirected file, several problems can occur. The program could receive an end-of-file (EOF) error when the disk is full. Many programs do not adequately check for EOF with stdout, and the user may not realize an error has occurred until the program has finished running. Another problem is that there is no provision to switch back to the screen. You can force your program to use the screen by opening a file called con: (under DOS on a PC), but doing so requires a lot of programming.

The following functions use stdout:

printf()	Performs a formatted write to stdout
putchar()	Writes a character to stdout
puts()	Writes the buffer to stdout
vprintf()	Performs a formatted write to stdout. The output is pointed to by a parameter-list pointer.

Each stdout function has a counterpart that can be used for any other stream file. And like the stdin functions, the stdout functions enable you to write code that is easier to read and understand.

The stderr File

The stderr file is similar to the stdout file; data written to stderr is displayed on the screen. The major difference is that stderr is used for error messages that you would not want redirected to a file if the user is using I/O redirection. You can use stderr to display messages to the user regardless of whether I/O redirection is used because stderr is never I/O redirected.

No functions use stderr directly. You can use fprintf() to write your error message:

```
fprintf(stderr,
    "The input file is in the old format. Run REFMT first");
```

The error message will not be redirected if the operating system's I/O redirection is in effect.

Always use stderr for the program's banner message (the message to the user that describes the program and lists the copyright, author, and so on) and error messages. If you develop one error message function that is always called when an error occurs, you can be sure that the message is written to the correct place—the screen and not a redirected file.

The stdaux File

The stdaux file's name is a bit confusing. What is the aux device? In ANSI C, the aux device is defined as the main serial communication port (not the console serial communication port). On a PC, aux is defined as COM1:, and stdaux writes to the COM1: port.

The short program in Listing 9.3, called STDAUX.C, writes 100 lines to the stdaux file. Before running this program, initialize the communications port. To do this under DOS on the PC, use the MODE command.

Listing 9.3. STDAUX.C.

```
/* STDAUX, written 1992 by Peter D. Hipson
 * This program uses the stdaux file. It should be run
 * only under DOS on a PC.
 */




#include <stdio.h>    // Make includes first part of the file
#include <string.h>   // For string functions
#include <stdlib.h>   // Standard include items
#include <process.h>  // For exit(), etc.


int main(           // Define main() and the fact that this program
    int     argc,   // uses the passed parameters
    char    *argv[],
```

continues

Listing 9.3. continued

```
        char    *envp[]
        );


int main(
    int     argc,
    char    *argv[],
    char    *envp[]
    )

{

int     i;

    for (i = 0; i < 100; i++)
    {
/*  Because stdaux is opened in the binary mode,
 *  CR/LF must be supplied explicitly, using \n\r
 */
        fprintf(stdaux,
            "Line %2d of 100 lines"
            " being written to stdaux by a program.\n\r",
            i);
    }


    return (0);
}
```

The stdprn File

The stdprn file is easy to understand. It provides a simple way to write to the system printer without having to explicitly open a file. The stdprn file cannot be redirected and therefore should be used only for items that will be printed, probably in response to a user request.

The short program in Listing 9.4, called STDPRN.C, writes to stdprn. Before running this program, be sure a printer is connected to the primary printer port and is online.

Listing 9.4. STDPRN.C.

```
/* STDPRN, written 1992 by Peter D. Hipson
 * This program  uses the stdprn file. It should be run
 * under DOS on a PC.
 */


#include <stdio.h>   // Make includes first part of file
#include <string.h>  // For string functions
#include <stdlib.h>  // Standard include items
#include <process.h> // For exit(), etc.


int main(          // Define main() and the fact that this program
    int     argc,  // uses the passed parameters
    char    *argv[],
    char    *envp[]
    );


int main(
    int     argc,
    char    *argv[],
    char    *envp[]
    )

{

int     i;

    for (i = 0; i < 50; i++)
    {
/* Because stdprn is opened in the binary mode,
 *  CR/LF must be supplied explicitly, using \n\r
 */
```

continues

Listing 9.4. continued

```
        fprintf(stdprn,
            "Line %2d of 50 lines"
            " being written to stdprn by a program.\n\r",
            i);
    }

/*  An explicit form feed is used to force a page eject
 *  if the printer is a laser printer
 */

    fprintf(stdprn, "\f");

    return (0);
}
```

This program shows how easy it is to use a printer from a C program. Listing 9.5 is a more flexible program—the user can choose the screen, the communications port, or the printer.

Listing 9.5. STDFILE.C.

```
/* STDFILE, written 1992 by Peter D. Hipson
 * This program prints to the selected destination. It
 * should be run under DOS on a PC.
 */


#include <stdio.h>   // Make includes first part of file
#include <string.h>  // For string functions.
#include <stdlib.h>  // Standard include items.
#include <process.h> // For exit(), etc.


int main(            // Define main() and the fact that this program
    int     argc,    // uses the passed parameters
    char    *argv[],
    char    *envp[]
    );
```

```c
int main(
    int     argc,
    char    *argv[],
    char    *envp[]
    )

{

FILE * OutputFile = NULL;

int     nFile = 0;
int     i;

    while (nFile < 1 || nFile > 3)
    {
        printf(
            "Which file to write to:\n"
            "    1 - stdprn (the printer)\n"
            "    2 - stdaux (the communications port)\n"
            "    3 - stdout (the console)\n"
            "  enter 1, 2 or 3: ");

        scanf("%d", &nFile);
    }

    switch(nFile)
    {
        case 1:
            OutputFile = stdprn;
            break;

        case 2:
            OutputFile = stdaux;
            break;

        case 3:
            OutputFile = stdout;
            break;
    }
```

continues

Listing 9.5. continued

```
    for (i = 0; i < 50; i++)
    {
/*  stdprn is opened in the binary mode, so a CR/LF
 *  must be supplied explicitly, using \n\r
 */
        fprintf(OutputFile,
            "Line %2d of 50 lines"
            " being written to user-selected destination by a program.\n\r",
            i);
    }

/*  Use an explicit form feed to force a page eject if the
 *  printer is a laser printer.
 */

    fprintf(OutputFile, "\f");

    return (0);
}
```

This program shows the effect of assigning standard file handles to a user-specified file. This technique enables you to have one output routine and several destinations. This is useful when you want the user to be able to preview a report or easily select a secondary printer connected to a communications port.

Low-Level I/O and File Handles

All file I/O functions described so far perform primarily high-level I/O, and all require stream files. (Functions that require stream files receive a FILE * structure pointer.)

You can also access a file more directly using low-level file I/O techniques. Before describing the details of these techniques, however, several important issues should be covered.

A file that has been opened as a stream file can be read and written to using low-level file I/O functions. To get the necessary integer file handle, you must use the fileno() function.

A low-level file can be used with stream functions by opening it with the `fdopen()` function. Be careful not to take a file that has been opened as a stream file, get its file handle, then open it a second time with `fdopen()`. You would then have to close the file twice.

The low-level file I/O functions are shown in Table 9.2. These functions generally have a stream file function counterpart.

Table 9.2. Low-level file functions.

Function	Description
close()	Closes the specified file.
creat()	Creates a new file.
dup()	Creates a new, duplicate file handle.
dup2()	Creates a new, duplicate file handle and sets the second (specified) file handle to the first file.
eof()	Tests for an end-of-file.
lseek()	Seeks (changes the read/write pointer) to a new place in the file.
open()	Opens an existing file.
read()	Reads an opened file.
sopen()	Opens a file in shared mode.
tell()	Returns the value of the read/write pointer.
write()	Writes data to a file that has been opened for output.

Before you use stream functions with a low-level file, be sure that you open the file using the correct stream function. Generally, it is best if you use one type of function with any specific file.

There are several reasons for using low-level functions, including the following:

- Low-level functions do not try to format data, read from a file, or write to a file.

- Low-level file I/O is not buffered. When an I/O statement is executed, what is written goes directly to the file. (This may slow the program's execution.)

Most programs benefit from the use of stream functions. The capability to open, read, and write any data object is present in both low-level files and stream files. The problems caused by buffering, if important, can be circumvented using the file flushing routines.

Standard Low-Level File Handles

Because `stdin`, `stdout`, `stdaux`, `stderr`, and `stdprn` are stream files, they can be referenced using the `fileno()` function. These files can also be used with low-level I/O functions directly, however. The file handle numbers for the standard stream files follows:

`stdin`	0
`stdout`	1
`stderr`	2
`stdaux`	3
`stdprn`	4

These low-level file numbers should not be used if possible. The `fileno()` function is more portable, especially when a program must run on different systems.

Console and Port I/O

Much of the direct access to the computer's terminal (the screen and keyboard) is system dependent. On a PC, you can have any of a number of keyboards, all of which have different keys, and different scan codes. Several functions interact more directly with the keyboard, and though not all are ANSI standard, they are often part of many C compilers. These functions are shown in Table 9.3.

You can easily simulate most console functions by using the stream functions and the predefined file handles. A few functions, however, have no equal. This section describes the console functions and how to use them.

Some of the most frequently used direct console functions are the character getting functions, `getch()` and `getche()`. The main difference between these two functions is that `getch()` does not echo the character pressed, and `getche()` does echo

the character. Although the screen functions can be used to read a keypress and echo it to the screen, you must use the getch() function to read a keypress without echoing it to the screen.

Table 9.3. Console I/O functions.

Console function	Description
cgets()	Gets a string from the console.
cprintf()	Performs a formatted print to the console.
cputs()	Writes a string to the screen.
cscanf()	Performs a formatted read from the console (keyboard).
getch()	Gets a character from the keyboard but does not echo the character to the screen.
getche()	Gets a character from the keyboard and echoes the character to the screen.
kbhit()	Returns immediately with the return code indicating whether a key has been pressed. Will not wait for a keypress.
putch()	Writes a character to the screen.
ungetch()	Allows one character to be pushed back to the keyboard. The character put back does not need to be the last character read. Only one character may be put back.

The next most commonly used function is the kbhit() function, which has no stream function counterpart. The kbhit() function enables you to poll the keyboard for a keypress. Many business applications have little use for this function. Games, however, run in real time, so they must check for user input without stopping the action. The kbhit() function enables a program to do just that.

Listing 9.6, ARCADE.C, does processing while waiting for keyboard input from the user. By a far stretch of the imagination, you could consider this program a simple arcade game.

Listing 9.6. ARCADE.C.

```c
/* ARCADE, written 1992 by Peter D. Hipson
 * This is a simple arcade game that uses console I/O.
 * It should be run under DOS on a PC. It also should
 * be compiled with Microsoft C or a compiler that
 * supports kbhit() and getch(). In addition, ANSI.SYS
 * should be loaded before using this program, and the
 * screen size is assumed to be 25 by 80.
 */


#include <stdio.h>    // Make includes first part of file
#include <conio.h>    // Console I/O functions
#include <string.h>   // For string functions
#include <stdlib.h>   // Standard include items
#include <process.h>  // For exit(), etc.
#include <time.h>     // To seed random numbers


/* ANSI.SYS screen control #defines follow: */

#define BOLD         "\x1B[1m"
#define NORMAL       "\x1B[0m"
#define RED          "\x1B[31m"
#define BLACK        "\x1B[30m"
#define GREEN        "\x1B[32m"

#define CLEAR_SCREEN "\x1B[2J"
#define CLEAR_EOL    "\x1B[K"

#define MOVE_CURSOR  "\x1B[%d;%df"

#define UP       '\x48'
#define DOWN     '\x50'
#define LEFT     '\x4B'
#define RIGHT    '\x4D'

#define MAX_HEIGHT  25
#define MAX_WIDTH   80

#define HALF_SECOND  (CLOCKS_PER_SEC / 2)
```

```
int main(           // Define main() and the fact that this
    int     argc,   // program uses the passed parameters
    char    *argv[],
    char    *envp[]
    );


int main(
    int     argc,
    char    *argv[],
    char    *envp[]
    )

{

char    chChar;

clock_t ClockTime;
clock_t OldClockTime;

int     i;
int     nHorizontal = 0;         /* Randomize for real game */
int     nVertical   = 0;         /* Randomize for real game */
int     nMoneyHorizontal = 10;   /* Randomize for real game */
int     nMoneyVertical   = 10;   /* Randomize for real game */
int     nPosition;

    OldClockTime = clock() / HALF_SECOND;

    srand((unsigned)time(NULL));

    printf(CLEAR_SCREEN);

    printf(MOVE_CURSOR, nMoneyVertical, nMoneyHorizontal);

    printf("$");

    printf(MOVE_CURSOR, nVertical, nHorizontal);

    printf("?");
```

continues

Listing 9.6. continued

```c
while(1)
{
    if (kbhit())
    {/* A key has been pressed, so process it as necessary */
        chChar = getch();

        if (chChar == (char)NULL)
        {
            chChar = getch();

            printf(MOVE_CURSOR, nVertical, nHorizontal);

            printf(" ");

            switch(chChar)
            {
                case DOWN:
                    if (++nVertical > MAX_HEIGHT)
                    {
                        --nVertical;
                    }
                    break;
                case UP:
                    if (--nVertical < 1)
                    {
                        ++nVertical;
                    }
                    break;
                case RIGHT:
                    if (++nHorizontal > MAX_WIDTH)
                    {
                        --nHorizontal;
                    }
                    break;
                case LEFT:
                    if (--nHorizontal < 1)
                    {
                        ++nHorizontal;
                    }
                    break;
```

```
            default:
                break;
        }

        printf(MOVE_CURSOR, nVertical, nHorizontal);

        if (nMoneyHorizontal == nHorizontal &&
            nMoneyVertical   == nVertical)
        {
            printf("\a");
        }

        printf("?");
    }
    else
    {
        if (chChar == '\x1b')
        {/* Exit on Esc keypress */
            printf(CLEAR_SCREEN);
            exit(4);
        }
    }
}
else
{/* No key has been pressed. Move the money. */
    ClockTime = clock() / HALF_SECOND;

    if (ClockTime != OldClockTime)
    {
        OldClockTime = ClockTime;

        printf(MOVE_CURSOR, nMoneyVertical, nMoneyHorizontal);

        printf(" ");  /* Erase the money */

        i = rand();

        switch(i % 4) /* Allow four states */
        {
            case 0:
                if (++nMoneyVertical > MAX_HEIGHT)
```

continues

Listing 9.6. continued

```
            {
                --nMoneyVertical;
            }
            break;
        case 1:
            if (--nMoneyVertical < 1)
            {
                ++nMoneyVertical;
            }
            break;
        case 2:
            if (++nMoneyHorizontal > MAX_WIDTH)
            {
                --nMoneyHorizontal;
            }
            break;
        case 3:
            if (--nMoneyHorizontal < 1)
            {
                ++nMoneyHorizontal;
            }
            break;

        default:
            break;
    }

    if (nMoneyHorizontal == nHorizontal &&
        nMoneyVertical   == nVertical)
    {
        --nMoneyHorizontal;
        --nMoneyVertical;
    }

    printf(MOVE_CURSOR, nMoneyVertical, nMoneyHorizontal);

    printf("$");   /* Display the money */

    printf(MOVE_CURSOR, nVertical, nHorizontal);
}
```

```
        }
    }

    return (0);
}
```

First the program and the screen are initialized. Standard stream I/O statements are used because they are easy to use. No sense in doing more work than is necessary! Then the screen is cleared, and the target (the dollar sign) is placed at position 10, 10. The chaser (the question mark) is then placed at position 0, 0, and the game begins.

A while loop polls the keyboard. When a key is pressed, kbhit() returns TRUE, allowing the program to read the keypress, as follows:

```
if (kbhit())
{/* A key has been pressed, so process it as necessary */
    chChar = getch();

    if (chChar == (char)NULL)
    {
        chChar = getch();
```

If the first call to getch() returns zero, an extended key (probably an arrow key) has been pressed. If the return is nonzero, an ASCII key has been pressed. The only nonextended key that interests us is ESC, which ends the game.

After a key has been pressed, a new location for the chaser is computed. If the chaser has landed on the target's position, the speaker beeps. Try playing the game— it's harder than it seems!

If no key has been pressed, the program checks how long it has been since the target moved. Every half second, if no key is pressed, the target moves one square in a random direction. This time period makes the game more playable. (Otherwise, on a fast CPU, the target would be all over the screen, and you could never hit it.)

All moves in ARCADE are kept in the bounds of the screen. In addition, the target cannot move to the same position as the chaser—the game should never lose by its own choice!

Direct Port I/O

This section assumes that you are programming on an IBM compatible PC. If you are using another type of computer, some of the discussion in this section may not apply.

Direct port I/O can be dangerous because the program is interacting with the hardware at a basic level. Because there is no error checking, you can seriously damage the information on your hard disk.

If you are writing software that uses direct port I/O, back up your hard disk!

Direct port I/O is system dependent, not only on the type of computer, but also on the computer's configuration. In this section, the assumption is that you are programming on an IBM compatible PC. If you are using another type of computer, this section may not apply.

The CPU uses the I/O ports to communicate with all the various peripherals, such as the communication ports, the printer ports, and the keyboard. Peripherals are connected to the CPU by *interface cards* (these may be part of the motherboard). The direct port I/O functions are shown in Table 9.4.

Table 9.4. Direct I/O functions.

I/O function	Description
inp()	Inputs a byte of data from the specified port
inpw()	Inputs two bytes of data from the specified port
outp()	Outputs a byte of data to the specified port
outpw()	Outputs two bytes of data to the specified port

The return type is always type int, so you should use only the first byte in functions that process byte-size data objects. Both output functions return the byte or word that was output. The input functions return the currently input byte or word.

The PC Printer Ports

The PC supports up to three printer ports. The addresses for the printer ports are in the BIOS data area, at segment 0040, as follows: 0040:0008 for LPT1, 0040:000A for LPT2, and 0040:000C for LPT3. Typical addresses for printer ports are 0x0378 or 0x03BC. Although there are standard addresses for the printer I/O, your program could use any I/O address that is defined by the system.

Listing 9.7, PRNPORT.C, prints to the printer a single string, followed by a form-feed character. (The form-feed character forces laser printers to print the page.) The program prints directly, without calling the DOS or the BIOS routines.

Listing 9.7. PRNPORT.C.

```
/* PRNPORT, written 1992 by Peter D. Hipson
 * This program prints directly to the printer's port.
 * The program should be run under DOS on a PC. If your
 * computer is not PC-compatible, do not run this program.
 * The program should also be compiled with Microsoft C.
 */

#include <stdio.h>    // Make includes first part of file
#include <conio.h>    // Console I/O functions
#include <string.h>   // For string functions
#include <stdlib.h>   // Standard include items
#include <process.h>  // For exit(), etc.
#include <time.h>     // To seed random numbers

#define MAKELONG(low, high) ((long)(((unsigned short int)(low)) \
  ¦ (((unsigned long int)((unsigned short int)(high))) << 16)))
#define MAKELP(sel, off)    ((void _far*)MAKELONG((off), (sel)))

/* Printer port definitions */
```

continues

Listing 9.7. continued

```c
#define BIOS_DATA_PAGE  0x0040
#define LPT1            0x0008

#define DATA_PORT     (nPort)
#define STATUS_PORT   (nPort + 1)
#define CONTROL_PORT  (nPort + 2)

#define STATUS_NORESP     0x01
#define STATUS_UNUSED1    0x02
#define STATUS_UNUSED2    0x04
#define STATUS_ERROR      0x08
#define STATUS_SELECTED   0x10
#define STATUS_NOPAPER    0x20
#define STATUS_ACK        0x40
#define STATUS_NOTBUSY    0x80

#define CONTROL_STROBE    0x01
#define CONTROL_AUTOFEED  0x02
#define CONTROL_INIT      0x04
#define CONTROL_SELECT    0x08
#define CONTROL_IRQ7      0x10
#define CONTROL_UNUSED1   0x20
#define CONTROL_UNUSED2   0x40
#define CONTROL_UNUSED3   0x80

/* End printer port definitions. */


int main(            // Define main() and the fact that this
    int     argc,    // program uses the passed parameters
    char    *argv[],
    char    *envp[]
    );

int PrintCharacter(char  chChar);
int PrinterStatus(void);
int main(
    int     argc,
    char    *argv[],
```

```
    char   *envp[]
    )


{


char   szNowIsTheTime[] = {
    "Now is the time for all good men to come to the aid...\f"};

int    nStatus;
int    i;


    if (!PrinterStatus())
    {
        printf("There was a printer error!\n");
        exit(4);
    }

    for (i = 0; i < strlen(szNowIsTheTime); i++)
    {
        if (PrintCharacter(szNowIsTheTime[i]) == 0)
        {
            printf("\nCouldn't print from '%s'\n",
                &szNowIsTheTime[i]);

            break;
        }
    }

    return (0);
}

int    PrintCharacter(
    char  chChar)


{

int _far    *pPrintPort;
int    nPort;
```

continues

Listing 9.7. continued

```
int     nStatus;

/*  The PC's printer port is at address 0040:0008
 *  (for LPT1:). If 0 is stored at that address,
 *  a printer port is not installed.
 */

    pPrintPort = MAKELP(BIOS_DATA_PAGE, LPT1);
    nPort = *pPrintPort;

    if (nPort == 0)
    {/* No printer is installed! */
        printf("No printer installed... WHY?\n");
        return(0);
    }

/*  Write the data byte to the printer's data lines */

    outp(DATA_PORT, chChar);

/*  Next, check to see if the printer is busy. */

    nStatus = inp(STATUS_PORT);

    if (!(nStatus & STATUS_NOTBUSY))
    {/* The printer is busy. You should wait and try again */
        printf("The printer is busy?\n");
        return(0);
    }

/*  Set the strobe line */
    outp(CONTROL_PORT, CONTROL_STROBE | CONTROL_INIT | CONTROL_SELECT);

/*  Clear the strobe line */
    outp(CONTROL_PORT, CONTROL_INIT | CONTROL_SELECT);
}


int     PrinterStatus()
```

```
{

int _far     *pPrintPort;
int     nPort;

int     nStatus;

/*  The PC's printer port is at address 0040:0008
 *  (for LPT1:). If 0 is stored at that address,
 *  a printer port is not installed.
 */

    pPrintPort = MAKELP(BIOS_DATA_PAGE, LPT1);
    nPort = *pPrintPort;

    if (nPort == 0)
    {/* No printer is installed! */
        printf("No printer installed... WHY?\n");
        return(0);
    }

    printf("Printer vector = %lp Printer port %4.4X\n",
        pPrintPort,
        nPort);

    nStatus = inp(DATA_PORT);

    printf("DATA port's contents %2.2X (last character that was
printed).\n",
        nStatus);

    nStatus = inp(STATUS_PORT);

    if (!(nStatus & STATUS_NORESP))
    {
        printf("The printer did not respond. \n");
    }
    else
    {
```

continues

Listing 9.7. continued

```
        printf("The printer is responding. \n");
    }

    if (!(nStatus & STATUS_ERROR))
    {
        printf("The printer is signaling an error. \n");
    }
    else
    {
        printf("The printer is signaling no errors.   \n");
    }

    if (nStatus & STATUS_SELECTED)
    {
        printf("The printer is currently selected. \n");
    }
    else
    {
        printf("The printer is not selected. \n");
    }

    if (nStatus & STATUS_NOPAPER)
    {
        printf("The printer is out of paper.\n");
    }
    else
    {
        printf("The printer has paper. \n");
    }

    if (nStatus & STATUS_ACK)
    {
        printf("The printer ACK line is set.\n");
    }
    else
    {
        printf("The printer ACK line is cleared.\n");
    }
```

```
    if (nStatus & STATUS_NOTBUSY)
    {
        printf("The printer is not busy.\n");
    }
    else
    {
        printf("The printer is currently busy. \n");
    }

    return(1);
}
```

The PRNPORT.C program shows how easy it is to print to a printer port using a high-level language such as C. Admittedly, this program cannot be used in its current state—the character print routines require more error checking and recovery. These improvements, however, would not be difficult to implement.

I have written custom printer drivers for the PC in C. Why? In one case, the printer (a special graphics printer with a high-speed interface) needed special timing and control signals, even though it used a Centronics type of connector and the same printer pins as other compatible printers.

A second use of the printer port is one that I think is more interesting than simply printing. In most PCs, the printer port is a bidirectional I/O port (it can both output data and read data) and as such can be used to communicate with all types of external devices.

A third use for custom drivers is for I/O boards that are not intended to be printer ports but have a similar structure. These boards are used for control and for special devices. It is not unusual for a special board to be used for graphic tablets (which might also use a serial port) or most tape drives, all of which need drivers.

You must write the driver in assembler (you can use in-line assembly if your compiler supports it) for the best control and performance. A C language driver is adequate, however, for initial development and for drivers with noncritical timing requirements.

The PC Communications Ports

The serial communications ports are more complex than the printer ports. First, they require more initialization because the speed (baud rate) and the format of the characters (number of bits) must be set. To make things easy, I have DOS initialize (in my AUTOEXEC.BAT file) all the communications ports to a known state.

Following are the addresses used by the PC communications ports. When a communications port is accessed, the first address used is referred to as the *I/O base address*. The communications port I/O address starts at 0x03F8 or 0x02F8 (COM1 and COM2) in most PCs. All addresses are accessed using input and output functions, either in C or assembler.

In the following discussion, the COM1 base I/O address of 0x3F8 is used. To access COM2, you must use the COM2 base I/O address of 0x2F8. To access a port other than COM1 or COM2, you must know the port's base I/O address. The addresses for COM1 through COM4 are stored in the BIOS data page as follows:

COM1	0000:0400
COM2	0000:0402
COM3	0000:0404
COM4	0000:0406

The UART (Universal Asynchronous Receiver/Transmitter) is the part of the communications port that converts a byte of data to a serial data stream. The UART in the PC's communications port has eight separate addresses. The following paragraphs and Table 9.5 describe each of these addresses.

Table 9.5. The serial board's I/O port usage.

Name	Address	Description	Name in SENDCOMM.C	Bits
Receive buffer	I/O base address + 0	Characters received may be retrieved from this I/O address. LCR_PORT bit 80 must be clear.	RBR_PORT 0–7	Eight bits of received data

Name	Address	Description	Name in SENDCOMM.C	Bits
Divisor register (LSB)	I/O base address + 0	Used to set the baud rate, which is determined using a 16-bit divisor. LCR_PORT bit 80 must be set.	DLL_PORT 0–7	Divisor's LSB (eight bits)
Transmit buffer	I/O base address + 1	Characters to be transmitted are output to this I/O address. LCR_PORT bit 80 must be clear.	THR_PORT 0–7	Eight bits of data to be transmitted
Divisor register (MSB)	I/O base address + 1	Used to set the baud rate, which is determined using a 16-bit divisor. LCR_PORT bit 80 must be set.	DLM_PORT 0–7	Divisor's MSB (eight bits)
Interrupt enable register	I/O base address + 2	Enables the conditions that cause the UART to generate an interrupt to be generated. When a specified bit is set and the condition occurs, an interrupt is generated.	IER_PORT 01	Received data available. A character has been received.
			02	Transmit holding register is empty. The character that was being sent has completed. A new character can now be sent.
			04	Receive line status. The receive line has changed.

continues

Table 9.5. continued

Name	Address	Description	Name in SENDCOMM.C	Bits
			08	MODEM status. The modem status line has changed.
			10	Not used
			20	Not used
			40	Not used
			80	Not used
Interrupt identifier register	I/O base address + 3	Tells the program what condition caused the interrupt.	IIR_PORT 01	If clear, an interrupt is pending
			02	Interrupt ID, bit 0
			04	Interrupt ID, bit 1
			08	Not used
			10	Not used
			20	Not used
			40	Not used
			80	Not used
Line control register	I/O base address + 4	Controls the format of the characters being transmitted, including the number of bits, the number of stop bits, and the parity. The divisor latch (see the divisor register) is also located at this address, bit 80.	LCR_PORT 01	Word length, bit 0
			02	Word length, bit 1
			04	Stop bits (clear = 1, set = 2)
			08	Parity enable

Name	Address	Description	Name in SENDCOMM.C	Bits
			10	Even parity
			20	Stick parity
			40	Set break
			80	Enable divisor latches
MODEM control register	I/O base address + 5	Sets the output control lines.	MCR_PORT 01 02 04 08 10 20 40 80	DTR RTS OUT1 OUT2 Loop back Not used Not used Not used
Line status register	I/O base address + 6	Status of various parameters.	LSR_PORT 01	Data has been received.
			02	Overrun error. The previous character received was not read by the computer and has been overwritten by the following character.
			04	Parity error. There was a parity error in the character being received.
			08	Framing error. The start/stop bits could not be detected correctly.
			10	Break interrupt. A break has been detected.
			20	Transmit buffer empty

continues

299

Table 9.5. continued

Name	Address	Description	Name in SENDCOMM.C	Bits
			40	Transmit shift register is empty. The output shift register is currently empty.
			80	Not used
MODEM status register	I/O base address + 7	Status of MODEM signal lines.	MSR_PORT 01	DCTS
			02	DDSR
			04	TERI
			08	DDCD
			10	CTS
			20	DSR
			40	RI (ring indicator)
			80	DCD

The receive buffer is located at base address + 0. The functionality of base address + 0 is controlled by bit 0x80 of LCR_PORT. If this bit is clear (zero), base address + 0 is used as the receive buffer.

The baud rate divisor register (LSB) is also located at base address + 0. The functionality of base address + 0 is controlled by bit 0x80 of LCR_PORT. If this bit is set, base address + 0 is used as the divisor register (LSB).

The transmit buffer is located at base address + 1. The functionality of base address + 1 is controlled by bit 0x80 of LCR_PORT. If this bit is clear (zero), base address + 1 is used as the transmit buffer.

The baud rate divisor register (MSB) is also located at base address + 1. The functionality of base address + 1 is controlled by bit 0x80 of LCR_PORT. If this bit is set, base address + 1 is used as the divisor register (MSB).

The interrupt enable register is located at base address + 2. Only the first four bits are used in this register.

The interrupt identifier register is located at base address + 3. It is used to tell the program what condition caused the interrupt.

The line control register is located at base address + 4. This register controls the character format and the mapping of the divisor latch (see offset +0 and +1).

The modem control register is located at base address + 5. This register is used to control the port's I/O connector control signals. These signals are then used to control the modem (or whatever else is connected to the port).

The line status register is located at base address + 6. It is used to pass to the program information regarding the status of the UART and the data being received.

The MODEM status register is located at base address + 7. The program uses this register to determine the status of the device connected to the port.

Note how the DLL and DLM registers (the speed registers) have the same address as the RBR and THR registers. This is accomplished with the divisor latch enable bit (0x80) of the LCR register. If this bit is set, these registers are used for the speed divisor. If this bit is cleared, these registers serve their other purpose.

A communications program can rely on the DOS MODE command setting the communications port parameters, or the program can set the parameters itself. Each of the port's registers may be read (except transmitted data), modified, and written back. This process of reading, modifying, and writing a register is all that is required to initialize the serial port.

Listing 9.8, SENDCOMM.C, sends a single string, followed by a LF/CR character pair, to COM1:. Before you run SENDCOMM.C, COM1: must be initialized with the DOS MODE command.

Listing 9.8. SENDCOMM.C.

```
/* SENDCOMM, written 1992 by Peter D. Hipson
 * This program outputs to the serial port. You should
 * run this program under DOS on a PC. If your computer
 * is not a PC-compatible, DO NOT RUN this program. Also,
 * the program should be compiled with Microsoft C.
 */


#include <stdio.h>    // Make includes first part of file
#include <conio.h>    // Console I/O functions
#include <string.h>   // For string functions
```

continues

Listing 9.8. continued

```c
#include <stdlib.h>  // Standard include items
#include <process.h> // For exit(), etc.
#include <time.h>    // To seed random numbers

#define MAKELONG(low, high) ((long)(((unsigned short int)(low)) \
  | (((unsigned long int)((unsigned short int)(high))) << 16)))
#define MAKELP(sel, off)    ((void _far*)MAKELONG((off), (sel)))

/* Comm port definitions */

#define BIOS_DATA_PAGE          0x0040
#define COM1                    0x0000

/* Receive a character port (read only) */
#define RBR_PORT                (nPort)
/* Send (transmit) a character port (write only) */
#define THR_PORT                (nPort)

/* Interrupt enable register */
#define IER_PORT                (nPort + 1)
#define RECEIVED_DATA_AVAILABLE 0x01
#define TRANSMIT_HOLD_EMPTY     0x02
#define RECIEVER_LINE_STATUS    0x04
#define MODEM_STATUS            0x08
/* Other bits undefined */

/* Interrupt identify register (read only) */
#define IIR_PORT                (nPort + 2)
#define INTERUPT_PENDING_0      0x01
#define INTERUPT_ID_BIT_1       0x02
#define INTERUPT_ID_BIT_2       0x04
/* Other bits undefined */

/* Line control register */
#define LCR_PORT                (nPort + 3)
#define WORD_LENGTH_SELECT_1    0x01  /* 00 = 5 bits, 01 = 6 bits */
#define WORD_LENGTH_SELECT_2    0x02  /* 10 = 7 bits, 11 = 8 bits */
#define NUMBER_STOP_BITS        0x04  /* 0 = 1 stop,  1 = 2 stop  */
#define PARITY_ENABLE           0x08
#define EVEN_PARITY_SELECT      0x10
```

```
#define STICK_PARITY              0x20
#define SET_BREAK                 0x40
#define DIVISOR_LATCH_BIT         0x80   /* For DLL and DLH access */
/* Other bits undefined */


/* Modem control register */
#define MCR_PORT                  (nPort + 4)
#define DTR                       0x01
#define RTS                       0x02
#define OUT_1                     0x04
#define OUT_2                     0x08
#define LOOP                      0x10
/* Other bits undefined */


/* Line status register */
#define LSR_PORT                  (nPort + 5)
#define DATA_READY                0x01
#define OVERRUN_ERROR             0x02
#define PARITY_ERROR              0x04
#define FRAMING_ERROR             0x08
#define BREAK_INTERUPT            0x10
#define TRANS_HOLDING_REGISTER    0x20
#define TRANS_SHIFT_REGISTER      0x40
/* Other bits undefined */


/* Modem status register */
#define MSR_PORT                  (nPort + 6)
#define DCTS                      0x01
#define DDSR                      0x02
#define TERI                      0x04
#define DDCD                      0x08
#define CTS                       0x10
#define DSR                       0x20
#define RI                        0x40
#define DCD                       0x80


/* Divisor latch least significant (sets speed) */
#define DLL_PORT                  (nPort + 0)
/* Bits 0 - 7 */
```

continues

Listing 9.8. continued

```
/* Divisor latch most significant (sets speed) */
#define DLM_PORT                (nPort + 1)
/* Bits 8 - 15 */

#define BAUD_50                 0x0900
#define BAUD_75                 0x0600
#define BAUD_110                0x0417
#define BAUD_134                0x0359
#define BAUD_150                0x0300
#define BAUD_300                0x0180
#define BAUD_600                0x00C0
#define BAUD_1200               0x0060
#define BAUD_1800               0x0040
#define BAUD_2000               0x003A
#define BAUD_2400               0x0030
#define BAUD_3600               0x0020
#define BAUD_4800               0x0018
#define BAUD_7200               0x0010
#define BAUD_9600               0x000C
#define BAUD_14400              0x0008
#define BAUD_19200              0x0006
#define BAUD_38400              0x0003
#define BAUD_56000              0x0002
#define BAUD_112000             0x0001


/* End serial port definitions */


int main(           // Define main() and the fact that this
    int     argc,   // program uses the passed parameters
    char    *argv[],
    char    *envp[]
    );

int SerialCharacter(char   chChar);
int SerialStatus(void);
int main(
    int     argc,
    char    *argv[],
```

```
    char    *envp[]
    )

{

char    szNowIsTheTime[] = {
    "Now is the time for all good men to come to the aid...\n\r"};

int     nStatus;
int     i;


    if (!SerialStatus())
    {
        printf("There was a serial error!\n");
        exit(4);
    }

    for (i = 0; i < strlen(szNowIsTheTime); i++)
    {
        if (SerialCharacter(szNowIsTheTime[i]) == 0)
        {
            printf("\nCouldn't send from character '%s'\n",
                &szNowIsTheTime[i]);

            break;
        }
    }

    return (0);
}

int     SerialCharacter(
    char  chChar)

{

int _far    *pSerialPort;
int     nPort;
```

continues

Listing 9.8. continued

```c
int     nStatus;

/*  The PC's serial port is at address 0040:0000
 *  (for COM1:). If a zero is stored at that address,
 *  a serial port is not installed.
 */
    pSerialPort = MAKELP(BIOS_DATA_PAGE, COM1);
    nPort = *pSerialPort;

    if (nPort == 0)
    {/* No serial port is installed! */
        printf("No serial installed... WHY?\n");
        return(0);
    }


/*  Write the data byte to the serial port's data lines.
 *  The program must wait until the last character
 *  has been sent because the simple hardware does not
 *  have a queue.
 */

    nStatus = inp(LSR_PORT);

    while (!(nStatus & TRANS_HOLDING_REGISTER))
    {/* Simply get the status again, which wastes time */
        nStatus = inp(LSR_PORT);
    }

    outp(THR_PORT, chChar);

    return(1);
}


int     SerialStatus()

{
```

```
int _far    *pSerialPort;
int    nPort;

int    nStatus;

/*  The PC's serial port is at address 0040:0000
 *  (for COM1:). If a zero is stored at that address,
 *  a serial port is not installed.
 */

    pSerialPort = MAKELP(BIOS_DATA_PAGE, COM1);
    nPort = *pSerialPort;

    if (nPort == 0)
    {/* No serial port is installed! */
        printf("No serial board installed... Why?\n");
        return(0);
    }

    printf("Serial vector = %lp Serial port %4.4X\n",
        pSerialPort,
        nPort);

    nStatus = inp(MCR_PORT);

    printf("MCR_PORT returned %2.2X\n", nStatus);

    if (nStatus & DTR)
    {
        printf("DTR is high. \n");
    }
    else
    {
        printf("DTR is low. \n");
    }

    if (nStatus & RTS)
    {
        printf("RTS is high. \n");
    }
```

continues

Listing 9.8. continued

```
else
{
    printf("RTS is low. \n");
}

nStatus = inp(IER_PORT);

printf("IER_PORT returned %2.2X\n", nStatus);

nStatus = inp(IIR_PORT);

printf("IIR_PORT returned %2.2X\n", nStatus);

nStatus = inp(LCR_PORT);

printf("LCR_PORT returned %2.2X\n", nStatus);

nStatus = inp(MCR_PORT);

printf("MCR_PORT returned %2.2X\n", nStatus);

nStatus = inp(LSR_PORT);

printf("LSR_PORT returned %2.2X\n", nStatus);

nStatus = inp(MSR_PORT);

printf("MSR_PORT returned %2.2X\n", nStatus);

return(1);
}
```

SENDCOMM is simple, in that it only displays the status of the registers, then sends the string. Following is the code that sends the characters:

```
nStatus = inp(LSR_PORT);

while (!(nStatus & TRANS_HOLDING_REGISTER))
{/* Simply get the status again, which wastes time */
```

```
        nStatus = inp(LSR_PORT);
    }

    outp(THR_PORT, chChar);
```

First, the program gets the port's status. If the `TRANS_HOLDING_REGISTER` bit is clear, the character can be sent. If the bit is set, the program waits for the hardware to send the current character, at which point the bit is cleared.

After the `TRANS_HOLDING_REGISTER` is clear, the program sends the character using a call to `outp()`. The hardware handles the serial transmission of the character in a serial format.

SENDCOMM.C is a simple character sending program. Receiving a character is just as easy. Listing 9.9, READCOMM.C, gets a character from the serial port, sends it back (echoes the character), and displays it on the terminal's screen.

Listing 9.9. READCOMM.C.

```
/* READCOMM, written 1992 by Peter D. Hipson
 * This program reads characters from the serial port.
 * You should run this program under DOS on a PC. If
 * your computer is not a PC-compatible, DO NOT RUN
 * this program. Also, the program should be compiled
 * with Microsoft C.
 */

#include <stdio.h>    // Make includes first part of file
#include <conio.h>    // Console I/O functions
#include <string.h>   // For string functions
#include <stdlib.h>   // Standard include items
#include <process.h>  // For exit(), etc.
#include <time.h>     // To seed random numbers

#define MAKELONG(low, high) ((long)(((unsigned short int)(low)) \
  ¦ (((unsigned long int)((unsigned short int)(high))) << 16)))
#define MAKELP(sel, off)    ((void _far*)MAKELONG((off), (sel)))

/* Comm port definitions */
```

continues

Listing 9.9. continued

```
#define BIOS_DATA_PAGE          0x0040
#define COM1                    0x0000

/* Receive a character port (read only) */
#define RBR_PORT                (nPort)
/* Send (transmit) a character port (write only) */
#define THR_PORT                (nPort)

/* Interrupt enable register */
#define IER_PORT                (nPort + 1)
#define RECEIVED_DATA_AVAILABLE 0x01
#define TRANSMIT_HOLD_EMPTY     0x02
#define RECIEVER_LINE_STATUS    0x04
#define MODEM_STATUS            0x08
/* Other bits undefined */

/* Interrupt identify register (read only) */
#define IIR_PORT                (nPort + 2)
#define INTERUPT_PENDING_0      0x01
#define INTERUPT_ID_BIT_1       0x02
#define INTERUPT_ID_BIT_2       0x04
/* Other bits undefined */

/* Line control register */
#define LCR_PORT                (nPort + 3)
#define WORD_LENGTH_SELECT_1    0x01  /* 00 = 5 bits, 01 = 6 bits */
#define WORD_LENGTH_SELECT_2    0x02  /* 10 = 7 bits, 11 = 8 bits */
#define NUMBER_STOP_BITS        0x04  /* 0 = 1 stop,  1 = 2 stop  */
#define PARITY_ENABLE           0x08
#define EVEN_PARITY_SELECT      0x10
#define STICK_PARITY            0x20
#define SET_BREAK               0x40
#define DIVISOR_LATCH_BIT       0x80  /* For DLL and DLH access */
/* Other bits undefined */

/* Modem control register */
#define MCR_PORT                (nPort + 4)
#define DTR                     0x01
#define RTS                     0x02
#define OUT_1                   0x04
```

```
#define OUT_2                    0x08
#define LOOP                     0x10
/* Other bits undefined */


/* Line status register */
#define LSR_PORT                 (nPort + 5)
#define DATA_READY               0x01
#define OVERRUN_ERROR            0x02
#define PARITY_ERROR             0x04
#define FRAMING_ERROR            0x08
#define BREAK_INTERUPT           0x10
#define TRANS_HOLDING_REGISTER   0x20
#define TRANS_SHIFT_REGISTER     0x40
/* Other bits undefined */


/* Modem status register */
#define MSR_PORT                 (nPort + 6)
#define DCTS                     0x01
#define DDSR                     0x02
#define TERI                     0x04
#define DDCD                     0x08
#define CTS                      0x10
#define DSR                      0x20
#define RI                       0x40
#define DCD                      0x80


/* Divisor latch least significant (sets speed) */
#define DLL_PORT                 (nPort + 0)
/* Bits 0 - 7 */


/* Divisor latch most significant (sets speed) */
#define DLM_PORT                 (nPort + 1)
/* Bits 8 - 15 */


/* Bits defined as 0xMMLL. MM is DLM. LL is DLL */

#define BAUD_50                  0x0900
#define BAUD_75                  0x0600
#define BAUD_110                 0x0417
#define BAUD_134                 0x0359
#define BAUD_150                 0x0300
```

continues

Listing 9.9. continued

```
#define BAUD_300            0x0180
#define BAUD_600            0x00C0
#define BAUD_1200           0x0060
#define BAUD_1800           0x0040
#define BAUD_2000           0x003A
#define BAUD_2400           0x0030
#define BAUD_3600           0x0020
#define BAUD_4800           0x0018
#define BAUD_7200           0x0010
#define BAUD_9600           0x000C
#define BAUD_14400          0x0008
#define BAUD_19200          0x0006
#define BAUD_38400          0x0003
#define BAUD_56000          0x0002
#define BAUD_112000         0x0001

/* End serial port definitions */

int main(            // Define main() and the fact that
    int     argc,    // this program uses the passed parameters
    char    *argv[],
    char    *envp[]
    );
int GetSerialCharacter(char   *chChar);
int SerialStatus(void);

int main(
    int     argc,
    char    *argv[],
    char    *envp[]
    )

{

char    chChar;

int     nStatus;
int     i;
```

```
    if (!SerialStatus())
    {
        printf("There was a serial error!\n");
        exit(4);
    }

    while(1)
    {
        if (kbhit())
        {/* Discard the keypress and end */
            (void)getch();
            break;
        }

        if (GetSerialCharacter(&chChar))
        {/* Print the received character, and get another */
            printf("%c", chChar);
        }
    }

    return (0);
}

int     GetSerialCharacter(
    char   *chChar)


{

int _far    *pSerialPort;
int     nPort;

int     nStatus;

/*  The PC's serial port is at address 0040:0000
 *  (for COM1:). If a zero is stored at that address,
 *  a serial port is not installed.
 */

    pSerialPort = MAKELP(BIOS_DATA_PAGE, COM1);
    nPort = *pSerialPort;
```

continues

Listing 9.9. continued

```
        if (nPort == 0)
        {/* No serial is installed! */
            printf("No serial installed...Why?\n");
            return(0);
        }

    /*  To read a character, the DATA_READY signal must be set
     *  (see the previous defines). This bit is in LSR_PORT.
     *  If DATA_READY is set, the program reads a character
     *  and returns TRUE.
     */

        nStatus = inp(LSR_PORT);

        if (nStatus & DATA_READY)
        {/* A character has been received. */
            *chChar = inp(RBR_PORT);

    /*  Echo the data byte back to the sender. The program
     *  must wait until the last character has been sent
     *  because the simple hardware does not have a queue.
     */

            nStatus = inp(LSR_PORT);

            while (!(nStatus & TRANS_HOLDING_REGISTER))
            {/* Simply get the status again, which wastes time */
                nStatus = inp(LSR_PORT);
            }

            outp(THR_PORT, *chChar);

            return(1);
        }

    return(0);
}


int     SerialStatus()
```

```
{

int _far    *pSerialPort;
int    nPort;

int    nTempStatus;
int    nStatus;

/*  The PC's serial port is at address 0040:0000
 *  (for COM1:). If a zero is stored at that address,
 *  a serial port is not installed.
 */

    pSerialPort = MAKELP(BIOS_DATA_PAGE, COM1);
    nPort = *pSerialPort;

    if (nPort == 0)
    {/* No serial is installed! */
        printf("No serial board installed...Why?\n");
        return(0);
    }

    printf("Serial vector = %lp Serial port %4.4X\n",
        pSerialPort,
        nPort);

    nStatus = inp(MCR_PORT);

    printf("MCR_PORT returned %2.2X\n", nStatus);

    if (nStatus & DTR)
    {
        printf("DTR is high. \n");
    }
    else
    {
        printf("DTR is low. \n");
    }
```

continues

Listing 9.9. continued

```
if (nStatus & RTS)
{
    printf("RTS is high. \n");
}
else
{
    printf("RTS is low. \n");
}

nStatus = inp(IER_PORT);

printf("IER_PORT returned %2.2X\n", nStatus);

nStatus = inp(IIR_PORT);

printf("IIR_PORT returned %2.2X\n", nStatus);

nStatus = inp(LCR_PORT);

printf("LCR_PORT returned %2.2X\n", nStatus);

nStatus = inp(MCR_PORT);

printf("MCR_PORT returned %2.2X\n", nStatus);

nStatus = inp(LSR_PORT);

printf("LSR_PORT returned %2.2X\n", nStatus);

nStatus = inp(MSR_PORT);

printf("MSR_PORT returned %2.2X\n", nStatus);

nTempStatus = inp(LCR_PORT);

outp(LCR_PORT, nTempStatus ¦ DIVISOR_LATCH_BIT);

nStatus = inp(DLM_PORT);

printf("DLM_PORT returned %2.2X\n", nStatus);
```

```
    nStatus = inp(DLL_PORT);

    printf("DLL_PORT returned %2.2X\n", nStatus);

    outp(LCR_PORT, nTempStatus);

    return(1);
}
```

READCOMM.C uses a simple loop to read the characters. The part of the program that does the reading is shown in bold in the following code fragment. The other parts of the code fragment echo code. Echoing received characters is optional and is usually controlled by the user.

```
    nStatus = inp(LSR_PORT);

    if (nStatus & DATA_READY)
    {/* A character has been received. */
        *chChar = inp(RBR_PORT);

/*  Echo the data byte to the sender. The program
 *  must wait until the last character has been sent
 *  because the simple hardware does not have a queue.
 */

        nStatus = inp(LSR_PORT);

        while (!(nStatus & TRANS_HOLDING_REGISTER))
        {/* Simply get the status again, which wastes time */
            nStatus = inp(LSR_PORT);
        }

        outp(THR_PORT, *chChar);
```

The READCOMM program also shows how to switch between the speed controlling ports, DLL and DLM. This is accomplished by setting the DIVISOR_LATCH_BIT bit in the LCR_PORT register, as follows:

```
    nTempStatus = inp(LCR_PORT);

    outp(LCR_PORT, nTempStatus | DIVISOR_LATCH_BIT);
```

```
nStatus = inp(DLM_PORT);

printf("DLM_PORT returned %2.2X\n", nStatus);

nStatus = inp(DLL_PORT);

printf("DLL_PORT returned %2.2X\n", nStatus);

outp(LCR_PORT, nTempStatus);
```

First, the program gets the current contents of the LCR_PORT and saves the contents in nTempStatus. Then the program writes to LCR_PORT with nTempStatus logically ORd with the DIVISOR_LATCH_BIT. This switches the meaning of RBR_PORT to DLL_PORT and the meaning of THR_PORT to DLM_PORT.

Be sure you reset LCR_PORT after you have finished setting (or checking) the baud rate. You set the baud rate using the identifiers prefaced with BAUD_ in either program.

Summary

In this chapter, you learned about input and output using C, and how to use both file I/O and port I/O.

- Files used for both program input and program output are vital to any program's operation.

- Text-based files can be read, printed, edited, and otherwise used without conversion by people. Text files usually contain only printable, newline, and form-feed characters.

- Binary files contain any bytes that a program must place in the file. Generally, a binary file is intended for use by the program or by other programs and cannot be edited, printed, or read.

- Using temporary work files, a programmer can extend a program's data storage space to almost the amount of free space on the disk. Work files can be text or binary, depending on the program's requirements.

- Stream files are supported by many functions, can be text or binary, and are usually buffered and formatted.

- Every C program has five opened files: stdin, stdout, stdaux, stdprn, and stderr. These files are opened as stream files.

- Low-level files are accessed with a minimum number of C functions and are usually unformatted and unbuffered.

- C compilers provide console functions to access the screen and keyboard.

- In PC compatible systems, your programs can access ports using C. This access allows direct interaction with the device, without DOS or the BIOS.

Data Management:
Sorts, Lists, and Indexes

Data management is what it's all about. Almost all computer programs manage data—even a simple computer game must manage and access data to update its list of current high scores.

Sorting, merging, and purging. Indexed files. Tree access methods. Everyone knows what sorting is, but the other terms may be unfamiliar. *Merging* is the process of combining two sorted files and creating a resultant, sorted file. *Purging* uses a sorted file to create a new file in which duplicate lines from the original file are eliminated. An *indexed* file (or in-memory data object) consists of two files: the main data file and a second, smaller index file. A tree access method offers fast searching and sorted access to data. (This chapter discusses B-trees.)

I'll use the creation of this book's index as an example of sorting, merging, and purging. For each chapter, I created a file in which each word is on a separate line (I simply changed all spaces to newline characters). I then sorted the file, then purged it, which eliminates all duplicate words (and makes the file size more manageable).

Then, I merged each chapter's file of unique words into one large file for the entire book. I then purged that file—even though each chapter's file contains only unique words, other chapters might contain some of these words too. After this final purge, I had a file of unique words in the book. After a quick session with an editor, I deleted any words that were not index material, leaving only the important words.

I used programs that I created to sort, merge, and purge as part of this chapter. The DOS SORT utility is limited to files under 64K, but the sort program in this chapter is limited only by the available memory. The merge and purge utilities are not part of DOS. I hope they prove to be valuable additions to your stable of programming tools.

Sorting

Sorting a file can be both easy and difficult. It's easy because C has a sort function called `qsort()` that is part of the library. This function's performance is acceptable. The difficult part is reading in the files and other programming overhead. You must provide a compare function that `qsort()` can use.

When you write a program in which you do not know the amount of data that the user will input, you must rely on dynamic memory allocation. This is not a problem with the `qsort()` function: you pass a single array of pointers to the data being sorted and, when `qsort()` returns, use the (now sorted) array of pointers to access the data in sorted order. When you use this technique with character strings, it reduces overhead and increases the program's performance because only the pointers are moved in memory, not the strings.

Listing 10.1, SORTFILE.C, sorts the input from `stdin` and writes the sorted results to `stdout`. If you use I/O redirection, the program could sort a file and place the results into a new file. Unlike the DOS SORT command, SORTFILE always sorts from column one. (Adding the capability to sort from any other column is an exercise I'll leave to you.)

Listing 10.1. SORTFILE.C.

```c
/*  SORTFILE, written 1992 by Peter D. Hipson
 *  This program sorts from stdin and sends the results
 *  to stdout. If your PC has memory models, you must
 *  compile with the LARGE model.
 */

#include <stdio.h>     // Make includes first part of file
#include <string.h>    // For string functions
#include <process.h>   // For exit(), etc.
#include <malloc.h>    // For malloc(), calloc(), realloc(), free()
#include <search.h>    // For qsort()...

int main(void); // Define main() and the fact that this program
                // does not use any passed parameters

int compare(void *arg1, void *arg2);


#define MAX_CHARACTERS 32767 /* Total maximum characters */
#define MAX_LINES       15500 /* Total maximum lines */
#define BIGEST_LINE     512   /* Largest line readable from keyboard */
#define MAX_BLOCKS      128   /* Allow 128 * MAX_CHARACTERS of memory */

/*  Although these variables are defined as external, they could
 *  be defined inside the function or allocated dynamically,
 *  depending on the program's needs and the available memory.
 */

char    szInput[BIGEST_LINE];
char    *szBuffer;
char    *pBlocks[MAX_BLOCKS];
char    *pBuffer[MAX_LINES];
int     nCurrentBlock = 0;
int     nBufferPointer = {MAX_CHARACTERS};
int     nLine = 0;

int main()

{
```

continues

Listing 10.1. continued

```
int    i;

/*  Use fprintf(stderr...) to force prompts and error messages
 *  to be displayed on the user's screen regardless of whether
 *  the output has been redirected.
 */

    fprintf(stderr,
        "\n"
        "Peter's SORTFILE: Sorts large files at the speed of light!\n"
        "\n"
        "    syntax: \n"
        "        sortfile <inputfile >outputfile \n"
        "\n"
        "    where: \n"
        "        the program's I/O is redirected\n\n");

    fprintf(stderr, "Reading input...\n");

    while (gets(szInput))
    {
        if ((nBufferPointer + strlen(szInput)) > MAX_CHARACTERS)
        { // The line won't fit! Allocate new memory:

            szBuffer = (char *)malloc(MAX_CHARACTERS);

            fprintf(stderr, "    Allocating buffer (32K).\n");
            nBufferPointer = 0;

            pBlocks[nCurrentBlock] = szBuffer;

            ++nCurrentBlock;

            if (szBuffer == NULL)
            {
            fprintf(stderr, "System sort memory exceeded, can't \
                            sort.\n");
```

```
                exit(16);
            }
        }

        pBuffer[nLine] = &szBuffer[nBufferPointer];

        strcpy(pBuffer[nLine], szInput);

// The + 1 skips over the terminating NULL in each string.
        nBufferPointer += strlen(szInput) + 1;

        if (++nLine >= MAX_LINES)
        { // Too many lines! End the program.
            fprintf(stderr, "Too many lines—cannot sort.\n");

            exit(16);
        }
    }

//
// Now sort the input lines
//

    fprintf(stderr, "Sorting, %d lines, in %d buffers.\n",
        nLine,
        nCurrentBlock);

    qsort((void *)pBuffer,
        (size_t)nLine,
        sizeof(char *),
        compare);

    fprintf(stderr, "Writing output...\n");

    for (i = 0; i < nLine; i++)
    {
        printf("%s\n", pBuffer[i]);
    }

    fprintf(stderr, "\n");
```

continues

Listing 10.1. continued

```
    for (i = 0; i < nCurrentBlock; i++)
    {
        free(pBlocks[i]);
    }

    return (0);
}


int compare(
    char **arg1,
    char **arg2)

{
    return strcmp(*(char**)arg1, *(char**)arg2);
}
```

Note the declaration of the `compare()` function:

```
int compare(char **arg1, char **arg2);
```

The function has two parameters. It receives its parameters as pointers to pointers to strings. Got that? You pass an array of pointers to strings, then `qsort()` passes pointers to elements in the array to compare. It compares the two pointers, and returns a value based on this comparison. The compare function returns zero if the two parameters are equal, less than zero if the first parameter is less than the second, and greater than zero if the first parameter is greater than the second.

Next are some defined identifiers:

```
#define MAX_CHARACTERS 32767 /* Total maximum characters */
#define MAX_LINES      16383 /* Total maximum lines */
#define BIGEST_LINE      512 /* Largest line readable from keyboard */
#define MAX_BLOCKS       128 /* Allow 128 * MAX_CHARACTERS of memory */
```

Memory is allocated in blocks of 32K using the `MAX_CHARACTERS` identifier. A maximum of 16K lines can be sorted (with a 4-byte pointer, about 16K pointers can fit in 64K). The largest line allowed is 512 bytes, and up to 128 calls can be made to the memory allocation functions (more than you'll find on a PC).

The external variables declared (they could be declared as internal static variables) define an input buffer, szBuffer[], a generic character pointer, an array of pointers to each block of memory (so that the blocks can be freed later), and an array of character pointers (*pBuffer[]) that point to each line that will be sorted:

```c
char    szInput[BIGEST_LINE];
char    *szBuffer;
char    *pBlocks[MAX_BLOCKS];
char    *pBuffer[MAX_LINES];
int     nCurrentBlock = 0;
int     nBufferPointer = {MAX_CHARACTERS};
int     nLine = 0;
```

The program receives its input from the keyboard and writes to the terminal. Therefore, if the program is used as a pipe or with I/O redirection, you must be sure that error messages do not get redirected. In Chapter 9, "Disk Files and Other I/O," you learned that the standard stream stderr does not get redirected, but stdout does. Therefore, if the program's output is written to stdout and messages to the user are written to stderr, you can be sure that messages to the user are not mixed with the program's output.

To access stderr, you use the fprintf(stderr,...); statement, as shown in the following code fragment:

```c
fprintf(stderr,
    "\n"
    "Peter's SORTFILE: Sorts large files at the speed of light!\n"
    "\n"
    "    syntax: \n"
    "        sortfile <inputfile >outputfile \n"
    "\n"
    "    where: \n"
    "        the program's I/O is redirected\n\n");

fprintf(stderr, "Reading input...\n");
```

After providing the opening messages to the user, the program reads the input from stdin. The C function gets() does fine in this context. After reading a line, the program checks whether there is enough room in the current buffer for the string. If there is not enough room, the program allocates a new buffer and displays a message that the buffer has been allocated:

```
while (gets(szInput))
{
    if ((nBufferPointer + strlen(szInput)) > MAX_CHARACTERS)
    { // The line won't fit! Allocate new memory:
        szBuffer = (char *)malloc(MAX_CHARACTERS);
        fprintf(stderr, "    Allocating buffer (32K).\n");
        nBufferPointer = 0;
        pBlocks[nCurrentBlock] = szBuffer;
        ++nCurrentBlock;
        if (szBuffer == NULL)
        {
        fprintf(stderr, "System sort memory exceeded--cannot \
                        sort.\n");
            exit(16);
        }
    }
```

Now that there is enough room in the buffer for the string, the program sets the pointer array (pBuffer[ ]) to the string's eventual location, then copies the string to the buffer. The intermediate buffer is used to help prevent buffer overflow (otherwise the program would have to stop filling a block of memory at least 512 bytes before the end of the block). The call to strcpy() does not take too much overhead. The program also updates the pointer into the block of memory, in preparation for the next string.

```
        pBuffer[nLine] = &szBuffer[nBufferPointer];

        strcpy(pBuffer[nLine], szInput);
// The + 1 skips over the terminating NULL in each string.
        nBufferPointer += strlen(szInput) + 1;
```

A bit of error checking comes next, to be sure that the program does not read in too many lines:

```
    if (++nLine >= MAX_LINES)
    { // Too many lines! End the program.
        fprintf(stderr, "Too many lines--cannot sort.\n");
        exit(16);
    }
}
```

After the input file had been read, the program calls qsort() to sort the file, using the compare (described previously):

```
qsort((void *)pBuffer,
    (size_t)nLine,
    sizeof(char *),
    compare);
```

When qsort() returns, the program uses printf() to write the final sorted output:

```
fprintf(stderr, "Writing output...\n");

for (i = 0; i < nLine; i++)
{
    printf("%s\n", pBuffer[i]);
}
```

Because the printf() output goes to stdout, the output could be redirected to a file. Finally, the blocks of memory are freed and the program ends:

```
for (i = 0; i < nCurrentBlock; i++)
{
    free(pBlocks[i]);
}
```

The compare function, which is called by qsort() in the main program, is simple. The program calls strcmp(). If you want the program to ignore case, you could call stricmp() instead. You could also create your own function to compare the strings, but C's functions work well enough.

```
int compare(
    char **arg1,
    char **arg2)

{
   return strcmp(*arg1, *arg2);
}
```

The SORTFILE program can sort files up to 500K, depending on the DOS version). You could use SORTFILE also with I/O redirection or as a filter with DOS's pipe operator, ¦.

Merging

No matter how much memory you have available, eventually you will want to sort a file that is too large. You could sort the file from the disk. Another method is to break the file into smaller parts that will fit in memory, sort these parts, then combine the sorted parts into a final sorted file that contains the sum of the parts. The process of breaking a file into smaller, more manageable parts, called a *sort/merge*, is a common technique on mainframes and minicomputers.

To keep the programs in this chapter as simple as possible (but wait until you see the BTREE program later in the chapter), I created separate merge and sort programs. Listing 10.2, MERGFILE.C, does not use stdin for its input because you must have two files to perform a merge.

Listing 10.2. MERGFILE.C.

```c
/* MERGFILE, written 1992 by Peter D. Hipson
 * This program merges two sorted files into one large
 * sorted file. If your PC has memory models, you must
 * compile with the LARGE model.
 */

#include <stdlib.h>    // For standard functions
#include <stdio.h>     // Make includes first part of file
#include <string.h>    // For string functions
#include <process.h>   // For exit(), etc.
#include <malloc.h>    // For malloc(), calloc(), realloc(), free()
#include <search.h>    // For qsort()...

int main(int argc, char *argv[], char *envp[]);

int compare(char **arg1, char **arg2);

#define BIGEST_LINE    512   /* The largest readable line      */
#define NEED_RECORD    1     /* A record is needed from the file */
#define END_OF_FILE    2     /* This file is finished          */
#define ALL_OK         3     /* No record needed; not EOF      */

/*  Although these variables are defined as external,
 *  they could be defined inside the function or
 *  allocated dynamically, depending on the program's
 *  needs and available memory.
 */
```

```
char    szInput1[BIGEST_LINE];
char    szInput2[BIGEST_LINE];

int main(
    int     argc,
    char    *argv[],
    char    *envp[]
    )

{

FILE    *InFile1;
FILE    *InFile2;
FILE    *OutFile;

char    szProgram[30];

/* Strings for _splitpath() (which parses a filename) */
char    szDrive[_MAX_DRIVE];
char    szDir[_MAX_DIR];
char    szFname[_MAX_FNAME];
char    szExt[_MAX_EXT];

int     i;
int     j;
int     nCompare = 0;
int     nFileOneStatus = NEED_RECORD;
int     nFileTwoStatus = NEED_RECORD;


/*  Use fprintf(stderr...) to force prompts and error messages
 *  to be displayed on the user's screen regardless of whether
 *  the output has been redirected.
 */
    _splitpath(argv[0],
        szDrive,
        szDir,
        szFname,
        szExt);
```

continues

Listing 10.2. continued

```c
    strncpy(szProgram, szFname, sizeof(szProgram) - 1);

    if (argc <= 3)
    {
        fprintf(stderr,
            "\n"
            "%s -\n"
            "\n"
            "Peter's MERGEFILE: Merges two sorted files into one!\n"
            "\n"
            "    syntax: \n"
            "       %s inputfile1 inputfile2 outputfile \n"
            "\n",
            szProgram,
            szProgram);

        return(16);
    }

    fprintf(stderr, "Reading input...\n");

    InFile1 = fopen(argv[1], "rt");
    InFile2 = fopen(argv[2], "rt");
    OutFile = fopen(argv[3], "wt");

    while (
        nFileOneStatus != END_OF_FILE ||
        nFileTwoStatus != END_OF_FILE)
    {
        switch(nFileOneStatus)
        {
            case NEED_RECORD: /* Read a record */
                if (fgets(szInput1, sizeof(szInput1), InFile1) == NULL)
                {
                    nFileOneStatus = END_OF_FILE;
                }
                else
                {
                    nFileOneStatus = ALL_OK;
```

```
        }
        break;

    case ALL_OK:       /* Nothing needed */
        break;

    case END_OF_FILE: /* Can't do anything */
        break;
}

switch(nFileTwoStatus)
{
    case NEED_RECORD: /* Read a record */
        if (fgets(szInput2, sizeof(szInput2), InFile2) == NULL)
        {
            nFileTwoStatus = END_OF_FILE;
        }
        else
        {
            nFileTwoStatus = ALL_OK;
        }
        break;

    case ALL_OK:       /* Nothing needed */
        break;

    case END_OF_FILE: /* Can't do anything */
        break;
}

if (nFileOneStatus == END_OF_FILE)
{
    if (nFileTwoStatus != END_OF_FILE)
    {
        fputs(szInput2, OutFile);
        nFileTwoStatus = NEED_RECORD;
    }
}
else
{
    if (nFileTwoStatus == END_OF_FILE)
    {
```

continues

Listing 10.2. continued

```
                        if (nFileOneStatus != END_OF_FILE)
                        {
                            fputs(szInput1, OutFile);
                            nFileOneStatus = NEED_RECORD;
                        }
                }
                else
                {
                    nCompare = strcmp(szInput1, szInput2);
                    if (nCompare < 0)
                    {/* File one is written */
                        fputs(szInput1, OutFile);
                        nFileOneStatus = NEED_RECORD;
                    }
                    else
                    {
                        if (nCompare > 0)
                        {/* File two is written */
                            fputs(szInput2, OutFile);
                            nFileTwoStatus = NEED_RECORD;
                        }
                        else
                        {/* They are the same; write both */
                            fputs(szInput1, OutFile);
                            fputs(szInput2, OutFile);
                            nFileOneStatus = NEED_RECORD;
                            nFileTwoStatus = NEED_RECORD;
                        }
                    }
                }
            }
    }

    fclose(InFile1);
    fclose(InFile2);
    fclose(OutFile);

    return (0);
}
```

Merging files is a simple process. Because this program does not use advanced techniques, I will dispense with the line-by-line analysis of the program's code and refer instead to the program's flowchart, shown in Figure 10.1.

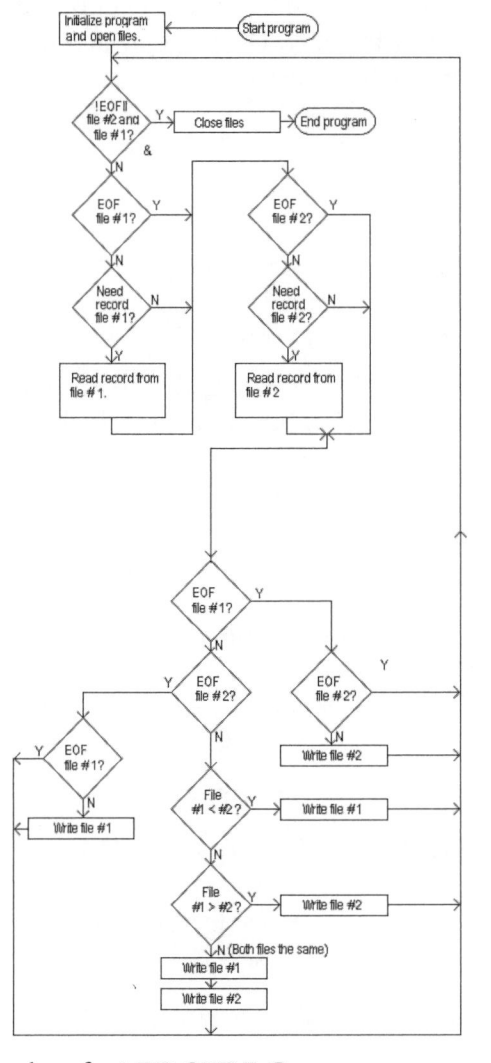

Figure 10.1. The flowchart for MERGFILE.C.

First, the program opens the two input files and the output file. If errors do not occur in this stage, the program reads a record from both input files. After the records are read, the program does its comparisons (taking into consideration possible end-of-file conditions), and writes the correct record. When the program reaches the end of both input files, it closes all the files and ends. It is a simple program that works quickly.

When writing a merge function, you must consider that one file may be (and usually is) shorter than the other. The merge program must be sure that the longer file's records are written to the output.

Purging

One often needed (and hard to find) program is a purge program, which is used to delete duplicates (sometimes called *de-dup*) from a file. You might want to delete duplicates, for example, from a mailing list or a word list.

The PURGFILE.C program in Listing 10.3 performs two functions. Part of the program works like MERGEFILE (Listing 10.2). Unlike MERGEFILE, however, PURGFILE does not write duplicates to the output file.

Listing 10.3. PURGFILE.C.

```
/*  PURGFILE, written 1992 by Peter D. Hipson
 *  This program merges and purges in one step. If your
 *  PC has memory models, you must compile with the
 *  LARGE model.
 */

#include <stdlib.h>   // For standard functions
#include <stdio.h>    // Make includes first part of file
#include <string.h>   // For string functions
#include <process.h>  // For exit(), etc
#include <malloc.h>   // For malloc(), calloc(), realloc(), free()
#include <search.h>   // For qsort()...

int main(int argc, char *argv[], char *envp[]);

int compare(char **arg1, char **arg2);

#define BIGEST_LINE    512   /* The largest readable line */
#define NEED_RECORD    1     /* A record is needed from the file */
```

```
#define END_OF_FILE    2    /* This file is finished */
#define ALL_OK         3    /* No record needed, not EOF */

/*  Although these variables are defined as external, they could
 *  be defined inside the function or allocated dynamically,
 *  depending on the program's needs and available memory.
 */

char    szInput[BIGEST_LINE];
char    szInput1[BIGEST_LINE];
char    szInput2[BIGEST_LINE];

int main(
    int     argc,
    char    *argv[],
    char    *envp[]
    )

{

FILE    *InFile1;
FILE    *InFile2;
FILE    *OutFile;

char    szProgram[30];

/* Strings for _splitpath(), which parses a file name */
char    szDrive[_MAX_DRIVE];
char    szDir[_MAX_DIR];
char    szFname[_MAX_FNAME];
char    szExt[_MAX_EXT];

int     i;
int     j;
int     nCompare = 0;
int     nFileOneStatus = NEED_RECORD;
int     nFileTwoStatus = NEED_RECORD;


/*  Use fprintf(stderr...) to force prompts and error messages to be
 *  displayed on the user's screen regardless of whether the output
```

continues

Listing 10.3. continued

```
 *  has been redirected.
 */

    _splitpath(argv[0],
        szDrive,
        szDir,
        szFname,
        szExt);

    strncpy(szProgram, szFname, sizeof(szProgram) - 1);

    if (argc <= 3)
    {
        fprintf(stderr,
            "\n"
            "%s -\n"
            "\n"
            "Peter's PURGEFILE: Merges two sorted files, \n"
            "    purging all duplicate lines!\n"
            "\n"
            "    inputfile1 and inputfile2 can be the same file,\n"
            "        if you want to de-dup only one file.\n"
            "\n"
            "    syntax: \n"
            "\n"
            "        %s inputfile1 inputfile2 outputfile \n"
            "\n",
            szProgram,
            szProgram);

        return(16);
    }

    InFile1 = fopen(argv[1], "rt");
    InFile2 = fopen(argv[2], "rt");
    OutFile = fopen(argv[3], "wt");

    while (
        nFileOneStatus != END_OF_FILE ||
        nFileTwoStatus != END_OF_FILE)
```

```
    {
        while(
            nFileOneStatus == NEED_RECORD ||
            nFileTwoStatus == NEED_RECORD)
        {
            switch(nFileOneStatus)
            {
                case NEED_RECORD: /* Read a record */
                    if (fgets(szInput, sizeof(szInput), InFile1) == NULL)
                    {
                        nFileOneStatus = END_OF_FILE;
                    }
                    else
                    {
                        if (strcmp(szInput, szInput1) != 0)
                        {
                            strcpy(szInput1, szInput);
                            nFileOneStatus = ALL_OK;
                        }
                    }

                    break;

                case ALL_OK:       /* Nothing needed */
                    break;

                case END_OF FILE: /* Can't do anything */
                    break;
            }

            switch(nFileTwoStatus)
            {
                case NEED_RECORD: /* Read a record */
                    if (fgets(szInput, sizeof(szInput), InFile2) == NULL)
                    {
                        nFileTwoStatus = END_OF_FILE;
                    }
                    else
                    {
                        if (strcmp(szInput, szInput2) != 0)
                        {
```

continues

Listing 10.3. continued

```
                          strcpy(szInput2, szInput);
                          nFileTwoStatus = ALL_OK;
                 }
            }
            break;

        case ALL_OK:      /* Nothing needed */
            break;

        case END_OF_FILE: /* Can't do anything */
            break;
    }
}

if (nFileOneStatus == END_OF_FILE)
{
    if (nFileTwoStatus != END_OF_FILE)
    {
        fputs(szInput2, OutFile);
        nFileTwoStatus = NEED_RECORD;
    }
}
else
{
    if (nFileTwoStatus == END_OF_FILE)
    {
        if (nFileOneStatus != END_OF_FILE)
        {
            fputs(szInput1, OutFile);
            nFileOneStatus = NEED_RECORD;
        }
    }
    else
    {
        nCompare = strcmp(szInput1, szInput2);
        if (nCompare < 0)
        {/* File one is written */
            fputs(szInput1, OutFile);
            nFileOneStatus = NEED_RECORD;
```

```
            }
            else
            {
                if (nCompare > 0)
                {/* File two is written */
                    fputs(szInput2, OutFile);
                    nFileTwoStatus = NEED_RECORD;
                }
                else
                {/* They are the same; write one and discard the
                 other. */
                    fputs(szInput1, OutFile);
                    nFileOneStatus = NEED_RECORD;
                    nFileTwoStatus = NEED_RECORD;
                }
            }
        }
    }
}

    fclose(InFile1);
    fclose(InFile2);
    fclose(OutFile);

    return (0);
}
```

Purging duplicate records from a single file is not difficult. First the program reads a line. Then the program discards the line if it is the same as the previous line, or saves the line if it is different from the previous line. PURGFILE performs a merge and a purge at the same time, however, making the program a bit more complex.

To use PURGFILE to purge a single file, you simply specify the same name twice or specify NUL: as the second filename. (A second filename must be specified to provide the output filename.)

The flowchart in Figure 10.2 shows how the PURGFILE program works. The program does not use advanced techniques, so this section looks only at the flowchart, rather than each line of code.

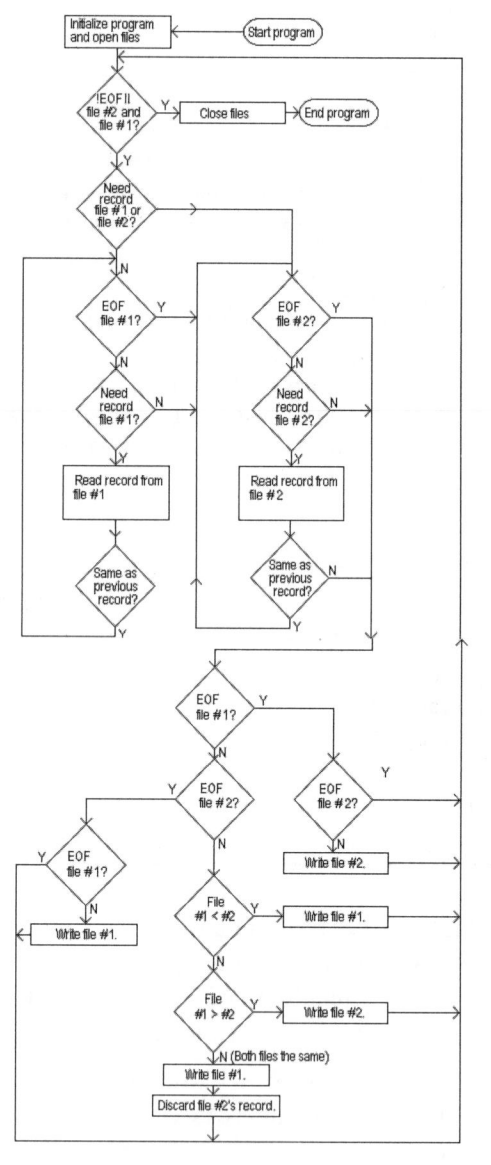

Figure 10.2. The flowchart for PURGFILE C.

As you can see in Figure 10.2, the program begins by opening the two input files and the output file. If there are no errors in the file-open stage, the program reads a record from each file (assuming that the program should read a record and that the program has not reached the end of the file).

After the records are read, the program makes its comparisons (taking into consideration possible end-of-file conditions), then writes the correct record. When the program has the same record from both files, it discards the second file's record, sets the flag indicating that it needs a new record from the second file, and saves the first file's record.

When the program reaches the end of both input files, it closes all the files and ends. It is a simple program that works quickly.

When you write a purge function, remember that a record might be repeated many times. When your program finds a duplicate and therefore reads a new record, it still must test to be sure that it has read a unique record. The program might be reading a third duplicate, for example, that must also be discarded.

Sorting, Merging, and Purging All in One

Usually, a single utility offers sort, merge, and purge functions. This type of utility will have one or two input filenames, sort the files, purge the duplicates, and provide a single output file.

A variation of a sort program is a sort that works on a file of any size. The process to create the ultimate sort follows:

1. Read the file, stopping at the end of the file or when there is no more free memory.

2. Sort this part of the file. Write the result of the sort to a temporary work file.

3. If the program has reached the end of the file and there are no more records to read in, the program renames step 2's work file to the output file's name and ends the program.

4. Again read the file, stopping when there is no more free memory or when the end of the file is reached.

5. Sort this part of the file. Write the result of the sort to a second temporary work file.

6. Merge the file created in step 2 with the file from step 5. Delete both of the files created by steps 2 and 5, and rename this new file using the name from step 2.

7. Go to step 3.

Linked Lists

A linked list is a group of data objects in which each object has a pointer to the next object in the group. Everything that you do with linked lists can be performed in memory or as part of a disk file.

Sometimes, sorting the data externally to the program (using the DOS SORT program) is not enough. When a user is entering data, it is never acceptable to stop the program, exit the program, run a sort, create a sorted file, then start the program again.

We have become accustomed to having the computer do the work for us, and rightly so. A program should not require the user to do anything that the program can perform without the user's intervention.

There are alternatives when data must be sorted. For example, when the user enters an item, the program can pause and use the qsort() function to insert the new item into the current database. If the database is large, however, the pause could be so long that you could go get lunch! Even a simple insert at the beginning of a list can be time consuming—every record in the database must be moved. The size and number of these records can be the critical factor.

Many programs must present the user's data in a sorted format. Because speed is critical, sorting each time the data is displayed usually is unacceptable—the data must be stored in sorted order.

Many programs work to keep as much of the user's current data as possible in memory. Searching a large quantity of data in memory should be not only quick, but instantaneous! If the data is not well organized, the search must be linear (record after record). On average, the program must look at half the records to find a matching record, assuming that the records are stored randomly.

In general, a linear search of a block of data or sorting after a data item has been added or edited is too slow and therefore inadequate.

The program's data must be organized better than the order in which it was entered. One way to organize is to use a linked list. In a linked list, you start with a pointer that points to, or identifies, the first member of the list. Each member (except the last) has a pointer that points to the next member in the list. The last member's pointer is a NULL pointer to indicate the end of the list. Often there is a separate pointer to the last member in the list—this enables you to add to the end of the list. A single linked list is shown in Figure 10.3.

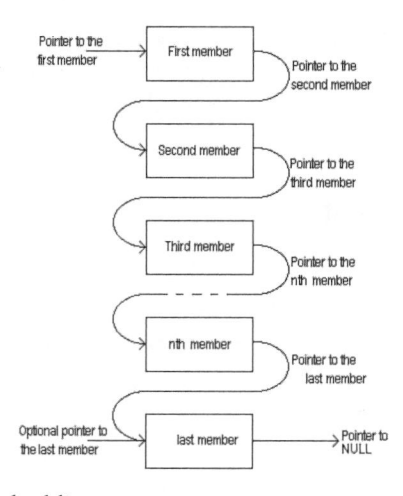

Figure 10.3. A single linked list.

When you add a new member to a linked list, the program simply follows the list until it finds the member that will precede the new member and inserts the new member at that point. When the program must display sorted data to the user, it uses the linked list pointers to find the necessary data. Because the links are already sorted, the program's performance is fast.

Using Dynamic Memory

Often you must rely on dynamic memory allocation (memory allocated using one of the memory allocation functions) because you cannot tell how much user data will be provided by the user. When allocating memory, the program must track each block of memory, usually with a linked list. In this situation, it may (or may not) be that the links are simply arranged in the order that the memory blocks are allocated. When a memory block is freed, it is removed from the linked list.

The example program in this section allocates memory blocks for each record that the user enters. These blocks are pointed to by links.

Disk-Based Lists

When you create a linked list as a disk-based file, the list's members must be the same size. If your program has different sized members of a single linked list, the best solution is to use a single union to create a single record of the correct size. The size of the union is determined by its largest member, so the members will be the same size.

Double Linked Lists

In a double linked list, each member has a pointer not only to its successor in the list, but also to its predecessor. Figure 10.4 shows how a double linked list is created. Notice that the pointer to the end of the list is mandatory. This pointer is necessary so that the end of the list can be accessed.

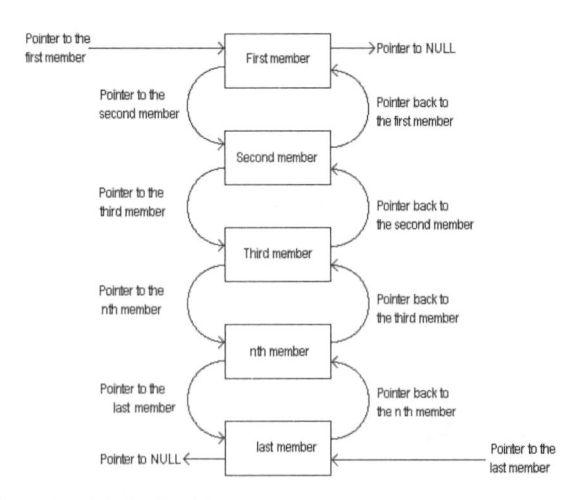

Figure 10.4. A double linked list.

Figure 10.5 shows the structure's list pointers. (Figure 10.5 and Figure 10.4 are the basis for Figures 10.6 through 10.9.)

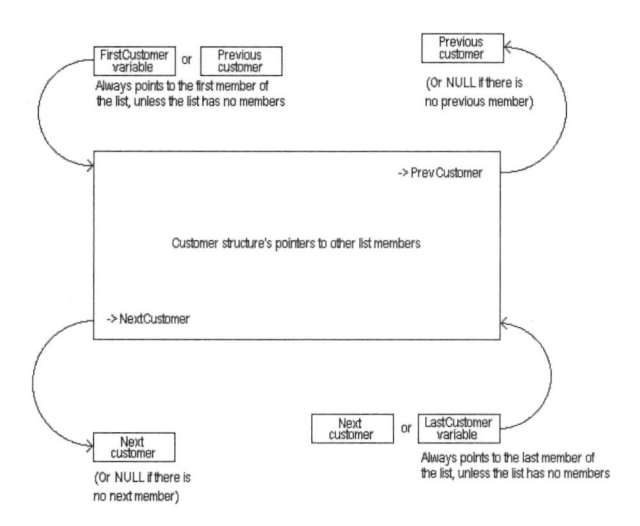

Figure 10.5. The CUSTOMER structure's linked list pointers.

You can perform a trick with a double linked list. When you add a member to a double linked list, the program can examine the key fields of the first and last members to determine whether the list should be traveled from the beginning or the end. This increases the program's performance. (It doesn't make sense to start at the first member if the new member will be added near the end of the list.)

Listing 10.4, the LINKLIST.C program, demonstrates the use of a double linked list with dynamically allocated members. The program is simple, without much optimization. The program always has sorted access to the items in the list.

Listing 10.4. LINKLIST.C.

```
/*  LINKLIST, written 1992 by Peter D. Hipson
 *  A double linked list program. This program has
 *  better error checking than the CDB program.
 *  To improve the program, make the ZIP code field a
 *  character field. A character field is better for ZIP
 *  codes because many non-US ZIP codes also
 *  contain letters.
 */
```

continues

Listing 10.4. continued

```c
#include <string.h>
#include <ctype.h>
#include <stdio.h>
#include <process.h>
#include <stdlib.h>

#define TRUE               1
#define FALSE              (!TRUE)

#define INCREMENT_AMOUNT   1 /* Add one record at a time */

#define CUSTOMER_RECORD    1
#define SUPPLIER_RECORD    2

/* Define the structure for the customer database. */

struct  _CUSTNAME;

typedef struct  _CUSTNAME {
    int     nRecordType;   // 1 == Customer record.
    struct _CUSTNAME *NextCustomer; // Link to next, or NULL if none
    struct _CUSTNAME *PrevCustomer; // Link to previous, or NULL if none
    char    szName[61];    // 60 chars for name; 1 for null at end
    char    szAddr1[61];   // 60 chars for address; 1 for null at end
    char    szAddr2[61];   // 60 chars for address; 1 for null at end
    char    szCity[26];    // 25 chars for city; 1 for null at end
    char    szState[3];    // 2-character state abbrev. plus null
    int     lZip;          // Print as %5.5ld for leading 0
    int     nRecordNumber; // Which record number?
    double  dSalesTotal;   // Amount the customer has purchased
    } CUSTNAME;

typedef CUSTNAME  near *NPCUSTNAME;
typedef CUSTNAME  *PCUSTNAME;

void    GiveHelp(void);

void    main()
```

```c
{

FILE      *DataFile;

PCUSTNAME    FirstCustomer = NULL;
PCUSTNAME    LastCustomer = NULL;
PCUSTNAME    Customer = NULL;
PCUSTNAME    TempCustomer = NULL;

char       szFileName[257];
char       szBuffer[257];

int        nNotDone = TRUE;
int        nRecord = 0;
int        nDebug = FALSE;
int        nNeedSaving = FALSE;

double     dSales = 0.0; /* Forces loading of floating-point support */

    printf("Please enter customer save file name: ");

    gets(szFileName);

    DataFile = fopen(szFileName, "wt");

    if (DataFile == NULL)
    {/* Test for file open. If the file can't be opened, exit with
      message. */
        printf("ERROR: File '%s' couldn't be opened.\n", szFileName);

        exit(4);
    }

    fclose(DataFile);

    printf("Demo of a linked list concepts\n"
        "\n"
        " Commands are:\n"
        "      A  -  Add a customer/supplier record.\n"
        "      D  -  Display current list.\n"
        "      X  -  Exit from program.\n"
```

continues

Listing 10.4. continued

```
            "      Z   -   Toggle debug mode.\n"
            "      ?   -   Display the command list."
            "      H   -   Display the command list."
            "      S   -   Save the list.\n"
        "\n"
        );

    nRecord = 0;

    while (nNotDone)
    {
        printf("Enter command (A, D+, D-, S)?");

        gets(szBuffer);

        switch(szBuffer[0])
        {
            case 'H': /* Give some help */
            case 'h':
            case '?':

                GiveHelp();

                break;

            case 'A': /* Add a record */
            case 'a':

                Customer = (PCUSTNAME)calloc(sizeof(CUSTNAME),
                    INCREMENT_AMOUNT);

                printf("Enter name %d: ", ++nRecord);
                gets(szBuffer);

                szBuffer[sizeof(Customer->szName) - 1] = '\0';
                strcpy(Customer->szName, szBuffer);

                if (strlen(Customer->szName) > 0)
                {/* Insert this record in the list, sorted by name. */
                    nNeedSaving = TRUE;
```

```
if (FirstCustomer == NULL)
{
    printf("It is first record \n");
    Customer->NextCustomer = NULL;
    Customer->PrevCustomer = NULL;

    FirstCustomer = Customer;
    LastCustomer = Customer;
    TempCustomer = NULL;
}
else
{
    TempCustomer = FirstCustomer;
}

while (TempCustomer)
{
    if (nDebug)
    {
        printf("TESTING FOR ADD: '%s' '%s'\n",
            Customer->szName,
            TempCustomer->szName);
    }

    if (strcmp(Customer->szName,
        TempCustomer->szName) < 0 ¦¦
        TempCustomer == LastCustomer)
    {
        if (strcmp(Customer->szName,
            TempCustomer->szName) < 0 &&
            TempCustomer == FirstCustomer)
        {
            if (nDebug)
            {
                printf("Assigning as first\n");
            }

            Customer->NextCustomer = FirstCustomer;
            FirstCustomer = Customer;
            Customer->PrevCustomer = NULL;
```

continues

Listing 10.4. continued

```
                    TempCustomer = Customer->NextCustomer;
                    TempCustomer->PrevCustomer = Customer;
                }
                else
                {
                    if (strcmp(Customer->szName,
                        TempCustomer->szName) > 0 &&
                        TempCustomer == LastCustomer)
                    {
                        if (nDebug)
                        {
                            printf("Assigning as last\n");
                        }

                        Customer->PrevCustomer =
                         LastCustomer;
                        LastCustomer = Customer;
                        Customer->NextCustomer = NULL;
                        TempCustomer = Customer-
                         >PrevCustomer;
                        TempCustomer->NextCustomer =
                        Customer;
                    }
                    else
                    {
                        if (nDebug)
                        {
                            printf("Assigning inside \
                                    list\n");
                        }

                        Customer->PrevCustomer =
                            TempCustomer->PrevCustomer;

                        Customer->NextCustomer =
                         TempCustomer;
                        TempCustomer->PrevCustomer =
                        Customer;
                        TempCustomer = Customer-
                         >PrevCustomer;
                        TempCustomer->NextCustomer =
                        Customer;
```

```
            }
        }

        TempCustomer = NULL;
    }
    else
    {
        TempCustomer = TempCustomer->NextCustomer;
    }
}

Customer->nRecordNumber = nRecord;

if (!nDebug)
{
    do
    {
        printf("Enter 1 for customer, 2 for supplier \
                ");
        gets(szBuffer);
        sscanf(szBuffer, "%d",   &Customer
        ->nRecordType);
    }
    while (Customer->nRecordType != CUSTOMER_RECORD
    &&
        Customer->nRecordType != SUPPLIER_RECORD);

    printf("Enter address line 1: ");
    gets(szBuffer);
    szBuffer[sizeof(Customer->szAddr1) - 1] = '\0';
    strcpy(Customer->szAddr1, szBuffer);

    printf("Enter address line 2: ");
    gets(szBuffer);
    szBuffer[sizeof(Customer->szAddr2) - 1] = '\0';
    strcpy(Customer->szAddr2, szBuffer);

    printf("Enter City: ");
    gets(szBuffer);
    szBuffer[sizeof(Customer->szCity) - 1] = '\0';
    strcpy(Customer->szCity, szBuffer);
```

continues

Listing 10.4. continued

```
                printf("Enter state postal abbreviation: ");
                gets(szBuffer);
                szBuffer[sizeof(Customer->szState) - 1] = '\0';
                strcpy(Customer->szState, szBuffer);

                printf("Enter ZIP code: ");
                gets(szBuffer);
                sscanf(szBuffer, "%ld",   &Customer->lZip);

                printf("Enter total sales: ");
                gets(szBuffer);
                sscanf(szBuffer, "%f",   &Customer->dSalesTotal);
            }
        }
        else
        {
            printf("\aSorry, name must not be blank!\n");
        }
        break;

    case 'Z': /* Debug mode toggle */
    case 'z':
        nDebug = !nDebug;
        break;

    case 'D': /* Display all records */
    case 'd':

        TempCustomer = FirstCustomer;

        printf("Display customers\n");

        while (TempCustomer)
        {
            if (nDebug)
            {
                printf(
                    "Name '%10s' Me %lp Next %lp Prev %lp\n",
                    TempCustomer->szName,
                    TempCustomer,
```

```
                    TempCustomer->NextCustomer,
                    TempCustomer->PrevCustomer);
        }
        else
        {
            printf(
                "Name '%10s' City '%10s' State '%2s' "
                "ZIP '%5.5ld'\n",
                TempCustomer->szName,
                TempCustomer->szCity,
                TempCustomer->szState,
                TempCustomer->lZip);
        }

        TempCustomer = TempCustomer->NextCustomer;
    }
    break;

case 'X': /* Exit; prompt for save if needed */
case 'x':

    nNotDone = FALSE;

    szBuffer[0] = '\0';

    while (nNeedSaving &&
        szBuffer[0] == '\0')
    {
        printf("\nSave the data? (y¦n)");

        gets(szBuffer);

        if (szBuffer[0] == 'n' ¦¦
            szBuffer[0] == 'N')
        {
            nNeedSaving = FALSE;
        }
        else
        {
            if (szBuffer[0] != 'y' &&
                szBuffer[0] != 'Y')
            {
```

continues

Listing 10.4. continued

```
                            printf("\nWrong answer, "
                                "please respond with 'y' or 'n'");

                            szBuffer[0] = '\0';
                        }
                    }
                }

            if (!nNeedSaving)
            {/* Do not need to save, so just exit */
                break;
            }

/*              Else fall through to save routines */

        case 'S': /* Save all records */
        case 's':

            printf("Saving customers\n");

            DataFile = fopen(szFileName, "wt");

            if (DataFile == NULL)
            {/* Test for file re-open; if file can't be opened, exit
             with message */
                printf("ERROR: File '%s' couldn't be opened.\n",
                    szFileName);

                exit(4);
            }

            TempCustomer = FirstCustomer;

            while (TempCustomer)
            {
                if (nDebug)
                {
                    fprintf(DataFile,
                        "Name '%10s' Me %lp Next %lp Prev %lp\n",
                        TempCustomer->szName,
```

```
                                TempCustomer,
                                TempCustomer->NextCustomer,
                                TempCustomer->PrevCustomer);
                    }
                    else
                    {
                        fprintf(DataFile,
                            "Name '%10s' City '%10s' State '%2s' "
                            "ZIP '%5.5ld'\n",
                            TempCustomer->szName,
                            TempCustomer->szCity,
                            TempCustomer->szState,
                            TempCustomer->lZip);
                    }

                    TempCustomer = TempCustomer->NextCustomer;
                }

                nNeedSaving = FALSE;

                fclose(DataFile);
                break;
        }
    }
}

void    GiveHelp()

{

    printf(
        "\n"
        "This program shows how a double linked list is created and\n"
        "used. It enables you to add records, display the list of\n"
        "records (which are always sorted by name), and save the\n"
        "list of records to the disk file.\n"
        "\n"
        "LINKLIST supports the following commands:\n");

    printf(
        "\n"
```

continues

Listing 10.4. continued

```
                "        A   -  Add a customer/supplier record.\n"
                "              Adds a record. Each added record is placed\n"
                "              in the list in the correct order. Added\n"
                "              records are sorted ·by name.\n");

    printf(
        "\n"
                "        D   -  Display current list.\n"
                "              Prints the current list of records in sorted\n"
                "              order. This list contains name and address\n"
                "              information or, in the debug mode, name and\n"
                "              pointer information.\n");

    printf(
        "\n"
                "        X   -  Exit from program.\n"
                "              Ends the program. If records have been added\n"
                "              and not saved, prompts for save. All saves\n"
                "              are made to the file specified when the\n"
                "              program was started.\n");

    printf(
        "\n"
                "        Z   -  Toggle debug mode.\n"
                "              Changes the information displayed for the\n"
                "              user. When on, debug mode shows where the newly\n"
                "              entered name is being placed in the list, and \
                              the\n"
                "              list pointers are displayed when a display command \
                              is\n"
                "              entered.\n");

    printf(
        "\n"
                "        ?   -  Display the command list.\n"
                "        H   -  Display the command list.\n"
                "              Displays this help information.\n");

    printf(
        "\n"
```

```
"    S   -  Save the list.\n"
"             Saves (to the specified save file) the current \
           list\n"
"             of records in sorted order. This list contains \
           name\n"
"             and address information or, in the debug mode,\n"
"             name and pointer information.\n"
"\n");


    printf(
        "Additional feature: This program includes a\n"
        "prompt to save when the exit command is given.\n"
        "This prompt is given only if the records have\n"
        "not been saved since the last added record.\n");

    printf(
        "Additional feature: This program has a debug mode so that\n"
        "the user can see how the program works. The debug mode \
         enables\n"
        "the user to print the linked list and its pointers.\n");


}
```

This program was developed from the CDB.C program, which was presented in Chapter 8, "Dynamic Memory Allocation." In this section, you look at the program, and the code that manages the linked list. First, in the following code fragment, is a nonspecific structure definition (yes, this is a definition, not a declaration) that creates the _CUSTNAME structure name:

```
struct _CUSTNAME;
```

This allows _CUSTNAME to be used in the declaration of the structure as a set of pointers, as the third and fourth lines in the following code show:

```
typedef struct _CUSTNAME {
    int     nRecordType;   // 1 == Customer record.
    struct _CUSTNAME *NextCustomer; // Link to next, or NULL if none
    struct _CUSTNAME *PrevCustomer; // Link to previous, or NULL if none
    char    szName[61];    // 60 chars for name; 1 for null at end
    char    szAddr1[61];   // 60 chars for address; 1 for null at end
```

```
char    szAddr2[61];    // 60 chars for address; 1 for null at end
char    szCity[26];     // 25 chars for city; 1 for null at end
char    szState[3];     // 2-character state abbrev. plus null
int     lZip;           // Print as %5.5ld for leading 0
int     nRecordNumber;  // Which record number?
double  dSalesTotal;    // Amount the customer has purchased
} CUSTNAME;
```

This section of the CUSTNAME structure declares members that point to the next member or the preceding member in the linked list.

The following code shows how the pointers to the first and last members in the linked list are defined:

```
PCUSTNAME    FirstCustomer = NULL;
PCUSTNAME    LastCustomer = NULL;
```

These lines could have been coded as

```
struct _CUSTNAME *FirstCustomer;
struct _CUSTNAME *LastCustomer;
```

I suggest that you use the pointer names defined (if you write your structure prototype as I do) when you create the typedef structure.

Next, a few pointers are created for the program to use when a member is created or inserted into the list:

```
PCUSTNAME    Customer = NULL;
PCUSTNAME    TempCustomer = NULL;
```

The next significant part of the program is the section for adding a record, which is called when the user enters the A command. First, the program allocates a block of memory to hold the CUSTNAME structure using calloc(), which initializes this memory to zero. (Remember, malloc() does not initialize memory.) After the memory has been allocated, the program prompts for the name to be added:

```
case 'A': /* Add a record */
case 'a':

    Customer = (PCUSTNAME)calloc(sizeof(CUSTNAME),
        INCREMENT_AMOUNT);

    printf("Enter name %d: ", ++nRecord);
    gets(szBuffer);
```

```
szBuffer[sizeof(Customer->szName) - 1] = '\0';
strcpy(Customer->szName, szBuffer);

if (strlen(Customer->szName) > 0)
```

If the user has entered a name (and not just pressed Return), this member must be added to the linked list. This program inserts members into the list in sorted order. Your program could insert members based on another criterion, for example, ZIP code or customer number.

Nothing prevents you from having two or more sets of links. You might have the list linked based on customer name, ZIP code, and customer number. Each additional key, however, slows the program's performance when a record is inserted and requires an additional two pointers for the customer structure (the preceding pointer and the next pointer). When you create a linked list with more than one set of links, simply treat each set of links as a separate linked list.

When a record is inserted into a linked list, there are four possible scenarios. One, the list might have nothing in it, and this is the initial member. Thus, both FirstCustomer and LastCustomer must be initialized to this member, as follows:

```
{/* Insert this record in the list, sorted by name. */
    nNeedSaving = TRUE;

    if (FirstCustomer == NULL)
    {
        printf("It is first record \n");
        Customer->NextCustomer = NULL;
        Customer->PrevCustomer = NULL;

        FirstCustomer = Customer;
        LastCustomer = Customer;
        TempCustomer = NULL;
    }
    else
    {
        TempCustomer = FirstCustomer;
    }
    while (TempCustomer)
    {
        if (nDebug)
        {
```

```
            printf("TESTING FOR ADD: '%s' '%s'\n",
                Customer->szName,
                TempCustomer->szName);
    }
```

If this is not the list's initial member, the program must go down the list searching for the correct insertion point. The record could be inserted in three places:

- At the beginning of the list, as the new first member.

- In the middle of the list.

- At the end of the list, as the last member.

Here is the code for inserting a member at the beginning of the list:

```
if (strcmp(Customer->szName,
    TempCustomer->szName) < 0 ||
    TempCustomer == LastCustomer)
{
    if (strcmp(Customer->szName,
        TempCustomer->szName) < 0 &&
        TempCustomer == FirstCustomer)
    {
        if (nDebug)
        {
            printf("Assigning as first\n");
        }

        Customer->NextCustomer = FirstCustomer;
        FirstCustomer = Customer;
        Customer->PrevCustomer = NULL;
        TempCustomer = Customer->NextCustomer;
        TempCustomer->PrevCustomer = Customer;
```

When the member will be the first member in the list, the program updates the FirstCustomer variable and the old first member. The FirstCustomer variable and the old first member's previous member pointer (->PrevCustomer) point to this new member. The new member's previous member pointer (->PrevCustomer) points to NULL, and the new member's next member pointer (->NextCustomer) points to the old first member (which has become the second member in the list).

In Figure 10.6, the bold lines show which pointers must be changed when a record is inserted in the beginning of the list. Compare this figure with Figure 10.4.

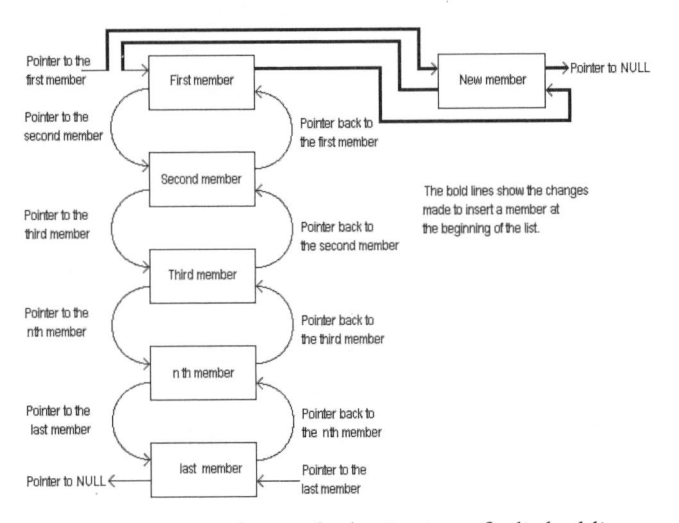

Figure 10.6. Inserting a new member at the beginning of a linked list.

When the member will be the last member in the list, the LastCustomer variable and the old last member must be updated:

```
}
else
{
    if (strcmp(Customer->szName,
        TempCustomer->szName) > 0 &&
        TempCustomer == LastCustomer)
    {
```

The LastCustomer variable and the old last member's next member pointer (->NextCustomer) will now point to the new member. The new member's next member pointer (->NextCustomer) will point to NULL, and the new member's previous member pointer (->PrevCustomer) will point to the old last member (which has become the next-to-last member in the list).

The bold lines in Figure 10.7 show which pointers must be changed when a record is inserted at the end of the list. Compare this figure with Figure 10.4.

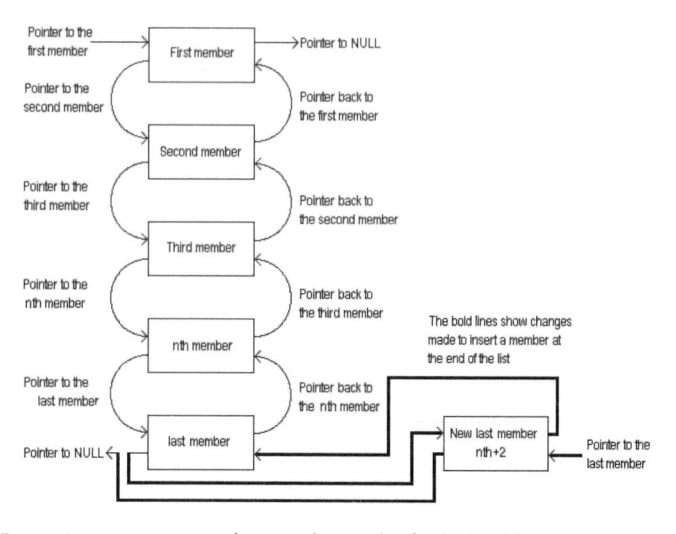

Figure 10.7. Inserting a new member at the end of a linked list.

The third insertion point is the middle of the list. Following is the code for inserting a member in the middle of the linked list:

```
if (nDebug)
{
    printf("Assigning as last\n");
}

Customer->PrevCustomer = LastCustomer;
LastCustomer = Customer;
Customer->NextCustomer = NULL;
TempCustomer = Customer->PrevCustomer;
TempCustomer->NextCustomer = Customer;
}
else
{
if (nDebug)
{
    printf("Assigning inside list\n");
}
```

The program must update what will be the previous customer's next member pointer (->NextCustomer) to point to the new member. The new member's prior member pointer (->PrevCustomer) will point to this previous customer member as

well. The program must also update what will be the next customer's prior member pointer (->PrevCustomer) to point to the new member. The new member's next member pointer (->NextCustomer) will point to this next customer member as well.

See Figure 10.8, which shows what is happening when a member is inserted into the middle of the list. The bold lines indicate which pointers must be changed when a record is inserted in the middle of the list. Compare this figure with Figure 10.4.

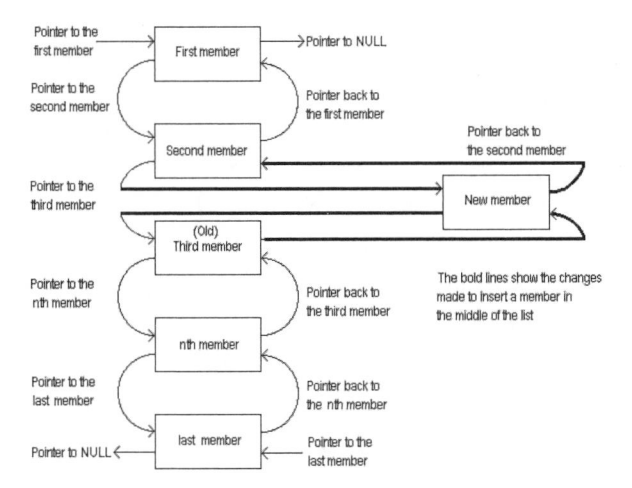

Figure 10.8. Inserting a new member in the middle of a linked list.

The user must provide the program with other information, such as the address, city, and state. The program can get this information after the record has been inserted into the list. (However, you could change the program so that the information is obtained before the record insertion.)

```
        Customer->PrevCustomer =
            TempCustomer->PrevCustomer;

        Customer->NextCustomer = TempCustomer;
        TempCustomer->PrevCustomer = Customer;
        TempCustomer = Customer->PrevCustomer;
        TempCustomer->NextCustomer = Customer;
    }
}
```

The code to display records in the list in sorted order is simple because the program maintains sorted links.

```
TempCustomer = FirstCustomer;

printf("Display customers\n");

while (TempCustomer)
{
    if (nDebug)
    {
        printf(
            "Name '%10s' Me %lp Next %lp Prev %lp\n",
            TempCustomer->szName,
            TempCustomer,
            TempCustomer->NextCustomer,
            TempCustomer->PrevCustomer);
    }
    else
    {
        printf(
            "Name '%10s' City '%10s' State '%2s' "
            "ZIP '%5.5d'\n",
            TempCustomer->szName,
            TempCustomer->szCity,
            TempCustomer->szState,
            TempCustomer->nZip);
    }

    TempCustomer = TempCustomer->NextCustomer;
}
break;
```

First, the program gets a pointer to the first member of the list and saves the pointer in FirstCustomer. When the first member of the linked list is obtained, it is displayed. The first member (and each following member, except the last one) has a pointer to the next member. The final member in the list has a pointer to NULL, which ends the while() loop. Just before the end of the while() loop, the pointer to the next customer record is assigned to TempCustomer. This allows the loop to display all the records.

The loop's output depends on the program's debug mode. In debug mode (used when the program is developed), the pointers are printed; otherwise, the names and addresses are printed.

With a linked list, it is easy to retrieve records in sorted order. Using multiple links, a program can retrieve records based on different criteria. A double linked list enables you to access the list in either forward order or backward order.

Linked lists do create a problem, however. The only way to access a specific member in the list is with a linear search. Because the list's members may be located randomly in memory, the only access you usually have to the list's members is to follow the chain of links. Therefore, finding a member in the middle of the list is not more efficient than finding a specific member in an unsorted list. Your program will know when the key field is greater than the member being tested, without searching the entire list. But you typically will be looking at approximately $n/2$ members (where n is the number of members in the list) to retrieve a specific member.

Indexing

Using an index to access data in a file is one way of gaining fast access to a large file of large data objects. Rarely can all of a user's data fit in memory at one time, so you must use a file as temporary or permanent storage.

With an index, the program's data is separated into two objects: the data and the index. The data is usually not arranged in a specific order; new records are added to the end of the block or the file. The index (there may be more than one index) is always sorted. It contains the minimum necessary to allow the program to access the data, typically a key value that the index is sorted on and a pointer to the corresponding data.

Figure 10.9 shows an indexed data file system that consists of a data file and two index files used to access the data. The records in this example are simple; many applications have thousands of bytes per record.

Each record in the data file is 183 bytes long. Each record contains a name, a company name, and an address that consists of the street, city, state, and ZIP code. The two index files are an index for the name field and an index for ZIP codes. Note that you cannot predict the order of records that do not have unique ZIP codes. In this example, either record with the ZIP code of 03468 could have been first.

The main factors for choosing an indexed data access system follow:

The main data file does not need to be sorted.

There can be more than one index, resulting in fast access to a given record.

Indexes can be created "on the fly," as the need arises.

The ZIP code index in Figure 10.9 has only 13 bytes per record. These short records can be sorted more quickly than the 183-byte records that make up the entire file.

The INDEX.C program in Listing 10.5 creates an indexed structure. This program writes records to a data file and retains an index array in memory. The array is then used to access the records.

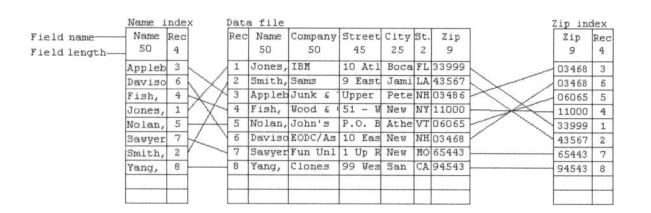

Figure 10.9. An indexed data file system.

Listing 10.5. INDEX.C.

```c
/*  INDEX, written 1992 by Peter D. Hipson
 *  This program shows indexed access to a file. It
 *  has better error checking than the CDB program in
 *  Chapter 8.
 */


#include <search.h>
#include <string.h>
#include <ctype.h>
#include <stdio.h>
#include <process.h>
#include <stdlib.h>


#define TRUE               1
#define FALSE              (!TRUE)


#define INCREMENT_AMOUNT   1 /* Add one record at a time */
#define INDEX_SIZE         400 /* Maximum number of records */


#define CUSTOMER_RECORD    1
#define SUPPLIER_RECORD    2
```

```
/* Define the structure for the customer database. */

struct  _CUSTNAME;

typedef struct  _CUSTNAME {
    int     nRecordType;    // 1 == Customer record
    struct  _CUSTNAME *NextCustomer; // Link to next, or NULL if none
    struct  _CUSTNAME *PrevCustomer; // Link to previous, or NULL if none
    char    szName[61];     // 60 chars for name; 1 for null at end
                            // In some cases, you would not need to
                            // duplicate this field in both the index and
                            // the record.
    char    szAddr1[61];    // 60 chars for address; 1 for null at end
    char    szAddr2[61];    // 60 chars for address; 1 for null at end
    char    szCity[26];     // 25 chars for city; 1 for null at end
    char    szState[3];     // 2-char state abbreviation plus null
    long    lZip;           // Use integer. Print as %5.5d for leading 0
    int     nRecordNumber;  // Which record number?
    double  dSalesTotal;    // Amount the customer has purchased
    } CUSTNAME;

typedef CUSTNAME  far   *FPCUSTNAME;
typedef CUSTNAME  near  *NPCUSTNAME;
typedef CUSTNAME        *PCUSTNAME;


typedef struct _INDEXREC {
    char    szName[61];     // 60 chars for name; 1 for null at end
    long    Customer;       // Pointer to customer record in file
    } CUSTINDEX;

typedef CUSTINDEX  far   *FPCUSTINDEX;
typedef CUSTINDEX  near  *NPCUSTINDEX;
typedef CUSTINDEX        *PCUSTINDEX;


void    GiveHelp(void);

int     compare(const void *, const void *);
```

continues

Listing 10.5. continued

```
void    main()

{

FILE        *DataFile;
FILE        *IndexFile;

PCUSTNAME   FirstCustomer = NULL;
PCUSTNAME   LastCustomer = NULL;
PCUSTNAME   Customer = NULL;
PCUSTNAME   TempCustomer = NULL;

PCUSTINDEX  CustIndex = NULL;
PCUSTINDEX  pTempCustIndex = NULL;
CUSTINDEX   TempCustIndex;

char        szIndexFile[257];
char        szDataFile[257];
char        szBuffer[257];
/* Strings for _splitpath(), which parses a file name */
char        szDrive[_MAX_DRIVE];
char        szDir[_MAX_DIR];
char        szFname[_MAX_FNAME];
char        szExt[_MAX_EXT];

int         i;
int         nDesiredRecord;
int         nNotDone = TRUE;
int         nRecord = 0;
int         nDebug = FALSE;
int         nNeedSaving = FALSE;

long        lFilePosition;

double      dSales = 0.0; /* Forces the loading of floating-point support
                            */
```

```
CustIndex = (PCUSTINDEX)calloc(sizeof(CUSTINDEX), INDEX_SIZE);

if (CustIndex == NULL)
{
    fprintf(stderr, "Couldn't allocate necessary index memory!\n");
    exit(16);
}

memset(CustIndex, 0, sizeof(CUSTINDEX));

Customer = (PCUSTNAME)calloc(sizeof(CUSTNAME), INCREMENT_AMOUNT);

if (Customer == NULL)
{
    fprintf(stderr, "Couldn't allocate necessary record memory!\n");
    exit(16);
}

printf(
    "Please enter customer save file name-\n"
    "Extensions of .DAT and .IND will be used: ");

gets(szBuffer);

_splitpath(szBuffer,
    szDrive,
    szDir,
    szFname,
    szExt);

strcpy(szIndexFile, szDrive);
strcat(szIndexFile, szDir);
strcat(szIndexFile, szFname);
strcat(szIndexFile, ".IND");

strcpy(szDataFile, szDrive);
strcat(szDataFile, szDir);
strcat(szDataFile, szFname);
strcat(szDataFile, ".DAT");
```

continues

Listing 10.5. continued

```
DataFile = fopen(szDataFile, "wb");

if (DataFile == NULL)
{/* Test for file open. If file can't be opened, exit with message.
 */
    printf("ERROR: Data file '%s' couldn't be opened.\n",
    szDataFile);

    exit(4);
}

fclose(DataFile);

IndexFile = fopen(szIndexFile, "wb");

if (IndexFile == NULL)
{/* Test for file open. If file can't be opened, exit with message.
 */
    printf("ERROR: Index file '%s' couldn't be opened.\n",
    szIndexFile);

    exit(4);
}

fclose(IndexFile);

printf("Demo of an indexed file/array.\n"
    "\n"
    " Commands are:\n"
    "       A   -  Add a customer/supplier record.\n"
    "       D   -  Display current list (from file).\n"
    "       X   -  Exit from program.\n"
    "       Z   -  Toggle debug mode.\n"
    "       ?   -  Display the command list.\n"
    "       H   -  Display the command list.\n"
    "\n"
    );

nRecord = -1;
```

```
while (nNotDone)
{
    printf("Enter command?");

    gets(szBuffer);

    switch(szBuffer[0])
    {
        case 'H': /* Give some help */
        case 'h':
        case '?':

            GiveHelp();

            break;

        case 'A': /* Add a record */
        case 'a':

            memset(Customer, 0, sizeof(CUSTNAME));

            printf("Enter name %d: ", ++nRecord);
            gets(szBuffer);

            szBuffer[sizeof(Customer->szName) - 1] = '\0';
            strcpy(Customer->szName, szBuffer);

            if (strlen(Customer->szName) > 0)
            {/* Insert this record in the list, sorted by name. */
                nNeedSaving = TRUE;

//              Add to file and index:

                Customer->nRecordNumber = nRecord;

                if (!nDebug)
                {
                    do
                    {
                        printf("Enter 1 for customer, 2 for supplier \
                            ");
```

continues

373

Listing 10.5. continued

```
                    gets(szBuffer);
                    sscanf(szBuffer, "%d",   &Customer-
                    >nRecordType);
        }
        while (Customer->nRecordType != CUSTOMER_RECORD
        &&
            Customer->nRecordType != SUPPLIER_RECORD);

        printf("Enter address line 1: ");
        gets(szBuffer);
        szBuffer[sizeof(Customer->szAddr1) - 1] = '\0';
        strcpy(Customer->szAddr1, szBuffer);

        printf("Enter address line 2: ");
        gets(szBuffer);
        szBuffer[sizeof(Customer->szAddr2) - 1] = '\0';
        strcpy(Customer->szAddr2, szBuffer);

        printf("Enter City: ");
        gets(szBuffer);
        szBuffer[sizeof(Customer->szCity) - 1] = '\0';
        strcpy(Customer->szCity, szBuffer);

        printf("Enter state postal abbreviation: ");
        gets(szBuffer);
        szBuffer[sizeof(Customer->szState) - 1] = '\0';
        strcpy(Customer->szState, szBuffer);

        printf("Enter ZIP code: ");
        gets(szBuffer);
        sscanf(szBuffer, "%d",   &Customer->nZip);

        printf("Enter total sales: ");
        gets(szBuffer);
        sscanf(szBuffer, "%f",   &Customer->dSalesTotal);
    }

    DataFile = fopen(szDataFile, "ab");

    if (DataFile == NULL)
    {
```

```c
                    printf(
                        "ERROR: Data file '%s' couldn't be "
                        "opened for update.\n",
                        szDataFile);

                    exit(4);
                }

                fseek(DataFile, 0, SEEK_END);

                CustIndex[nRecord].Customer = ftell(DataFile);
                strcpy(CustIndex[nRecord].szName, Customer->szName);

                printf("Index    %d '%s' is at '%ld'\n",
                    nRecord,
                    CustIndex[nRecord].szName,
                    CustIndex[nRecord].Customer);

                fwrite(Customer, sizeof(CUSTNAME), 1, DataFile);

                fclose(DataFile);
            }
            else
            {
                printf("\aSorry, name must not be blank!\n");
            }
            break;

        case 'Z': /* Debug mode toggle */
        case 'z':
            nDebug = !nDebug;
            break;

        case 'D': /* Display a record */
        case 'd':

            printf("Display customer (total %d).\n", nRecord + 1);

            qsort(CustIndex,
                nRecord + 1,
                sizeof(CUSTINDEX),
                compare);
```

continues

Listing 10.5. continued

```c
for (i = 0; nDebug && i <= nRecord; i++)

{/* In debug mode, display the sorted index list. */
    printf("Record %2d szName '%s'\n",
        i,
        CustIndex[i].szName);
}

memset(Customer, 0, sizeof(CUSTNAME));
memset(&TempCustIndex, 0, sizeof(CUSTINDEX));

printf("Enter name");
gets(TempCustIndex.szName);

printf("Searching with a linear search\n");

nDesiredRecord = -1;

for (i = 0; i <= nRecord; i++)
{/* Linear search; could be bsearch() */
    if (stricmp(TempCustIndex.szName,
        CustIndex[i].szName) == 0)
    {
        nDesiredRecord = i;
        break;
    }
}

if (nDesiredRecord >= 0)
{
    DataFile = fopen(szDataFile, "rb");

    if (DataFile == NULL)
    {
        printf(
            "ERROR: Data file '%s' couldn't be  \
             opened.\n",
            szDataFile);
```

```
            exit(4);
        }

    fseek(DataFile,
        CustIndex[nDesiredRecord].Customer, SEEK_SET);

    fread(Customer, sizeof(CUSTNAME), 1, DataFile);

    printf(
        "Name '%10s' City '%10s' State '%2s' "
        "ZIP '%5.5d'\n",
        Customer->szName,
        Customer->szCity,
        Customer->szState,
        Customer->nZip);

    fclose(DataFile);
}
else
{
    printf("LINEAR SEARCH: Sorry, the name '%s' couldn't \
            be found\n",
        TempCustIndex.szName);
}

printf("Searching with a binary search\n");

if ((pTempCustIndex = (PCUSTINDEX)bsearch(&TempCustIndex,
    CustIndex,
    nRecord + 1,
    sizeof(CUSTINDEX),
    compare)) != NULL)
{
    DataFile = fopen(szDataFile, "rb");

    if (DataFile == NULL)
    {
        printf(
            "ERROR: Data file '%s' couldn't be \
            opened.\n",
            szDataFile);
```

continues

Listing 10.5. continued

```
                    exit(4);
            }

            fseek(DataFile,
                pTempCustIndex->Customer, SEEK_SET);

            fread(Customer, sizeof(CUSTNAME), 1, DataFile);

            printf(
                "Name '%10s' City '%10s' State '%2s' "
                "ZIP '%5.5d'\n",
                Customer->szName,
                Customer->szCity,
                Customer->szState,
                Customer->nZip);

            fclose(DataFile);
        }
        else
        {
            printf("BSEARCH: Sorry, the name '%s' couldn't be \
                    found\n",
                TempCustIndex.szName);
        }

        break;

    case 'X': /* Exit; prompt for save if needed. */
    case 'x':

        nNotDone = FALSE;

        szBuffer[0] = '\0';

        while (nNeedSaving &&
            szBuffer[0] == '\0')
        {
            printf("\nSave the data? (y¦n)");
```

```
        gets(szBuffer);

        if (szBuffer[0] == 'n' ||
            szBuffer[0] == 'N')
        {
            nNeedSaving = FALSE;
        }
        else
        {
            if (szBuffer[0] != 'y' &&
                szBuffer[0] != 'Y')
            {
                printf("\nWrong answer, "
                    "please respond with 'y' or 'n'");

                szBuffer[0] = '\0';
            }
        }
    }

    if (!nNeedSaving)
    {/* Don't need to save, so just exit */
        break;
    }

/*          Else fall through to the save routines */

case 'S': /* Save all records */
case 's':

    printf("Saving customer index file.\n");

    IndexFile = fopen(szIndexFile, "wb");

    if (IndexFile == NULL)
    {/* Test for file open. If file can't be opened, exit
     with message. */
        printf("ERROR: Index file '%s' couldn't be \
                opened.\n",
            szIndexFile);
```

continues

379

Listing 10.5. continued

```
                }
                else
                {
                    fwrite(CustIndex,
                        sizeof(CUSTINDEX) * (nRecord + 1),
                        1,
                        IndexFile);

                    fclose(IndexFile);

                    nNeedSaving = FALSE;
                }
                break;

            default:
                printf("\aUnknown operation '%c'\n",
                    szBuffer[0]);
                break;

        }
    }
}


int     compare(
    PCUSTINDEX CustIndex1,
    PCUSTINDEX CustIndex2)

{

//    Uncomment the following printf() to see how qsort and qsearch work.
//
//    printf("Comparing %s and %s\n",
//        CustIndex1->szName,
//        CustIndex2->szName);

    return(stricmp(
        ((PCustIndex) CustIndex1)->szName,
        ((PCustIndex) CustIndex2)->szName));
}
```

```
void    GiveHelp()

{

    printf(
        "\n"
        "This program shows how an indexed file list is created and\n"
        "used. It enables you to add records, display a specified\n"
        "record, and save the list of records to the disk file.\n"
        "\n"
        "INDEX supports the following commands:\n");

    printf(
        "\n"
        "      A   -  Add a customer/supplier record.\n"
        "             Adds a record. Each added record is placed\n"
        "             in the list in the correct order.\n");

    printf(
        "\n"
        "      D   -  Display current list.\n"
        "             Prints the user-specified record. This\n"
        "             command lists the name and address\n"
        "             information, assuming the name has been found.\n");

    printf(
        "\n"
        "      X   -  Exit from program.\n"
        "             Ends the program. If records or the index have\n"
        "             not been saved, will prompt for save. All saves \
        are\n"
        "             made to the file specified when the program was \
        started.\n");

    printf(
        "\n"
        "      Z   -  Toggle debug mode.\n"
        "             Changes the information displayed for the\n"
        "             user. When on, debug mode shows the sorted\n"
        "             index list.\n");
```

continues

Listing 10.5. continued

```
printf(
    "\n"
    "    ?   -  Display the command list.\n"
    "    H   -  Display the command list.\n"
    "           Displays this help information.\n");

printf(
    "\n"
    "    S   -  Save the list.\n"
    "           If records and the index have not been saved, this \
option\n"
    "           saves the records the user has entered. All saves \
are made\n"
    "           to the file specified when the program was \
started.\n");

printf(
    "Additional feature: In this program includes a prompt\n"
    "to save when the exit command is given. (This prompt\n"
    "is given only when the records have not been saved since\n"
    "the last added record).\n");

printf(
    "Additional feature: This program has a debug mode so that\n"
    "the user can see how the program works. This debug mode \
allows\n"
    "the user to print the linked list and its pointers.\n");

}
```

First the CUSTNAME structure (which is identical to the structure used in many of the other example programs) is defined. Then an index on the customer's name is defined.

In general, the field you are indexing on should be unique (although this is not a requirement). When you use the index to retrieve records, a unique field ensures that only one name is returned for each requested search, which can make your program simpler because is does not have to process multiple matches.

The definition of the index structure follows:

```
typedef struct _INDEXREC {
    char    szName[61];    // 60 chars for name, 1 for null at end.
    long    Customer;      // Pointer to actual customer record in file.
    } CUSTINDEX;


typedef CUSTINDEX  far  *FPCUSTINDEX;
typedef CUSTINDEX  near *NPCUSTINDEX;
typedef CUSTINDEX       *PCUSTINDEX;
```

Pointers are defined for the structure, like any other typedef'd structure. A compare() function is also defined for use when sorting (and searching) the index. The advantage of an indexed file is that it is always sorted. However, you can avoid re-sorting the entire index when a record is added or an index field is changed. A typical trick is to retain the existing records in the sorted index, and when a record is added or changed, add it to a special area at the end of the index. If a binary search of the sorted portion of the index does not find the record, a linear search is used on the special section of nonsorted records. When the count of records in the unsorted section exceeds a predetermined value, the program re-sorts the index.

Linear Search Versus Binary Search

A linear search starts with the first record in the list or file, and reads each record until it finds a match to the key or the file ends. In a linear search, the list or file does not need to be sorted, and the records in the list do not have to be in any particular order.

A binary search proceeds as follows:

1. The binary search starts with the middle item in the list. If the key is less than the selected item, the binary search takes the item halfway between the current item and the beginning of the list. If the key is greater than the selected item, the binary search takes the item halfway between the current item and the end of the list. With one comparison, the binary search eliminates half of the file.

2. If the key is less than the item found in step 1, the half less than the item is selected. If the key is greater than the item found in step 1, the half that is

---

greater than the item is selected. Of this half, the middle item is then again selected.

3. This process is repeated until a match is found or it is shown that the key is not part of the list.

For example, suppose the key (the item you want to find) is 5. Your list contains the following numbers: 1, 2, 5, 12, 23, 24, 34, 35, 38, 45, 47, 50, 60, 65, 66, 76, 78, and 80. The first selection is 38 (the middle item in the list). Because 5 is less than 38, the next selection is 23, (halfway between 1 and 38). Because 5 is smaller than 23, the next selection is 5 (halfway between 1 and 23). This is a match, so the search stops.

The maximum number of comparisons with a binary search is small—in a file of 65,000 items, at most only 16 comparisons must be made. With a linear search, an average of 32,000 comparisons are required.

The winner? A binary search is always the winner when the list can be (or is) sorted. If the list cannot be sorted, a linear search must be performed.

Fortunately, the C compiler provides a binary search function called bsearch(). This function requires a sorted list and the address of a compare function. The bsearch() and bsort() functions use the same compare function, so that only one compare function needs to be written when using either bsearch() or bsort(). In our sorting and searching, we are working with an array of index records, and these index records are what must be dealt with by the compare function. Because with bsort() and bsearch() the compare is passed the address of the array members, the compare function is defined as accepting two pointers to CUSTINDEX structures.

```
int    compare(const void *, const void*);
```

When the user wants to add a record to the customer database, the program first uses memset() to clear the Customer structure. It then prompts for the name. If the user enters a name, the program processes it.

The code for adding a record follows:

```
case 'A': /* Add a record */
case 'a':
```

```
            memset(Customer, 0, sizeof(CUSTNAME));

            printf("Enter name %d: ", ++nRecord);
            gets(szBuffer);

            szBuffer[sizeof(Customer->szName) - 1] = '\0';
            strcpy(Customer->szName, szBuffer);

            if (strlen(Customer->szName) > 0)
            {/* Insert this record in the list, sorted by name. */
                nNeedSaving = TRUE;

//              Add to file and index:

                Customer->nRecordNumber = nRecord;
```

To add the record to the database, the program first opens the database file. The file is closed when it is not in use so that the database is as safe as possible if the computer fails. If you do not close files in your program, you should at least call fflush() after every write to the file.

The file is opened in the append mode so that existing records are not lost. If the file were opened in the write mode, the operating system would delete the contents of the file.

```
DataFile = fopen(szDataFile, "ab");

if (DataFile == NULL)
{
    printf(
        "ERROR: Data file '%s' couldn't be "
        "opened for update.\n",
        szDataFile);

    exit(4);
}
```

After the file is opened, the program goes to the end of the file:

```
fseek(DataFile, 0, SEEK_END);
```

The ftell() function returns the current file pointer for the record that will be added. This value is assigned to the index array's pointer to this record. Next, strcpy() copies the key into the index array:

```
CustIndex[nRecord].Customer = ftell(DataFile);
strcpy(CustIndex[nRecord].szName, Customer->szName);
```

After the index has been set up, the program writes the record to the database and closes the file:

```
fwrite(Customer, sizeof(CUSTNAME), 1, DataFile);

fclose(DataFile);
```

When the user requests a record, the program searches for the record using both a linear search and the bsearch() function. I used both search techniques in Listing 10.5 simply to show how they are implemented; your program should use one or the other (probably bsearch() because it is easy to implement and fast).

To use a binary search, the index must be sorted. When the user wants the names displayed, the program sorts the index list. The programmer can choose to sort the index either as names are added (which slows the process of adding names) or when the sorted index list is used. This program would have been better if it included a flag to indicate when the list was already sorted.

The following code shows how a record is retrieved and displayed:

```
case 'D': /* Display a record */
case 'd':

    printf("Display customer (total %d).\n", nRecord + 1);

    qsort(CustIndex,
        nRecord + 1,
        sizeof(CUSTINDEX),
        compare);

    for (i = 0; nDebug && i <= nRecord; i++)
    {/* In debug mode, display the sorted index list. */
        printf("Record %2d szName '%s'\n",
            i,
            CustIndex[i].szName);
    }
```

In the debug mode, the program first shows the programmer the index list. This display is useful when you want to see the results of the sort.

386

Following the display of the index list, the user is prompted to provide a name to search for:

```
memset(Customer, 0, sizeof(CUSTNAME));
memset(&TempCustIndex, 0, sizeof(CUSTINDEX));

printf("Enter name");
gets(TempCustIndex.szName);

printf("Searching with a linear search\n");
```

After the user enters a name, the program does a linear search. This search starts at the first name, then searches each name in order, until either the list ends or the name is found:

```
nDesiredRecord = -1;

for (i = 0; i <= nRecord; i++)
{/* Linear search; could be bsearch() */
    if (stricmp(TempCustIndex.szName,
        CustIndex[i].szName) == 0)
    {
        nDesiredRecord = i;
        break;
    }
}
```

If the supplied key name is found, the program opens the database file (read mode) and uses fseek() to find the correct record. After finding the record, the program reads it in and displays the information for the user. If the supplied key name is not found, the program simply gives the user a message that the name wasn't found.

```
if (nDesiredRecord >= 0)
{
    DataFile = fopen(szDataFile, "rb");

    if (DataFile == NULL)
    {
        printf(
            "ERROR: Data file '%s' couldn't be opened.\n",
            szDataFile);
```

```
        exit(4);
    }

    fseek(DataFile,
        CustIndex[nDesiredRecord].Customer, SEEK_SET);

    fread(Customer, sizeof(CUSTNAME), 1, DataFile);

    printf(
        "Name '%10s' City '%10s' State '%2s' "
        "ZIP '%5.5d'\n",
        Customer->szName,
        Customer->szCity,
        Customer->szState,
        Customer->nZip);

        fclose(DataFile);
    }
    else
    {
        printf("LINEAR SEARCH: Sorry, the name '%s' couldn't be found\n",
            TempCustIndex.szName);
    }
```

After the linear search is finished, the program does a binary search. This search is performed with one statement:

```
if ((pTempCustIndex = (PCUSTINDEX)bsearch(&TempCustIndex,
    CustIndex,
    nRecord + 1,
    sizeof(CUSTINDEX),
    compare)) != NULL)
{
```

If the supplied key name is found, the program opens the database file (read mode) and use fseek() to find the correct record. After seeking to the record, the program reads it in and displays the information for the user. If the supplied key name is not found, the program displays a message that the name wasn't found.

```
DataFile = fopen(szDataFile, "rb");

if (DataFile == NULL)
{
```

```
        printf(
            "ERROR: Data file '%s' couldn't be opened.\n",
            szDataFile);

        exit(4);
    }


    fseek(DataFile,
        pTempCustIndex->Customer, SEEK_SET);


    fread(Customer, sizeof(CUSTNAME), 1, DataFile);


    printf(
        "Name '%10s' City '%10s' State '%2s' "
        "ZIP '%5.5d'\n",
        Customer->szName,
        Customer->szCity,
        Customer->szState,
        Customer->nZip);


    fclose(DataFile);
    }
    else
    {
        printf("BSEARCH: Sorry, the name '%s' couldn't be found\n",
            TempCustIndex.szName);
    }


break;
```

When the program ends (or when the user requests a save), the index array is
saved to a file. The index array in the saved file could be re-read into the index array
later when the user reuses the data file. To conserve on disk space, the program writes
only the index entries that have been used, not the entire index array.

```
case 'S': /* Save all records */
case 's':

    printf("Saving customer index file.\n");

    IndexFile = fopen(szIndexFile, "wb");
```

```
        if (IndexFile == NULL)
        {/* Test for file open. If file can't be opened, exit with message.
         */
            printf("ERROR: Index file '%s' couldn't be opened.\n",
                szIndexFile);
        }
        else
        {
            fwrite(CustIndex,
                sizeof(CUSTINDEX) * (nRecord + 1),
                1,
                IndexFile);
            fclose(IndexFile);

            nNeedSaving = FALSE;
```

A quick look at the compare function shows that the szName members of the index array are being compared using stricmp(). I have included a (commented out) printf() that shows how the sort and the search use the compare function.

```
int     compare(
    PCUSTINDEX CustIndex1,
    PCUSTINDEX CustIndex2)

{

//    Uncomment the following printf() to see how qsort and qsearch work.
//
//    printf("Comparing %s and %s\n",
//        CustIndex1->szName,
//        CustIndex2->szName);

    return(stricmp(
        CustIndex1->szName,
        CustIndex2->szName));
}
```

Indexes can reside permanently in a disk file. The index for large databases can be much too large to fit into memory. To search a disk-based index, you must write a binary search function. Typically, such a function would know—by a global variable or a passed parameter—the number of records in the index, the size of the index records, and the index file's name or file handle.

Your disk-based bsearch function would then read the middle record. Compute this record's position using an fseek(). For example:

```c
/*  The code assumes that more than one record is in
 *  the index file.
 */


long    lFirstRecord = 0;
long    lLastRecord = lTotalRecords;
long    lCurrentRecord = ((lLastRecord - lFirstRecord) / 2);
long    lOffset = lLastRecord - lFirstRecord;

    while(lOffset > 0)
    {
        lCurrentRecord = ((lLastRecord - lFirstRecord) / 2);

        fseek(IndexFile, lCurrentRecord *
            sizeof(CUSTINDEX) * (lCurrentRecord), SEEK_SET);

//      Read the record into Index (not shown)

        if (Key < Index) /* This compare depends on Key's data type */
        {
            lLastRecord = lCurrentRecord;
        }

        if (Key > Index) /* This compare depends on Key's data type */
        {
            lFirstRecord = lCurrentRecord;
        }

        if (Index == Key) /* This compare depends on Key's data type */
        {
            return(lCurrentRecord);
        }

        lTotalRecords = lLastRecord - lFirstRecord;
        lOffset = lLastRecord - lFirstRecord;

    }
```

```
/*  The record was not found! */

    return (-1);
```

This binary search function is simplified. I did not show the reading of the index file, nor are the compares accurate because they assume that Index and Key are numeric, which may not be true.

Indexing a file can greatly enhance the access to specific records, especially when a record must be accessed using more than one key (or index) value.

Fixed-field Disk Files

The best examples of fixed-field disk files are files created using a structure. Because the structure's length is fixed and each member's location is known, you can always determine the location of any structure and its members in the file.

I recommend reading a file written with a structure into an identical structure. After the data is placed in the structure, you can work on it using the individual structure members. A possible exception to the reading of individual records is when a large block of the file is read into a structure array, and the array is searched for the correct key or another data object.

Many of the example programs write fixed-field files. For example, the INDEX.C program (Listing 10.5) creates two fixed-field files.

B-trees

None of the data management techniques in this chapter have addressed the problem of a data list that changes frequently, must be searched quickly, and is too large to constantly re-sort. Some problems with the techniques covered so far include:

- A linked list presents data that appears to be sorted, but the list can be searched only with a linear search.

- An indexed list is easy to search, but it must be resorted when an index value is added, deleted, or changed.

The solution is to use the B-tree technique, a different method of storing data. The B-tree technique arranges data in a structured format. Figure 10.10 shows some

sample data (used also in the "Linear Search Versus Binary Search" sidebar), and its organization in a B-tree.

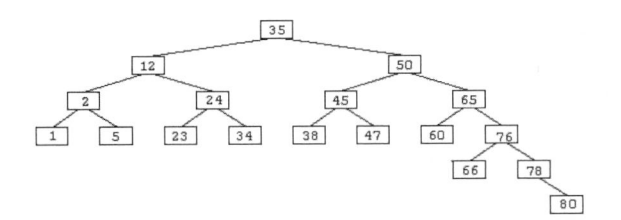

Figure 10.10. A B-tree's organization.

Data organization in a B-tree resembles an upside down tree. Usually, the first data object has a key that half of the remaining data keys are less than (called the left side) and the other half of the data keys are greater than (called the right side). The tree continues in the same manner for all remaining data objects.

The following terms are used when discussing B-trees:

Node	A data item in a B-tree.
Root node	The first node in a B-tree.
Left side	Data items on the left side are less than the current data item.
Right side	Data items on the right side are greater than the current data item.
Balance	How well the tree is organized. (Most B-trees exhibit some imbalance.)

Figure 10.11 shows these terms and their relationships.

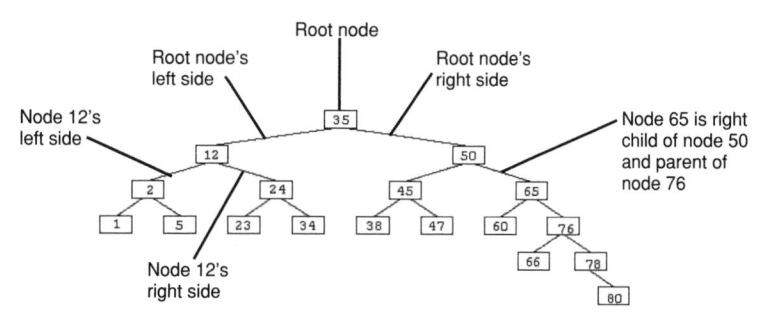

Figure 10.11. B-tree terms and relationships.

B-trees present some problems to the programmer, such as the following:

As records are added to the tree, it must be reorganized to ensure that each node has a balanced number of data objects on its right and left sides.

When a B-tree member is changed or deleted, the tree must be reorganized to eliminate the hole that is created. This reorganization can be complete, which rebalances the tree, or partial, which may create a dummy member to take the place of the missing member.

When sorted data objects are added to the B-tree, the tree's balance suffers unless the tree is reorganized.

When programming a B-tree implementation from scratch, you must have the following functionality:

`AddRecord()`	Adds a record to the B-tree. If a record with the key being added exists, you must decide what action to take: add the record as a duplicate record, have and increment an occurrence counter, or do not add the duplicate record.
`DeleteRecord()`	Deletes a record in the B-tree. The B-tree must be reorganized, or a dummy record must be inserted to replace the deleted record. Using a dummy record usually implies that there is a deleted flag field.

| SearchRecord() | Searches for a key value and returns the information necessary to access the record. This function could return the record structure if desired. |
| PrintTree() | Debugging tool. This function is needed if you are creating your own B-tree functions, but is normally not used in a final program. |

There are a number of supporting functions as well. These functions are not always present in any specific B-tree implementation.

Listing 10.6, the BTREE.C program, implements a basic B-tree structure. The program contains the following functions:

Search()	Finds a record in the B-tree.
SearchAndAdd()	Finds a record in the B-tree; if the key does not exist, the record is added.
Insert()	Inserts a record into the B-tree.
CopyItem()	Copies a node to another node.
NewItem()	Creates a new node.
TreePrint()	Prints the current tree.
DeleteItem()	Deletes a node from the current B-tree.
UnderFlow()	Used by DeleteItem() to adjust the B-tree when an item has been deleted.
Delete()	Used by DeleteItem() to delete items from the B-tree.
PrintHelp()	Prints a help screen.

Listing 10.6. BTREE.C.

```
/*  BTREE.C
 *  This is a simple B-tree program. It should be compiled
 *  under ANSI C.
 *  [BTREE.C of JUGPDS Vol.19]
 */
```

continues

Listing 10.6. continued

```c
#include <stdlib.h>     // For standard functions
#include <stdio.h>      // Make includes first part of file
#include <string.h>     // For string functions
#include <process.h>    // For exit(), etc.
#include <malloc.h>     // For malloc(), calloc(), realloc(), free()
#include <search.h>     // For qsort()
#include <time.h>       // To initialize the random-number functions


/*  B-tree search and add, find, and delete
 *  Adapted from
 *     ALGORITHMS+DATA STRUCTURES=PROGRAMS by N. Wirth
 *
 *  Implemented for BDS  C by H. Katayose (JUG-CP/M No.179)
 *  Implemented for ANSI C by P. Hipson    (CUG)
 */

/* PAGE_SIZE is better at 8 (less memory fragmentation) */

#define PAGE_SIZE        2
#define HALF_PAGE_SIZE   (PAGE_SIZE / 2)

#define PAGE             struct _page
#define ITEM             struct _item

#define ROOT     0
#define RIGHT    1
#define LEFT     2

#define TRUE     (1)
#define FALSE    (0)

/* Storage allocation structures used by malloc() */

struct _header
{
    struct  _header     *_ptr;
    unsigned            _size;
};
```

```
struct _header  _base;      /* Declare this external data to  */
struct _header  *_allocp;   /* be used by malloc() */


/* B-tree structures */

struct _item
{
    int     nKeyValue;
    PAGE    *RightReference;
    int     nCount;
};

struct _page
{
    int     nItemCount;
    PAGE    *LeftReference;
    ITEM    Item[PAGE_SIZE];
};

/* Function prototypes */

int     Search(int nKeyValue, int * nLevelCount, PAGE *a, ITEM *v);
int     SearchAndAdd(int nKeyValue, PAGE *a, ITEM *v);
int     Insert(PAGE *a, int  i, ITEM *u, ITEM *v);
int     CopyItem(ITEM *DestinationItem, ITEM *SourceItem);
int     NewItem(PAGE **Page);
int     TreePrint(PAGE *p, int l, int nRightLeft, int nPosition);
int     DeleteItem(int  nKeyValue, PAGE *a);
int     UnderFlow(PAGE *c, PAGE *a, int s);
int     Delete(PAGE *p, PAGE *a, int k);
void    PrintHelp(void);

/* The main program */

int main()

{

int     i;
int     j;
```

continues

Listing 10.6. continued

```
int     nKeyValue;
int     h;
int     nLevelCount = 0;

char    chOperation;
char    szCommand[132];

PAGE    *q;
PAGE    *root;
ITEM    u;


    printf("\n\nBTREE: Demo program for B-trees\n"
        "\n"
        "Command are:\n"
        "   A # - Adds key # (integer 0 - 32767).\n"
        "   D # - Deletes key # (integer 0 - 32767).\n"
        "   S # - Searches for key # (integer 0 - 32767).\n"
        "   R # - Adds # random keys (integer 0 - 2000).\n"
        "   H   - Prints a help screen.\n"
        "   T   - Prints the current B-tree structure.\n"
        "   X   - Exits, after a confirming prompt.\n\n");

    root = NULL;

    while (TRUE)
    {
        printf("\n\nCommand ?");

        gets(szCommand);

        sscanf(szCommand, "%c %d", &chOperation, &nKeyValue);

        switch(chOperation)
        {
            case 'h':
            case 'H':
                PrintHelp();
                break;
```

```
case 'r':
case 'R':
    printf("ADDING %d NODES\n", nKeyValue);

    srand((unsigned)time(NULL));

    if (nKeyValue > 2000)
    {
        nKeyValue = 2000;
    }

    for (i = 0; i < nKeyValue; i++)
    {
        j = rand();

        if (SearchAndAdd(j, root, &u))
        {
            q = root;
            NewItem(&root);
            root->nItemCount = 1;
            root->LeftReference = q;
            CopyItem(&root->Item[0], &u);
        }
    }

    TreePrint(root, 0, ROOT, 0);
    break;

case 's':
case 'S':
    nLevelCount = 0;

    if ((Search(nKeyValue, &nLevelCount, root, &u)))
    {
        printf("SEARCH KEY %d found by searching %d \
                levels\n",
            nKeyValue,
            nLevelCount);
    }
    else
    {
```

continues

Listing 10.6. continued

```c
            printf("SEARCH KEY %d NOT FOUND searching %d \
                    levels\n",
                nKeyValue,
                nLevelCount);
        }


        break;

    case 'a':
    case 'A':
        printf("ADD KEY %d\n", nKeyValue);

        if (SearchAndAdd(nKeyValue, root, &u))
        {
            q = root;
            NewItem(&root);
            root->nItemCount = 1;
            root->LeftReference = q;
            CopyItem(&root->Item[0], &u);
        }

        TreePrint(root, 0, ROOT, 0);

        break;

    case 't':
    case 'T':

        printf("PRINT TREE\n");

        TreePrint(root, 0, ROOT, 0);

        break;

    case 'd':
    case 'D':

        printf("DELETE KEY %d\n", nKeyValue);
```

```
            if (DeleteItem(nKeyValue, root))
            {
                if (root->nItemCount == 0)
                {
                    q = root;
                    root = q->LeftReference;
                }
            }

            TreePrint(root, 0, ROOT, 0);

            break;

        case 'x':
        case 'X':

            printf("Confirm exit, y¦n:");

            scanf("%c", &chOperation);

            if (chOperation == 'y' ¦¦
                chOperation == 'Y')
            {
                exit(0);
            }

            break;

        default:
            printf("\aUnknown operation '%c'\n",
                chOperation);
            break;
        }
    }

    return(0);
}

int Search(
    int     nKeyValue,
    int     *nLevelCount,
```

continues

Listing 10.6. continued

```
        PAGE    *a,
        ITEM    *v)


    {

    int     i;

    ITEM    u;

    //    printf("Search()...\n");

        if (a == NULL)
        {
            return(FALSE);
        }

        for (i = 0; i < a->nItemCount && nKeyValue > a->Item[i].nKeyValue;
            i++)
        {
            ;
        }

        if (nKeyValue == a->Item[i].nKeyValue && i < a->nItemCount)
        {
            return(TRUE);
        }
        else
        {
            ++(*nLevelCount);

            return(Search(nKeyValue, nLevelCount,
                i ? a->Item[i - 1].RightReference : a->LeftReference, &u));
        }
    }


    int SearchAndAdd(
        int nKeyValue,
        PAGE    *a,
        ITEM    *v)
```

```
{

int    i;

ITEM   u;

//    printf("SearchAndAdd()...\n");

    if (a == NULL)
    {
        v->nKeyValue = nKeyValue;
        v->nCount = 1;
        v->RightReference = NULL;
        return TRUE;
    }

    for (i = 0; i < a->nItemCount && nKeyValue > a->Item[i].nKeyValue;
        i++)
    {
        ;
    }

    if (nKeyValue == a->Item[i].nKeyValue && i < a->nItemCount)
    {
        a->Item[i].nCount++;
    }
    else
    {
        if (SearchAndAdd(nKeyValue,
            i ? a->Item[i - 1].RightReference : a->LeftReference, &u))
        {
            return (Insert(a, i, &u, v));
        }
    }

    return FALSE;
}


int Insert(
    PAGE    *a,
```

continues

Listing 10.6. continued

```
        int     i,
        ITEM    *u,
        ITEM    *v)


{

PAGE    *b;
int     j;
int     h;

//    printf("Insert()...\n");

    if (a->nItemCount < PAGE_SIZE)
    {
        for (j = a->nItemCount; j >= i + 1; j—)
        {
            CopyItem(&a->Item[j], &a->Item[j - 1]);
        }

        ++a->nItemCount;

        CopyItem(&a->Item[i], u);

        return(FALSE);
    }
    else
    {/* Page a is full. Split it and assign the emerging item to v. */

        NewItem(&b);

        if (i <= HALF_PAGE_SIZE)
        {
            if (i == HALF_PAGE_SIZE)
            {
                CopyItem(v, u);
            }
            else
            {
                CopyItem(v, &a->Item[HALF_PAGE_SIZE - 1]);
```

```
            for (j = HALF_PAGE_SIZE - 1; j >= i + 1; j--)
            {
                CopyItem(&a->Item[j], &a->Item[j - 1]);
            }

            CopyItem(&a->Item[i], u);
        }

        for (j = 0; j <= HALF_PAGE_SIZE - 1; j++)
        {
            CopyItem(&b->Item[j], &a->Item[j + HALF_PAGE_SIZE]);
        }
    }
    else
    {
        i -= HALF_PAGE_SIZE;
        CopyItem(v, &a->Item[HALF_PAGE_SIZE]);

        for (j = 0; j <= i - 2; j++)
        {
            CopyItem(&b->Item[j], &a->Item[j + HALF_PAGE_SIZE + 1]);
        }

        CopyItem(&b->Item[i - 1], u);

        for (j = i; j <= HALF_PAGE_SIZE - 1; j++)
        {
            CopyItem(&b->Item[j], &a->Item[j + HALF_PAGE_SIZE]);
        }
    }

    if (HALF_PAGE_SIZE == 0)
    {
        a->nItemCount = 1;
        b->nItemCount = 1;
    }
    else
    {
        a->nItemCount = HALF_PAGE_SIZE;
        b->nItemCount = HALF_PAGE_SIZE;
    }
```

continues

405

Listing 10.6. continued

```c
            b->LeftReference = v->RightReference;
            v->RightReference = b;
        }

        return(TRUE);
}


int CopyItem(
    ITEM    *DestinationItem,
    ITEM    *SourceItem)

{

//    printf("CopyItem()...\n");

    DestinationItem->nKeyValue      = SourceItem->nKeyValue;
    DestinationItem->RightReference = SourceItem->RightReference;
    DestinationItem->nCount         = SourceItem->nCount;

    return(0);
}


int NewItem(
    PAGE    **Page)

{

//    printf("NewItem()...\n");

    if ((*Page = (PAGE *)malloc(sizeof(**Page))) == NULL)
    {
        fprintf(stderr, "Couldn't allocate memory!\n");

        exit(16);
    }

/*  malloc() doesn't initialize storage, so we do. */
```

```c
        memset(*Page, 0, sizeof(**Page));

    return(0);
}


int TreePrint(
    PAGE    *Page,
    int     nLevel,
    int     nRightLeft,
    int     nPosition)
{

int     i;
int     j;

    if (Page != NULL)
    {
        for (i = 0; i < Page->nItemCount; i++)
        {
            switch(nRightLeft)
            {
                case ROOT: /* Should have only one root */
                    printf("\n");
                    printf("(ROOT   %2d) ", nLevel);
                    break;

                case LEFT: /* Happens all the time */
                    printf("(L %2d   %2d) ", nLevel, nPosition);
                    break;

                case RIGHT:/* Happens all the time */
                    printf("(R %2d   %2d) ", nLevel, nPosition);
                    break;

                default:   /* Should never happen */
                    printf("ERROR       ");
                    break;
            }
```

continues

407

Listing 10.6. continued

```c
                for (j = 0; j < nLevel; j++)
                {/* Adjust the starting column for the variable */
                    printf(".....");
                }


                printf("%5d \n", Page->Item[i].nKeyValue);


                if (Page->Item[i].RightReference != NULL)
                {
                    TreePrint(Page->Item[i].RightReference,
                        nLevel + 1, RIGHT, i + 1);
                }
            }

        if (Page->LeftReference != NULL)
        {
            TreePrint(Page->LeftReference, nLevel + 1, LEFT, 0);
        }
    }

    return(0);
}


int DeleteItem(
    int   nKeyValue,
    PAGE *a)

{

int     i;
int     k;
int     l;
int     r;

PAGE    *q;
```

```
//    printf("DeleteItem()...\n");

    if (a == NULL)
    {
        printf("Key is not in tree! Cannot delete this key.\n");
        return FALSE;
    }
    else
    {/* Binary array search */
        for (l = 0, r = a->nItemCount - 1; l <= r; )
        {
            k = (l + r) / 2;
            if (nKeyValue <= a->Item[k].nKeyValue)
            {
                r = k - 1;
            }
            if (nKeyValue >= a->Item[k].nKeyValue)
            {
                l = k + 1;
            }
        }

        q = (r == -1) ? a->LeftReference : a->Item[r].RightReference;

        if (l - r > 1)
        {/* Found; now delete Item[k] */
            if (q == NULL)
            {/* a is a terminal page    */
                -(a->nItemCount);

                for (i = k; i < a->nItemCount; i++)
                {
                    CopyItem(&a->Item[i], &a->Item[i + 1]);
                }

                return (a->nItemCount < HALF_PAGE_SIZE);
            }
            else
            {
                if (Delete(q, a, k))
                {
```

continues

Listing 10.6. continued

```c
                    return(UnderFlow(a, q, r));
                }
            }
        }
        else
        {
            if (DeleteItem(nKeyValue, q))
            {
                return UnderFlow(a, q, r);
            }
        }
    }
}


int UnderFlow(
    PAGE    *c,
    PAGE    *a,
    int     s)

{

PAGE    *b;

int     i;
int     k;
int     mb;
int     mc;

//    printf("UnderFlow()...\n");

    mc = c->nItemCount;

    if (s < mc - 1)
    {
        ++s;

        b = c->Item[s].RightReference;
        mb = b->nItemCount;
```

```
k = (mb - HALF_PAGE_SIZE + 1) / 2;

CopyItem(&a->Item[HALF_PAGE_SIZE - 1], &c->Item[s]);

a->Item[HALF_PAGE_SIZE - 1].RightReference = b->LeftReference;

if (k > 0)
{
    for(i = 0; i < k - 1; i++)
    {
        CopyItem(&a->Item[i + HALF_PAGE_SIZE], &b->Item[i]);
    }

    CopyItem(&c->Item[s], &b->Item[k - 1]);
    c->Item[s].RightReference = b;
    b->LeftReference = b->Item[k - 1].RightReference;
    mb -= k;

    for (i = 0; i < mb; i++)
    {
        CopyItem(&b->Item[i], &b->Item[i + k]);
    }

    b->nItemCount = mb;
    a->nItemCount = HALF_PAGE_SIZE - 1 + k;

    return(FALSE);
}
else
{
    for (i = 0; i <  HALF_PAGE_SIZE; i++)
    {
        CopyItem(&a->Item[i + HALF_PAGE_SIZE], &b->Item[i]);
    }

    for (i = s; i < mc; i++)
    {
        CopyItem(&c->Item[i], &c->Item[i + 1]);
    }
```

continues

Listing 10.6. continued

```
                    a->nItemCount = PAGE_SIZE;
                    c->nItemCount = mc - 1;
            }
    }
    else
    {
        b = (s == 0) ? c->LeftReference : c->Item[s - 1].RightReference;
        mb = b->nItemCount + 1;
        k = (mb - HALF_PAGE_SIZE) / 2;

        if (k > 0)
        {
            for(i = HALF_PAGE_SIZE - 2; i >= 0; i--)
            {
                CopyItem(&a->Item[i + k], &a->Item[i]);
            }

            CopyItem(&a->Item[k - 1], &c->Item[s]);
            a->Item[k - 1].RightReference = a->LeftReference;
            mb -= k;

            for (i = k - 2; i >= 0; i--)
            {
                CopyItem(&a->Item[i], &b->Item[i + mb]);
            }

            a->LeftReference = b->Item[mb].RightReference;
            CopyItem(&c->Item[s], &b->Item[mb - 1]);
            c->Item[s].RightReference = a;
            b->nItemCount = mb - 1;
            a->nItemCount = HALF_PAGE_SIZE - 1 + k;

            return(FALSE);
        }
        else
        {
            CopyItem(&b->Item[mb], &c->Item[s]);
            b->Item[mb].RightReference = a->LeftReference;
```

```
                for (i = 0; i < HALF_PAGE_SIZE - 1; i++)
                {
                    CopyItem(&b->Item[i + mb], &a->Item[i]);
                }

                b->nItemCount = PAGE_SIZE;
                c->nItemCount = mc - 1;
            }
        }

        return(TRUE);
    }


    int Delete(
        PAGE    *p,
        PAGE    *a,
        int     k)

    {
    PAGE    *q;

    //    printf("Delete()...\n");

        if ((q = p->Item[p->nItemCount - 1].RightReference)!= NULL)
        {
            if (Delete(q, a, k))
            {
                return(UnderFlow(p, q, p->nItemCount - 1));
            }
        }
        else
        {
            p->Item[p->nItemCount - 1].RightReference = a
            ->Item[k].RightReference;
            CopyItem(&a->Item[k], &p->Item[p->nItemCount - 1]);

            —(p->nItemCount);

            return(p->nItemCount < HALF_PAGE_SIZE);
        }
    }
```

continues

Listing 10.6. continued

```c
void PrintHelp()

{

    printf(
        "\n\nBTREE: Demo program for B-trees\n"
        "\n"
        "Command are:\n"
        "    A # - Adds key # (integer 0 - 32767).\n"
        "    D # - Deletes key # (integer 0 - 32767).\n"
        "    S # - Searches for key # (integer 0 - 32767).\n"
        "    R # - Adds # random keys (integer 0 - 2000).\n"
        "    H   - Prints a help screen.\n"
        "    T   - Prints the current B-tree structure.\n"
        "    X   - Exits, after a confirming prompt.\n\n");


    printf("\n"
        "All keys (the items that are placed in the tree) are \
        integers,\n"
        "ranging from 0 to 32767. Each item is added to the tree when \
        the\n"
        "Add command is issued.\n");

    printf("\n"
        "A new key is added with the Add command. Enter an A and an\n"
        "integer value.\n");

    printf("\n"
        "An existing key can be deleted by using the Delete command.\n"
        "Enter a D followed by an integer key value. If the value \
        entered\n"
        "is not a valid key, the program will tell you so.\n");

    printf("\n"
        "When you search for a key, the tree is traversed. If the key\n"
        "is found, the level where it was found is provided. If the \
        key\n"
        "is not found, a message is printed.\n");
```

```
        printf("\n"
            "The Repeat command is used to build a table of random keys. \
             The\n"
            "rand() function is called the specified number of times. No\n"
            "test for duplicates is made, but duplicates for random-number\n"
            "counts of less than several hundred are infrequent.\n");

        printf("\n"
            "To print the entire tree structure, use the Tree command. \
             This\n"
            "command is entered as a T. There are no parameters for "
            "this command.\n");

        printf("\n"
            "To end the program, use the Exit command. Enter an X, with no\n"
            "parameters. You will be prompted to confirm that you want to\n"
            "exit.\n");

        printf("\n"
            "If you don't enter the key (or count for Repeat), the \
             previous\n"
            "value for the count is used.\n");


}
```

The BTREE program arranges its tree in a way that you might not expect. The memory allocation functions could be called for each node, but this would be inefficient. Rather, each allocated block has from two to eight nodes. (You could have more than eight, but the B-tree's performance might suffer.) I chose a block that would contain two data items (or nodes).

```
/* PAGE_SIZE is better at 8 (less memory fragmentation).*/

#define PAGE_SIZE        2
#define HALF_PAGE_SIZE   (PAGE_SIZE / 2)
```

Three structures are created for the B-tree. First, a structure is created for the malloc() function:

```
/* Storage allocation structures used by malloc() */
```

```
struct _header
{
    struct  _header     *_ptr;
    unsigned            _size;
};

struct _header  _base;      /* Declare this external data to  */
struct _header  *_allocp;   /* be used by malloc() */
```

The next structure, called _item, contains information specific to each data item (node) in the B-tree. This is the structure that would contain your item-specific data, such as the node's key (this is an integer in the example program, but it could be a character string as well), a pointer to a structure containing the item's data, or an index into a file that would have the item's data.

```
struct  _item
{
    int     nKeyValue;
    PAGE    *RightReference;
    int     nCount;
};
```

The third structure, _page, forms the building block for the B-tree. This structure contains a count of items (from 1 to PAGE_SIZE), the block's left branch, and an array of PAGE_SIZE Items. The nItemCount variable indicates how many of the items are used.

```
struct  _page
{
    int     nItemCount;
    PAGE    *LeftReference;
    ITEM    Item[PAGE_SIZE];
};
```

The majority of BTREE.C's main function processes keyboard input. This code is similar to the code in other example programs, so this section describes only the three most important blocks. The first block is executed when the user searches for a record. The Search() function is called, and is passed parameters that include the key the user is searching for and the root node for the B-tree.

```
case 's':
case 'S':
    nLevelCount = 0;
```

```
if ((Search(nKeyValue, &nLevelCount, root, &u)))
{
    printf("SEARCH KEY %d found by searching %d levels\n",
        nKeyValue,
        nLevelCount);
}
else
{
    printf("SEARCH KEY %d NOT FOUND searching %d levels\n",
        nKeyValue,
        nLevelCount);
}

break;
```

The `SearchAndAdd()` function searches for the item. If the item cannot be found, `SearchAndAdd()` adds the user's key to the B-tree. This function returns TRUE if the item was not added because the B-tree does not exist yet. If the B-tree does not exist yet, the B-tree is created and the item is added as the root of the node.

```
case 'a':
case 'A':
    printf("ADD KEY %d\n", nKeyValue);

    if (SearchAndAdd(nKeyValue, root, &u))
    {
        q = root;
        NewItem(&root);
        root->nItemCount = 1;
        root->LeftReference = q;
        CopyItem(&root->Item[0], &u);
    }

    TreePrint(root, 0, ROOT, 0);

    break;
```

The `DeleteItem()` function is called when the user wants to delete a key. If the item being deleted is the current root, `DeleteItem()` returns TRUE, signaling that a new root must be created from another node.

```
case 'd':
case 'D':
```

```
        printf("DELETE KEY %d\n", nKeyValue);

        if (DeleteItem(nKeyValue, root))
        {
            if (root->nItemCount == 0)
            {
              q = root;
              root = q->LeftReference;
            }
        }

        TreePrint(root, 0, ROOT, 0);

        break;
```

Let's look at some of the functions that do the work in the BTREE program. The Search() function simply follows the tree, starting at the given node, until the specified key is found or it is known that the key is not in the B-tree. The Search() function works recursively: it calls itself each time it searches a node and does not find a match for the specified key. By calling itself, Search() can use a simple function to perform a search to any level:

```
int Search(
    int     nKeyValue,
    int     *nLevelCount,
    PAGE    *a,
    ITEM    *v)

{

int     i;

ITEM    u;

//    printf("Search()...\n");

    if (a == NULL)
    {
        return(FALSE);
    }

    for (i = 0; i < a->nItemCount && nKeyValue > a->Item[i].nKeyValue;
```

```
i++)
    {
        ;
    }

    if (nKeyValue == a->Item[i].nKeyValue && i < a->nItemCount)
    {
        return(TRUE);
    }
```

Search uses a simple integer comparison to check for a match. If the key had been a character string, you could use a call to strcmp() or some other character comparison function.

The recursive call to Search() follows. The recursion is performed by using a comparison of the variable i and by passing the current node's right or left node to search.

```
    else
    {
        ++(*nLevelCount);

        return(Search(nKeyValue, nLevelCount,
            i ? a->Item[i - 1].RightReference : a->LeftReference, &u));
    }
}
```

The SearchAndAdd() function is similar to the Search() function. When Search() ends, however, it simply returns a flag showing that the key was not found. When SearchAndAdd() returns, it adds the key to the current B-tree.

```
int SearchAndAdd(
    int  nKeyValue,
    PAGE  *a,
    ITEM  *v)

{

int  i;

ITEM  u;

//   printf("SearchAndAdd()...\n");
```

If the function was passed a NULL pointer, the program is preparing to add this key to a node. Then SearchAndAdd() prepares to add the key as the node, and returns TRUE to tell the caller that a node has been created.

The root node is created in the main program because the root node is "owned" by the main program, not by the B-tree functions:

```
if (a == NULL)
{
    v->nKeyValue = nKeyValue;
    v->nCount = 1;
    v->RightReference = NULL;
    return TRUE;
}
```

The following code, which is similar to the code in Search(), is used to find a match:

```
for (i = 0; i < a->nItemCount && nKeyValue > a->Item[i].nKeyValue;
    i++)
{
    ;
}

if (nKeyValue == a->Item[i].nKeyValue && i < a->nItemCount)
{
```

In the following code, if a match is found, a counter of matches is incremented. This allows our version of B-tree to have duplicate keys, with only one copy of the key kept in memory.

```
    a->Item[i].nCount++;
}
else
{
    if (SearchAndAdd(nKeyValue,
        i ? a->Item[i - 1].RightReference : a->LeftReference, &u))
    {
```

If the SearchAndAdd() function does not find the key, the Insert() function adds the key to the B-tree (in the correct place), as follows:

```
        return (Insert(a, i, &u, v));
    }
}
```

```
    return FALSE;
}
```

The `Insert()` function adds the current key value to the passed node by computing the number of items in the current block. If the block is too full, the function splits it into two blocks:

```
int Insert(
    PAGE    *a,
    int     i,
    ITEM    *u,
    ITEM    *v)

{

PAGE    *b;
int     j;
int     h;

//    printf("Insert()...\n");

    if (a->nItemCount < PAGE_SIZE)
    {
        for (j = a->nItemCount; j >= i + 1; j—)
        {
            CopyItem(&a->Item[j], &a->Item[j - 1]);
        }

        ++a->nItemCount;

        CopyItem(&a->Item[i], u);

        return(FALSE);
    }
    else
    {/* Page a is full. Split it and assign the emerging item to v. */

        NewItem(&b);

        if (i <= HALF_PAGE_SIZE)
        {
            if (i == HALF_PAGE_SIZE)
            {
```

```
            CopyItem(v, u);
        }
        else
        {
            CopyItem(v, &a->Item[HALF_PAGE_SIZE - 1]);

            for (j = HALF_PAGE_SIZE - 1; j >= i + 1; j--)
            {
                CopyItem(&a->Item[j], &a->Item[j - 1]);
            }

            CopyItem(&a->Item[i], u);
        }

        for (j = 0; j <= HALF_PAGE_SIZE - 1; j++)
        {
            CopyItem(&b->Item[j], &a->Item[j + HALF_PAGE_SIZE]);
        }
    }
    else
    {
        i -= HALF_PAGE_SIZE;
        CopyItem(v, &a->Item[HALF_PAGE_SIZE]);

        for (j = 0; j <= i - 2; j++)
        {
            CopyItem(&b->Item[j], &a->Item[j + HALF_PAGE_SIZE + 1]);
        }

        CopyItem(&b->Item[i - 1], u);

        for (j = i; j <= HALF_PAGE_SIZE - 1; j++)
        {
            CopyItem(&b->Item[j], &a->Item[j + HALF_PAGE_SIZE]);
        }
    }

    if (HALF_PAGE_SIZE == 0)
    {
        a->nItemCount = 1;
        b->nItemCount = 1;
```

```
        }
        else
        {
            a->nItemCount = HALF_PAGE_SIZE;
            b->nItemCount = HALF_PAGE_SIZE;
        }


        b->LeftReference = v->RightReference;
        v->RightReference = b;
    }

    return(TRUE);
}
```

The CopyItem() function copies information from the source item to the destination item. In the days of non-ANSI C, structures could not be assigned to each other. ANSI C supports structure assignments, however, so you could replace CopyItem() with assignment statements.

```
int CopyItem(
    ITEM    *DestinationItem,
    ITEM    *SourceItem)

{

//    printf("CopyItem()...\n");

    DestinationItem->nKeyValue      = SourceItem->nKeyValue;
    DestinationItem->RightReference = SourceItem->RightReference;
    DestinationItem->nCount         = SourceItem->nCount;

    return(0);
}
```

The NewItem() function is used to create a new node. NewItem() uses malloc() to allocate memory for the new node, then clears the memory.

```
int NewItem(
    PAGE    **Page)

{
```

```
//    printf("NewItem()...\n");

    if ((*Page = (PAGE *)malloc(sizeof(**Page))) == NULL)
    {
        fprintf(stderr, "Couldn't allocate memory!\n");

        exit(16);
    }

/*  malloc() doesn't initialize storage, so we do... */

    memset(*Page, 0, sizeof(**Page));

    return(0);
}
```

The TreePrint() function prints the B-tree. This function knows which level it is being called for and prints this information with the current node's values.

```
int TreePrint(
    PAGE    *Page,
    int     nLevel,
    int     nRightLeft,
    int     nPosition)
{

int     i;
int     j;
```

If TreePrint() is called with a NULL node, it does nothing. Otherwise, TreePrint() prints the level, prints whether it is the left or right node of its parent, and indents the node's numeric value (its key value) by four spaces for each level.

```
if (Page != NULL)
{
    for (i = 0; i < Page->nItemCount; i++)
    {
        switch(nRightLeft)
        {
            case ROOT: /* Should have only one root */
                printf("\n");
                printf("(ROOT   %2d) ", nLevel);
                break;
```

```
        case LEFT: /* Happens all the time */
            printf("(L %2d    %2d) ", nLevel, nPosition);
            break;

        case RIGHT:/* Happens all the time */
            printf("(R %2d    %2d) ", nLevel, nPosition);
            break;

        default:   /* Should never happen */
            printf("ERROR        ");
            break;
    }

    for (j = 0; j < nLevel; j++)
    {/* Adjust the starting column for the variable */
        printf(".....");
    }
```

After the necessary header information is displayed, the key value is printed. Remember, the key does not need to be an integer. If it was a character string, you would probably have to change the following line:

```
printf("%5d \n", Page->Item[i].nKeyValue);
```

After printing the key value, TreePrint(), like Search(), calls itself recursively, and is passed information on whether the right node or the left node is being followed:

```
    if (Page->Item[i].RightReference != NULL)
    {
        TreePrint(Page->Item[i].RightReference,
            nLevel + 1, RIGHT, i + 1);
    }
    }

    if (Page->LeftReference != NULL)
    {
        TreePrint(Page->LeftReference, nLevel + 1, LEFT, 0);
    }
}

return(0);
}
```

The DeleteItem() function deletes a node. DeleteItem() first checks that a node and an item to be deleted have been passed.

```c
int DeleteItem(
    int   nKeyValue,
    PAGE *a)


{

int     i;
int     k;
int     1;
int     r;

PAGE    *q;

//    printf("DeleteItem()...\n");

    if (a == NULL)
    {
        printf("Key is not in tree! Cannot delete this key.\n");
        return(FALSE);
    }
    else
```

Remember binary searches from earlier in the chapter? The following binary search uses the same technique: halving the list you are searching, depending on the result of the comparison of a given node and the user's key:

```c
{/* Binary array search */
    for (1 = 0, r = a->nItemCount - 1; 1 <= r; )
    {
        k = (1 + r) / 2;
        if (nKeyValue <= a->Item[k].nKeyValue)
        {
            r = k - 1;
        }
        if (nKeyValue >= a->Item[k].nKeyValue)
        {
            1 = k + 1;
        }
    }
```

```
        q = (r == -1) ? a->LeftReference : a->Item[r].RightReference;

    if (l - r > 1)
    {/* Found; now delete Item[k] */
        if (q == NULL)
        {/* a is a terminal page   */
            --(a->nItemCount);

            for (i = k; i < a->nItemCount; i++)
            {
                CopyItem(&a->Item[i], &a->Item[i + 1]);
            }

            return (a->nItemCount < HALF_PAGE_SIZE);
        }
        else
        {
            if (Delete(q, a, k))
            {
                return(UnderFlow(a, q, r));
            }
        }
    }
    else
    {
        if (DeleteItem(nKeyValue, q))
        {
            return(UnderFlow(a, q, r));
        }
    }
  }
}
```

The UnderFlow() function readjusts the B-tree. It shifts the remaining nodes, attempting to keep the B-tree as balanced as possible:

```
int UnderFlow(
    PAGE    *c,
    PAGE    *a,
    int     s)

{...}
```

DeleteItem() calls the Delete() function to delete the node. This function takes care of some of the housekeeping because there can be more than one key per block.

```
int Delete(
    PAGE    *p,
    PAGE    *a,
    int     k)

{...}
```

The rest of this section describes ways to make some of the routines in BTREE more generic (or more specific, depending on how you look at things).

First, the key is changed to a character field (16 characters long). Then a new field called lFileIndex is added to each node; this field is an index to a file's record. To use this new field, Search() should return it as one of its parameters. The lFileIndex field should be set when calling SearchAndAdd().

The rest of this section describes the changes you must make to the B-tree functions. Change all references to the functions for the nKeyValue variable to reflect both the new variable's type and the change in its name.

Use a new parameter to change the SearchAndAdd() function and the Search() function so that they pass back the lFileIndex variable.

Change TreePrint() so that it prints the lFileIndex variable in the debug mode.

Change the main function so that it can handle a character-based key.

Make the following changes to the program's source code. The Item structure should have the following variables:

```
struct  _item
{
    char    szKeyValue[16];
    long    lFileIndex;
    PAGE    *RightReference;
    int     nCount;
};
```

Change all references to nKeyValue to reflect the new data type of szKeyValue. This means changing references such as the following:

```
for (i = 0; i < a->nItemCount && nKeyValue > a->Item[i].nKeyValue; i++)
```

to

```
for (i = 0; i < a->nItemCount &&
    strcmp(szKeyValue, a->Item[i].szKeyValue) > 0; i++)
```

and changing the reference

```
if (nKeyValue == a->Item[i].nKeyValue && i < a->nItemCount)
```

to

```
if (strcmp(szKeyValue, a->Item[i].szKeyValue) == 0 &&
        i < a->nItemCount)
```

Both of these references are in the `Search()` function.

In the `SearchAndAdd()` function, change

```
v->nKeyValue = nKeyValue;
```

to

```
strcpy(v->szKeyValue, nKeyValue);
```

and change

```
for (i = 0; i < a->nItemCount && nKeyValue > a->Item[i].nKeyValue; i++)
```

to (as in `Search()`)

```
for (i = 0; i < a->nItemCount &&
    strcmp(szKeyValue, a->Item[i].szKeyValue) > 0; i++)
```

and the reference

```
if (nKeyValue == a->Item[i].nKeyValue && i < a->nItemCount)
```

to

```
if (strcmp(szKeyValue, a->Item[i].szKeyValue) == 0 &&
        i < a->nItemCount)
```

In `CopyItem()`, change

```
DestinationItem->nKeyValue     = SourceItem->nKeyValue;
```

to the following (with an added line for the new `lFilePointer` structure member):

```
strcpy(DestinationItem->szKeyValue, SourceItem->szKeyValue);
DestinationItem->lFilePointer   = SourceItem->lFilePointer;
```

In the `DeleteItem()` function, change

```
if (nKeyValue <= a->Item[k].nKeyValue)
```

to

```
if (strcmp(szKeyValue, a->Item[k].szKeyValue) <= 0)
```

and change

```
if (nKeyValue >= a->Item[k].nKeyValue)
```

to

```
if (strcmp(szKeyValue, a->Item[k].szKeyValue) >= 0)
```

These changes are simple to make. Should the key be some other data type, similar changes would have to be made.

Summary

In this chapter, you learned about data management.

- Data often must be sorted. You can perform a sort externally by using files and calling DOS's sort program or by calling another commercial sort routine.

- If data can be sorted in memory, you can use the C qsort() function.

- There is no provision for merging sorted data files under DOS, but this chapter presented a merge utility you can use.

- Most operating systems do not have a command for purging a data file of duplicates. This chapter presented a purge utility for this purpose.

- Linked lists organize data so that it may be retrieved in a specified order (usually sorted). Each member in a linked list has a pointer to the next member in the list. Usually, this pointer is the only way to find the members of a linked list.

- Linked lists can be used to group data based on a specific attribute.

- In a double linked list, the current data object is linked both with its successor and its predecessor.

- Indexed files enable a programmer to sort a much smaller set of data, which is then used to access specific data objects. Each record in the index file needs to contain only the key value and a pointer to its corresponding data object.

- A single data file may have more than one index file, each one indexing a different data file field.

- A B-tree organizes data so that specific data items are accessed easily.

- B-tree programs work with in-memory and file-based data structures. For acceptable performance, however, the tree must be in memory.

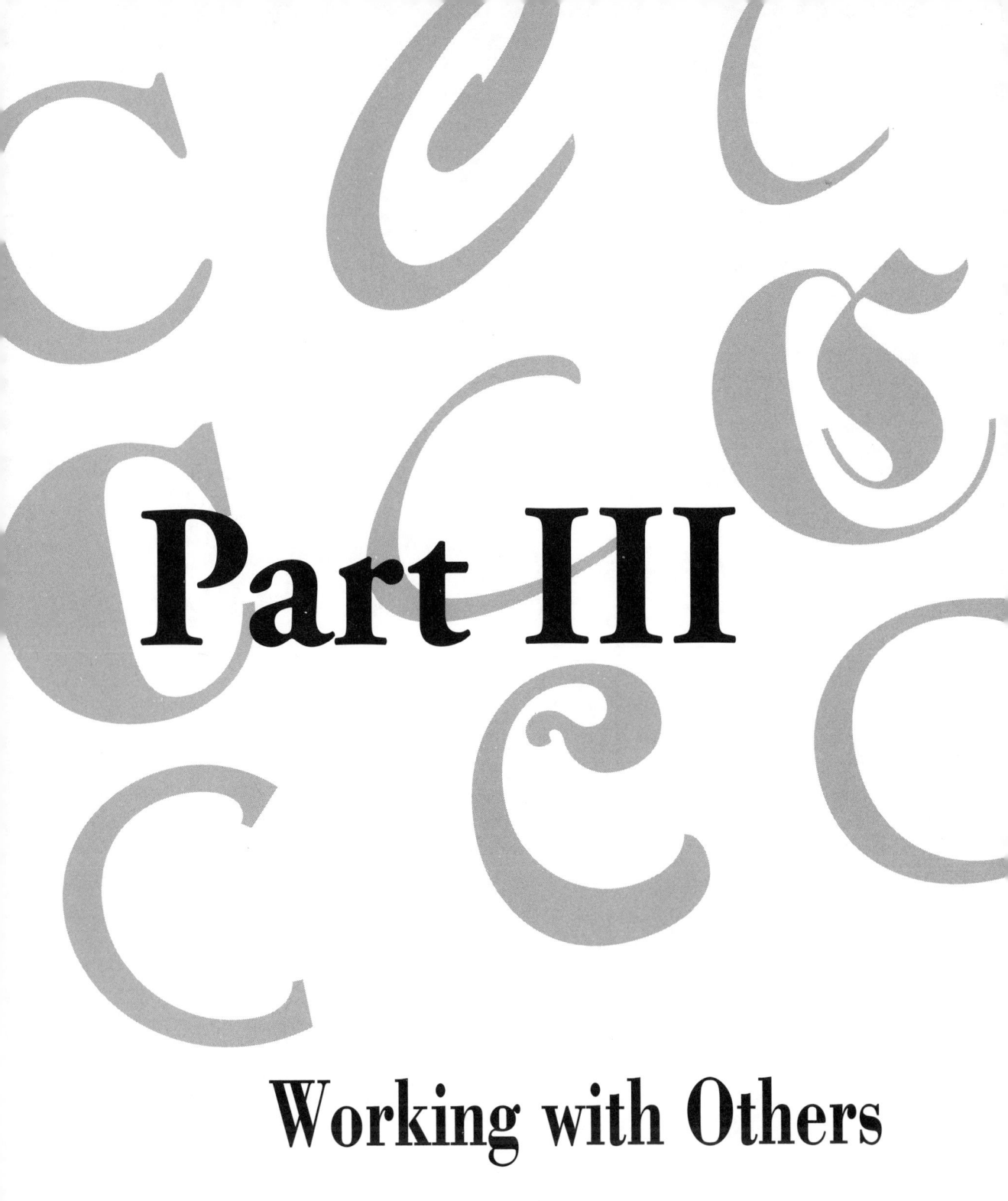

Part III

Working with Others

C and Other Languages

Many discussions in previous chapters did not pertain to a particular compiler. In this chapter, almost everything is dependent on the type of compiler. As in other chapters, I assume that you are using a Microsoft compiler. However, I have noted when something applies to a Borland or a Watcom compiler.

Nothing in the ANSI standard restricts C programs from containing functions written in another language. If your compiler is not covered, do not assume that you cannot mix languages. Most compilers include at least a provision for writing functions in assembly.

You may be asking why anyone would mix languages when C can do almost anything. Here are some good reasons:

You have a library of application-specific functions written in another computer language, such as Pascal or FORTRAN. For mathematical applications, FORTRAN still has many advantages.

You must create a function that is faster than what an optimizing compiler can produce. With assembly, you can directly control the computer's CPU and get every ounce of performance out of it. (Remember, though, that it is easy to create assembly functions that are not as efficient as a function written in C and compiled with the compiler's optimization turned on.)

Your project is on a tight schedule, so you must purchase a library of functions to save development time.

When you purchase a library of functions, be sure it includes the source code. You cannot depend on the supplier of the code to respond to your needs, and without source code you are on your own. I have never used code written by someone else without making at least one change. As well, if the supplier goes out of business, you can keep your product running if you have source code.

> Peter's rule: When you buy a library of functions, get the source code. If it is unavailable, look for a different product.

Other Languages

This chapter considers four languages other than C: assembly, BASIC, FORTRAN, and Pascal. All have been around for many years and are standardized. If your program must interface with a language not mentioned in this chapter, do not despair. Check whether the language you are using calls functions in a manner similar to one of the languages described here.

Table 11.1 shows the types of routines for each language. The major difference is that in FORTRAN a function returns a value, but a subroutine does not have a return value. When a function executes, a dummy variable with the same name as the function is created to hold the return value. (An example of this is shown in Listing 11.7, later in this chapter.)

Table 11.1. Routine types for different languages.

Language value	Returns a value	Has no return
assembly	Procedure	Procedure
BASIC	FUNCTION	Subprogram
C	function	(void) function
FORTRAN	FUNCTION	SUBROUTINE
Pascal	Function	Procedure

Do not ignore your C compiler's power. Almost all C compilers produce a mixed (or perhaps a pure) assembly listing of the functions being compiled. Typical assembly-listing options that you can use are shown in Table 11.2.

Table 11.2. C compiler assembly-listing options.

Option	Description	Compiler
/Fa	Produces an assembly output file	Microsoft
/Fc	Produces a mixed object and source listing file	Microsoft
/Fl	Produces an object listing file	Microsoft
/S	Produces a mixed assembly/source listing file	Borland C++
WDISASM (a stand-alone program)	Produces (with options) assembly/object listing files	Watcom

If you use the options listed for Microsoft compilers, you must use the full compiler, not QuickC or QuickC for Windows. Neither of the QuickC compilers produces an assembly or object listing.

Watcom's utility (WDISASM) has a number of options documented in the manual. It can disassemble .OBJ files produced by any Microsoft compatible compiler (one that produces compatible .OBJ files). You must check that the disassembly is correct, however, because not all .OBJ files disassemble correctly. Sometimes, disassembly by hand (a long and tedious process) is the only way to find out what the compiler did for a given block of code.

Do not overlook using the DOS DEBUG command to look at .EXE and .OBJ files. It has a crude disassembler, and it can help you see what is happening. Most debuggers can provide a disassembly listing as well.

Some compilers (such as Watcom's C/386) do not provide an assembly listing, but do come with a utility program to produce assembly. In Watcom, for example, the WDISASM utility disassembles an .OBJ file.

You can save hours of programming if you use the compiler's assembly listing option to produce an assembly program that is compatible with C programs. You can save time also if you already know the arguments that are passed to the function. Create a dummy function with as much of the necessary functionality as possible, then use the output of the compiler's assembly listing as the starting point for your assembly routine.

Assembly

Assembly is not a language. Rather, it is a method to use the CPU's native machine language. You must specify everything when writing in assembly: where data objects come from, where they will go, the basic operations, and so on. To use assembly language, you must be very familiar with how the CPU works.

Listing 11.1, CALLASM, is a simple example of how assembly works. It is written in assembly, and can be linked with the C libraries.

Listing 11.1. CALLASM.ASM.

```
;
;   CALLASM.ASM:  This program calls the C printf() function
;                 and prints a string on the terminal.
;
                NAME    CALLASM
                EXTRN   _printf:BYTE                ; Prototype for
printf()
                EXTRN   __acrtused:BYTE             ; Used to initialize C
                                                    ;  startup code
DGROUP          GROUP   _DATA,CONST,_BSS            ; Establish the DGROUP
_TEXT           SEGMENT WORD PUBLIC 'CODE'          ; Name the code
                                                    ;  segment _TEXT
                ASSUME  CS:_TEXT,DS:DGROUP,SS:DGROUP
                PUBLIC  _main                       ; Our function is
                                                    ;  main()
_main:          mov     word ptr nCount,0000H       ; Initialize nCount to
                                                    ;  zero
                mov     ax,offset DGROUP:szBuffer   ; Get address of
                                                    ;  szBuffer[]
                push    ax                          ; Push on stack as the
                                                    ;  last\parameter to
printf()
                mov     ax,offset DGROUP:L1         ; Get format string
                                                    ;  address
                push    ax                          ; Push on stack as the
                                                    ;  next parameter to
                                                    ;  printf()
                call    near ptr _printf            ; Now call printf()
                add     sp,0004H                    ; Discard printf()'s
                                                    ;  parameters
                mov     word ptr nCount,ax          ; Save printf()'s
                                                    ;  return value
                                                    ; Done, return to
                                                    ;  caller
_TEXT           ENDS

_DATA           SEGMENT WORD PUBLIC 'DATA'          ; Set up the data
                                                    ;  segment
```

continues

Listing 11.1. continued

```
                                                  ; PUBLIC is the same
                                                  ;   as C's
                                                  ; extern variables
                PUBLIC   szBuffer                 ; szBuffer is a public
                                                  ;   name
                PUBLIC   nCount                   ; nCount is a public
                                                  ;   name
szBuffer        LABEL    BYTE
                DB       "This is an assembly program."
                DB       0aH,00H                  ; append the \n for
                                                  ;   newline
nCount          LABEL    BYTE
                DB       00H,00H                  ; nCount, init to zero
_DATA           ENDS

CONST           SEGMENT WORD PUBLIC 'CONST'
L1              LABEL    BYTE
                DB       "%s",00H                 ; Our format string, a
                                                  ;   constant, in the
                                                  ;   CONST
                                                  ;   segment
CONST           ENDS

_BSS            SEGMENT WORD PUBLIC 'BSS'         ; The BSS segment is
                                                  ;   used
                                                  ;   by C to find the
                                                  ;   stack and
                                                  ;   has other uses,
                                                  ;   including
                                                  ;   storage for global
                                                  ;   variables
                                                  ;   not initialized
                                                  ;   explicitly
_BSS            ENDS                              ;   by the program

                END                              ; End of our program
```

Nobody recommends that you write an assembly program that calls C functions. Instead, write the program as a C program, then call the functions coded in assembly from C.

FORTRAN

FORTRAN was the first programming language developed, although the first compilers were created by Grace Hopper in the early 1950s. These compilers were simple and inefficient, and the "languages" they supported were never named.

FORTRAN (short for FORmula TRANslation) can trace its roots to the early 1950s, when John Backus and Irving Ziller at IBM set out to develop a new computer language for the soon to be released IBM 704 computer. The development team grew to many more members, and in April 1957, they completed the first FORTRAN compiler.

The IBM 704 was the first computer to implement floating point in hardware. Until that time, computers used software emulation to perform floating-point math.

A typical FORTRAN program is shown in Listing 11.2, DEMO.FOR.

Listing 11.2. DEMO.FOR.

```
* DEMO.FOR
* A simple, typical FORTRAN program. This program
* is equivalent to the standard HELLO.C program.

*2345678----

      program   hello

      print *, 'Hello (FORTRAN)'

      end
```

Pascal

Pascal is taught extensively at schools and universities, but has never caught on in a nonacademic environment, mostly due to the lack of good compilers. Apple released a UCSD Pascal system for the Apple II, but the implementation was crude and almost impossible to use productively, requiring a custom operating system incompatible with the existing Apple II operating system. Pascal became popular on PCs due only to the efforts of Borland, who released a good and inexpensive compiler called Turbo Pascal.

Although Pascal is still used today (and some Pascal compilers, most notably Turbo Pascal, remain), you will seldom see libraries of Pascal code that you will want to include in your C application. It is more likely you will have to convert a Pascal program to C. This conversion is easier if you can call Pascal functions from the C code, and convert each function one at a time. A typical Pascal program is shown in Listing 11.3.

Listing 11.3. HELLO.PAS.

```
/*  HELLO.PAS
 *  A simple, typical Pascal program. This program
 *  is equivalent to the standard HELLO.C program.
 */

program hello

begin

    writeln('Hello, from Pascal');

end.
```

The example program looks very much like a C program. The comments are delimited in the same manner (using /* and */), statements end with a semicolon, and the begin and end keywords are similar to braces in C.

BASIC

BASIC (Beginner's All-Purpose Symbolic Instruction Code) is the first language used by most beginning programmers. It is simple and easy to learn, but not used for serious programming due to its limitations.

There are few reasons to interface BASIC code with C and even fewer methods. Several BASIC compilers are available, but none produce code compatible with C code created with a C compiler. The best way to interface BASIC and C is to convert the BASIC code to C, producing a new program that is bound to be better than the original.

A simple BASIC program is shown in Listing 11.4, HELLO.BAS. It's the shortest example of a hello program!

Listing 11.4. HELLO.BAS.

```
PRINT "Hello"
```

Calling Other Languages from C

Usually, you write the main body of your program in C. Then you may use a few functions written in another language because you want to enhance the speed of the program (assembly code can be much faster than code written in a higher level language) or because you do not want to rewrite the functions in C.

This section describes how to create a basic C application and how to call a function created in another language. First, the main program is created in C, as shown in Listing 11.5, CALLNOTC.C. This program calls a non-C function called `max()` to determine the maximum of two numbers.

Listing 11.5. CALLNOTC.C.

```
/* CALLNOTC program, written 1992 by Peter D. Hipson */

Listing 11.5./* This C program calls C, FORTRAN, or assembly */
```

continues

Listing 11.5. continued

```c
#include <stdio.h>
#include <stddef.h>
#include <stdlib.h>
#include <string.h>
#include <time.h>

int  cdecl   maximum(int nVar1, int nVar2);


int    main()

{
int    nVar1 = 0;
int    nVar2 = 1;

char   szBuffer[256];

    printf("Enter the same number twice to end\n");


    while(nVar1 != nVar2)
    {
        printf("Enter two integers, separated with blanks");

        gets(szBuffer);

        sscanf(szBuffer, "%d %d", &nVar1, &nVar2);

        printf("The values entered are %d and %d. The larger is %d\n",
            nVar1,
            nVar2,
            maximum(nVar1, nVar2));
    }

    return(0);

}

/* This is maximum() written in C */
int    maximum(
```

```
int     nVar1,
int     nVar2)

{

    if (nVar1 < nVar2)
    {
        return(nVar2);
    }
    else
    {
        return(nVar1);
    }
}
```

In the maximum() function, four lines of code do most of the work: a compare and two return values. Many programmers consider multireturns in a single function to be poor programming style. I do not agree, but I do not use goto except to a single label near the end of the function just before the cleanup code.

To see what a typical C compiler does with the maximum() function, look at the following output from the Microsoft C 7.00 compiler (without optimization):

```
                _maximum:
    *** 00008a 55          push    bp
    *** 00008b 8b ec        mov bp,sp
    *** 00008d 81 ec 00 00       sub sp,OFFSET L00390
    *** 000091 56          push    si
    *** 000092 57          push    di
; ; Line 50     if (nVar1 < nVar2)
    *** 000093 8b 46 06     mov ax,WORD PTR 6[bp]
    *** 000096 39 46 04     cmp WORD PTR 4[bp],ax
    *** 000099 7c 03 e9 00 00      jge L00387
; ; Line 51     {
; ; Line 52         return(nVar2);
    *** 00009e 8b 46 06     mov ax,WORD PTR 6[bp]
    *** 0000a1 e9 00 00     jmp L00386
; ; Line 53     }
; ; Line 54     else
    *** 0000a4 e9 00 00     jmp L00388
                L00387:
; Line 54     else (continued...)
```

continues

Listing 11.5. continued

```
; ; Line 55     {
; ; Line 56        return(nVar1);
   *** 0000a7  8b 46 04    mov ax,WORD PTR 4[bp]
   *** 0000aa  e9 00 00    jmp L00386
; ; Line 57     }
                  L00388:
; ; Line 58}
; Line 58 (end of the function, cleanup:)
                  L00386:
   *** 0000ad  5f          pop di
   *** 0000ae  5e          pop si
   *** 0000af  8b e5       mov sp,bp
   *** 0000b1  5d          pop bp
   *** 0000b2  c3          ret OFFSET 0
Local Size: 2
; Line 0
```

Next, Microsoft C's /0x (maximum optimize) switch was turned on so that you could see what a compiler can do using maximum optimization. The following output was produced:

```
                  _maximum:
   *** 00007a  55          push    bp
   *** 00007b  8b ec       mov bp,sp
;    nVar1 = 4
;    nVar2 = 6
   *** 00007d  8b 56 04    mov dx,WORD PTR [bp+4]   ;nVar1
   *** 000080  8b 5e 06    mov bx,WORD PTR [bp+6]   ;nVar2
;|***    if (nVar1 < nVar2)
; Line 50
   *** 000083  3b da       cmp bx,dx
   *** 000085  7e 05       jle $I433
;|***    {
;|***         return(nVar2);
; Line 52
   *** 000087  8b c3       mov ax,bx
   *** 000089  5d          pop bp
   *** 00008a  c3          ret
   *** 00008b  90          nop
```

```
;|***     }
;|***     else
; Line 54
                  $I433:
;|***     {
;|***         return(nVar1);
; Line 56
   *** 00008c  8b c2      mov ax,dx
;|***     }
;|*** }
; Line 58
   *** 00008e  5d         pop bp
   *** 00008f  c3         ret


_maximum   ENDP
_TEXT   ENDS
END
;|***
;|*** // #endif
```

Notice that the optimized code is slightly smaller and a bit more complex. This code might be more difficult to debug, but this drawback is unimportant because code is seldom debugged at the machine-language level after optimization.

Calling Assembly from C

Can a programmer using assembly language write a smaller, faster function than the compiler? To test this, I wrote the maximum() function in assembly. So that I would not be biased by looking at what the compiler produced for optimized code, I wrote the assembly function before I produced the two listings of maximum() shown in the preceding section.

Listing 11.6 is my version of maximum(). It is a bit shorter and faster than the version from the compiler, even when the compiler version is fully optimized.

Listing 11.6. MAXIMUM.ASM.

```
;
;  A hand optimized assembly function for C.
;  cmacros.inc are a handy group of macros that make
```

continues

Listing 11.6. continued

```
;   writing C-compatible functions easier.
;

include          e:\windev\include\cmacros.inc


;
; int maximum(int, int);
;
;  This version was optimized by hand for both
;  minimum size and fastest execution. The
;  compiler's code is twice as long.
;
;
                 NAME    MAXIMUM
DGROUP           GROUP   _DATA
_TEXT            SEGMENT WORD PUBLIC 'CODE'
                 ASSUME  CS:_TEXT,DS:DGROUP,SS:DGROUP
                 PUBLIC  _maximum
_maximum:        enter   0000H,00H

                 mov     ax,word ptr +6H[bp]
                 cmp     word ptr +4H[bp],ax
                 jle     short L6

                 mov     ax,word ptr +4H[bp]


L6:              nop                         ;Handy label target...
                 leave
                 ret
_TEXT            ENDS


_DATA            SEGMENT WORD PUBLIC 'DATA'
_DATA            ENDS


                 END
```

In my version of `maximum()`, I used the `enter` and `leave` operands, which are useful for creating functions called by higher level languages such as C.

One of the tested values is returned in `AX`. If the value in `AX` is the larger of the two values, `AX` does not need to be reloaded and can just return that value. Otherwise, the other value is placed in `AX` and then returned.

Because this version is optimized by hand, it executes faster and makes better use of memory. For more complex functions, however, this improvement is more difficult to obtain. By breaking your assembly code into smaller and smaller parts and analyzing the resultant code, you can be confident that it will be faster without performing some extensive benchmarks.

Calling FORTRAN and Pascal from C

Writing `maximum()` in FORTRAN is an easy task, as shown in Listing 11.7. Optimization is less of a concern in FORTRAN than in assembly because FORTRAN is a high-level language. Not all C compilers support FORTRAN functions.

Listing 11.7. The maximum() function in FORTRAN.

```
*
*   The C function maximum() written in FORTRAN
*

        integer function maximum(nVar1, nVar2)
        integer*2 nVar1, nVar2

        maximum = nVar2

        if (nVar1 .gt. nVar2) maximum = nVar1

        end
```

When this function is called from C, the calling C program file must tell the C compiler that the function is written in FORTRAN. This is accomplished by properly declaring the `maximum()` function:

```
int __fortran maximum(int, int);
```

The call fails if the function is not declared correctly (using the `__fortran` keyword) because of the way that the arguments are passed to a FORTRAN program's functions. Except for the differences in languages, functions written in FORTRAN and in Pascal are handled the same way.

Calling C Functions from Other Languages

The opposite of calling from C a function written in another language is calling from a second language a function written in C. There are several problems in doing this. For example, many C library functions rely on the execution of C initialization code, which may not be present when a program written in another language calls a C function. You can partially alleviate this problem in assembly by writing the program's main function in C, thereby forcing the assembly program to behave like a C program.

A C program can grow quite large when it is linked, so many programmers write in assembly to keep the program smaller. If the C function called from another language does not make any calls to C library functions, no library functions are included in the executable program. This makes the program smaller and eliminates the task of ensuring that C has properly initialized itself.

This section presents a few examples of other languages calling a C function. These examples use CALLNOTC.C (Listing 11.5), which was used also in the previous section. The `maximize()` function is written in C (see Listing 11.8), and the main, calling program is written in another language. Because `maximize()` does not call any other functions, I did not have to address the issue of calling C's startup code. However, I have included the necessary mechanism to initialize C, in case you need it.

Listing 11.8. MAXIMUM.C.

```
/* MAXIMUM.C function, written 1992 by Peter D. Hipson */

/* This is a C function called by FORTRAN or assembly */

#include <stdio.h>
#include <stddef.h>
```

```
#include <stdlib.h>
#include <string.h>
#include <time.h>

int   cdecl   maximum(int nVar1, int nVar2);


int     maximum(
    int     nVar1,
    int     nVar2)

{
    if (nVar1 < nVar2)
    {
        return(nVar2);
    }
    else
    {
        return(nVar1);
    }
}
```

The maximum() function could be written in assembly, but some other function that must do special things such as interact with hardware might have to be written in assembly.

Calling C from Assembly

An assembly program can call a C function, subject to either of two conditions. One, the C library must be linked with the assembly program. Any C functions called (CALLNOTC, in Listing 11.5, calls several) are processed by library functions, whose references must be resolved.

Two, the C library's startup code must be included and called. With Microsoft C, this is accomplished by linking with the necessary library (I used SLIBCE.LIB in developing CALLNOTC.ASM, in Listing 11.9) and defining the external symbol, _acrtused. When the startup code from the C library is executed, it properly initializes the C environment.

Listing 11.9. CALLNOTC.ASM.

```
;/* CALLNOTC program, written 1992 by Peter D. Hipson */
;
;/* This is an assembly program that calls FORTRAN or assembly */
;
;#include <stdio.h>
;#include <stddef.h>
;#include <stdlib.h>
;#include <string.h>
;#include <time.h>
;
;int  cdecl   maximum(int nVar1, int nVar2);
;


; Enable 386 instruction set

.386

                NAME    callnotc

; maximum(), sscanf(), gets(), and printf() are called

                EXTRN   _maximum:BYTE
                EXTRN   _sscanf:BYTE
                EXTRN   _gets:BYTE
                EXTRN   _printf:BYTE

; _acrtused is used to initialize C at runtime

                EXTRN   __acrtused:BYTE

;  The datagroup is _DATA (misc data), CONST (constants),
;  and _BSS (uninitialized data)

DGROUP          GROUP   _DATA,CONST,_BSS

_TEXT           SEGMENT WORD PUBLIC USE16 'CODE'
                ASSUME  CS:_TEXT,DS:DGROUP,SS:DGROUP

;  The program's main function, called by C's startup code.
;  Microsoft C naming conventions require the underscore
```

```
;   prefix. Other compilers may use an underscore
;   following the name.

                PUBLIC  _main

_main:          push    bp          ; Start up, save registers,
                mov     bp,sp       ; and get ready to run
                sub     sp,0000H
                push    si
                push    di

; Initialize nVar1 and nVar2 so that they are not the same!

                mov     word ptr -104H[bp],0000H
                mov     word ptr -106H[bp],0001H

; Call to printf(szMsg1);

                mov     ax,offset DGROUP:szMsg1
                push    ax
                call    near ptr _printf
                add     sp,0002H

                jmp     near ptr Loop1

; Loop back to Loop1

Loop1:          mov     ax,offset DGROUP:szMsg2
                push    ax
                call    near ptr _printf
                add     sp,0002H

                lea     ax,-102H[bp]
                push    ax
                call    near ptr _gets
                add     sp,0002H

                lea     ax,-106H[bp] ; nVar2's address
                push    ax
                lea     ax,-104H[bp] ; nVar1's address
                push    ax
```

continues

Listing 11.9. continued

```
                mov     ax,offset DGROUP:szScanFormat
                push    ax
                lea     ax,-102H[bp]    ; szBuffer (auto var on stack)
                push    ax
                call    near ptr _sscanf
                add     sp,0008H

                push    word ptr -106H[bp]  ; nVar2
                push    word ptr -104H[bp]  ; nVar1
                call    near ptr _maximum
                add     sp,0004H

                push    ax
                push    word ptr -106H[bp]  ; nVar2
                push    word ptr -104H[bp]  ; nVar1
                mov     ax,offset DGROUP:szPrintFormat
                push    ax
                call    near ptr _printf
                add     sp,0008H

                mov     ax,word ptr -106H[bp]
                cmp     word ptr -104H[bp],ax
                je      short AllDone       ; We are finished
                jmp     near ptr Loop1      ; Go around another time
AllDone:        mov     ax,0000H            ; A zero return code
                jmp     near ptr Dummy
Dummy:          pop     di                  ; Clean up and go home
                pop     si
                mov     sp,bp
                pop     bp
                ret
_TEXT           ENDS


_DATA           SEGMENT WORD PUBLIC USE16 'DATA'
```

```
szMsg1          LABEL   BYTE
                DB      "Enter the same number twice to end", 0AH, 00H
szMsg2          LABEL   BYTE
                DB      "Enter two integers, separated with blanks", 00H
szScanFormat    LABEL   BYTE
                DB      "%d %d", 00H
szPrintFormat   LABEL   BYTE
                DB      "The values entered are %d and %d, "
                DB      "the larger is %d",0AH, 00H
_DATA           ENDS

CONST           SEGMENT WORD PUBLIC USE16 'CONST'
CONST           ENDS

_BSS            SEGMENT WORD PUBLIC USE16 'BSS'
_BSS            ENDS

                END
```

The program calls not only the C function (maximum()), but also a number of other library functions, including printf(), gets(), and scanf(). These functions form the basic I/O for the program. DOS I/O interrupt routines could have been called directly, but because they do not do formatted I/O, the program would have to convert the typed characters to integer numbers and convert the numbers back to characters for output.

To summarize, write the main program in C (or another high-level language) if possible. Then write in assembly the routines whose speed or size is critical. When using an advanced compiler (such as Microsoft's C 7.0), you can control how much of the library code is included, the arrangement of the program's segments (whether there are separate data and code segments or a single segment for both), and the allocation and use of memory.

When programming on a PC (under DOS), do not forget the available DOS services. These services, listed in Table 11.3, are accessed using the Int 21 instruction. If you are using a different operating system, it should have similar functions.

Table 11.3. MS-DOS Int 21 function codes.

Function (hex)	Function (decimal)	Description	DOS version
00H	0	Terminate the current program or process.	1.0+
01H	1	Read a character from the console (with echo to screen).	1.0+
02H	2	Write a character to the screen.	1.0+
03H	3	Read a character from AUX:.	1.0+
04H	4	Write a character to AUX:.	1.0+
05H	5	Send output to the printer.	1.0+
06H	6	Perform I/O from the console; DOS does not process the characters.	1.0+
07H	7	Get a character from the keyboard, waiting for a keypress if no character is available; the character is not processed by DOS.	1.0+
08H	8	Get a character from the keyboard, waiting for a keypress if no character is available.	1.0+
09H	9	Print a string to the console; the string is terminated with a dollar sign.	1.0+
0AH	10	Read a character string (a line, typed by the user, up to a carriage return) from the keyboard.	1.0+

Function (hex)	Function (decimal)	Description	DOS version
0BH	11	Test to see whether a character is available from the keyboard.	1.0+
0CH	12	Discard the contents of the input buffer, and get the input.	1.0+
0DH	13	Reset the specified disk drive.	1.0+
0EH	14	Make the specified drive the current drive.	1.0+
0FH	15	Open a file.	1.0+
10H	16	Close a file.	1.0+
11H	17	Find the first file meeting the provided specification.	1.0+
12H	18	Find the next file after using Int 0x11.	1.0+
13H	19	Delete the specified file.	1.0+
14H	20	Perform a sequential read.	1.0+
15H	21	Perform a sequential write.	1.0+
16H	22	Create a new file.	1.0+
17H	23	Rename a file.	1.0+
18H	24	Reserved.	
19H	25	Get the current drive.	1.0+
1AH	26	Set the Disk Transfer Address (DTA).	1.0+
1BH	27	Get the current default drive data.	1.0+

continues

Table 11.3. continued

Function (hex)	Function (decimal)	Description	DOS version
1CH	28	Get data for the specified drive.	2.0+
1DH	29	Reserved	
1EH	30	Reserved	
1FH	31	Reserved	
20H	32	Reserved	
21H	33	Random file read.	1.0+
22H	34	Random file write.	1.0+
23H	35	Get the size of the specified file.	1.0+
24H	36	Set the file's current position.	1.0+
25H	37	Set an interrupt vector.	1.0+
26H	38	Create a new Program Segment Prefix (PSP).	1.0+
27H	39	Random block read.	
28H	40	Random block write.	1.0+
29H	41	Parse a filename into a valid DOS filename	1.0+
2AH	42	Get the date.	1.0+
2BH	43	Set the date.	1.0+
2CH	44	Get the time.	1.0+
2DH	45	Set the time.	1.0+
2EH	46	Set the write verify flag.	1.0+
2FH	47	Get the Disk Transfer Address (DTA).	2.0+

Function (hex)	Function (decimal)	Description	DOS version
30H	48	Get the DOS version	2.0+
31H	49	Terminate-and-Stay-Resident (TSR).	2.0+
32H	50	Reserved	
33H	51	Get or set the break flag, and get the boot drive.	2.0+
34H	52	Reserved	
35H	53	Get the interrupt vector.	2.0+
36H	54	Get the drive allocation information.	2.0+
39H	57	Create a directory.	2.0+
3AH	58	Delete a directory.	2.0+
3BH	59	Set the current directory.	2.0+
3CH	60	Create a file.	2.0+
3DH	61	Open a file.	2.0+
3EH	62	Close a file.	2.0+
3FH	63	Read from a file (can also read from a device).	2.0+
40H	64	Write to a file (can also read from a device).	2.0+
41H	65	Delete a file.	2.0+
42H	66	Set the file pointer.	2.0+
43H	67	Get (or set) a file's attributes.	2.0+
44H	68	IOCTL processing.	2.0+
45H	69	Duplicate a file handle.	2.0+
46H	70	Redirect a file handle.	2.0+

continues

459

Table 11.3. continued

Function (hex)	Function (decimal)	Description	DOS version
47H	71	Get the current directory.	2.0+
48H	72	Allocate a memory block.	2.0+
49H	73	Release a memory block.	2.0+
4AH	74	Resize a memory block.	2.0+
4BH	75	Execute (run) a program (EXEC).	2.0+
4CH	76	Terminate a process with a return code (which can be tested in a batch file).	2.0+
4DH	77	Get the return code from a child process.	2.0+
4EH	78	Find the first file.	2.0+
4FH	79	Find the next file, after finding the first file.	2.0+
50H	80	Reserved	
51H	81	Reserved	
52H	82	Reserved	
53H	83	Reserved	
54H	84	Get the verify flag.	2.0+
55H	85	Reserved	
56H	86	Rename a file.	2.0+
57H	87	Get (or set) the file date and time.	2.0+
58H	88	Get (or set) the allocation strategy.	3.0+

Function (hex)	Function (decimal)	Description	DOS version
59H	89	Get extended error information following a DOS error.	3.0+
5AH	90	Create a temporary file.	3.0+
5BH	91	Create a new file.	3.0+
5CH	92	Lock (or unlock) a file region.	3.0+
5DH	93	Reserved	
5EH	94	Get the machine name, get (or set) the printer setup.	3.1+
5FH	95	Device redirection.	3.1+
60H	96	Reserved	
61H	97	Reserved	
62H	98	Get the Program Segment Prefix (PSP) address.	3.0+
63H	99	Get the DBCS lead byte only table.	2.25
64H	100	Reserved	
65H	101	Get the extended country information.	3.3+
66H	102	Get (or set) the code page.	3.3+
67H	103	Set the file handle count.	3.3+
68H	104	Commit a file.	3.3+
69H	105	Reserved	
6AH	106	Reserved	
6BH	107	Reserved	
6CH	108	Extended open file.	4.0+

Calling C from FORTRAN and Pascal

A C function is called from a FORTRAN or a Pascal program in a manner similar to the way any other type of function is called from FORTRAN or Pascal. The main program must be told that the function is written in C (so that the parameters are passed properly), and C library functions must not be called.

Because C is not the language of the main program, the C initialization code cannot be called, which means the C library functions cannot be called. This restriction can limit the usefulness of a C function; you may decide that it is easier to write the entire program in one language.

All the Things that Can Go Wrong

When you mix languages in your programming, you can easily get things mixed up. Much of the discussion in this section is specific to Microsoft's C compilers. However, other compilers often behave in a similar manner. Borland's C compilers, for example, offer similar methods for argument passing.

Following are some of the more common things that can ruin your day:

If you are calling a C function from another language, you must tell the compiler the calling convention. You can tell C that a function will be using FORTRAN calling conventions, then call the function from a FORTRAN program without telling the FORTRAN program that the function is written in C. If the function is written in C with C's calling conventions, however, the calling program must know this.

When assembly is called from C, the parameters must be read from the stack in the correct order. A C function expects its arguments to be passed in right to left order. A FORTRAN or a Pascal function expects arguments in a left to right order.

A function using the C calling conventions expects its caller to clean the arguments from the stack. A FORTRAN or a Pascal function takes the arguments from the stack itself.

The value being returned must be in the correct place. Generally, AX is used for 2-byte return values, and AX and DX are used for 4-byte return values.

The compiler modifies the function's name. If it is a C function, an underscore is added (either before or after the name, depending on the compiler) and its case is not changed. If it is a FORTRAN or a Pascal function, an underscore is not added and the name is converted to uppercase. When calling C functions from assembly, the underscore is often forgotten, leading to unresolved references.

When accessing a multidimensional array, C and Pascal vary the subscripts in row-major order. FORTRAN and BASIC vary them in column-major order.

The C array `nArray[2][10][20]` is typically `nArray(20,10,2)` in FORTRAN.

In C, arrays are indexed from zero. In FORTRAN, arrays typically are indexed from one. In Pascal, the lower bound is specified by the programmer. Exceeding the bounds of an array is common in mixed C/FORTRAN/Pascal code because the initial starting points for the bounds differ.

Do not call C library code from a program that has a main procedure written in FORTRAN or Pascal.

Do not call library functions from a function written in a language different from the language of the main program. It may be possible to call the main program language's library functions, but make sure that you use the correct calling conventions.

In all, mixed language programming is not used frequently. It is complex and prone to subtle failures that may be difficult to find and correct. Mixed language programming should be used as a last resort.

Looking at Data

Each programming language views data a little differently. Table 11.4 is a cross-reference of simple data types used in C, BASIC, FORTRAN, and Pascal. The similarity in the data types of FORTRAN and Pascal shows the common roots between those two languages.

Table 11.4. Data types.

C/C++	BASIC	FORTRAN	Pascal
short	*variable*%	INTEGER*2	INTEGER2
int	INTEGER		INTEGER
unsigned short	(unsigned not supported)	(unsigned not supported)	WORD
unsigned (see unsigned long and unsigned short)			
long	*variable*& LONG	INTEGER*4 INTEGER (default)	INTEGER4
unsigned long	(unsigned not supported)	(unsigned not supported)	(unsigned not supported)
float	*variable*! *variable* SINGLE	REAL*4 REAL	REAL4 REAL
double	*variable*# DOUBLE	REAL*8 DOUBLE PRECISION	REAL8
long double			
unsigned char		CHARACTER*1 (not the same as LOGICAL) LOGICAL *2 LOGICAL *4	CHAR

Because BASIC does not predeclare scalar variables, a variable's type is indicated by a suffix code (%, &, !, or #). If the suffix is missing, the variable is assumed to be a real (floating-point) variable.

Variables are classified according to

- *Type* (what is stored in them), such as integer, character, or floating point

- *Size* (how large they are)

If you picture a variable as a certain number of bytes holding a certain type of data, you can easily convert from one language's variable types to another.

Names and Limits

C allows a longer name length (the number of characters in a name that are significant) than FORTRAN. In C, the limit is 32 characters for internal names and 6 characters for external names. With some versions of FORTRAN, the limit is 6 characters for internal or external names.

When an external name is processed by C compilers, an underscore is usually added before or after the name. When programming in languages that do not use this convention, you must explicitly add the underscore. In Listing 11.9, for example, the `printf()` library function is called. The referenced name is `_printf` because the compiler prefixes the name with an underscore, and you must do the same. A FORTRAN or Pascal identifier does not have an added underscore.

When an external identifier is used in FORTRAN, the case of the name will have been changed to uppercase. This can create problems when linking the program, depending on the linker's options. If you use the `/NOIGNORECASE` option (which tells the linker that the case of the identifiers must match) when you create a mixed language program, the linker may generate unresolved reference errors for names in the wrong case.

Summary

In this chapter, you learned about mixed language programming.

- Programs written in C can call functions written in assembly, FORTRAN, Pascal, and BASIC, provided the compiler supports mixed language calls to the language to be called.

- A function written in C can be called from other languages. When a C function is called from an assembly program, library functions can be called provided the C startup code is incorporated into the assembly program. If the other language is not assembly, however, the C library functions cannot be used.

- You must consider how each of the variable types, especially arrays, are handled between C and other languages. Do not exceed the bounds of an array. Arrays in FORTRAN are indexed starting with one; arrays in C are indexed starting with zero.

- The FORTRAN compiler converts all external identifiers in FORTRAN programs to uppercase. C and assembly external identifiers can be mixed case.

- Arguments for a C function are placed on the stack in the opposite order of arguments in FORTRAN or Pascal.

- With most C compilers, it is easy to write the shell of an assembly function in C, compile it with an assembly listing option, and convert the assembly listing to an assembly file. This ensures that the parameters, calling protocol, and return values are correctly coded.

C and Databases

Computers generally do two things: number management and data management. Most end users (nonprogrammers) manage data or numbers, and most of the software tools they use are related to these two tasks.

Number management is usually performed using a spreadsheet program. Spreadsheets are complex programs that enable a person to manipulate numeric data, generate what-if scenarios, create reports, and so on. Because spreadsheet programs have become standardized, there are a limited number of add-on products.

With data management systems, the story is different. Many custom add-on programs directly interact with the database program and with files created with the database program.

This chapter covers the interaction of C programs with database programs and the use of the data files created with database programs. When the name dBASE is mentioned, the information usually applies to most other compatible programs, such as FoxBase.

Products such as R:Base and Oracle are incompatible with dBASE. You can write callable C functions for use with R:Base, but the real power when using R:Base files comes from a library of functions (available from Microrim, which supplies R:Base) that allow C programs to access R:Base database files using the same command functionality as the R:Base interactive commands.

Interfacing with dBASE-Compatible Programs

The primary way to interface with database programs is with Clipper, a dBASE-compatible compiler (just like a C compiler). Clipper is not a C compiler, however, so some of the calling conventions are different.

For example, a C function called from a Clipper program (Summer 1987 version) does not receive its arguments directly. Clipper places the arguments in external variables, and the called function must make assignments from these external variables.

Because there are no interfacing standards, the procedures for interfacing C with a database program differ depending on the product. Knowing how to interface C with dBASE, for example, will not help you interface C with Clipper, FoxBase, or Paradox.

Using dBASE Files Directly

Rather than using Clipper, dBASE, or another database program to access a dBASE file, it is more common to include in a program the support to directly access a dBASE and dBASE-compatible file.

There are three main versions of dBASE that you must work with. The dBASE II program is old and rarely used. dBASE III is more common, is still used extensively, and is the standard that other programs follow when creating a dBASE-compatible file. The dBASE IV program is the latest of the dBASE programs that you might encounter. This chapter covers dBASE III and dBASE IV's file features that are compatible with dBASE III.

Accessing a file created by dBASE is as easy as accessing any other file. The format of a simple dBASE file is shown in Figure 12.1. This figure shows the layout of the file header, the column headers, and the data.

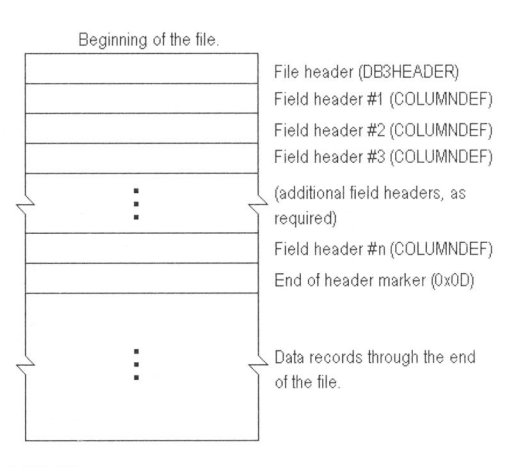

Figure 12.1. A dBASE file.

This chapter does not describe the special features of dBASE IV or how to access indexes. By the end of this chapter, however, you should be able to read a dBASE file and create a file that dBASE can read.

The dBASE file format is simple. Using a program such as DUMP, you could easily dump a simple dBASE file and determine the use of each file variable. So that you do not have to do this, however, this section describes the two structures that make up the file's header.

The first structure (called DB3HEADER in Listing 12.1) defines the file header and describes the dBASE file. This information enables you to determine the file's contents, such as the file's record layout, the number of records in the file, the date the file was updated, and the version of dBASE that created the file.

```
#pragma pack 1 /* Pack to byte boundaries */
typedef struct    {
/*  Bit fields are arranged from least significant
    to most significant */
    unsigned int   bfVersion:7;
    unsigned int   bfHasMemo:1;
    unsigned int   bYear:8;
    unsigned char  bMonth;
    unsigned char  bDay;
    long int       lNumberRecords;
    short int      nFirstRecordOffset;
    short int      nRecordLength;
```

```
unsigned char  szReserved[20];
} DB3HEADER;
```

The main header structure has a series of bit field variables. This allows a direct test of the memo field bit, which is otherwise difficult to access, as follows:

```
unsigned short int   bfVersion:7;
```

The bfVersion variable is a 7-bit bit field. Its value designates the version of dBASE that created the database file. For most dBASE-compatible files, bfVERSION contains one of the values in Table 12.1.

Table 12.1. Version codes for dBASE-compatible files.

File type	Description
0x02	dBASE II file. Generally incompatible with dBASE III.
0x03	dBASE III or FoxBase file. The file could have been created with dBASE IV, but the file is compatible with dBASE III.
0x04	dBASE IV file, partially compatible with dBASE III file I/O routines.
0x75	FoxBase file. The memo file bit is usually set (see discussion of bfHasMemo).
0x0B	dBASE IV file. Memo file bit is usually set (see discussion of bfHasMemo).

Generally, a value of 3 in the version field (bfversion) means that the file is compatible with dBASE III. If the bfHasMemo variable (a single bit) is True, a .DBT memo file is included:

```
unsigned short int   bfHasMemo:1;
```

The functions in this chapter do not access memo files, so this bit and any memo fields can be ignored.

ANSI standards require a bit field to be defined as a short int, so the bYear byte-sized variable (the year that the database was last updated) is included as the final eight bits in the bit field:

```
unsigned short int   bYear:8;
```

This prevents us from taking the address of this variable, but we never need its address. (If we needed the address of bYear, we could define a union to map a variable to this address.)

The bMonth byte variable contains the month the database was last updated:

```
unsigned char   bMonth;
```

The bDay byte variable contains the day the database was last updated:

```
unsigned char   bDay;
```

The lNumberRecords variable contains the number of database records in the database. The program uses this value to determine how many records must be read.

```
long int        lNumberRecords;
```

The number of fields in each record and the location of the first record is computed with the nFirstRecordOffset variable:

```
unsigned short int      nFirstRecordOffset;
```

Because a file seek operation requires a long type, you must cast this variable to a long. A short int is used because a dBASE header is never more than 64K.

The nRecordLength variable holds the length of each record in the database:

```
short int       nRecordLength;
```

The first byte of each record is a flag field. This flag field contains a blank if the record is not deleted, or * if it has been deleted.

The reserved fields should not be used or modified. Generally, they contain zeros:

```
unsigned char   szReserved[20];
```

After the header is read, the column definition records (often called field definition records) can be read. There is one column definition record for each column in the database.

You usually do not know how many columns will be defined in a database when you write your program (and please do not guess a "really large number"). Therefore, the program must compute the number of column definitions by reading the information in the file header.

Each column definition is contained in a structure as shown:

```
typedef struct    {
    char            szColumnName[11];
    char            chType;
    long            lFieldPointer;
    unsigned char   byLength;
    unsigned char   byDecimalPlace;
    char            szReserved[14];
    } COLUMNDEF;
```

The first field, szColumnName, contains the name of the column as a standard C string (terminated with \0). This name may be up to 10 characters long, leaving a final 11th byte to hold the terminating \0.

```
char            szColumnName[11];
```

The column type is coded in the single character member called chType:

```
char            chType;
```

This code can contain any of the characters shown in Table 12.2. The field definition characters in Table 12.2 are valid for dBASE III. For other versions of dBASE, other fields may be defined.

Table 12.2. dBASE column definition characters.

Value	Identifier	Description
N	NUMERIC_FIELD	The field is a number, either integer (if the decimal places are 0) or floating point.
C	CHARACTER_FIELD	The field is a character string.
L	LOGICAL_FIELD	The field is logical, containing Y, y, N, n, T, t, F, or f
M	MEMO_FIELD	The field is a pointer to a 512-byte memo field in the .DBT file, so the file position is computed as 512 times the field's value. A memo field has a fixed length of 512 bytes.
D	DATE_FIELD	The field is a date formatted as YYYYMMDD.

Value	Identifier	Description
F	FLOAT_FIELD	The field is a floating-point number. (Not found in all database programs because this type is not dBASE III-compatible).
P	PICTURE_FIELD	The field is in picture format. (Not found in all database programs because this type is not dBASE III-compatible.)

The lFieldPointer member is used by some versions of dBASE as the displacement of the field in the record:

```
long            lFieldPointer;
```

Because you should not depend on this field being set, the field offsets are computed based on the sizes of the previous fields. For most versions of dBASE, lFieldPointer is initialized to zero. Many programs that create a dBASE-compatible file use this field for their own purposes—whether this is a good idea is up to you, the programmer.

The byLength member contains the length of the field:

```
unsigned char  byLength;
```

This length is the only indicator of where one field ends and the other begins. The sum of byLength for each column, plus 1 for the record status byte, equals the file header's nRecordLength member. (The record status byte is also called the deleted flag byte and is the first byte in every record.)

The program uses the byDecimalPlace member to determine the format of the numbers in the column. If the value of byDecimalPlace is zero, the numbers in the column are integer. If the value is greater than zero, the numbers are floating point. Because decimal places are stored in the database, you can use simple scanf() calls to read the column's value. If necessary, the column's value can be saved for later display of the number.

```
unsigned char  byDecimalPlace;
```

Finally, 14 bytes of space in the column definition are unused and marked as reserved. You should not use these bytes:

```
char            szReserved[14];
```

473

Reading dBASE and dBASE-Compatible Files

Reading dBASE-compatible files is a simple process. These files consist of a file header, column headers, and data. They are organized in a fixed manner, have a simple structure, and have data that is generally in an ASCII format, easily read into a set of variables using sscanf() function calls.

To read a dBASE file, you need only a simple program. Listing 12.1, DBREAD.C, reads a dBASE III file and prints each record's raw data to the screen.

Listing 12.1. DBREAD.C.

```
/* DBREAD, written 1992 by Peter D. Hipson */
/* This program reads dBASE III files. /*

#include <stdio.h>
#include <stddef.h>
#include <stdlib.h>

/* Some defines useful for dBASE files: */

/* Actual record status defines (first byte of each record) */
#define DELETED_RECORD '*'
#define USABLE_RECORD ' '

/* Field (column) definitions (capital letters, please) */

#define NUMERIC_FIELD      'N'
#define CHARACTER_FIELD    'C'
#define LOGICAL_FIELD      'L'
#define MEMO_FIELD         'M'
#define DATE_FIELD         'D'
#define FLOAT_FIELD        'F'
#define PICTURE_FIELD      'P'

/* End of dBASE defines */

#pragma pack(1) /* Pack to byte boundaries */

typedef struct   {
```

```
/*  Bitfields are arranged from least significant to most significant */
    unsigned int    bfVersion:7;
    unsigned int    bfHasMemo:1;
    unsigned int    bYear:8;
    unsigned char   bMonth;
    unsigned char   bDay;
    long int        lNumberRecords;
    short int       nFirstRecordOffset;
    short int       nRecordLength;
    unsigned char   szReserved[20];
    } DB3HEADER;


typedef struct   {
    char            szColumnName[11];
    char            chType;
    long            lFieldPointer;
    unsigned char   byLength;
    unsigned char   byDecimalPlace;
    char            szReserved[14];
    } COLUMNDEF;


int    main()

{

FILE    *DBFile;

DB3HEADER   db3Header;

COLUMNDEF    *ColumnDef;

unsigned char * pBuffer;

char    szFileName[25];

int     i;
int     nColumnCount = 0;
int     nResult;
```

continues

475

Listing 12.1. continued

```
long    lCurrentRecord = 0;

double  dSales = 0.0; /* Forces loading of floating point support.*/



    printf("sizeof(DB3HEADER) = %d\n", sizeof(DB3HEADER));
    printf("sizeof(COLUMNDEF) = %d\n", sizeof(COLUMNDEF));

    printf("Please enter customer database name: ");

    gets(szFileName);

    DBFile = fopen(szFileName, "rb");

    if (DBFile == NULL)
    {
        fprintf(stderr,
            "ERROR: File '%s' couldn't be opened.\n", szFileName);

        exit(4);
    }

    nResult = fread((char *)&db3Header,
        sizeof(DB3HEADER),
        1,
        DBFile);

    if (nResult != 1)
    {
        if (!feof(DBFile))
        {
            fprintf(stderr, "ERROR: File '%s', read error (Database \
                            header).\n",
                szFileName);

            fclose(DBFile);

            exit(4);
        }
```

```
        else
        {
            fprintf(stderr, "Unexpected end of database file '%s'.\n",
                szFileName);

            fclose(DBFile);

            exit(4);
        }
    }

    if (db3Header.bfHasMemo)
    {
        printf("There is a .DBT memo\n");
    }
    else
    {
        printf("There is no a .DBT memo\n");
    }

    printf("Created with version %d of dBASE. \n",
        db3Header.bfVersion);

    if (db3Header.bfVersion != 3 &&
        db3Header.bfVersion != 4)
    {
        printf("The version of dBASE that created this file "
            "may not be compatible.\n");
    }

    printf("Updated last on: %d/", db3Header.bMonth);
    printf("%d", db3Header.bDay);
    printf(" 19%d\n", db3Header.bYear);

    printf("There are %ld records in the database. \n",
        db3Header.lNumberRecords);

    printf("The first record starts at byte %d. \n",
        db3Header.nFirstRecordOffset);

    printf("Each record is %d bytes long. \n",
        db3Header.nRecordLength);
```

continues

Listing 12.1. continued

```c
        printf("The reserved field contains '%s' \n",
            db3Header.szReserved);

        nColumnCount =
            (db3Header.nFirstRecordOffset - sizeof(DB3HEADER)) /
            sizeof(COLUMNDEF);

        printf("There are %d columns in each record. \n", nColumnCount);

    /*  Now allocate memory for each of the column definitions: */

        ColumnDef = (COLUMNDEF *)calloc(sizeof(COLUMNDEF), nColumnCount);

        if (ColumnDef == (COLUMNDEF *)NULL)
        {
            fprintf(stderr,
                "Couldn't allocate memory for the column definitions \n");

            fclose(DBFile);

            exit(4);
        }

        nResult = fread((char *)ColumnDef,
            sizeof(COLUMNDEF),
            nColumnCount,
            DBFile);

        if (nResult != nColumnCount)
        {
            if (!feof(DBFile))
            {
                fprintf(stderr, "ERROR: File '%s', read error (Column \
                                definitions).\n",
                    szFileName);

                fclose(DBFile);

                exit(4);
            }
```

```
    else
    {
        fprintf(stderr, "Unexpected end of database file '%s'"
            " while reading column definitions.\n",
            szFileName);

        fclose(DBFile);

        exit(4);
    }
}

printf("Column definitions: \n");

for (i = 0; i < nColumnCount; i++)
{
    printf("Name: '%10.10s' ", ColumnDef[i].szColumnName);

    switch(ColumnDef[i].chType)
    {
        case NUMERIC_FIELD: /* Number field */
            printf(" (Numeric)\n");
            break;

        case CHARACTER_FIELD: /* Character field */
            printf(" (Character)\n");
            break;

        case LOGICAL_FIELD: /* Logical (using 'Y', 'N', etc */
            printf(" (Logical)\n");
            break;

        case MEMO_FIELD: /* Memo Index field */
            printf(" (Memo file .DBT Index)\n");
            break;

        case DATE_FIELD: /* Date in YYYYMMDD format */
            printf(" (Date in YYYYMMDD)\n");
            break;
```

continues

479

Listing 12.1. continued

```
                case FLOAT_FIELD: /* Floating point field */
                    printf(" (Floating point)\n");
                    break;

                case PICTURE_FIELD: /* Date in YYYYMMDD format */
                    printf(" (Picture format)\n");
                    break;

                default: /* Unknown type of field */
                    printf(" (Field type unknown)\n");
                    break;
            }

        printf("Length: %d\n", ColumnDef[i].byLength);
        printf("DecimalPoint: %d\n", ColumnDef[i].byDecimalPlace);
        printf("Reserved '%s'\n", ColumnDef[i].szReserved);
    }

/*  Next allocate the buffer to hold a database record
 *  We add a byte for the terminating \0, which is not supplied by
 *  dBASE as part of the record.
 */

    pBuffer = (unsigned char *)calloc(sizeof(char),
        db3Header.nRecordLength + 1);

    if (pBuffer == (unsigned char *)NULL)
    {
        fprintf(stderr,
            "Couldn't allocate memory for the column buffer\n");

        fclose(DBFile);

        exit(4);
    }

    nResult = fseek(DBFile,
        (long)db3Header.nFirstRecordOffset, SEEK_SET);

    if (nResult != 0)
```

```c
{
    if (!feof(DBFile))
    {
        fprintf(stderr, "ERROR: File '%s', seek error.\n",
            szFileName);

        fclose(DBFile);

        exit(4);
    }
    else
    {
        fprintf(stderr, "Unexpected end of database file '%s'"
            " while reading record.\n",
            szFileName);

        fclose(DBFile);

        exit(4);
    }
}

for (lCurrentRecord = 0;
    lCurrentRecord < db3Header.lNumberRecords;
    ++lCurrentRecord)
{
    nResult = fread((char *)pBuffer,
        db3Header.nRecordLength, 1, DBFile);

    if (nResult != 1)
    {
        if (!feof(DBFile))
        {
            fprintf(stderr, "ERROR: File '%s', read error \
                            (records).\n",
                szFileName);

            fclose(DBFile);

            exit(4);
        }
        else
```

continues

Listing 12.1. continued

```c
        {
            fprintf(stderr, "Unexpected end of database file '%s'"
                " while reading records.\n",
                szFileName);

            fclose(DBFile);

            exit(4);
        }
    }

    pBuffer[db3Header.nRecordLength] = '\0';

/*  Where we print inside the switch, a program that would use the
 *      database records would parse, and read each field, probably
 *      using a built format string and a call to sscanf().
 */

    switch(pBuffer[0])
    {
        case USABLE_RECORD: /* Valid, undeleted record */
            printf("Record  '%s'\n", &pBuffer[1]);
            break;

        case DELETED_RECORD: /* Record has been deleted. Usually,
                                    you'd ignore it. */
            printf("Deleted '%s'\n", &pBuffer[1]);
            break;

        default: /* The record's status is unknown */
            printf("Unknown '%s'\n", &pBuffer[1]);
            break;
    }
}

return(0);

}
```

In DBREAD, first the file is opened, then the file header is read into the DB3HEADER structure. The information placed in this structure is used to read the column definitions and the data records.

Next, the program allocates the memory for the column definitions by computing the number of columns:

```
nColumnCount =
    (db3Header.nFirstRecordOffset - sizeof(DB3HEADER)) /
    sizeof(COLUMNDEF);
```

The calloc() function uses the nColumnCount variable to allocate the required memory. The column definitions are saved for later use.

```
ColumnDef = (COLUMNDEF *)calloc(sizeof(COLUMNDEF), nColumnCount);
```

After the memory is allocated, the column definitions are read. A loop is not necessary; the program uses one read in which the number of bytes is computed from the size of the structure and the number of columns in the database:

```
nResult = fread((char *)ColumnDef,
    sizeof(COLUMNDEF),
    nColumnCount,
    DBFile);
```

After all the columns have been read (determined by the return value from a call to the fread() function), the program can process them as required. In this simple example, the information is printed to the screen. A for() loop is an easy and effective way to process the columns:

```
for (i = 0; i < nColumnCount; i++)
{
    printf("Name: '%10.10s' ", ColumnDef[i].szColumnName);
```

When the format of the records has been determined, the program can process the records in the dBASE file. First, a buffer must be allocated to hold the records. The buffer's size is known (or can be computed from the size of each record, not forgetting the byte for the record's status):

```
pBuffer = (unsigned char *)calloc(sizeof(char),
    db3Header.nRecordLength + 1);
```

Because we do not use dBASE's index files, we accept the records in the order that they are stored in the file, using a simple for() loop. Before reading the records, I recommend that you do a seek to the known point where the first record can be found.

This is necessary because dBASE adds a carriage return (0x0D) after the column definitions and may well add another extra byte. This point is found in the file header, in the `nFirstRecordOffset` member of the `DB3HEADER` structure.

```
nResult = fseek(DBFile,
    (long)db3Header.nFirstRecordOffset, SEEK_SET);
```

The program is now at the position of the first record in the dBASE file, so it can read each record:

```
for (lCurrentRecord = 0;
    lCurrentRecord < db3Header.lNumberRecords;
    ++lCurrentRecord)
{
    nResult = fread((char *)pBuffer,
        db3Header.nRecordLength, 1, DBFile);
```

As each record is read, the first byte tells you the status of the record. If the first byte is a blank, the record is not deleted. If the byte is *, the record has been deleted and should not be processed (unless you are writing a deleted record processor!).

Creating dBASE and dBASE-Compatible Files

With a little care, you can read a dBASE file or create a dBASE-compatible file without difficulty. The process of creating a dBASE-compatible file is basically the reverse of reading a file.

Listing 12.2, DBWRITE.C, is a simple program that creates a simple dBASE III-compatible .DBF file. This file can be read by any program that can read dBASE files.

Listing 12.2. DBWRITE.C.

```
/* DBWRITE, written 1992 by Peter D. Hipson   */
/* This program creates a dBASE-compatible file. */
/* Derived from DBREAD.C */

#include <stdio.h>
#include <stddef.h>
#include <stdlib.h>
#include <string.h>
#include <time.h>
```

```c
/* Some defines that are useful for dBASE files: */

/* Record status defines (first byte of each record) */
#define DELETED_RECORD '*'
#define USABLE_RECORD ' '

/* Field (column) definitions (capital letters, please) */
#define NUMERIC_FIELD      'N'
#define CHARACTER_FIELD    'C'
#define LOGICAL_FIELD      'L'
#define MEMO_FIELD         'M'
#define DATE_FIELD         'D'
#define FLOAT_FIELD        'F'
#define PICTURE_FIELD      'P'

/* End of dBASE defines */

#pragma pack(1) /* Pack to byte boundaries */

typedef struct   {
/*  Bit fields are arranged from least significant to most significant */
    unsigned int    bfVersion:7;
    unsigned int    bfHasMemo:1;
    unsigned int    bYear:8;
    unsigned char   bMonth;
    unsigned char   bDay;
    long int        lNumberRecords;
    short int       nFirstRecordOffset;
    short int       nRecordLength;
    unsigned char   szReserved[20];
    } DB3HEADER;


typedef struct   {
    char            szColumnName[11];
    char            chType;
    long            lFieldPointer;
    unsigned char   byLength;
    unsigned char   byDecimalPlace;
    char            szReserved[14];
    } COLUMNDEF;
```

continues

Listing 12.2. continued

```
int     main()

{

FILE     *DBFile;

DB3HEADER    db3Header;

struct _DBRECORD {
    char     sStatus[1]; /* Status does not count as a member */
    char     sName[40];
    char     sAddr1[40];
    char     sAddr2[40];
    char     sCity[20];
    char     sState[2];
    char     sZip[5];
    } OurRecord;

char         *pOurRecord;

COLUMNDEF    ColumnDef[6]; /* Six members in OurRecord */

char         szBuffer[200];   /* Work buffer */
char         szTime[26];

char         szFileName[25];

int          i;
int          nColumnCount = 0;
int          nResult;

long         lCurrentRecord = 0;

double       dSales = 0.0; /* Forces loading of floating-point support */

struct tm    *NewTime;
time_t       aClock;

/* Step 1. Determine the layout of the columns (fields). In this
 *          example, they are predefined. In other programs, you
```

```
*           might determine the column layout by prompting the user
*           or by examining the user's data.
*/

    printf("Please enter new database name: ");

    gets(szFileName);

    DBFile = fopen(szFileName, "wb");

    if (DBFile == NULL)
    {
        fprintf(stderr,
            "ERROR: File '%s' couldn't be opened.\n", szFileName);

        exit(4);
    }

/* Step 2. Initialize and write the header record.
 */

    time( &aClock );

    NewTime = localtime(&aClock);

    memset(&db3Header, 0, sizeof(db3Header));

    /* Make it dBASE III-compatible */
    db3Header.bfVersion = 3;

    /* Make it a database with no memo fields */
    db3Header.bfHasMemo = 0;

    /* Set the date to now, but UPDATE when closing */
    /* because date may have changed */
    db3Header.bYear = NewTime->tm_year;
    db3Header.bMonth = (unsigned char)(NewTime->tm_mon + 1);
    db3Header.bDay   = (unsigned char)NewTime->tm_mday;

    /* No records in the database yet */
    db3Header.lNumberRecords = 0;
```

continues

Listing 12.2. continued

```
        /* File header, plus column headers, plus a byte for the carriage
           return */
        db3Header.nFirstRecordOffset = sizeof(DB3HEADER) + sizeof(ColumnDef)
                                    + 2;

        /* Make it the size of a record in the database */
        db3Header.nRecordLength = sizeof(OurRecord);

        nResult = fwrite((char *)&db3Header,
            sizeof(DB3HEADER),
            1,
            DBFile);

        if (nResult != 1)
        {
            fprintf(stderr, "ERROR: File '%s', write error (Database \
                            header).\n",
                szFileName);

            fclose(DBFile);

            exit(4);
        }

    /* Step 3. Initialize the column headers using the information from step
       1.*/

        memset(ColumnDef, 0, sizeof(ColumnDef));

    /*  Do the following for each column, either inline or using a loop */

        strcpy(ColumnDef[0].szColumnName, "Name");
        ColumnDef[0].chType = CHARACTER_FIELD;
        ColumnDef[0].byLength = sizeof(OurRecord.sName);
        ColumnDef[0].byDecimalPlace = 0;

        strcpy(ColumnDef[1].szColumnName, "Address1");
        ColumnDef[1].chType = CHARACTER_FIELD;
        ColumnDef[1].byLength = sizeof(OurRecord.sAddr1);
```

```
    ColumnDef[1].byDecimalPlace = 0;

    strcpy(ColumnDef[2].szColumnName, "Address2");
    ColumnDef[2].chType = CHARACTER_FIELD;
    ColumnDef[2].byLength = sizeof(OurRecord.sAddr2);
    ColumnDef[2].byDecimalPlace = 0;

    strcpy(ColumnDef[3].szColumnName, "City");
    ColumnDef[3].chType = CHARACTER_FIELD;
    ColumnDef[3].byLength = sizeof(OurRecord.sCity);
    ColumnDef[3].byDecimalPlace = 0;

    strcpy(ColumnDef[4].szColumnName, "State");
    ColumnDef[4].chType = CHARACTER_FIELD;
    ColumnDef[4].byLength = sizeof(OurRecord.sState);
    ColumnDef[4].byDecimalPlace = 0;

    strcpy(ColumnDef[5].szColumnName, "Zipcode");
    ColumnDef[5].chType = CHARACTER_FIELD;
    ColumnDef[5].byLength = sizeof(OurRecord.sZip);
    ColumnDef[5].byDecimalPlace = 0;

    nResult = fwrite((char *)ColumnDef,
        sizeof(ColumnDef),
        1,
        DBFile);

    if (nResult != 1)
    {
        fprintf(stderr, "ERROR: File '%s', write error (Column \
                        headers).\n",
            szFileName);

        fclose(DBFile);

        exit(4);
    }

/* Step 4. Write a carriage return (and a NULL) to meet dBASE standards
 */
```

continues

Listing 12.2. continued

```c
        nResult = fwrite((char *)"\x0D\0",
            sizeof(char) * 2,
            1,
            DBFile);

        if (nResult != 1)
        {
            fprintf(stderr, "ERROR: File '%s', write error (Column \
                            headers).\n",
                szFileName);

            fclose(DBFile);

            exit(4);
        }

        db3Header.nFirstRecordOffset = (int)ftell(DBFile);

    /* Step 5. Get some records for the database. */

        memset(&OurRecord, 0, sizeof(OurRecord));

        printf("Enter the name: (or no name to end)");
        gets(szBuffer);
        strncpy(OurRecord.sName, szBuffer, sizeof(OurRecord.sName));

        while (strlen(szBuffer) > 0)
        {
            OurRecord.sStatus[0] = USABLE_RECORD;

            printf("Enter address line 1: ");
            gets(szBuffer);
            strncpy(OurRecord.sAddr1, szBuffer, sizeof(OurRecord.sAddr1));

            printf("Enter address line 2:");
            gets(szBuffer);
            strncpy(OurRecord.sAddr2, szBuffer, sizeof(OurRecord.sAddr2));

            printf("Enter city:");
```

```c
        gets(szBuffer);
        strncpy(OurRecord.sCity, szBuffer, sizeof(OurRecord.sCity));

        printf("Enter state (2 characters only):");
        gets(szBuffer);
        strncpy(OurRecord.sState, szBuffer, sizeof(OurRecord.sState));

        printf("Enter Zipcode:");
        gets(szBuffer);
        strncpy(OurRecord.sZip, szBuffer, sizeof(OurRecord.sZip));

/*      dBASE records do not contain NULLs, but are padded with
 *      blanks instead, so we convert the NULLs to spaces
 */

        pOurRecord = (char *)&OurRecord;

        for (i = 0; i < sizeof(OurRecord); i++)
        {
            if (pOurRecord[i] == '\0')
            {
                pOurRecord[i] = ' ';
            }
        }

        nResult = fwrite((char *)&OurRecord,
            sizeof(OurRecord),
            1,
            DBFile);

        if (nResult != 1)
        {
            fprintf(stderr, "ERROR: File '%s', write error (Column \
                        headers).\n",
                szFileName);

            fclose(DBFile);

            exit(4);
        }
        else
        {
```

continues

Listing 12.2. continued

```
                ++db3Header.lNumberRecords;
        }

        memset(&OurRecord, 0, sizeof(OurRecord));

        printf("Enter the name: (or no name to end)");
        gets(szBuffer);
        strncpy(OurRecord.sName, szBuffer, sizeof(OurRecord.sName));
    }

/* Step 6. Update the file header with the current time and
 *         the number of records.
 */

    time( &aClock );

    NewTime = localtime(&aClock);

    /* Set the date to now */
    db3Header.bYear = NewTime->tm_year;
    db3Header.bMonth = (unsigned char)(NewTime->tm_mon + 1);
    db3Header.bDay   = (unsigned char)NewTime->tm_mday;

    /* The number of records is already set */

    nResult = fseek(DBFile, (long)0, SEEK_SET);

    if (nResult != 0)
    {
        fprintf(stderr, "ERROR: File '%s', seek error (rewrite of \
                        header).\n",
            szFileName);

        fclose(DBFile);

        exit(4);
    }

    nResult = fwrite((char *)&db3Header,
        sizeof(DB3HEADER),
```

```
        1,
        DBFile);

    if (nResult != 1)
    {
        fprintf(stderr, "ERROR: File '%s', write error (Database header \
                        rewrite).\n",
            szFileName);

        fclose(DBFile);

        exit(4);
    }

/* Finished. Close the file and end the program.
 */

    fclose(DBFile);

    return(0);
}
```

Your program that *creates* a dBASE file must do the following, in order:

1. Determine the record layout. This may have been already defined by the application's requirements, or you may be using information supplied by the user. Each field must have a type and a length.

2. Initialize and write a dBASE file header (our DB3READ structure). You must initialize the record size (sum of fields plus the leading record deleted byte), the pointer to the first record, usually the byte after the end of header byte (see step 4), the date, and the time.

3. Initialize and write the field headers (our COLUMNDEF structure). Be sure you specify the field's name, length, and type.

4. Write the end of the header byte (0x0D); following the header byte with a NULL byte (0x00) is optional.

5. Write the records placed in the file at creation time. Be sure the deleted flag is set to blank so that the initial records are not deleted.

6. Seek to the beginning of the file and reset the file header's number of records count, date, and time. (The date and time are reset because they have changed since they were last written.) Rewrite the file header.

Each of these six steps were followed in DBWRITE.C and are indicated by comments in the program.

Updating dBASE and dBASE-Compatible Files

When you update a dBASE file, I suggest that you update a copy of the original file. If you update the original file, you risk damaging the original file if your program crashes. I never work on the only copy of a file. Instead, I copy the original .DBF file to a .BAK file or a temporary work file.

The steps for updating a dBASE file follow:

1. Read the file header and the column (field) header records.

2. Read the file's data records if necessary. Append to the file any new records that the user creates. If the user is deleting a record, mark it with the * delete flag in the first column (the deleted field) of the data record. Modify records as necessary. When modifying a record, many programs mark the original record as deleted, then make the changed record a new record. Although this technique is acceptable, the database file may grow excessively if many records are changed.

3. Write the updated file header record with a new date and record count.

Using a dBASE-compatible file structure increases your program's flexibility because the user can use other utilities (including a database program) to manipulate the data files.

Summary

In this chapter, you learned about interfacing C with database programs and with files created by dBASE-compatible programs.

• Database programs are one of the most common computer applications.

• The most common database file format is the dBASE III format. It is simple and easy to use.

- A dBASE III .DBF file can be read using two structures, as shown in the chapter.

- A dBASE III file can be created using simple C functions.

- A .DBF file can contain deleted records. It is possible to write a program that recreates the database and undeletes the deleted records—if the database has not been packed and the space that the deleted records occupied has not been lost.

All About Header Files

Header files are a feature of the C language that helps the programmer write better programs. There are two types of header files: the files that the programmer writes and the files that come with your compiler. This chapter covers fifteen standard C header files. First, though, the chapter reviews the usage of function prototypes and how to make your prototypes more effective.

> The terms *header file* and *include file* are commonly used interchangeably. There are no differences between the two—header files *are* include files.

Function Prototypes

One of the most valuable improvements to C is the addition of function prototypes. A *function prototype* specifies the order and types of arguments that will be passed to a function. It specifies also the type of the function's return value, if the function returns a value. In early versions of C, the compiler would accept any arguments to a function.

Suppose that a function called `MultFloat()` accepts two `float` arguments and returns the product of the two arguments as a `float`. Using an early version of C that does not have function prototypes, you could pass two integers to `MultFloat()`. These arguments would be passed unchanged, and `MultFloat()`—unaware of the wrong argument types—would return a bogus value or signal a floating-point error.

A function prototype consists of three major parts:

- The return value. If the function returns nothing, the prototype should have a return type of `void`.

- The function's name. I recommend that you use mixed case and no under-scores. Underscores can be a problem with linkers that allow only six signifi-cant characters.

- The function's parameters. Be explicit about size and type when possible. If you can, include the variable name that will be used by the function because the name implies what the argument does.

The function prototype is the declaration of the function. The function itself is defined (and has a body) later in the program or in a different source file.

Following is a function prototype for a function that compares two strings:

```
int OurStrCmp(void far *, void far *);
```

In this function prototype, a function returns an integer. The size of this integer is unimportant and therefore undefined—it could be `short` or `long`, depending on the compiler's default integer size. If the size of the returned value is important, you must specify the size. `OurStrCmp()` returns a value that is only less than zero, zero, or greater than zero.

Both of the parameters passed to the function are defined as pointers to type `void`. Here, the `void` type means the pointers have no specific type, and any pointer type can be passed. If your function expects only a character string pointer, specify this in your function prototype. If the arguments will not be modified when passing pointers, specify this also using the `const` keyword.

Because `OurStrCmp()` only compares strings, the prototype could be more specific. Rewriting the function prototype for `OurStrCmp()` results in the following:

```
short int OurStrCmp(const char far *, const char far *);
```

Now the function prototype is more complete. However, let's add the variable names to make it more readable:

```
short int OurStrCmp(const char far * szStringA,
                    const char far * szStringB);
```

This prototype is more detailed and allows the compiler to check the types of the arguments passed to the function. In addition, when the function is created, the prototype is used to check whether the function has been properly declared.

If you write your prototypes like the one presented here, the easiest way to write the function for that prototype is to start with the prototype, delete the ending semicolon, and add the function's opening and closing braces. Although many prototypes are written on one line, a function's declaration is commonly written with each argument on a new line, as follows:

```
short int OurStrCmp( /* Returns the result of the compare */
    const char far * szStringA, /* The first string to compare */
    const char far * szStringB) /* The second string to compare */

{

/* The body of the function */

} /* end:   OurStrCmp() */
```

This function declaration fully documents the return value and the parameters.

When you create a header file, provide for the possibility that the header file is included more than once. A typical way to do this is to create an identifier; if the identifier exists, the header file has already been included. This could be coded as follows:

```
#ifndef  _MYHEADER
#define  _MYHEADER
/* Other lines in this header file */
#endif /* _MYHEADER   */
```

The `_MYHEADER` identifier must remain unique. This technique prevents errors from symbols defined more than once.

The ANSI C Header Files

ANSI C compilers contain a number of standard header files. These files are used for specific purposes—try not to include header files if you will not be using their functionality. For example, if your program does not have any time-based functions, including time.h will not improve your program but will slow the compiler.

Table 13.1 lists some common identifiers. The table includes both defined identifiers and those that are integral parts of the C language.

Table 13.1. Typical header file identifiers.

Identifier	Description
size_t	An identifier that is guaranteed to hold the size of any definable data object. This identifier is usually defined as type unsigned int.
far	With segmented (PC 80x86) architecture, a 32-bit pointer. Usually consists of a segment (or selector) and an offset.
near	With segmented (PC 80x86) architecture, a 16-bit pointer. Usually consists of an offset, without any segment (or selector) information. The object being identified is in the default segment.
__FILE__	The filename of the current file (and header files that have been included).
__LINE__	The current line number of the current file. Each included header file has its own number.
const	A modifier that tells the compiler that the variable should be treated as a constant and should not be modified.
volatile	A modifier that tells the compiler that the variable may be changed in a way that the compiler cannot detect. Examples of undetectable changes are when the variable is modified by an interrupt handler or by a function that uses setjmp().

The rest of this chapter describes the standard C header files. Header files specific to particular C compilers are not included in the discussion. To learn about compiler-specific header files, refer to your compiler's documentation and look at the files themselves.

Your compiler may not contain all the header files described in this chapter. If that is the case, the contents of the header file (or files) are probably included in another header file. A likely choice is the `stdlib.h` file, which often serves as a catchall.

The assert.h File (ANSI)

The `assert.h` header file is used for the `assert()` macro. Note that `assert()` is *always* implemented as a macro and is never directly implemented as a function.

You can test a condition with the `assert()` macro. If the condition tests as TRUE, nothing happens. If the condition tests as FALSE, the following message is printed to `stderr`:

Assertion failed: *condition, filename, linenumber*

The *condition* is printed as a text string, along with the source file name and the current line number in the current file. After the message is printed, the program calls `abort()` to end the program—a failed `assert()` definitely ends your program!

To turn off the effect of the `assert()` macro, you must define the NDEBUG identifier. When this identifier is defined, `assert()` evaluates as `((void)0)`, which is effectively nothing.

The typical definition of the `assert()` macro is

```
#define assert(exp)((exp) ? (void) 0 : \
  _assert(#exp,_ _FILE_ _,_ _LINE_ _) )
```

If the expression evaluates to FALSE, the condition, filename and line number in the `assert()` macro are passed to a function. If the condition evaluates to TRUE, the macro evaluates to `((void)0)`.

The `assert()` macro is a valuable tool when you are debugging your program, but you must remember to define NDEBUG when creating the production version of the program.

The ctype.h File (ANSI)

The ctype.h header file contains the character conversion functions that work with a single character. For conversion functions that use strings, see the string.h header file. A character can be classified as any one of the types shown in Table 13.2.

Table 13.2. Common character type identifiers not part of the ANSI standard.

Identifier	Description
_UPPER	An uppercase letter
_LOWER	A lowercase letter
_DIGIT	A digit (0–9)
_SPACE	A tab, a carriage return, a newline, a vertical tab, or a form feed
_PUNCT	A punctuation character
_CONTROL	A control character
_BLANK	A space character
_HEX	A hexadecimal digit (0–9, a–f, A–F)

The following functions are defined in the ctype.h header file. Although these functions are defined with a parameter type of int, they are typically passed a parameter of char. The compiler performs the necessary conversion.

isalpha()	Returns TRUE if the character is alphabetic
isupper()	Returns TRUE if the character is uppercase
islower()	Returns TRUE if the character is lowercase
isdigit()	Returns TRUE if the character is a numeric digit
isxdigit()	Returns TRUE if the character is a hexadecimal digit
isspace()	Returns TRUE if the character is a whitespace character
ispunct()	Returns TRUE if the character is a punctuation character

isalnum()	Returns TRUE if the character is alphabetic or numeric
isprint()	Returns TRUE if the character is a printable character
isgraph()	Returns TRUE if the character is a nonspace printable character
iscntrl()	Returns TRUE if the character is a control character
toupper()	Converts the character to uppercase
tolower()	Converts the character to lowercase
_tolower()	Converts the character to lowercase
_toupper()	Converts the character to uppercase

Many of these functions are also defined as macros. See Table 13.3. These macros are used unless they are undefined using the #undef statement, which must be included after the ctype.h header file is included.

Table 13.3. Character classification macros.

Macro	Definition
isalpha(_c)	((_ctype+1)[_c] & (_UPPER¦_LOWER))
isupper(_c)	((_ctype+1)[_c] & _UPPER)
islower(_c)	((_ctype+1)[_c] & _LOWER)
isdigit(_c)	((_ctype+1)[_c] & _DIGIT)
isxdigit(_c)	((_ctype+1)[_c] & _HEX)
isspace(_c)	((_ctype+1)[_c] & _SPACE)
ispunct(_c)	((_ctype+1)[_c] & _PUNCT)
isalnum(_c)	((_ctype+1)[_c] & (_UPPER¦_LOWER¦_DIGIT))
isprint(_c)	((_ctype+1)[_c] & (_BLANK¦_PUNCT¦_UPPER¦_LOWER¦_DIGIT))
isgraph(_c)	((_ctype+1)[_c] & (_PUNCT¦_UPPER¦_LOWER¦_DIGIT))
iscntrl(_c)	((_ctype+1)[_c] & _CONTROL)

continues

503

Table 13.3. continued

Macro	Definition
toupper(_c)	((islower(_c)) ? _toupper(_c) : (_c))
tolower(_c)	((isupper(_c)) ? _tolower(_c) : (_c))
_tolower(_c)	((_c)-'A'+'a')
_toupper(_c)	((_c)-'a'+'A')
__isascii(_c)	((unsigned)(_c) < 0x80)
__toascii(_c)	((_c) & 0x7f)

The character classification macros reference an array of bytes called _ctype. The bits in this array are set based on the character's classification. This allows a fast test of a character's attributes in a macro.

Both the toupper() and tolower() functions return the correctly converted character or the supplied character if there is no conversion. It is no longer necessary to check whether the character is uppercase or lowercase first.

The errno.h File (ANSI)

The errno.h header file has identifiers for the error codes returned by the errno() function. C compilers may define different values for each identifier, so you should never hard code an integer constant—use the identifier instead.

The errno() function is generally coded as a function, then defined to appear as a variable called errno. Table 13.4 lists the common values for errno.

Table 13.4. Typical errno values.

Error code	Description
E2BIG	The argument list is too long.
EACCES	You cannot access the file, probably because the file is not compatible with your request or the file has an attribute (such as read only) that is incompatible with your request.

Error code	Description
EAGAIN	You cannot create any more child processes.
EBADF	The specified file number is invalid (probably not a currently opened file), or the file is opened in a mode incompatible with the requested action.
EDEADLOCK	The resource could not be locked (after a preset number of tries), and a resource deadlock would occur.
EDOM	The argument to a math function is not in the domain of the function.
EEXIST	The file that is to be created already exists.
EINVAL	The specified argument is invalid.
EMFILE	Too many files are open.
ENOENT	The file or directory cannot be found.
ENOEXEC	The file that was to be executed was not an executable file.
ENOMEM	There is not enough RAM.
ENOSPC	The disk drive is full.
ERANGE	The argument to a math function was too large, resulting in a partial or total loss of significance.
EXDEV	An attempt was made to rename (using rename()) a file to a new directory on a different drive.

Other errno values are specific to the environment or compiler. The use of errno is generally defined in a function's error conditions. For example, the description for the read() function includes information that errno may be set to EBADF if a bad file handle is encountered.

Include   <io.h>, <errno.h>

Syntax   int read(int handle, void *buffer, unsigned int
                   count);

Returns	The number of bytes read or 0 at the end-of-file if the function was successful. Returns -1 if the function was not successful.

errno: EBADF

The float.h File (ANSI)

The floating-point header file, float.h, includes important information about the implementation's floating-point capabilities. This header file was discussed in Chapter 2, "Data Types, Constants, Variables, and Arrays."

The float.h header file is important to any program that uses floating-point math.

As the following list shows, most of the float.h header file deals with various constants. You can use these constants if necessary. For example, I use the FLT_MIN value to indicate a value that is missing (which is different from a zero value in my program).

DBL_DIG	For a data type of float, the number of decimal digits of precision
DBL_EPSILON	For a data type of float, the smallest value such that 1.0 + DBL_EPSILON != 1.0
DBL_MANT_DIG	For a data type of double, the number of bits in the mantissa
DBL_MAX	For a data type of double, the maximum value
DBL_MAX_10_EXP	For a data type of double, the maximum decimal exponent
DBL_MAX_EXP	For a data type of double, the maximum binary exponent
DBL_MIN	For a data type of double, the minimum positive value
DBL_MIN_10_EXP	For a data type of double, the minimum decimal exponent

DBL_MIN_EXP	For a data type of double, the minimum binary exponent
FLT_DIG	For a data type of float, the number of decimal digits of precision
FLT_EPSILON	For a data type of float, the smallest value such that 1.0 + FLT_EPSILON != 1.0
FLT_MANT_DIG	For a data type of float, the number of bits in the mantissa
FLT_MAX	For a data type of float, the maximum value
FLT_MAX_10_EXP	For a data type of float, the maximum decimal exponent
FLT_MAX_EXP	For a data type of float, the maximum binary exponent
FLT_MIN	For a data type of float, the minimum positive value
FLT_MIN_10_EXP	For a data type of float, the minimum decimal exponent
FLT_MIN_EXP	For a data type of float, the minimum binary exponent
FLT_RADIX	For a data type of float, the exponent radix
FLT_ROUNDS	For a data type of float, addition rounding
LDBL_DIG	For a data type of long double, the number of decimal digits of precision
LDBL_EPSILON	For a data type of long double, the smallest value such that 1.0 + LDBL_EPSILON != 1.0
LDBL_MANT_DIG	For a data type of long double, the number of bits in the mantissa
LDBL_MAX	For a data type of long double, the maximum value
LDBL_MAX_10_EXP	For a data type of long double, the maximum decimal exponent

LDBL_MAX_EXP	For a data type of long double, the maximum binary exponent
LDBL_MIN	For a data type of long double, the minimum positive value
LDBL_MIN_10_EXP	For a data type of long double, the minimum decimal exponent
LDBL_MIN_EXP	For a data type of long double, the minimum binary exponent

The io.h File

The io.h header file supplements the stdio.h header file of ANSI C. The file, as shown in this book, is used with various Microsoft versions of C. The io.h header file contains various low-level I/O function prototypes.

The limits.h File (ANSI)

All parts of the C language contain limits. Many of the limits that apply to floating-point math are in the float.h header file. The integer limits are in the limits.h header file and are shown in the following list:

CHAR_BIT	The number of bits in a char
SCHAR_MIN	The minimum signed char value
SCHAR_MAX	The maximum signed char value
UCHAR_MAX	The maximum unsigned char value
CHAR_MIN and SCHAR_MIN	The minimum char value
CHAR_MAX and SCHAR_MAX	The maximum char value
MB_LEN_MAX	The maximum number of bytes in a multibyte char
SHRT_MIN	The minimum (signed) short value

SHRT_MAX	The maximum (signed) short value
USHRT_MAX	The maximum unsigned short value
INT_MIN	The minimum (signed) int value
INT_MAX	The maximum (signed) int value
UINT_MAX	The maximum unsigned int value
LONG_MIN	The minimum (signed) long value
LONG_MAX	The maximum (signed) long value
ULONG_MAX	The maximum unsigned long value

Rather than hard code numeric values for these values, always use the identifiers.

The locale.h File (ANSI)

There are more ways to tell the time than there are hours in a day. Many countries have a special way of writing the time and date, and sometimes one country has more than one way to specify the time or date.

The locale.h header file defines how time and dates are formatted for the current country. You can set the locale by calling the C setlocale() function, with one of the parameters in Table 13.5 as the first parameter. The second parameter is either the character string "C" (for United States defaults) or " " for the native country's defaults. Any other string for the second parameter depends on the implementation of the compiler.

Table 13.5. Locale identifiers used with the lconv structure.

Identifier	Description
LC_ALL	Sets all categories.
LC_COLLATE	Sets the collate order. Used by strcoll() and strxfrm()
LC_CTYPE	Sets the character set queries for ctype.h
LC_MONETARY	Sets the display format for currency. No C functions use this information.

continues

Table 13.5. continued

Identifier	Description
LC_NUMERIC	Sets the display format for numbers. Used by `printf()` and `scanf()` type functions.
LC_TIME	Sets the display format for the time. This affects `strftime()`, `ctime()`, and `asctime()`.

The `localeconv()` function returns a pointer to the internal `lconv` structure, which contains the formatting information. The format and contents of `lconv` depend on the compiler, and as such are not documented here.

Although you can get a pointer to the `lconv` structure, you must use the `setlocale()` function to modify it rather than modify it directly. This limits your direct use of the structure to read only. Save the information pointed to by `localeconv()` in a buffer in your program because the structure pointed to by `localeconv()` may change or move.

The malloc.h File

Your system may have a header file called `malloc.h`. This header supplements the `stdlib.h` header file that is part of ANSI C. The `malloc.h` header file contains functions, identifiers, and other things that deal with memory allocation.

The math.h File (ANSI)

The `math.h` header file defines prototypes for the various floating-point functions. The `math.h` file and the `errno.h` file are often included with the `float.h` header file.

The memory.h File

The memory.h header file contains function prototypes for the memory functions and buffer manipulation functions. Many ANSI C compilers include these functions in the string.h header file. See Table 13.6.

Table 13.6. Memory functions.

Function	Description
memchr()	Returns a pointer to the first byte in a block matching the specified character
memcmp()	Compares two blocks of memory, returning any differences
memcpy()	Copies two *nonoverlapping* blocks of memory
memmove()	Copies two blocks of memory, which may or may not overlap
memset()	Fills a block of memory with the specified byte

The memory functions are used in much the same way as the string functions. Memory functions, however, work with a specific length; string functions expect a terminating NULL to mark the end of the string.

The search.h File

The search.h header file contains function prototypes for the search and sort routines. Many ANSI C compilers contain these functions in the stdlib.h header file. The search function, bsearch(), performs a binary search. The sort function, qsort(), performs a quick sort. Both functions require a user-written compare function.

The setjmp.h File (ANSI)

The setjmp() and longjmp() functions are defined in the setjmp.h header file. The ANSI C standard defines setjmp() as a macro. However, some compiler producers have written setjmp() as a function.

The signal.h File (ANSI)

ANSI C uses a signal to tell the program that an error has occurred. The signal.h header file defines the conditions that are trapped and optionally passed to the program. See Table 13.7.

Table 13.7. Signal values.

Value	Description
SIGINT	An interrupt, such as a Ctrl-C keypress. Required by ANSI.
SIGILL	An illegal instruction or an anomaly in the program's execution that is usually caused by corrupted memory. Required by ANSI.
SIGFPE	A floating-point error or another math error exception. Required by ANSI.
SIGSEGV	An attempt to access memory was made that the program does not allow. Required by ANSI.
SIGTERM	The program was requested to end (probably caused by the operating system shutting down). Required by ANSI.
SIGBREAK	A Ctrl-Break sequence.
SIGABRT	Abnormal termination, perhaps triggered with a call to abort(). Required by ANSI.

The two functions that deal with signaling are raise(), which triggers a signal condition, and signal(), which sets up the handler for the error condition.

The stdarg.h File (ANSI)

The stdarg.h header file has been designed to replace the varargs.h header file. Generally, you cannot mix these two header files in the same source file.

An important part of C programming is the capability to use a variable number of arguments. Just think of how printf() or scanf() would work without this capability.

If your program uses the stdarg.h header file, a function with a variable number of arguments must have at least one fixed (always present) argument. This fixed argument is passed to the va_start() routine to enable access to the variable arguments.

The program in Listing 13.1, VARGS.C, shows two ways to use a variable number of arguments. The OurErrors() function shows the use of vfprintf() as well. Because the vfprintf() is new, many programmers do not fully understand it yet.

Listing 13.1. VARGS.C

```c
/* VARGS, written 1992 by Peter D. Hipson */
/* This program demonstrates stdarg.h     */

#include <limits.h>
#include <stdarg.h>
#include <stdio.h>
#include <stdlib.h>

#define TRUE              1
#define FALSE             (!TRUE)

int     AddList(int nFirst, ...);
int     OurErrors(char * OutputFormat, ...);

void    main()

{

int     nSum;
```

continues

Listing 13.1. continued

```c
    nSum = AddList(10, 20, 30, 40, 50, 60, 70, 80, 90, INT_MIN);

    (void)OurErrors("%s - %d, %s\n", "First", nSum, "Second");

}

int     AddList(
    int nFirst,
    ...)

{

int     nReturnValue = nFirst;
int     nThisValue;

va_list Arguments;

    va_start(Arguments, nFirst);

    while((nThisValue = va_arg(Arguments, int)) != INT_MIN)
    {
        nReturnValue += nThisValue;
    }

    va_end(Arguments);

    return(nReturnValue);
}


int     OurErrors(
    char * OutputFormat,
    ...)

{

va_list Arguments;

    va_start(Arguments, OutputFormat);
```

```
vfprintf(stderr, OutputFormat, Arguments);

va_end(Arguments);

return(0);

}
```

The stddef.h File (ANSI)

The stddef.h header file is one of the more important header files for the C compiler. This header file contains many common constants, identifiers, types, and variables, for example, NULL and offsetof(). The NULL identifier is defined as zero or as a pointer that is guaranteed to point to nothing. The offsetof() macro determines the offset from the beginning of a structure to a given member. Most nontrivial programs should include stddef.h.

The stdio.h File (ANSI)

Most of the higher level I/O functions are in the stdio.h header file. This file is used in most (if not all) programs, because a program without I/O is rather uncommunicative!

One item defined in stdio.h is the structure that the FILE* type points to. Note, however, that you should never modify this structure's members.

Also defined in stdio.h are the constants that fseek() uses, including SEEK_CUR (the current file position), SEEK_END (the end of the file), and SEEK_SET (the beginning of the file).

The stdio.h header file also contains the prototypes for the various I/O functions and the standard file identifiers—stdin, stdout, stderr, stdaux, and stdprn.

The stdlib.h File (ANSI)

The stdlib.h header file contains the definitions and declarations for commonly used library functions. These library functions are usually found in the stdlib.h header file because they do not fit elsewhere or cannot be placed in other header files for technical reasons. This section describes some of the functions in the stdlib.h header file.

String Conversion

The string conversion functions convert strings to their numeric equivalent. The conversion process is performed in accordance with the locale settings, so that the thousands separator (a comma in the United States) may be recognized. The three ANSI functions for string conversion are strtod(), strtol(), and strtoul().

Memory Allocation

If a compiler does not have a separate memory allocation header file (such as malloc.h), the memory allocation functions are defined in stdlib.h.

Random Numbers

The C random number function is called rand(). The random numbers may be seeded using srand(). The sequence of random numbers repeats, however, if srand() receives the same seed each time. A common trick is to seed the random numbers with the current time or the elapsed time between two (or more) keystrokes.

Communications with the Operating System

You can issue operating system commands with the system() function. This function's behavior is not defined by ANSI C, with two exceptions. If the system() function is called with a NULL parameter, it returns TRUE if a command interpreter is present. If the system() parameter is called with NULL and signal() returns zero, you cannot issue commands to the operating system.

You can use the atexit() function to tell the operating system which functions should be called when the program ends. Although you can include functions, they cannot be removed after installation.

You can use abort() to end your program. Regardless of the use of the SIGABORT signal error handler, abort() will not return to the caller.

Search Functions

The bsearch() function is often defined in stdlib.h. Why bsearch() is defined here and qsort() is not is beyond me.

Integer Math

ANSI C has two integer math functions. These functions enable you to divide two integer values, and provide both a quotient and a remainder in one call. As well, these functions produce more predictable results than the division operator.

Multibyte Characters

Because ANSI C supports multibyte character sets (useful for languages that do not use the roman character set), there are functions to support character sets that have more than 256 characters. These characters are represented with a two-byte sequence, and their values depend on both the compiler and the language. You must read your compiler's documentation to determine which functions are provided and how to use them.

The string.h File (ANSI)

The various string manipulation functions are defined in the string.h header file. This file also contains various memory functions (such as the ones found in the memory.h header file).

The time.h File (ANSI)

The time functions are in the time.h header file. ANSI C added the strftime() function to the C language, which helps you format a time string.

The varargs.h File

In most C compilers, the stdarg.h header file has been replaced with the varargs.h header file. You usually cannot mix these two header files in the same source file.

Summary

In this chapter, you learned about the ANSI standard header files.

- Although there are standards for header files, most compilers add header files that offer additional functionality (such as graphics) or split the functionality of existing ANSI header files into several new files (such as Microsoft's use of the memory.h header file).

- The varargs.h and the stdarg.h files both define the passing of a variable number of arguments to a function. In general, the stdarg.h header file is considered the ANSI standard way to pass a variable number of arguments.

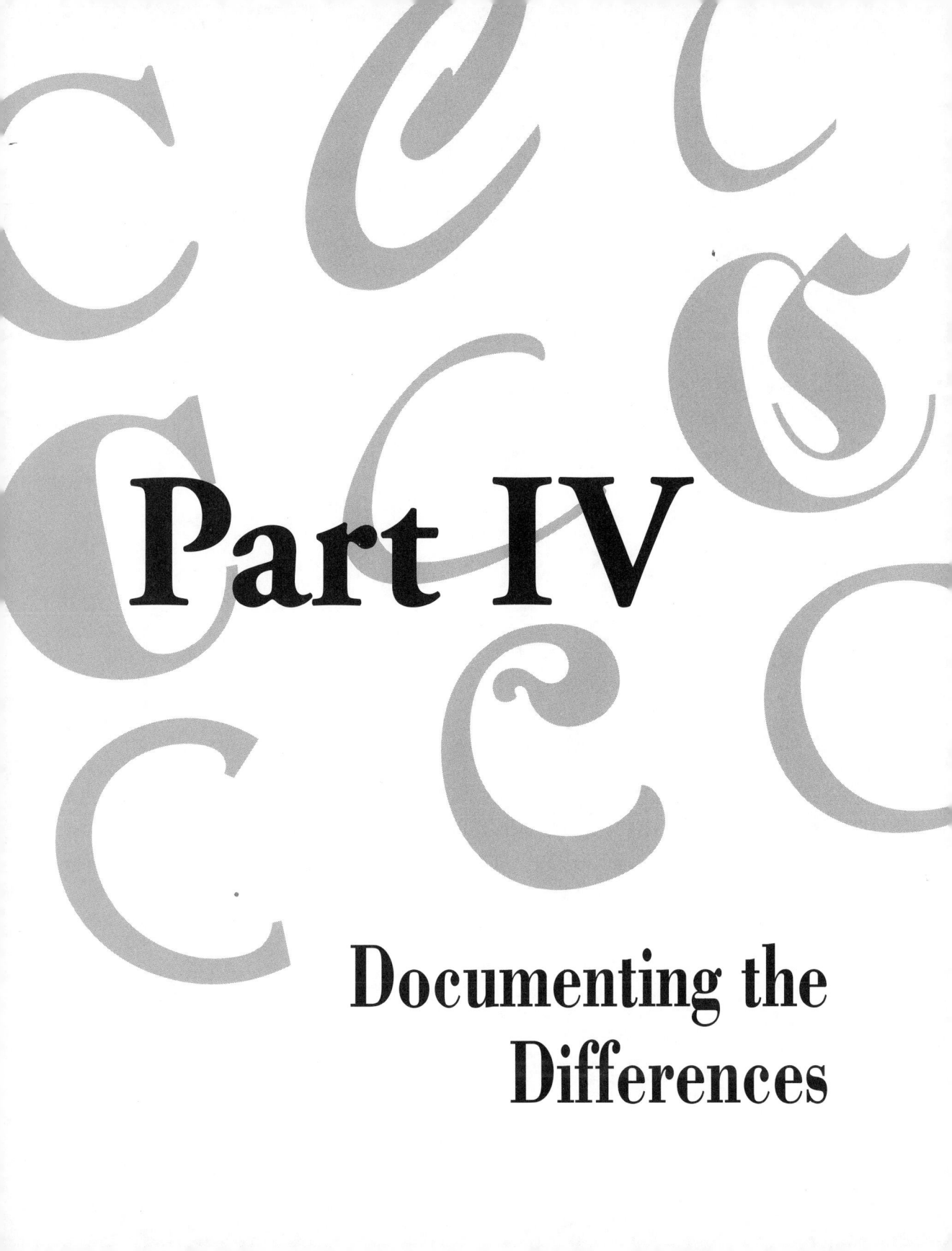

Part IV

Documenting the Differences

ANSI C's Library Functions

This chapter presents the ANSI C standard functions. I have not included functions that are not ANSI—there are several hundred additional non-ANSI functions that vary both in function and implementation between different compilers. For the non-ANSI functions, it is preferable to use the documentation that is supplied with the compiler because there may be differences between different implementations of a non-ANSI function that you would not expect.

Functions

The ANSI C libarary functions are presented below in alphabetical order.

abort()

Header:	process.h & stdlib.h
Syntax:	`void abort(void);`
Description:	Aborts (ends) the current program or process.
Parameters:	None.
Returns:	Does not return to caller.

Example:	`if (nDisaster)`
	`{`
	`abort();`
	`}`

Note:	Generally, use `abort()` only if recovery is not possible. Open files will probably be lost and any work entered by the user and not saved cannot be recovered.

abs()

Header:	math.h & stdlib.h
Syntax:	`int abs(int nValue);`
Description:	Returns the absolute value of the provided parameter.
Parameters:	`nValue`—A signed integer whose absolute value is desired.
Returns:	Returns the absolute value of the provided parameter.
Example:	`printf("abs(-20) = %d\n", abs(-20));` `/* Will print: abs(-20) = 20 */`

acos()

Header:	math.h
Syntax:	`double acos(double dValue);`
Description:	Provides the principal arc cosine of *dValue*.
Parameters:	*dValue*—Type double, ranging -1 to 1.
Returns:	Arc cosine, a value between zero and 3.1415926.
Example:	`dArcCos = acos(0.4);` `/* dArcCos will be 1.047 */`
Note:	Sets `errno` to `EDOM` if the parameter passed is outside the allowed range.

asctime()

Header:	time.h
Syntax:	`char * asctime(const struct tm *` `                    TimePointer);`
Description:	Converts time as contained in parameter `TimePointer` to a character string. The string's format follows the example: `Wed Jun 24 22:21:00 1992\n\0`.
Parameters:	A pointer to a properly initialized time structure.
Returns:	A character pointer to a string. You should copy this string to your program's own memory if you wish to save it.

Example:	`struct tm tmTime;`
	`time_t lTime;`
	
	`    time(&lTime);`
	`    tmTime = localtime(&ltime);`
	`    printf("Time: '%s'", asctime(&tmTime);`

Note:	Initialize the time structure (tm in the example) using `time()` and `localtime()`.

523

asin()

Header:	math.h
Syntax:	`double asin(double dValue);`
Description:	Returns the arcsine of parameter *dValue*.
Parameters:	*dValue*—Which must be in the range of -1 and 1.
Returns:	The arcsine of *dValue*.
Example:	`dArcSine = asin(0.5);` `/* dArcSine will be 0.5236 */`

assert()

Header:	assert.h
Syntax:	`void assert(unsigned nConditional);`
Description:	The `assert()` macro prints a message.
Parameters:	*nConditional*—A conditional expression, such as `(nCount < 0)`.
Returns:	No return value.
Example:	`assert(nCount < 0);`
Note:	If the conditional expression evaluates to 0, then a message containing the conditional expression, the source filename, and line number is printed to `stderr`, and the program ends.

atan()

Header:	math.h
Syntax:	`double atan(double dValue);`
Description:	Returns the arctangent of *dValue*.
Parameters:	*dValue*—The value for which arctangent is desired.

Returns:	The arctangent of *dValue*.
| Example: | ```
double  dTangent
    dTangent = atan(0.25);
``` |
| Note: | Also see atan2(). |

atan2()

Header:	math.h
| Syntax: | ```
double atan2(double dValue1, double
                 dValue2);
``` |
Description:	Returns the arctangent of *dValue1* and *dValue2*.
Parameters:	*dValue1*—The first value whose arctangent is desired.
	dValue2—The second value whose arctangent is desired.
Returns:	The arctangent of *dValue1* and *dValue2*.
| Example: | ```
double  dTangent
    dTangent = atan2(0.25, 3.2);
``` |
| Note: | Also see atan(). |

atexit()

Header:	stdlib.h
| Syntax: | ```
int atexit(void (* function)(void));
``` |
Description:	Tells the system to call *function* when the program ends.
Parameters:	*function*—Pointer to the function to be called.
Returns:	Zero if atexit() is successful.
| Example: | ```
atexit(OurExitFunction);
``` |
| Note: | Functions are called in a last in, first out manner. There is no way to remove a function once it has been passed using atexit(). |
```

atof()

Header:	math.h & stdlib.h
Syntax:	`double atof(const char * szString);`
Description:	Converts characters to a double value.
Parameters:	*szString*—Pointer to a string containing the character representation of the double number.
Returns:	A double value.
Example:	`    dValue = atof("1234.56");` `/* dValue will be 1234.56 */`
Note:	Conversion continues until the first invalid character is reached. You can test `errno` to determine any errors that occurred.

atoi()

Header:	stdlib.h
Syntax:	`int atoi(const char * szString);`
Description:	Converts characters to a short integer value.
Parameters:	*szString*—Pointer to a string containing the character representation of the integer.
Returns:	A short integer.
Example:	`    nValue = atoi("1234");` `/*  nValue will be 1234 */`
Note:	Conversion continues until the first invalid character is reached. You can test `errno` to determine any errors that occurred.

atol()

Header:	stdlib.h
Syntax:	`long atol(const char * szString);`

Description:	Converts characters to a long (32-bit) integer.
Parameters:	*szString*—Pointer to a string containing the character representation of the integer.
Returns:	A long integer.
Example:	

```
    lValue = atol("12345678");
/*  lValue will be 12345678 */
```

Note:	Conversion continues until the first invalid character is reached. You can test errno to determine any errors that occurred.

bsearch()

Header:	search.h & stdlib.h
Syntax:	

```
void * bsearch((void *key, const void *base,
                size_t num, size_t width,
                int (*compare)(const void *elem1,
                               const void
                               *elem2));
```

Description:	Searches a sorted list for the given key value.
Parameters:	*key*—Pointer to the key value to search for.
	base—Pointer to the array to search.
	num—Number of elements in the array being searched.
	width—Size of an element in the array being searched.
	compare—Pointer to a function that is doing the compare.
Returns:	Either a pointer to a matching element or NULL if the key was not found in the list.
Example:	

```
/* See Chapter 10, "Data Management: Sorts, Lists,
    and Indexes."*/
```

Note:	The array to be searched must be sorted; if it is not, the results are undefined.

calloc()

Header:	malloc.h & stdlib.h
Syntax:	`void * calloc(size_t nCount, size_t nSize);`
Description:	Allocates an array.
Parameters:	*nCount*—Number of elements.
	nSize—Size of each array element.
Returns:	Either a pointer to the array or NULL if the memory couldn't be allocated.
Example:	`int     *pOurArray;`
	`pOurArray = calloc(100, sizeof(int));`
Note:	The `calloc()` function initializes the memory to zero.

ceil()

Header:	math.h
Syntax:	`double ceil(double dValue);`
Description:	Returns the smallest integer value not less than *dValue*.
Parameters:	*dValue*—Number for which the ceiling value is desired.
Returns:	The integer ceiling value, converted to a double.
Example:	`dCeil = ceil(-2.2);`
	`/* dCeil will be -2.0 */`
Note:	See `floor()`.

clearerr()

Header:	stdio.h
Syntax:	`void clearerr(FILE * filepointer);`
Description:	Clears an existing end of file or other error condition for the given file.

528

Parameters:	*filepointer*—Pointer to a stream file.
Returns:	No return value.
Example:	

```
if (ferror(OpenFile))
{
    clearerr(OpenFile);
}
```

Note:	See `ferror()` and `fopen()`.

clock()

Header:	time.h
Syntax:	`clock_t clock(void);`
Description:	Provides the number of clock ticks (amount of CPU time) used by the program since it started.
Parameters:	None.
Returns:	CPU time.
Example:	

```
printf("CPU time is %d\n", clock() /
        CLOCKS_PER_SEC);
```

Note:	The time returned is not elapsed time, but actual CPU time. In multitasking systems, returned time varies greatly from elapsed time. You convert this time returned by dividing it with the macro `CLOCKS_PER_SEC` which is defined in time.h.

cos()

Header:	math.h
Syntax:	`double cos(double dValue);`
Description:	Returns the cosine of *dValue* (in radians).
Parameters:	*dValue*—Value to compute the cosine of.
Returns:	Cosine of *dValue*.

Example:	```dReturned = cos(0.5)``` ```/* dReturned will be 0.877583 */```
Note:	When *dValue* is a large value, the result may not be significant.

cosh()

Header:	math.h
Syntax:	```double cosh(double dValue);```
Description:	Returns the hyperbolic cosine of *dValue* (in radians).
Parameters:	*dValue*—Value to compute the hyperbolic cosine of.
Returns:	Hyperbolic cosine of *dValue*.
Example:	```dReturned = cosh(0.5)``` ```/* dReturned will be 1.1276 */```
Note:	When *dValue* is a large value, the result may not be significant.

ctime()

Header:	time.h
Syntax:	```char * ctime(const time_t * TimeBuffer);```
Description:	Converts the time pointed to by *TimeBuffer* into a printable format.
Parameters:	*TimeBuffer*—Pointer to a data object of type ```time_t```, properly initialized (perhaps by using ```time()```).
Returns:	Pointer to a character string, which is formatted as the example: ```Fri Jun 26 15:17:00 1992\n\0```
Example:	```time_t OurTime = time(NULL);``` ``` printf(ctime(&OurTime));```
Note:	This function is equal to calling ```asctime(localtime(TimeBuffer))```.

difftime()

Header:	time.h
Syntax:	`double difftime(time_t starttime, time_t endtime);`
Description:	Computes and returns the difference between *starttime* and *endtime* (in seconds).
Parameters:	*startime*—Time interval start.
	endtime—Time interval end.
Returns:	Double time difference, in seconds.
Example:	

```
time_t StartTime = time(NULL);
time_t EndTime;
char    szBuffer[100];

    printf("Wait a few seconds, and press
            return\n");
    gets(szBuffer);
    EndTime = time(NULL);
    printf("You waited %f seconds\n",
            difftime(EndTime, StartTime));
```

Note:	Don't forget that the difference is in seconds.

div()

Header:	stdlib.h
Syntax:	`div_t div(int numerator, int denominator);`
Description:	Returns both the quotient and remainder from the division of *numerator* by *denominator*.
Parameters:	*numerator*—Integer value to be divided.
	denominator—Integer value to divide by.
Returns:	Structure `div_t` containing the result of the division.

Example: `div_t    DivResult;`

                 `DivResult = div(100, 3);`

Note: Also see `ldiv()`.

exit()

Header: process.h & stdlib.h

Syntax: `void exit(int nExitCode);`

Description: Causes the program to end.

Parameters: *nExitCode*—An integer passed back to the parent process.

Returns: Does not return.

Example: `exit(0);`

Note: On MS-DOS systems, only the low order byte of *nExitCode* is available.

exp()

Header: math.h

Syntax: `double exp(double dValue);`

Description: Returns the exponential value of *dValue*, such that $\exp(x)=e^x$.

Parameters: *dValue*—Value whose exponential value is desired.

Returns: Exponential value of *dValue*.

Example: `double   dExp;`
                 `    dExp = exp(.5);`
                 `/* dExp will be 1.6487 */`

Note: An ERANGE error occurs if *dValue* is too large.

fabs()

Header:	math.h
Syntax:	`double fabs(double dValue);`
Description:	Returns the absolute value of *dValue*.
Parameters:	*dValue*—Double for which absolute value is desired.
Returns:	The absolute value of *dValue*.
Example:	`double dAbs = fabs(-0.2);` `/* dAbs will be 0.2 */`
Note:	Also see `abs()`.

fclose()

Header:	stdio.h
Syntax:	`int fclose(FILE * OpenFile);`
Description:	Closes the open stream file pointed to by *OpenFile*.
Parameters:	*OpenFile*—Pointer to a `FILE` structure.
Returns:	Zero if the function is successful.
Example:	`fclose(OpenFile);`
Note:	If the function fails, then `errno` contains the error code.

feof()

Header:	stdio.h
Syntax:	`int feof(FILE * OpenFile);`
Description:	Tests for an end of file condition on *OpenFile*.
Parameters:	*OpenFile*—Pointer to a `FILE` structure for an opened file.
Returns:	A non-zero if the file is at end of file.

Example:
```
int    nEndOfFile = feof(OpenFile);
/* nEndOfFile is zero if not end of file */
```

Note: Also see clearerr() for clearing the end of file condition.

ferror()

Header: stdio.h

Syntax: `int ferror(FILE * OpenFile);`

Description: Tests for any error conditions for the stream file OpenFile.

Parameters: OpenFile—Pointer to a FILE structure for an opened file.

Returns: A non-zero if there is an error associated with OpenFile.

Example:
```
int    nError = ferror(OpenFile);
/* nError will be zero if no errors. */
```

Note: Also see clearerr() for clearing errors.

fflush()

Header: stdio.h

Syntax: `int fflush(FILE * OpenFile);`

Description: For output files, fflush() writes any unwritten characters in the file's buffer to the file. For input files, fflush() will undo the last ungetc(). If OpenFile is NULL, then all open files are flushed.

Parameters: OpenFile—Pointer to a FILE structure for an opened file or NULL for all files.

Returns: A non-zero if an error is associated with OpenFile.

Example:
```
int    nError = fflush(OpenFile);
/* nError is zero if no errors in flushing.
   */
```

Note: Also see clearerr() for clearing errors. Frequently flushing output files helps prevent data loss if the computer crashes.

fgetc()

Header:	stdio.h
Syntax:	`int fgetc(FILE * OpenFile);`
Description:	Gets the next character from *OpenFile*.
Parameters:	*OpenFile*—Pointer to a FILE structure for an opened input file.
Returns:	The next character from *OpenFile*, or EOF if either an error occurs or the end-of-file is reached.

Example:	`char  chChar = (char)fgetc(OpenFile);`
	`/* chChar contains the next character`
	`    from the file. */`

Note:	Also see clearerr() for clearing errors. Getting single characters at a time can be inefficient; if possible, use fgets() to get an entire line at a time.

fgetpos()

Header:	stdio.h
Syntax:	`int fgetpos(FILE * OpenFile, fpos_t *` `                Position);`
Description:	Saves the current position of *OpenFile* in the variable pointed to by *Position*.
Parameters:	*OpenFile*—Pointer to a FILE structure for an opened input file.
	Position—Pointer to a variable of type fpos_t.
Returns:	A non-zero if there is an error.

Example:	`fpos_t   Position;`
	`    fgetpos(OpenFile, &Position);`
	`/* Position will contain the file current`
	`    position. */`

Note:	Usually, you use fseek() to reset the file to the point indicated by *Position*.

fgets()

Header:	stdio.h
Syntax:	`char * fgets(char * szBuffer, int BufferSize, FILE * OpenFile);`
Description:	Gets a string from the file, stopping when either a newline character is encountered or `BufferSize` - 1 characters have been read.
Parameters:	`szBuffer`—Buffer to store characters in.
	`BufferSize`—Size of the buffer.
	`OpenFile`—Pointer to a `FILE` structure for an opened input file.
Returns:	`NULL` if an error occurs; otherwise, `szBuffer` is returned.
Example:	`char    szBuffer[100];`
	`    gets(szBuffer, sizeof(szBuffer),`
	`        OpenFile);`
Note:	A newline character is never discarded. Don't assume there will always be a newline character; test to be sure.

floor()

Header:	math.h
Syntax:	`double floor(double dValue);`
Description:	Returns the largest integer (converted to double) that is not greater than `dValue`.
Parameters:	`dValue`—Value to use for the computation.
Returns:	Double value representing the largest integer not larger than `dValue`.
Example:	`double dFloor = floor(3.14159);`
	`/* dFloor will be 3.0 */`
Note:	See ceil().

fmod()

Header:	math.h
Syntax:	`double fmod(double x, double y);`
Description:	Returns the remainder of x / y.
Parameters:	x—Numerator, double value to be divided.
	y—Denominator, double value to divide by.
Returns:	Remainder of the division.
Example:	`double    dMod = fmod(3.14159, 3.0);`
	`/* dMod will be 0.14159 */`
Note:	If y is non-zero, then the result has the same sign as x.

fopen()

Header:	stdio.h
Syntax:	`FILE * fopen(const char * szFileName, const` `            char * Mode);`
Description:	Opens the file, using the filename and mode provided.
Parameters:	`szFileName`—Pointer to a character string containing a valid filename.
	`Mode`—Pointer to a character string containing the mode descriptor characters.
Returns:	Pointer to a `FILE` structure for the file that was opened or `NULL` if the file couldn't be opened.
Example:	`FILE * OurFile;` `    OurFile = fopen("ourfile.dat", "r");`
Note:	The mode characters include those shown in Table 14.1, which follows. Each character can be used with other characters except where indicated otherwise.

537

Table 14.1. File opening mode letter descriptions.

Mode Character	Description
r	Read (cannot be used with write, w, or append, a).
w	Write (cannot be used with read, r, or append, a).
a	Append (cannot be used with read, r, or write, w).
b	Binary (cannot be used with text, t).
t	Text (cannot be used with binary, b).
+	Opens for both read and write (used with read and write). With write, truncates file to zero length.

fprintf()

Header:	stdio.h
Syntax:	`int fprintf(FILE * OpenFile, const char * szFormat, ...);`
Description:	Does formatted output to the file pointed to by `OpenFile`.
Parameters:	`OpenFile`—Pointer to an open stream (text mode) file.
	`szFormat`—A format descriptor string.
Returns:	Number of characters written. If negative, then an error occurred.
Example:	`fprintf(stderr, "The number one is" "%d\n", 1);`
Note:	See the section on `printf()` format codes at the end of this chapter.

fputc()

Header:	stdio.h
Syntax:	`int fputc(int nCharacter, FILE * OpenFile);`

Description:	Writes the character contained in *nCharacter* to the file pointed to by *OpenFile*.

Parameters: *nCharacter*—Character to be written.

                     OpenFile—Pointer to an opened file.

Returns: The character written or EOF if an error occurs.

Example:

```
fputc('!', stderr);
fputc('\n', stderr);
```

Note: Use errno to determine what error occurred.

fputs()

Header: stdio.h

Syntax:

```
int fputs(const char * szBuffer, FILE *
          OpenFile);
```

Description: Writes the string pointed to by *szBuffer* to the file specified.

Parameters: *szBuffer*—Pointer to a string to be written.

                     OpenFile—Pointer to an opened file.

Returns: EOF if an error occurs, otherwise a non-negative value.

Example:

```
fputs("Now is the time...\n", stderr);
```

Note: Also see fprintf().

fread()

Header: stdio.h

Syntax:

```
size_t fread(void * Array, size_t
             ElementSize, size_t
             NumberElements, FILE *
             OpenFile);
```

Description: Reads an array from the file.

539

Parameters:	*Array*—Pointer to the array (which may be a character array).
	ElementSize—Size of each element in the array.
	NumberElements—Number of elements in array.
	OpenFile—Pointer to an opened file.
Returns:	Number of elements read.
| Example: | ```
int    nTimes[20];
    fread(nTimes, sizeof(nTimes[0]),
        sizeof(nTimes) / sizeof(nTimes[0]),
        OpenFile);
``` |
| Note: | The number of elements read may be less than the number requested. |

free()

Header:	malloc.h & stdlib.h
| Syntax: | ```
void free(void * Pointer);
``` |
Description:	Frees the memory (which was allocated with `calloc()` or `malloc()`) pointed to by *Pointer*.
Parameters:	*Pointer*—Pointer to a dynamically allocated memory block.
Returns:	No return value.
| Example: | ```
int   *nArray = calloc(20, sizeof(int));
    free(nArray);
``` |
| Note: | See `calloc()` and `malloc()`. |

freopen()

Header:	stdio.h
| Syntax: | ```
FILE * freopen(const char * szFileName,
               const char * szMode, FILE *
               OpenFile);
``` |

Description:	Allows a specific file to be associated with an already opened file. Usually used to allow `stdin`, or one of the other pre-opened standard files, to be associated with a specific file.
Parameters:	*szFileName*—Pointer to the filename of the file to be opened.
	szMode—Mode string (see `fopen()` for details).
	OpenFile—Pointer to an opened file.
Returns:	Pointer to a `FILE` structure.
Example:	

```
FILE * File = freopen("OurFile.dat", "r",
                            stdin);
/* scanf() will now read from 'OurFile.dat'
    */
```

Note:	Also see `fopen()`.

frexp()

Header:	math.h
Syntax:	

```
double frexp(double dValue, int *
                nExponent);
```

Description:	Normalizes a floating point number and places the exponent in the integer pointed to by *nExponent*.
Parameters:	*dValue*—Floating point value to be normalized.
	nExponent—Pointer to an integer to hold the exponent (2 raised to the .power *nExponent*).
Returns:	The parameter *dValue* normalized.
Example:	

```
int     nExponent;
double  dNormal = frexp(3.14159,
                            &nExponent);
/* dNormal will be 0.785398, nExponent will
    be 2 */
```

Note:	In the preceding example 0.785398 * (2 * 2) = 3.14159.

fscanf()

Header:	stdio.h
Syntax:	`int fscanf(FILE * OpenFile, const char *` `        szFormat, ...);`
Description:	Reads formatted input from the specified stream (text mode) file, with the format of the input determined by the format string pointed to by `szFormat`.
Parameters:	`OpenFile`—Pointer to an opened file. `szFormat`—Format string (see the section on format strings below).
Returns:	Number of arguments scanned or EOF if the end of the stream was reached.
Example:	`fscanf(OpenFile, "%s %d", szBuffer,` `        &nCount);`
Note:	`fscanf()` has a variable number of arguments determined by the format string.

fseek()

Header:	stdio.h
Syntax:	`int fseek(FILE * OpenFile, long lOffset, int` `        nOrigin);`
Description:	Moves the file pointer for the specified file to the position specified by `lOffset` relative to the origin specified by `nOrigin`.
Parameters:	`OpenFile`—Pointer to an opened file. `lOffset`—Where to move the file pointer. `nOrigin`—Origin point from which to compute the new file pointer position.
Returns:	Zero if the function is successful, non-zero if it fails.

Example:	`fseek(OpenFile, 2561, SEEK_CUR);` `/* Skip the next 256 bytes */`
Note:	Table 14.2 lists the valid seek origins.

Table 14.2. File seek origins.

Origin point	Description
SEEK_SET	From the start of the file (a negative value for the offset value is not acceptable).
SEEK_CUR	From the current position of the file's pointer (either a negative or positive value for the offset value is acceptable).
SEEK_END	From the end of the file (a negative value for the offset value is acceptable).

You cannot seek before the beginning of a file, but you can seek past the end of the file.

fsetpos()

Header:	stdio.h
Syntax:	`int fsetpos(FILE * OpenFile, const fpos_t *` `Position);`
Description:	Sets a file's position, using the `fpos_t` variable filled in using `fgetpos()`.
Parameters:	*OpenFile*—Pointer to an opened file.
	Position—Pointer to an `fpos_t` data object, filled in using `fgetpos()`.
Returns:	Zero if successful, otherwise a non-zero value.

Example:

```
fpos_t   Position;

    Position = 100;

/* Position is now at byte 100. */
            fsetpos(OpenFile, &Position);
```

Note: Also see fgetpos().

ftell()

Header: stdio.h

Syntax: `long ftell(FILE * OpenFile);`

Description: Returns the current read or write point for the specified file.

Parameters: *OpenFile*—Pointer to an opened file.

Returns: The read or write position for the file.

Example: `long    lPosition = ftell(OpenFile);`

Note: The result received from `ftell()` can later be used with `fseek()`.

fwrite()

Header: stdio.h

Syntax:
```
size_t fwrite(const void * Array, size_t
              ElementSize, size_t
              NumberElements, FILE *
              OpenFile);
```

Description: Writes *NumberElements* of *Array* to the specified file.

Parameters: *Array*—Pointer to an array (often a character string).

              ElementSize—Size of each element in the array.

              NumberElements—Number of elements to write.

              OpenFile—Pointer to an opened file.

Returns: Number of elements written. If the returned value is less than *NumberElements* then an error occurred.

| Example: | ```
int    nArray[] = {1,2,3,4,5,6,7,8,9};
    fwrite(nArray,
        sizeof(nArray[0]),
        sizeof(nArray) / sizeof(nArray[0]),
        OpenFile);
``` |

Note: Check errno if an error occurred, to determine what the error is.

getc()

Header:	stdio.h
Syntax:	int getc(FILE * OpenFile);
Description:	Gets the next character from the specified file.
Parameters:	OpenFile—Pointer to an opened file.
Returns:	The character retrieved from the file or EOF if there is an error.
| Example: | ```
char    chChar;
    chChar = (char)getc(stdin);
/* Gets one character from the keyboard */
``` |
| Note: | This function is generally equal to fgetc() except that it may be implemented as a macro. |

getchar()

Header:	stdio.h
Syntax:	int getchar(void);
Description:	Gets the next character from stdin.
Parameters:	None.
Returns:	The next character from stdin.
| Example: | ```
char    chChar;
    chChar = getchar();
``` |
| Note: | This function is the same as using getc(stdin). |
```

gets()

Header:	stdio.h
Syntax:	`char * gets(char * szBuffer);`
Description:	Gets the next line from `stdin`, until either the end of the `stdin` file is reached or until a newline character is encountered.
Parameters:	`szBuffer`—Pointer to a character string to hold the characters read.
Returns:	Pointer to `szBuffer` or `NULL` if an end of file condition is encountered.
Example:	`char   szBuffer[100];` `    gets(szBuffer);`
Note:	Careful: There is no check for buffer overrun! It may be better to use `fgets()` rather than this function.

gmtime()

Header:	time.h
Syntax:	`struct tm * gmtime(const time_t *` `                   TimeValue);`
Description:	Breaks down `TimeValue` and places the result into the `tm` structure.
Parameters:	`TimeValue`—Pointer to a `time_t` variable.
Returns:	A returned pointer to a structure of type `tm`.

Example:	`tm    TimeStruct;`
	`time_t  OurTime;`
	
	`    OurTime = time(NULL);`
	`    TimeStruct = (tm*)gmtime(&OurTime);`

Note:	Remember to consider the effects of different time zones and daylight savings time.

isalnum()

Header:	ctype.h
Syntax:	`int isalnum(int Character);`
Description:	Tests to see if the specified character is an alphanumeric character (a–z, A–Z, or 0–9).
Parameters:	*Character*—The character to be tested.
Returns:	A non-zero if the character is alphanumeric or a zero if it is not.
Example:	

```
if (isalnum('a'))
     printf("'a' is alphanumeric \n");
```

Note:	See isalpha().

isalpha()

Header:	ctype.h
Syntax:	`int isalpha(int Character);`
Description:	Tests to see if the specified character is an alphabetic character (a–z or A–Z).
Parameters:	*Character*—The character to be tested.
Returns:	A non-zero if the character is alphabetic or a zero if it is not.
Example:	

```
if (isalpha('a'))
     printf("'a' is alphabetic \n");
```

Note:	See isalnum().

iscntrl()

Header:	ctype.h
Syntax:	`int iscntrl(int Character);`
Description:	Tests to see if the specified character is a control character ('\x00'–'\x1f').

Parameters:	*Character*—The character to be tested.
Returns:	A non-zero if the character is a control character or a zero if it is not.
| Example: | ```
if (iscntrl('\a'))
        printf("'\a' is a control character"
                " (the bell?) \n");
``` |
| Note: | See isalpha(). |

isdigit()

Header:	ctype.h
Syntax:	int isdigit(int *Character*);
Description:	Tests to see if the specified character is a numeric digit (0–9).
Parameters:	*Character*—The character to be tested.
Returns:	A non-zero if the character is a numeric digit or a zero if it is not.
| Example: | ```
if (isdigit('1'))
        printf("'1' is a digig \n");
``` |
| Note: | See isalnum(). |

isgraph()

Header:	ctype.h
Syntax:	int isgraph(int *Character*);
Description:	Tests to see if the specified character is a printable character (except a space).
Parameters:	*Character*—The character to be tested.
Returns:	A non-zero if the character is printable, or a zero if it is not.
| Example: | ```
if (isgraph(chChar))
        putc(chChar);
``` |
| Note: | To test for a blank character, use isspace(). |
```

islower()

Header:	ctype.h
Syntax:	`int islower(int Character);`
Description:	Tests to see if the specified character is lowercase (a–z).
Parameters:	`Character`—The character to be tested.
Returns:	A non-zero if the character is lowercase or a zero if it is not.
Example:	

```
    if (islower(chChar))
  putc(chChar);
```

Note:	Also see `isupper()`.

isprint()

Header:	ctype.h
Syntax:	`int isprint(int Character);`
Description:	Tests to see if the specified character is a printable character (including spaces).
Parameters:	`Character`—The character to be tested.
Returns:	A non-zero if the character is printable, or a zero if it is not.
Example:	

```
    if (isprint(chChar))
        putc(chChar);
```

Note:	To test for all characters except for a blank character, use `isgraph()`.

ispunct()

Header:	ctype.h
Syntax:	`int ispunct(int Character);`
Description:	Tests to see if the specified character is valid punctuation, such as the period (.), comma (,), or exclamation point (!).

Parameters: *Character*—The character to be tested.

Returns: A non-zero if the character is punctuation or a zero if it is not.

Example:

```
if (ispunct(chChar))
    putc(chChar);
```

Note: None.

isspace()

Header: ctype.h

Syntax: `int isspace(int Character);`

Description: Tests to see if the specified character is a valid whitespace character.

Parameters: *Character*—The character to be tested.

Returns: A non-zero if the character is a valid whitespace character or a zero if it is not.

Example:

```
if (isspace(chChar))
    putc(chChar);
```

Note: To test for a non-blank character, use isgraph(). Valid whitespace characters include those shown in Table 14.3:

Table 14.3. Valid whitespace characters.

Character	Description (hex value)
' '	The space character.
'\f'	The form feed character (\x0C').
'\n'	The newline character (\x0A').
'\r	The carriage return character (\x0D').
'\t	The tab character (\x09').
'\v	The vertical tab character (\x0B').

isupper()

Header:	ctype.h
Syntax:	`int isupper(int Character);`
Description:	Tests to see if the specified character is uppercase (A–Z).
Parameters:	`Character`—The character to be tested.
Returns:	A non-zero if the character is uppercase or a zero if it is not.

Example:

```
if (isupper(chChar))
    putc(chChar);
```

Note:	To test for a lowercase character, use `islower()`.

isxdigit()

Header:	ctype.h
Syntax:	`int isxdigit(int Character);`
Description:	Tests to see if the specified character is a valid hexadecimal digit character (a–f, A–F, and 0–9).
Parameters:	`Character`—The character to be tested.
Returns:	A non-zero if the character is a valid hexadecimal digit or a zero if it is not.

Example:

```
if (isxdigit(chChar))
    putc(chChar);
```

Note:	To test for a decimal-only digit, use `isdigit()`.

labs()

Header:	math.h & stdlib.h
Syntax:	`long labs(long lValue);`
Description:	Returns the absolute value of `lValue`.

Parameters:	*lValue*—The value for which absolute value is desired.
Returns:	Absolute value of *lValue*.
Example:	

```
long   lReturned;
    lReturned = labs(-234556);
```

Note:	Also see abs().

ldexp()

Header:	math.h
Syntax:	double ldexp(double *lValue*, int *nPower*);
Description:	Multiplies a floating point value by two raised to *nPower*(lValue * 2nPower).
Parameters:	*lValue*—Value to multiply.
	nPower—Power to raise two by.
Returns:	(*lValue* * (2 * *nPower*))
Example:	

```
    if (ldexp(.785398, 2) == 3.14259)
    printf("It works!\n");
```

Note:	See frexp().

ldiv()

Header:	stdlib.h
Syntax:	ldiv_t ldiv(long *numerator*, long *denominator*);
Description:	Returns both the quotient and remainder from the division of *numerator* by *denominator*.
Parameters:	*numerator*—Long integer value to be divided.
	denominator—Long integer value to divide by.

Returns:	Structure `ldiv_t` containing the result of the division.
Example:	`ldiv_t    DivResult;`
	`    DivResult = ldiv(100, 3);`
Note:	Also see `div()`.

localeconv()

Header:	locale.h
Syntax:	`struct lconv * localeconv(void);`
Description:	Returns the structure type `lconv` filled in with appropriate values for the location.
Parameters:	None.
Returns:	Pointer to an `lconv` structure.
Example:	`lconv    OurConversions;`
	`    OurConversions = (lconv *)localeconv();`
Note:	See `setlocale()` for more information.

localtime()

Header:	time.h
Syntax:	`struct tm * localtime(const time_t *`
	`                        TimeValue);`
Description:	Breaks down *TimeValue*, and places the result into the `tm` structure.
Parameters:	*TimeValue*—Pointer to a `time_t` variable.
Returns:	A pointer to a returned structure of type `tm`.
Example:	`tm    TimeStruct;`
	`time_t  OurTime;`
	`    OurTime = time(NULL);`
	`    TimeStruct = (tm *)localtime(&OurTime);`

553

Note:	Remember to consider the effects of different time zones and daylight savings time.

log()

Header:	math.h
Syntax:	`double log(double dValue);`
Description:	Computes the natural logarithm (base e) of `dValue`.
Parameters:	`dValue`—Value to compute the natural logarithm of.
Returns:	Logarithm of `dValue`.
Example:	

```
    printf("Log of 3.14159 is %f",
           log(3.14159));
/* Log of 3.14159 is 1.144729 */
```

Note:	See `log10()`.

log10()

Header:	math.h
Syntax:	`double log10(double dValue);`
Description:	Computes the logarithm (base 10) of `dValue`.
Parameters:	`dValue`—Value to compute the logarithm of.
Returns:	Logarithm of `dValue`.
Example:	

```
    printf("Log10 of 3.14159 is %f",
           log10(3.14159));
/* Log10 of 3.14159 is 0.49715 */
```

Note:	See `log()`.

longjmp()

Header:	setjmp.h

Syntax:	void longjmp(jmp_buf *jumpbuffer*, int *nReturnCode*);
Description:	Restores the environment to what was saved in *jumpbuffer* by setjmp(), which causes execution to continue from the call to setjmp(), with setjmp() returning *nReturnCode*.
Parameters:	*jumpbuffer*—Buffer of type jmp_buf initialized by setjmp().
	nReturnCode—Value that setjmp() returns when longjmp() is called.
Returns:	longjmp() does not return, execution continues with setjmp().
Example:	See Figure 14.1 for an example.
Note:	See setjmp().

As Figure 14.1 shows, the error handler usually uses longjmp() to get past a part of the program that is causing an error. Since this error handler doesn't have any access to the failing function's variables, it cannot make any changes or set any flags.

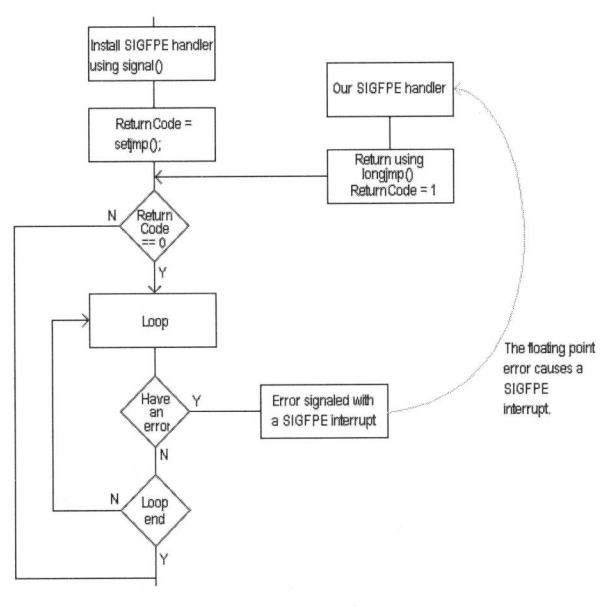

Figure 14.1. Program flow using setjmp() and longjmp().

malloc()

Header:	malloc.h & stdlib.h
Syntax:	`void * malloc(size_t SizeToAllocate);`
Description:	Allocates memory (uninitialized).
Parameters:	*SizeToAllocate*—Size of the memory block to allocated.
Returns:	Pointer to the memory block allocated or NULL if the memory could not be allocated..
Example:	`int  * nArray;`

```
nArray = (int *)malloc
         (sizeof(int) * 500);
memset(nArray, 0, sizeof(int) * 500)
```

Note:	Memory allocated using `malloc()` is never initialized; however, memory allocated using `calloc()` is.

mblen()

Header:	stdlib.h
Syntax:	`int mblen(const char * szString, size_t` `        nCount);`
Description:	Examines *nCount* characters, starting from the location pointed to by *szString*, looking for the number of bytes in the next multibyte character.
Parameters:	*szString*—Pointer to the first byte of the multibyte character.
Returns:	Zero if *szString* is NULL, -1 if this is not a multibyte character or the number of characters in the multibyte character.
Example:	`int   nCount;` `    nCount = mblen(szString, 3);`
Note:	See the other multibyte character functions, which follow.

mbstowcs()

Header:	stdlib.h
Syntax:	size_t mbstowcs(wchar_t * *pWideChar*, const char * *szString*, size_t *nCount*);
Description:	Converts the multibyte characters pointed to by *szSting* into wide character codes and places the result into *pWideChar*, converting up to *nCount* characters.
Parameters:	*pWideChar*—Pointer to a string buffer to receive the wide character conversion.
	szString—Source multibyte character string.
	nCount—Size of *pWideChar*.
Returns:	Number of characters converted or -1 if an error occurs.
Example:	No example provided.
Note:	Also see mblen() and mbtowc().

mbtowc()

Header:	stdlib.h
Syntax:	int mbtowc(wchar_t * *pWideChar*, const char * *pMultiByte*, size_t *nCount*);
Description:	Converts a single multibyte character pointed to by *pMultiByte* into a wide character code and places the result into *pWideChar*, examining up to *nCount* characters.
Parameters:	*pWideChar*—Pointer to a buffer to receive the wide character conversion.
	pMultiByte—Source multibyte character string.
	nCount—Size of *pWideChar*.

Returns: Number of characters converted or -1 if an error occurs.

Example: No example provided.

Note: Also see `mblen()` and `mbtowcs()`.

memchr()

Header: memory.h & string.h

Syntax:
```
void * memchr(const void * szString, int
                chChar, size_t nLength);
```

Description: Searches for the first occurrence of *chChar* in *szString* limiting the search to the first *nLength* characters.

Parameters: *szString*—Pointer to the string to search.

                chChar—Character to search for.

                nLength—Number of characters to search in *szString*.

Returns: Pointer to the located character or NULL if it cannot be found.

Example:
```
char    szString[] = {"Now is the time for
                        all good men"};

    printf("Is it the time %s",
        memchr(szString, 'f',
        strlen(szString));
/* Will print Is it the time for all good men */
```

Note: See `memcmp()` and `memset()`. Notice that `memchr()` doesn't assume the string is a NULL terminated character string.

memcmp()

Header: memory.h & string.h

Syntax:
```
int memcmp(const void * pBuffer1, const void
                * pBuffer2, size_t nLength);
```

Description: Compares up to *nLength* characters of *pBuffer1* with *pBuffer2*,

Parameters:	*pBuffer1*—Pointer to the first buffer.
	pBuffer2—Pointer to the second buffer.
	nLength—Number of bytes to compare.
Returns:	Zero if they are equal, < 0 if *pBuffer1* is less than *pBuffer2*, or > 0 if *pBuffer1* is greater than *pBuffer2*.
Example:	

```
char    szString1[] = {"Now is all the time
                           for all good men"};
char    szString2[] = {"Now is not the time
                           for all good men"};

    if (memcmp(szString1, szString2,
        strlen(szString1)) == 0)
    {
        printf("'%s' '%s' are equal",
            szString1,
            szString2);
    }
/* Will not print since the strings are not
   equal */
```

Note:	See memchr() and memset(). Notice that memcmp() doesn't assume the string is a NULL terminated character string.

memcpy()

Header:	memory.h & string.h
Syntax:	void * memcpy(void * *pDestination*, const void * *pSource*, size_t *nLength*);
Description:	Copies *nLength* bytes from *pSource* to *pDestination*. Source and destination must not overlap.
Parameters:	*pDestination*—Pointer to the destination buffer.
	pSource—Pointer to the source buffer.
	nLength—Number of bytes to copy.

Returns:	The pointer *pDestination*.

Example:

```
char    szString1[] = {"Now is all the time
                        for all good men"};
char    szString2[] = {"Now is not the time
                        for all good men"};

    memcpy(szString1, szString2,
        strlen(szString2));
    printf("'%s' and '%s'",
        szString1,
        szString2);
```

Note: See `memmove()` and `memset()`. Notice that `memcpy()` should not be used where the source and destination overlap.

memmove()

Header:	string.h

Syntax:

```
void * memmove(void * pDestination, const
              void * pSource, size_t
              nLength);
```

Description: Copies *nLength* bytes from *pSource* to *pDestination*. Source and destination may overlap.

Parameters: *pDestination*—Pointer to the destination buffer.

pSource—Pointer to the source buffer.

nLength—Number of bytes to copy.

Returns: The pointer *pDestination*.

Example:

```
char    szString1[100] = {"Now is all the
                          time for all good
                          men"};
char    szString2[100] = {"Now is not the
                          time for all good
                          men"};
```

```
memmove(&szString2[10], szString2,
        strlen(szString2));
printf("'%s'",
    szString2);
```

Note: See `memcpy()` and `memset()`. Notice that `memcpy()` should not be used where the source and destination overlap, while `memmove()` works correctly when there is overlap; however, this function may be slower.

memset()

Header: memory.h & string.h

Syntax:
```
void * memset(void * pBuffer, int nByte,
                size_t nLength);
```

Description: Fills *nLength* bytes of *pBuffer* with *nByte*.

Parameters: *pBuffer*—Buffer that is to be filled.

nByte—Byte to fill the buffer with.

nLength—How many bytes to fill.

Returns: The pointer *pBuffer*.

Example:
```
int    * Array;
    Array = (int *)malloc
            (sizeof(int) * 100);
    memset(Array, 0, sizeof(int) * 100);
/* Zeros out the allocated array */
```

Note: This function is very useful to initialize both auto and allocated data objects, which are not otherwise initialized.

mktime()

Header: time.h

Syntax:
```
time_t mktime(struct tm * Time);
```

Description:	Converts the `tm` time structure to calendar time (Coordinated Universal Time). If the values are out of range, they are adjusted as necessary.
Parameters:	*Time*—Pointer to a tm time structure.
Returns:	A `time_t` structure.
Example:	

```
struct tm Time;
    memset(Time, 0, sizeof(Time);
/* fill in Time with values */
    mktime(&Time);
```

Note:	Also see `time()`.

modf()

Header:	math.h
Syntax:	

```
double modf(double dValue, double *
                dIntegral);
```

Description:	Computes the fractional and integral parts of *dValue*.
Parameters:	*dValue*—Real number for which integral and fractional parts are desired.
	dIntegral—Pointer to a double that will receive the integral part of *dValue*.
Returns:	The fractional part of *dValue*.
Example:	

```
double  dIntegral;
double  dFractional = modf(4.1234,
                        &dIntegral);
/* dIntegral will be 4, dFractional will be 0.1234 */
```

Note:	See `fmod()`.

offsetof()

Header:	stddef.h

Syntax:	`size_t offsetof(composite `*`Structure`*`, name` `Member);`
Description:	Returns the offset (in bytes) of *Member* from the beginning of *Structure*.
Parameters:	*Structure*—A structure.
	Member—A member in *Structure*.
Returns:	Offset in bytes.

Example:	`struct tm Time;`
	`    printf("the offset of tm_year is %d",`
	`        offsetof(struct tm, tm_year));`

Note:	Remember that *Structure* is the type name, not the variable name.

perror()

Header:	stdio.h & stdlib.h
Syntax:	`void perror(const char * `*`szPrefix`*`);`
Description:	Prints an error message corresponding to errno to stderr. If *szPrefix* is not NULL, that string is prefixed to the message printed.
Parameters:	
Returns:	Zero if successful, otherwise a non-zero value.

Example:	`/* Set errno to an error value (usually set by a library`
	`function) */`
	`    errno = EACCES;`
	`    perror("DUMMY ERROR HERE");`
	
	`/* prints: DUMMY ERROR HERE: Permission denied   */`

pow()

Header:	math.h
Syntax:	`double pow(double x, double y);`
Description:	Raises *x* to the power *y*.
Parameters:	*x*—Number to raise to power *y*.
	y—Power to raise *x* to.
Returns:	*x* to the power *y*.
Example:	

```
    printf("3 to the power 5 = %f\n",
            pow(3.0, 5.0));
/* Prints: 3 to the power 5 = 243.000000  */
```

Note:	See `exp()`.

printf()

Header:	stdio.h
Syntax:	`int printf(const char * szFormat, ...);`
Description:	Prints, to `stdout` formatted output as defined by `szFormat`.
Parameters:	`szFormat`—A format descriptor string.
Returns:	Number of characters written. If negative, then an error occurred.
Example:	

```
    printf("The number one is %d\n", 1);
```

Note:	See the section on `printf()` format codes at the end of this chapter.

putc()

Header:	stdio.h
Syntax:	`int putc(int nChar, FILE * OpenFile);`
Description:	Writes `nChar` to the stream file `OpenFile`.

Parameters:	*nChar*—Character to be written.
	OpenFile—Pointer to an opened file.
Returns:	Character *nChar* if successful, otherwise EOF.
Example:	`putc('A', stdout);`
Note:	Same as `fputc()` except that `putc()` can be implemented as a macro.

putchar()

Header:	stdio.h
Syntax:	`int putchar(int nChar);`
Description:	Writes *nChar* to the stream file stdout.
Parameters:	*nChar*—Character to be written.
Returns:	Character *nChar* if successful, otherwise EOF.
Example:	`putchar('A');`
Note:	Same as `fputc(nChar, stdout)` except that `putc()` can be implemented as a macro.

puts()

Header:	stdio.h
Syntax:	`int puts(const char * szString);`
Description:	Writes *szString* to the stream file stdout.
Parameters:	*szString*—Pointer to the character string to be written.
Returns:	Non-zero positive value if successful, otherwise EOF.
Example:	`putchar("Now is the time.\n");`
Note:	Also see `fputs()` and `putc()`.

565

qsort()

Header:	search.h & stdlib.h

Syntax:	```void qsort(void * Array, size_t```
	 ``` NumberElements, size_t```
	 ``` ElementSize, int (*compare)```
	 ``` (const void *, const void *));```

Description:	Sorts *Array* using a quicksort method.
Parameters:	*Array*—Pointer to an array to be sorted (can be an array of any type).
	NumberElements—Number of elements in *Array* to be sorted.
	ElementSize—Size of each element in *Array*.
	Compare—Pointer to a function to do compare of array elements.
Returns:	No return value.
Example:	See Chapter 10, "Data Management: Sorts, Lists, and Indexes."
Note:	With a creative *Compare* function, qsort() can do any sort imaginable.

raise()

Header:	signal.h
Syntax:	```int raise(int nException);```
Description:	Simulates occurrence of an error condition.
Parameters:	*nException*—The error condition that is to be signaled.
Returns:	Zero if successful, otherwise a non-zero value.
Example:	```raise(SIGINT);```
Note:	This function is most useful when you have installed your own exception handler. See signal().

rand()

Header:	stdlib.h
Syntax:	`int rand(void);`
Description:	Returns a pseudorandom number in the range of zero to `RAND_MAX` (usually 32767).
Parameters:	None
Returns:	Random number.
Example:	`int   nRandom = rand();` `/* nRandom will be a random number */`
Note:	Don't forget to seed the random number using `srand()`.

realloc()

Header:	malloc.h & stdlib.h
Syntax:	`void * realloc(void * pBuffer, size_t` `               nNewSize);`
Description:	Changes the size of the buffer pointed to by *pBuffer*.
Parameters:	*pBuffer*—Pointer to an allocated buffer. *nNewSize*—New size for the buffer (either smaller or larger).
Returns:	Pointer to a new buffer, with *pBuffer*'s contents copied to it or `NULL` if a new buffer could not be allocated.

Example:	`char  * pBuffer = malloc(sizeof(char) * 100);`
	`    strcpy(pBuffer,`
	`    "Now is the time for all good men");`
	`/* now shrink it... */`
	`    pBuffer = realloc`
	`(pBuffer, strlen(pBuffer) + 1);`
	`/* This example shrinks the buffer to fit the contents`
	`*/`

Note:	Always save the pointer in case the buffer can't be resized. Never refer to the old pointer after this function successfully returns.

remove()

Header:	io.h & stdio.h
Syntax:	`int remove(const char * szFileName);`
Description:	Deletes the file with name that is pointed to by *szFileName*.
Parameters:	*szFileName*—Pointer to a character string containing the name of an existing file.
Returns:	Zero if successful, otherwise a non-zero value.
Example:	`remove("test.dat");`
Note:	Be careful to not delete a file that is currently opened because the results may be unpredictable.

rename()

Header:	io.h & stdio.h
Syntax:	`int rename(const char * szOldName, const char * szNewName);`
Description:	Renames files.
Parameters:	*szOldName*—Pointer to a string that contains the old filename.
	szNewName—Pointer to a string containing the new filename.
Returns:	Zero if successful, otherwise a nonzero value.
Example:	`rename("OldData.Dat", "NewData.Dat");`
Note:	Very useful under PC DOS because it allows renaming a file to a different directory.

rewind()

Header:	stdio.h
Syntax:	`void rewind(FILE * OpenFile);`

Description:	Resets the file pointer for *OpenFile* to the beginning of the file.
Parameters:	*OpenFile*—Pointer to an opened file.
Returns:	No return value.
Example:	`rewind(OpenFile);`
Note:	Much the same as calling `fseek(`*OpenFile*`, 0, SEEK_SET)`.

scanf()

Header:	stdio.h
Syntax:	`int scanf(const char * `*szFormat*`, ...);`
Description:	Reads from `stdin` formatted input.
Parameters:	*szFormat*—Pointer to a string containing format codes.
Returns:	Number of items that were scanned and stored or `EOF` if the end of the file was encountered.

Example:	`int   i;`
	`    scanf("%d", &i);`
	`/* i will be whatever (numeric) value`
	`    entered */`

Note:	See the section on `scanf()` format codes at the end of this chapter.

setbuf()

Header:	stdio.h
Syntax:	`void setbuf(FILE * `*OpenFile*`, char *` `              `*pBuffer*`);`
Description:	Sets a buffer for the file *OpenFile*.
Parameters:	*OpenFile*—Pointer to an opened file.
	pBuffer—Pointer to a buffer of at least `BUFSIZ` bytes.
Returns:	No return value.

Example:
```
char    szBuffer[123];
char * pBuffer = malloc(BUFSIZ);

    setbuf(stdin, pBuffer);

    printf("enter a string\n");

    gets(szBuffer);

    printf("enter a second string\n");

    gets(szBuffer);

    printf("'%s'\n", pBuffer);
```

Note: Be sure the buffer is large enough (use BUFSIZ).

setjmp()

Header: setjmp.h

Syntax: `int setjmp(jmp_buf jumpbuffer);`

Description: Saves the environment to *jumpbuffer*, which then can be used by longjmp() to return to the point saved.

Parameters: *jumpbuffer*—a buffer of type jmp_buf.

Returns: setjmp() returns zero when being initialized or the return code specified by longjmp(), which will not be zero.

Example: See Figure 14.2 for an example.

Note: See longjmp().

As Figure 14.2 shows, the error handler usually uses longjmp() to get past a part of the program that is causing an error. Because this error handler doesn't have any access to the failing function's variables, it cannot make any changes or set any flags.

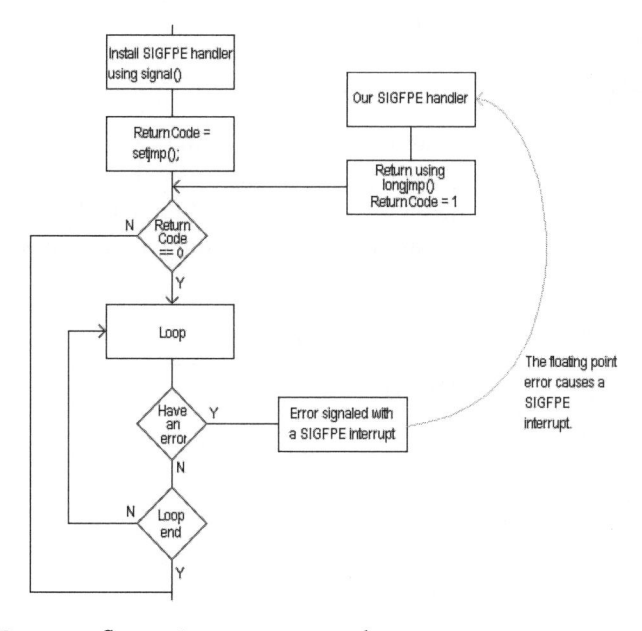

Figure 14.2. Program flow using setjmp() and longjmp().

setlocale()

Header:	locale.h
Syntax:	char * setlocale(int *Category*, const char * *Locale*);
Description:	Sets the *category* for the *locale*.
Parameters:	*Category*—Category to set (see Table 14.4).
	Locale—The locale to set.

Returns: String indicating the current locale.

Example: `setlocale(LC_ALL, "C");`

Note: Because most compilers and operating systems support only the "C" locale, this function doesn't have an effect. As new locales are added, this function will be more useful. Check the documentation supplied with your compiler for other information.

Table 14.4. Locale categories.

Category	Description
LC_ALL	Entire environment.
LC_MONETARY	Money format.
LC_COLLATE	Collate sequence.
LC_NUMERIC	Number format.
LC_CTYPE	Character handling.
C_TIME	Time-related items

setvbuf()

Header: stdio.h

Syntax: `int setvbuf(FILE * OpenFile, char * pBuffer,`
              `              int nMode, size_t nSize);`

Description: Sets a buffer for the file `OpenFile`.

Parameters: `OpenFile`—Pointer to an opened file.

              `pBuffer`—Pointer to a buffer.

              `nMode`—Mode for the file buffer (see Table 14.5).

              `nSize`—Buffer.

Returns: Zero if successful, otherwise a nonzero value.

Example:
```
char    szBuffer[123];
char * pBuffer = malloc(BUFSIZ * 2);

    setvbuf(stdin, pBuffer, _IOFBF, BUFSIZ *
            2);

    printf("enter a string\n");

    gets(szBuffer);

    printf("enter a second string\n");

    gets(szBuffer);

    printf("'%s'\n", pBuffer);
```

Note: Be sure the buffer is large enough to be effective. Table 14.5 shows
                 the allowable modes.

Table 14.5. Function setvbuf()'s modes.

Mode	Description
IOFBF	The input and output will be fully buffered.
IOLBF	The output will be line buffered (buffer is flushed when a newline is encountered or the buffer is full).
IONBF	No buffering is performed (All parameters except *OpenFile* and *nMode* are ignored).

signal()

Header: signal.h

Syntax:
```
void (* signal(int nSignal,
              void (* function)(int) ))(int);
```

Description: Tells the system to call *function* whenever the error condition specified by *nSignal* is raised by either an error condition or the `raise()` function.

Parameters: *nSignal*—The error condition to be modified.

                function—The function to be called when the error condition is raised. See Table 14.6 for other values for *function*.

Returns: `SIG_ERR` if an error occurs, otherwise the previous signal handler.

If *function* is one of the defined constants shown in Table 14.6, then the action described will be taken. Notice that after the error condition occurs, `signal()` must again be called because the system first makes a call to `signal(nSignal, SIG_DFL)`.

Table 14.6. Signal predefined actions.

Defined value	Description
`SIG_DFL`	The default action will occur.
`SIG_IGN`	The condition will be ignored.
`SIG_ACK`	Used in some systems to tell the operating system the handler is ready to receive the next error signal.

sin()

Header: math.h

Syntax: `double sin(double dValue);`

Description: Computes the sine of *dValue*.

Parameters: *dValue*—Value to compute the sine of.

Returns: The sine of *dValue*.

Example:
```
dValueSine=sin(.5);
/* dValueSine will be 0.4794 */
```

Note: See acos(), asin(), and cos().

sinh()

Header: math.h

Syntax: `double sinh(double dValue);`

Description: Computes the hyperbolic sine of `dValue`.

Parameters: `dValue`—Value to compute the hyperbolic sine of.

Returns: The hyperbolic sine of `dValue`.

Example: `dValueSine = sinh(.5);/* dValueSine will be 0.5210 */`

Note: See acos(), asin(), and cos().

sprintf()

Header: stdio.h

Syntax:
```
int sprintf(char * pBuffer,
            const char * szFormat, ...);
```

Description: Prints, to the buffer pointed to by `pBuffer`, formatted output as defined by `szFormat`.

Parameters: `pBuffer`—Pointer to a destination buffer.

     `szFormat`—A format descriptor string.

Returns: Number of characters written. If negative, then an error occurred.

Example:
```
char    szBuffer[100];
sprintf(szBuffer,
            "The number one is %d\n", 1);
```

Note: Be sure the destination buffer is large enough. See the section on format codes at the end of this chapter.

sqrt()

Header:	math.h
Syntax:	`double sqrt(double dValue);`
Description:	Computes the square root of *dValue*.
Parameters:	*dValue*—Value for which square root is desired.
Returns:	Square root of *dValue*.
Example:	`double dSquareRoot = sqrZXt(2);` `/* dSquareRoot will be 1.41 */`
Note:	The argument must not be negative.

srand()

Header:	stdlib.h
Syntax:	`void srand(unsigned int nSeed);`
Description:	Seeds (sets the starting point) of the random number generator.
Parameters:	*nSeed*—A seed value.
Returns:	No return value.
Example:	`srand((unsigned)time(NULL));`
Note:	The sequence of numbers returned by `rand()` is identical if identical seeds are used. Using the `time()` function assures a reasonably random starting point.

sscanf()

Header:	stdio.h
Syntax:	`int sscanf(const char * szInput,` `        const char * szFormat, ...);`
Description:	Reads from the buffer pointed to by *szInput*, formatted input.

Parameters:	*szInput*—Pointer to a buffer containing the string to be read.
	szFormat—Pointer to a string containing format codes.
Returns:	Number of items that were scanned and stored or EOF if the end of the file was encountered.
Example:	``` int i; char szInput[] = {"1 2 3 4"}; scanf(szInput, "%d", &i); /* i will be 1 */ ```
Note:	See the section on scanf() format codes at the end of this chapter.

strcat()

Header:	string.h
Syntax:	``` char * strcat(char * szDestination, const char * szSource); ```
Description:	Concatenates the string pointed to by *szSource* to *szDestination*.
Parameters:	*szDestination*—String that will have *szSource* appended to it.
	szSource—The string to append to *szDestination*.
Returns:	Pointer *szDestination*.
Example:	``` char szString[100] = {"Now is the time"}; strcat(szString, " for all good men"); /* szString will be Now is the time for all good men */ ```
Note:	Be sure the destination is large enough to hold the resultant string and that it has been properly initialized. The destination can be a string of zero length.

strchr()

Header:	string.h
Syntax:	``` char * strchr(const char * szString, int chChar); ```

Description:	Searches for the first occurrence of *chChar* in *szString*.
Parameters:	*szString*—Pointer to the string to be searched.
	chChar—Character to search for.
Returns:	Pointer to the first occurrence of *chChar* or NULL if it is not found.

Example:

```
char szString[100] =
{"Now is the time for all good men"};

    printf("Not the time %s",
            strchr(szString, 'f'));
/* Will print Not the time for all good men */
```

Note:	See memchr().

strcmp()

Header:	string.h

Syntax:

```
int strcmp(const char * szString1,
            const char * szString2);
```

Description:	Compares two strings and returns a value indicating if they are equal or if one is less than the other.
Parameters:	*szString1*—The first string to compare.
	szString2—The second string to compare.
Returns:	Zero if they are equal, < 0 if *szString1* is less than *szString2*, or > 0 if *szString1* is greater than *szString2*.

Example:

```
char    szString1[] =
{"Now is all the time for all good men"};
char    szString2[] =
{"Now is not the time for all good men"};

    if (strcmp(szString1, szString2) == 0)
    {
        printf("'%s' '%s' are equal",
            szString1,
```

```
                                      szString2);
            }
   /* Will not print since the strings are not equal
      */
```

Note: See memchr(). Notice that memcmp() doesn't assume the string is a
              NULL terminated character string.

strcoll( )

Header: string.h

Syntax: int strcoll(const char * szString1, const char *
                          szString2);

Description: Compares two strings using the collating sequence selected by
                   setlocale() and returns a value indicating whether they are
                   equal or if one is less than the other.

Parameters: szString1—The first string to compare.

                   szString2—The second string to compare.

Returns: Zero if they are equal, < 0 if szString1 is less than szString2, or
                   > 0 if szString1 is greater than szString2.

Example:
```
char    szString1[] =
{"Now is all the time for all good men"};
char    szString2[] =
{"Now is not the time for all good men"};

    if (strcoll(szString1, szString2) == 0)
    {
        printf("'%s' '%s' are equal",
            szString1,
            szString2);
    }
/* Will not print since the strings are not equal
   */
```

Note: See memchr(). Notice that memcmp() doesn't assume the string is a
              NULL terminated character string. This function is equal to strcmp()
              when the default collating sequence specified by locale "C" is used.

strcpy( )

Header:	string.h
Syntax:	`char * strcpy(char * szDestination,` `                const char * szSource);`
Description:	Copies the string to *szDestination* that is pointed to by *szSource*.
Parameters:	*szDestination*—A string that has *szSource* copied to it.
	szSource—The string copied to *szDestination*.
Returns:	Pointer *szDestination*.

Example:	`char szString[100] = {"Now is the time"};`
	`    strcpy(szString, " for all good men");`
	`/* szString will be for all good men */`

Note:	Be sure the destination is large enough to hold the resultant string.

strcspn( )

Header:	string.h
Syntax:	`size_t strcspn(const char * szString,` `                const char * szChars);`
Description:	Returns the length of the initial string that does not contain any characters found in *szChars*.
Parameters:	*szString*—Pointer to a string to be searched.
	szChars—String containing characters to be searched for.
Returns:	Length of the initial string that contains no characters from *szChars*, up to the length of *szString*.

Example:	`char   szString[100] =`
	`{"Now is the time for all good men."};`
	`int    nCount = strcspn(szString, "fzx");`
	
	`    printf("Never a good time %s",`
	`        &szString[nCount]);`

```
/* will print Never a good time for all good men.
  */
```

Note: Also see strspn().

strerror( )

Header: string.h

Syntax: `char * strerror(int nError);`

Description: Returns a pointer to a string describing the error contained in
                 nError.

Parameters: *nError*—Error value (usually from errno).

Returns: Pointer to an error message or a message indicating a message
                 doesn't exist for this error.

Example: ```
                 printf("Had an error: %s\n",
                            strerror(ENOMEM));
                 ```

Note:            See errno and the header file errno.h.

# strftime( )

Header:          time.h

Syntax:          ```
                 size_t strftime(char * szBuffer, size_t
                            nBufferSize, const char *
                            szFormat, const struct tm * Time);
                 ```

Description: Prints to *szBuffer* the time contained in *Time* according to the
                 format specified in *szFormat* (see Table 14.7 for the format
                 characters).

Parameters: *szBuffer*—Pointer to the destination buffer that will receive the
                 formatted time string.

                 nBufferSize—Size of *szBuffer*.

                 szFormat—Pointer format string.

                 Time—Pointer to a tm time structure.

Returns: The number of characters placed in *szBuffer* or NULL if an error occurs.

Example:

```
time_t   OurTime;

OurTime = time(NULL);

strftime(szBuffer, sizeof(szBuffer),
        "Today is %A %B %d, %Y",
    localtime(&OurTime));
    printf("%s\n", szBufer);
/* Will print Today is Friday June 26, 1992 */
```

Note: See the format characters in Table 14.7. This function makes the creation of attractive time displays easy.

Table 14.7. Function strftime()'s format codes.

Format	Description
%a	Abbreviated weekday name.
%A	Full weekday name.
%b	Abbreviated month name.
%B	Full month name.
%c	Full date and time (like ctime()) representation appropriate for the locale.
%d	Numeric day of the month.
%H	Hour in 24–hour format (00–23).
%I	Hour in 12–hour format (01–12).
%j	Day of the year (001–366).
%m	Month (01–12).
%M	Minute (00–59).
%p	AM/PM indicator for a 12–hour clock.
%S	Seconds (00–61).

%U	Week of the year as a decimal number; Sunday is taken as the first day of the week (00–53).
%w	Day of the week, (0–6; Sunday is 0).
%W	Week of the year; Monday is taken as the first day of the week (00–53).
%x	Date representation for current locale.
%X	Time representation for current locale.
%y	Year without the century (00–99).
%Y	Year with the century.
%z	Time zone name or abbreviation; no characters if time zone is unknown.
%%	Percent sign.

strlen()

Header:	string.h
Syntax:	`size_t strlen(const char * szString);`
Description:	Returns the length of a string.
Parameters:	*szString*—Pointer to the string for which length is desired.
Returns:	Number of characters in *szString* (excluding the terminating NULL).
Example:	```char szString[100] =```

```
char  szString[100] =
"Now is the time for all good programmers to..."};
    printf("Length of '%s' is \n %d",
            szString, strlen(szString));
/* the length printed is 46 */
```

Note:	This function returns the number of characters in the string, not the defined size. To get the defined size, use `sizeof()`.

strncat()

Header:	string.h
Syntax:	`char * strncat(char * szDestination, const char * szSource, size_t nCount);`
Description:	Concatenates *nCount* characters of string pointed to by *szSource* to *szDestination*.
Parameters:	*szDestination*—String that will have *szSource* appended to it.
	szSource—String to append to *szDestination*.
	nCount—Number of characters from *szSource* to append.
Returns:	Pointer *szDestination*.

Example:	`char szString[100] = {"Now is the time"};`
	`    strncat(szString, " for all good men", 15);`
	`/* szString will be Now is the time for all good m`
	`    */`

Note:	Be sure the destination is large enough to hold the resultant string, and that it has been properly initialized. The destination can be a string of zero length.

strncmp()

Header:	string.h
Syntax:	`int strncmp(const char * szString1, const char * szString2, size_t nCount);`
Description:	Compares up to *nCount* characters of the two strings and returns a value indicating whether they are equal or if one is less than the other.
Parameters:	*szString1*—The first string to compare.
	szString2—The second string to compare.
	nCount—Number of characters to compare.

Returns:	Zero if they are equal, < 0 if *szString1* is less than *szString2*, or > 0 if *szString1* is greater than *szString2*.

Example:

```
char    szString1[] =
{"Now is all the time for all good men"};
char    szString2[] =
{"Now is all the time for all Bad men"};

    if (strncmp(szString1, szString2, 20) == 0)
    {
        printf("'%s' '%s' are equal",
            szString1,
            szString2);
    }
/* Will print since the strings are equal
   for the first 20 characters*/
```

Note: See strcmp().

strncpy()

Header:	string.h

Syntax:
```
char * strncpy(char * szDestination, const char *
                    szSource, size_t nCount);
```

Description:	Copies to *szDestination* up to *nCount* characters from the string pointed to by *szSource*.

Parameters: *szDestination*—String that will have *szSource* copied to it.

szSource—String copied to *szDestination*.

nCount—Number of characters to copy.

Returns: Pointer *szDestination*.

Example:
```
char szString[100] = {"Now is the time"};
    strncpy(szString, " for all good men", 10);
/* szString will be for all g */
```

Note: Be sure the destination is large enough to hold the resultant string.

strpbrk()

Header:	string.h
Syntax:	char * strpbrk(const char * *szString*, const char * *szCharacters*);
Description:	Finds the first occurrence of any character from *szCharacters* found in *szString*.
Parameters:	*szString*—Pointer to a string to search.
	szCharacters—Pointer to a string containing characters to search for.
Returns:	Pointer to the first character found in *szString* that is in *szCharacters*.
Example:	

```
char    szString1[] =
{"Now is all the time for all good men"};
char   * pChars;

    pChars = strpbrk(szString1, "fzxy");

    if (pChars)
    {
        printf("found at '%s'\n",
            pChars);
    }
/* Will print found at 'for all good men' */
```

strrchr()

Header:	string.h
Syntax:	char * strrchr(const char * *szString*, int *chChar*);
Description:	Finds the last occurrence of *chChar* found in *szString*.
Parameters:	*szString*—Pointer to a string to search.
	chChar—Character to search for.

Returns:	Pointer to the last occurrence of *chChar* found in *szString*.
Example:	

```
char    szString1[] =
{"Now is all the time for all good men"};
char    * pChars;

    pChars = strrchr(szString1, 'a');

    if (pChars)
    {
        printf("found at '%s'\n",
            pChars);
    }

/* Will print found at 'all good men' */
```

strspn()

Header:	string.h
Syntax:	size_t strspn(const char * szString, const char * szChars);
Description:	Returns the length of the initial string that contains characters found in *szChars*.
Parameters:	*szString*—Pointer to a string to be searched.
	szChars—String containing characters that must be contained.
Returns:	Length of the initial string that contains only characters from *szChars*, up to the length of *szString*.
Example:	

```
char    szString[100] =
{"Now is the time for all good men."};
char    szOutput[100];

    memset(szOutput, 0, sizeof(szOutput));

    strncpy(szOutput, szString,
        strspn(szString, "woN si teh"));
```

```
        printf("%s",
            szOutput);
    /* will print Now is the ti  */
```

Note: Also see strcspn().

strstr()

Header: string.h

Syntax:
```
char * strstr(const char * szString, const char *
                szCharacters);
```

Description: Finds the first occurrence of *szCharacters* in *szSting*.

Parameters: *szString*—Pointer to the string to search.

                   szCharacters—Pointer to the characters to search for.

Returns: Pointer to the point where the characters were found.

Example:
```
char    szString[100] =
{"Now is the time for all good men."};

    printf("'%s'", strstr(szString, "me"));
/* will print 'me for all good men.' */
```

Note: Basically a search for a substring in a string function.

strtod()

Header: stdlib.h

Syntax:
```
double strtod(const char * szString,
                char ** pEnd);
```

Description: Converts the string to a floating point number, stopping when an
                   invalid character has been reached. The stopping point is stored
                   in the variable pointed to by *pEnd* if *pEnd* is not NULL.

Parameters: *szString*—Pointer to the string to convert.

                   pEnd—Pointer to a string pointer.

Returns: The floating point number converted.

Example:
```
double  dValue;
char    szString[100] =
{"123.34 Now is the time for all good men."};
char   * pEnd;

    dValue = strtod(szString, &pEnd);

    printf("Converted %f stopped at '%s'\n",
        dValue,
        pEnd);

/*
 * Prints: Converted 123.340000 stopped at
 ' Now is the time for all good men.'
 */
```

Note: See strtol().

strtok()

Header: string.h

Syntax: char * strtok(char * *szString*, const char *
                szTokenSep);

Description: Breaks the string pointed to by *szString* into tokens, when each token is separated by one (or more) of the characters found in *szTokenSep*.

Parameters: *szString*—Pointer to a string to break into tokens. This string will be modified, so use a copy if necessary.

szTokenSep—Pointer to a string of token separators.

Returns: Pointer to a token from *szString*.

Example:
```
char    szString[100] =
{"Now is the time for all good men."};
char    szTokens[] = {" ."};
char   * pToken;
```

```
                         printf("'%s'\n", szString);

                         pToken = strtok(szString, szTokens);

                         do
                         {
                             printf("Token '%s'\n", pToken);
                         } while (pToken = strtok(NULL, szTokens));

                         printf("'%s'\n", szString);

                     /*
                      * Prints:
                      *    'Now is the time for all good men.'
                      *    Token 'Now'
                      *    Token 'is'
                      *    Token 'the'
                      *    Token 'time'
                      *    Token 'for'
                      *    Token 'all'
                      *    Token 'good'
                      *    Token 'men'
                      *    'Now'
                      */
```

Note: Don't forget that this function modifies the string passed.

strtol()

Header: stdlib.h

Syntax:
```
long strtol(const char * szString, char ** pEnd,
            int nBase);
```

Description: Converts the string to a long integer number, stopping when an invalid character has been reached. The stopping point is stored in the variable pointed to by *pEnd* if *pEnd* is not NULL. The parameter *nBase* determines what base is used and must be either 0 or 2 through 36. If *nBase* is zero, then the base of the

number is determined from the number's format—if the number starts with 0x or 0X, then it is base 16; if it starts with a zero, then base 8 is assumed; otherwise it is decimal based.

Parameters: *szString*—Pointer to the string to convert.

pEnd—Pointer to a string pointer.

nBase—Base of the number to be converted.

Returns: The long integer converted.

Example:
```
long    lValue;
char    szString[100] =
{"123.34 Now is the time for all good men."};
char    * pEnd;

    lValue = strtol(szString, &pEnd, 0);

    printf("Converted %ld stopped at '%s'\n",
        lValue,
        pEnd);

/*
 * Prints: Converted 123 stopped at
 '.34 Now is the time for all good men.'
 */
```

Note: See strtoul().

strtoul()

Header: stdlib.h

Syntax:
```
unsigned long int strtoul(const char * szString,
                          char ** pEnd,
                          int nBase);
```

Description: Converts the string to an unsigned long integer number, stopping when an invalid character is reached. The stopping point is stored in the variable pointed to by *pEnd* if *pEnd* is not NULL. The parameter *nBase* determines what base is used and must be

591

either 0 or 2 through 36. If *nBase* is zero, then the base of the number is determined from the number's format; if the number starts with 0x or 0X, then it is base 16; if it starts with a zero, then base 8 is assumed; otherwise it is decimal based.

Parameters: *szString*—Pointer to the string to convert.

pEnd—Pointer to a string pointer.

nBase—Base of the number to be converted.

Returns: The long integer converted.

Example:
```
unsigned long   lValue;
char    szString[100] =
{"123.34 Now is the time for all good men."};
char    * pEnd;

    lValue = strtoul(szString, &pEnd, 0);

    printf("Converted %ld stopped at '%s'\n",
        lValue,
        pEnd);

/*
 * Prints: Converted 123 stopped at '.34 Now is the time
for all good men.'
 */
```

Note: See strtol().

strxfrm()

Header: string.h

Syntax: size_t strxfrm (char * *szDestination*, const char *
szSource, size_t *nLength*);

Description: Copies the string pointed to by *szSource* to the buffer pointed to by *szDestination*, using the collating sequence set by setlocale (). The function is identical to strncpy() when the locale is "C",

except the string is not padded with NULL characters when *szSource* is shorter than *nLength*.

Parameters:	*szDestination*—Pointer to a buffer where *szSource* will be copied to.

szSource—Pointer to a string to copy and convert.

nLength—Maximum number of characters to copy and convert.

Returns: Length of the converted string.

Example:
```
char    szSource[100] =
{"Now is the time for all good men."};
char    szDestination[100];

    strxfrm(szDestination, szSource,
            strlen(szSource));

    printf("Converted \n'%s' \nto \n'%s'\n",
        szSource,
        szDestination);

/*
 * Prints:
 *   Converted
 *   'Now is the time for all good men.'
 *   to
 *   'Now is the time for all good men.'
 */
```

Note: See strncpy()

system()

Header: process.h & stdlib.h

Syntax: `int system(const char * szCommand);`

Description: Passes the string pointed to by *szCommand* to the operating system's command processor.

Parameters:	*szCommand*—Pointer to a string containing an operating system command, or NULL to determine if there is a command processor.
Returns:	If *szCommand* is NULL, non-zero if there is a command processor, otherwise a zero value. If *szCommand* is not NULL, then zero if there was no error, or a non-zero value if the command processor couldn't be loaded.

Example:

```
/* Check for command processor, and do a dir command if
present */
    if (system(NULL))
    {
        system("dir *.*");
    }
```

Note:	Most operating systems have a loadable command processor.

tan()

Header:	math.h
Syntax:	`double tan(double dValue);`
Description:	Returns the tangent of *dValue*, measured in radians.
Parameters:	*dValue*—Value for which tangent is desired.
Returns:	The tangent of *dValue*.

Example:

```
double  dResult;

    dResult = tan(1.5);

/* dResult will be 14.10142  */
```

Note:	Also see tanh().

tanh()

Header:	math.h
Syntax:	`double tanh(double dValue);`

Description:	Returns the hyperbolic tangent of *dValue*, measured in radians.
Parameters:	*dValue*—Value for which hyperbolic tangent is desired.
Returns:	The hyperbolic tangent of *dValue*.
Example:	

```
double  dResult;

    dResult = tanh(1.5);

/* dResult will be 0.905148  */
```

Note:	Also see tan().

time()

Header:	time.h
Syntax:	time_t time(time_t * TimeValue);
Description:	Returns the current calendar time encoded into a time_t type.
Parameters:	*TimeValue*—Pointer to a type time_t, which if not NULL, will also receive the time.
Returns:	The current time.
Example:	

```
char    szBuffer[100];
time_t  OurTime;

    OurTime = time(NULL);

    strftime(szBuffer, sizeof(szBuffer),
            "Today is %A %B %d, %Y",
        localtime(&OurTime));

    printf("%s\n", szBuffer);

/* Will print Today is Saturday June 27, 1992 */
```

Note:	Also see strftime() and ctime(). The function time()'s parameter is often NULL as shown in the preceding example.

tmpfile()

Header:	stdio.h
Syntax:	`FILE * tmpfile(void);`
Description:	Creates a temporary work file and opens it for update. This file is removed by the system either when it is closed or the program ends.
Parameters:	None.
Returns:	Handle to a file or NULL if the function fails.
Example:	`FILE * TempWork = tmpfile();`
Note:	Be careful not to close the file in error because this removes the file.

tmpnam()

Header:	stdio.h
Syntax:	`char * tmpnam(char * szFileName);`
Description:	Creates a save name for a temporary work file. This function is used when `tmpfile()` cannot be used, such as in situations where the file must be closed for some reason.
Parameters:	*szFileName*—Pointer to a buffer to hold the filename. This buffer must be at least L_tmpnam characters long.
Returns:	Pointer to the filename buffer. If *szFileName* is NULL, then the buffer is a static internal buffer.

Example:	`char    szBuffer[L_tmpnam];`
	
	`tmpnam(szBuffer);`
	
	`printf("The temporary work file is '%s'\n",`
	`        szBuffer);`

Note:	Don't forget to remove the file when the program ends.

tolower()

Header:	ctype.h & stdlib.h
Syntax:	`int tolower(int chChar);`
Description:	Converts *chChar* to lowercase if it was originally uppercase. If *chChar* was not uppercase, then it is returned unchanged.
Parameters:	*chChar*—Uppercase letter to be converted to lowercase.
Returns:	The character converted to lowercase.
Example:	

```
        printf("'A' in lowercase is '%c'\n",
                tolower('A');
/* Will print 'A' in lowercase is 'a' */
```

Note:	See toupper().

toupper()

Header:	ctype.h & stdlib.h
Syntax:	`int toupper(int chChar);`
Description:	Converts *chChar* to uppercase if it was originally lowercase. If *chChar* was not lowercase, then it is returned unchanged.
Parameters:	*chChar*—Lowercase letter to be converted to uppercase.
Returns:	The character converted to uppercase.
Example:	

```
        printf("'a' in uppercase is '%c'\n",
                toupper('a');
/* Will print 'a' in uppercase is 'A' */
```

Note:	See tolower().

ungetc()

Header:	stdio.h
Syntax:	`int ungetc(int chChar, FILE * OpenFile);`

Description: This function pushes back a character to the file *OpenFile* (which was opened for input).

Parameters: *chChar*—Character to be pushed back to the file.

                OpenFile—Pointer to an opened file.

Returns: The character that was pushed back.

Example:
```
char     szBuffer[129];

    printf("Please press the 'b' key: ");

    szBuffer[0] = (char)getc(stdin);

    ungetc('A', stdin);

    szBuffer[1] = (char)getc(stdin);

    printf("szBuffer has %2.2s\n", szBuffer);
/* Will print szBuffer has bA (if you type a 'b'
   at the prompt) */
```

Note: The character need not be the same one as was last read. You may ungetc() only one character before the character is read or discarded (by a call to fseek(), fsetpos(), or rewind()).

va_arg()

Header: stdarg.h

Syntax:
```
type va_arg(va_list param, type);
```

Description: Obtains the next argument from a list of variable arguments to a function.

Parameters: *param*—Parameter list pointer.

                type—Type of the next (to be fetched) parameter.

Returns: Value of the parameter being fetched.

Example:
```
/* Program VARGS, written 17 June 1999 by Peter D.
```

```
    Hipson */

#include <limits.h>
#include <stdarg.h>
#include <stdio.h>
#include <stdlib.h>

#define TRUE                    1
#define FALSE                   (!TRUE)

int     AddList(int nFirst, ...);
int     OurErrors(char * OutputFormat, ...);

void    main()

{

int     nSum;

    nSum = AddList(10, 20, 30, 40, 50, 60, 70, 80,
                    90, INT_MIN);

    (void)OurErrors("%s - %d, %s\n", "First",
                    nSum, "Second");

}

int     AddList(
    int nFirst,
    ...)

{

int     nReturnValue = nFirst;
int     nThisValue;

va_list Arguments;

    va_start(Arguments, nFirst);
```

```
        while((nThisValue = va_arg(Arguments, int)) !=
            INT_MIN)
        {
            nReturnValue += nThisValue;
        }

        va_end(Arguments);

        return(nReturnValue);
    }


    int     OurErrors(
        char * OutputFormat,
        ...)

    {

    va_list Arguments;

        va_start(Arguments, OutputFormat);

        vfprintf(stderr, OutputFormat, Arguments);

        va_end(Arguments);

        return(0);

    }
```

Note: See Chapter 13, "All About Header Files," for more information.

va_end()

Header: stdarg.h

Syntax: `void va_end(va_list param);`

Description: Ends the processing of the variable number of arguments.

Parameters:	*param*—Variable argument list.
Returns:	No return value.
Example:	(See va_arg(), preceding function described.)
Note:	See Chapter 13, "All About Header Files," for more information.

va_start()

Header:	stdarg.h
Syntax:	`void va_start(va_list param, previous);`
Description:	Starts processing of a variable number of arguments.
Parameters:	*param*—va_list variable, used by the va_ functions.
	previous—Name of the last fixed parameter being passed to the called function.
Returns:	No return value.
Example:	(See va_arg(), previously described.)
Note:	See Chapter 13, "All About Header Files," for more information.

vfprintf()

Header:	stdio.h
Syntax:	`int vfprintf(FILE * OpenFile, const char * szFormat, va_list VarArgs);`
Description:	Prints to the specified file by using arguments passed by another function.
Parameters:	*OpenFile*—Pointer to an opened file.
	szFormat—Pointer to a string containing format information.
	VarArgs—Variable argument list.
Returns:	Number of characters written or a negative value if there was an error.

Example:

```
/* Program VARGS, written 17 June 1999 by
   Peter D. Hipson */

#include <limits.h>
#include <stdarg.h>
#include <stdio.h>
#include <stdlib.h>

int     OurErrors(char * OutputFormat, ...);

void    main()

{

int     nSum = 100;

    (void)OurErrors("%s - %d, %s\n",
                    "First", nSum, "Second");

}

int     OurErrors(
    char * OutputFormat,
    ...)

{

va_list Arguments;

    va_start(Arguments, OutputFormat);

    vfprintf(stderr, OutputFormat,
             Arguments);

    va_end(Arguments);

    return(0);

}
```

Note: See vprintf().

vprintf()

Header: stdio.h

Syntax: int vprintf(const char * *szFormat*, va_list
                            VarArgs);

Description: Prints to stdout using arguments passed by another function.

Parameters: *szFormat*—Pointer to a string containing format information.

VarArgs—Variable argument list.

Returns: Number of characters written or a negative value if there was an error.

Example:
```
/* Program VARGS, written 17 June 1992 by
   Peter D. Hipson */

#include <limits.h>
#include <stdarg.h>
#include <stdio.h>
#include <stdlib.h>

int     OurOutput(char * OutputFormat, ...);

void    main()

{

int     nSum = 100;

    (void)OurOutput("%s - %d, %s\n",
                        "First", nSum, "Second");

}

int OurOutput(
    char * OutputFormat,
            ...)

{

va_list Arguments;

    va_start(Arguments, OutputFormat);

    vprintf(OutputFormat, Arguments);

    va_end(Arguments);

    return(0);

}
```

Note: See vfprintf().

vsprintf()

Header:	stdio.h
Syntax:	int vsprintf(char * *szBuffer*, const char * *szFormat*, va_list *VarArgs*);
Description:	Prints, using arguments passed by another function, to the buffer pointed to by *szBuffer*.
Parameters:	*szBuffer*—Pointer to a buffer to write to.
	szFormat—Pointer to a string containing format information.
	VarArgs—Variable argument list.
Returns:	Number of characters written or a negative value if there was an error.
Example:	

```
/* Program VARGS, written 17 June 1992 by
   Peter D. Hipson */

#include <limits.h>
#include <stdarg.h>
#include <stdio.h>
#include <stdlib.h>

int     OurOutput(char * OutputBuffer,
                  char * OutputFormat, ...);

void    main()

{

char    szBuffer[100];
int     nSum = 100;

    (void)OurOutput(szBuffer,
                    "%s - %d, %s\n",
                    "First", nSum, "Second");

    printf("%s", szBuffer);

}

int     OurOutput(
    char * OutputBuffer,
```

```
        char * OutputFormat,
        ...)

{

va_list Arguments;

    va_start(Arguments, OutputFormat);

    vsprintf(OutputBuffer, OutputFormat,
            Arguments);

    va_end(Arguments);

    return(0);

}
```

Note: See vfprintf() and vprintf().

wcstombs()

Header: stdlib.h

Syntax:
```
size_t wcstombs(char * szDestination,
                const wchar_t * pWideChars,
                size_t nSize);
```

Description: Converts the wide characters in the buffer pointed to by *pWideChars* to multibyte characters. Stores up to *nSize* characters in *szDestination*.

Parameters: *szDestination*—Pointer to a buffer to receive the multibyte characters.

    pWideCharacters—Pointer to a buffer containing the wide characters to be converted.

    nCount—Size of *szDestination*.

Returns: Number of characters converted.

Example:
```
wcstombs(szBuffer, szWideChars,
        sizeof(szBuffer));
```

Note: See wctomb().

wctomb()

Header:	stdlib.h
Syntax:	`int wctomb(char * szDestination, const wchar_t WideChar);`
Description:	Converts a single wide character in the buffer pointed to by *pWideChars* to a multibyte character.
Parameters:	*szDestination*—Pointer to a buffer to receive the multibyte characters.
	WideChar—Wide character to be converted.
Returns:	Number of bytes resulting from the conversion.
Example:	`wctomb(szBuffer, szWideChar[0]);`
Note:	See `wcstombs()`.

printf() Format Codes

The `printf()` family of functions—`printf()`, `fprintf()`, `sprintf()`, `vprintf()`, `vfprintf()`, and `vsprintf()`— uses a format string to describe the format of the output. This format string enables the programmer to specify what is output.

The format string specifies the variables and how they are output. Because these functions use a variable number of arguments, the function doesn't know what variables have been passed except to look at the format string. Making an error in one variable's type often causes problems with the variables that follow.

How is a variable formatted? The first character in a format specifier is a percent sign, `%`. This format specifier has the following fields:

```
%[flags][size][.precision][prefix]type
```

The `flags` field is optional. Four values are allowed in this field, as shown in Table 14.8.

Table 14.8. Flags used with printf() family of functions.

Flag character	Description
'-'	Left justify the output field within the width defined.
'+'	Signed, positive values are always prefixed with a plus sign. Negative values are prefixed with a minus sign.
' '	Signed, positive values are always prefixed with a blank. Negative values are prefixed with a negative sign.
'#'	Alternate conversion adds a leading zero for octal values, a '0x' or '0X' for hexadecimal values, forces a floating point number to always have a decimal point, and removes floating point trailing zeros.

The following section describes each type of printf() field, and the meanings for size, .precision, and prefix fields. Because all these fields depend on the type field, the table is organized with subheads for each type.

c

The c type tells printf() to output a single character. This field is affected by the following:

flags

Only the - (left justify) flag is used. If the width field specifies a width greater than one, then the character can be either right justified (default) or left justified (using the left justify flag).

width

Specifies the width of the output.

.precision

Ignored if present.

prefix

Ignored if present.

d and i

The d and i type tells printf() to output a signed decimal integer. This field is affected by the following:

flags

All flags as shown in Table 14.8 affect a field of this type.

width

Specifies the minimum width. If the formatted result is less than the width, then it is padded with blanks. If the formatted result is greater than the width, then the width is ignored, and the formatted output's actual width is used.

.precision

The precision specifies the minimum number of digits to appear. This causes output that has fewer than the number of digits of width to be padded on the left with zeros.

prefix

The prefix allows specification of a short or long integer. Use h to specify a short (16-bit) integer, and l to specify a long (32-bit) integer. The default is to the default size for an integer for the system.

e and E

The e and E types tell printf() to output a floating point number, using an exponential format. This output takes the form of [-]d.ddde[+¦-]ddd. If the E type

is specified, then the form taken is `[-]d.dddE[+¦-]ddd` with an uppercase E used to indicate the exponent.

This field is affected by the following:

flags

All `flags` as shown in Table 14.8 affect a field of this type.

width

Specifies the minimum width. If the formatted result is less than the width, then it is padded with blanks. If the formatted result is greater than the width, then the width is ignored and the formatted output's actual width is used.

.precision

Specifies the number of digits that follow the decimal point in the mantissa.

prefix

Two prefixes are recognized. The `l` prefix specifies the value is a `double`. The `L` prefix specifies the value is a `long double`. When a `float` is passed as a parameter, it is always passed as a `double` (unless it is cast as a `float`, which is not recommended).

f

The `f` type tells `printf()` to output a floating point number. This field is affected by the following:

flags

All `flags` as shown in Table 14.8 affect a field of this type.

width

Specifies the minimum width. If the formatted result is less than the width, then it is padded with blanks. If the formatted result is greater than the width, then the width is ignored and the formatted output's actual width is used.

609

.precision

Specifies the number of digits that follow the decimal point.

prefix

Two prefixes are recognized. The l prefix specifies the value is a double. The L prefix specifies the value is a long double. When a float is passed as a parameter, it is always passed as a double (unless it is cast as a float, which is not recommended).

g and G

The g and G types tell printf() to output using either the f, e, or E types, depending on the value of the argument. The e type is used if the exponent for the conversion would be less than -4 or greater than the precision. Trailing zeros are removed, and the decimal point appears only if there is a decimal part of the number. See the f, e, or E types for more information.

n

The n type tells printf() to save the current number of characters written so far to the variable pointed to by the argument. No modifiers are allowed with the n type.

o

The o type tells printf() to output a decimal number in octal (base 8) format. This field is affected by the following:

flags

All flags as shown in Table 14.8 affect a field of this type.

width

Specifies the minimum width. If the formatted result is less than the width, then it is padded with blanks. If the formatted result is greater than the width, then the width is ignored, and the formatted output's actual width is used.

.precision

The precision specifies the minimum number of digits to appear. This causes output that has fewer than the number of digits of width to be padded on the left with zeros.

prefix

The prefix allows specification of a short or long integer. Use h to specify a short (16-bit) integer and 1 to specify a long (32-bit) integer. The default is to the default size for an integer for the system.

p and P

The p and P types tell printf() to output a pointer. The pointer is printed in hexadecimal notation, in a format that may be machine dependent. The case of the type is used to specify the case of the hexadecimal digits. This field is affected by the following:

flags

All flags as shown in Table 14.8 affect a field of this type.

width

Specifies the minimum width. If the formatted result is less than the width, then it is padded with blanks. If the formatted result is greater than the width, then the width is ignored, and the formatted output's actual width is used.

.precision

The precision specifies the minimum number of digits to appear. This causes output that has fewer than the number of digits of width to be padded on the left with zeros.

prefix

With compilers that have segmented memory (and memory models) the prefix allows specification of near or far pointers. Use F to specify a far (or long) pointer and N to specify a near (or short) pointer. The default is to the default pointer type for the program.

s

The s type tells `printf()` to output a string. This field is affected by the following:

flags

All `flags` as shown in Table 14.8 affect a field of this type except for the + (for plus sign) and the ' ' (a blank, again for signs).

width

The width specifier defines the minimum width. If the string is longer than the width and no `.precision` value is specified, then the output expands to the size of the string.

.precision

Specifies the maximum number of characters to be output. If the string being printed is larger than the `width` specification, then it will be truncated to `.precision` size.

prefix

With compilers that have segmented memory (and memory models) the prefix allows specification of a near or far pointer. Use F to specify a far (or long) pointer and N to specify a near (or short) pointer. The default is to the default pointer type for the program.

u

The u type tells `printf()` to output an unsigned decimal integer. This field is affected by the following:

flags

All `flags` as shown in Table 14.8 affect a field of this type, except there can never be a minus sign.

width

Specifies the minimum width. If the formatted result is less than the width, then it is padded with blanks. If the formatted result is greater than the width, then the width is ignored and the formatted output's actual width is used.

.precision

The precision specifies the minimum number of digits to appear. This causes output that has fewer than the number of digits of width to be padded on the left with zeros.

prefix

The prefix allows specification of a short or long integer. Use h to specify a short (16-bit) integer and l to specify a long (32-bit) integer. The default is to the default size for an integer for the system.

x and X

The x and X types tell printf() to output an unsigned, hexadecimal integer. The case of the hexadecimal digits matches the case of the type field. This field is affected by the following:

flags

All flags as shown in Table 14.8 affect a field of this type.

width

Specifies the minimum width. If the formatted result is less than the width, then it is padded with blanks. If the formatted result is greater than the width, then the width is ignored and the formatted output's actual width is used.

.precision

The precision specifies the minimum number of digits to appear. This causes output that has fewer than the number of digits of width to be padded on the left with zeros.

prefix

The prefix allows specification of a short or long integer. Use h to specify a short (16-bit) integer and 1 to specify a long (32-bit) integer. The default is to the default size for an integer for the system.

scanf() format codes

The scanf() family of functions—scanf(), fscanf(), and sscanf()—uses a format string to describe the format of the input. This format string allows the programmer to specify what is read. All arguments passed to these functions that are to receive values are passed as addresses. Failure to provide addresses causes the program to fail.

The format string specifies what the variables will be when they are filled in, their types, and the format of the input data. Because these functions use a variable number of arguments, the function doesn't know what variables have been passed except to look at the format string.

How is a variable formatted? The first character in a format specifier is a percent sign, %. This format specifier has the following fields:

```
%[*][width][typelength]type
```

The * specifies that the next field of type is to be skipped. The specification of type is important to ensure the field is correctly skipped.

The optional specification width specifies the maximum width that is scanned for this field. The field may well be shorter than width, depending on the type specification.

The typelength specifier provides information about the size of the object that receives the input. Using an 'h' character specifies a short (16-bit) object while the '1' character specifies a long (32-bit) object. When used with floating point arguments, the '1' character specifies a long double object (its size being implementation dependent).

c

The c type tells scanf() to input one (or more) characters, which may include whitespace characters (the s type does not include whitespace characters). This field is affected by the following:

width

Specifies the width of the input field. If not specified, then the width is assumed to be one character.

typelength

None allowed.

d

The d type tells scanf() to input a signed decimal integer. This field is affected by the following:

width

Specifies the maximum width.

typelength

The typelength specifier provides information about the size of the object that receives the input. Using an 'h' character specifies a short (16-bit) object while the 'l' character specifies a long (32 bit) object.

o

The o type tells scanf() to input a decimal number in octal (base 8) format. This field is affected by the following:

width

Specifies the maximum width.

typelength

The `typelength` specifier provides information about the size of the object that will receive the input. Using an 'h' character specifies a short (16-bit) object while the 'l' character specifies a long (32-bit) object.

x

The x type tells `scanf()` to input an unsigned, hexadecimal integer. This field is affected by the following:

width

Specifies the maximum width.

typelength

The `typelength` specifier provides information about the size of the object that receives the input. Using an 'h' character specifies a short (16-bit) object, while the 'l' character specifies a long (32-bit) object.

i

The i type tells `scanf()` to input a signed decimal integer, which may be in a decimal, octal, or hexadecimal format. The first characters in the string are examined, and if they are 0x, then the number is assumed to be base hexadecimal. If there is a leading 0 with no following x, then the base is assumed to be octal. If the leading character is not a 0, then the number is assumed to be decimal. This field is affected by the following:

width

Specifies the maximum width.

typelength

The typelength specifier provides information about the size of the object that receives the input. Using an 'h' character specifies a short (16-bit) object, while the 'l' character specifies a long (32-bit) object.

u

The u type tells scanf() to input an unsigned decimal integer. This field is affected by the following:

width

Specifies the maximum width.

typelength

The typelength specifier provides information about the size of the object that receives the input. Using an 'h' character specifies a short (16-bit) object, while the 'l' character specifies a long (32-bit) object.

e, f, and g

The e, f, and g types tell scanf() to input a floating point number.

This field is affected by the following:

width

Specifies the maximum width.

typelength

With floating point arguments, the 'l' character specifies a long double object (its size being implementation dependent).

n

The n type tells scanf() to save the current number of characters scanned so far to the variable pointed to by the argument. No modifiers are allowed with the n type.

p

The p and P types tell scanf() to input a pointer. The pointer is scanned in hexadecimal notation, in a format that may be machine dependent. This field is affected by the following:

width

Specifies the maximum width.

typelength

No typelength specifier is used.

s

The s type tells scanf() to input a character string, which consists of a group of nonwhitespace characters. Input is assigned up to the first whitespace character. This field is affected by the following:

width

Specifies the maximum width.

typelength

No typelength specifier is used.

[...]

The [...] type tells scanf() to input a character string, consisting of all characters that are found in the brackets. Prefixing the characters with a ^ causes all characters that are not in the group to be read.

Typically, this input format is used to read strings that contain blanks or other whitespace characters. This field is affected by the following:

width

Specifies the maximum width.

typelength

No typelength specifier is used.

Summary

This chapter covered the various ANSI standard library functions:

- The functions are prototyped in the standard header files.

- Programmers must be careful to pass the correct parameters to those functions that take a variable number of arguments (such as printf()) because the compiler cannot check argument types.

- About 150 non-ANSI functions are available with many compilers. Using the non-ANSI function may create problems when the program is ported to a different compiler.

Preprocessor Directives

To help you gain a better understanding of how a C compiler produces the object module, this chapter looks at the process of compiling. Most compilers take the following steps, in this order:

1. Preprocess the input file, in this order:

    a. Process the #preprocessor directives.

    b. Strip comments from the source (as necessary).

    c. Expand all macros.

2. The syntax checker processes the file to check for syntax errors.

3. The code generator generates the necessary object module.

All preprocessor commands begin with a pound symbol (#). It must be the first nonblank character, and for readability, a preprocessor directive should begin in column 1. Notice that a defined identifier is always a macro and can be referred to in that way.

The C preprocessor offers four operators to help you in creating macros (see the section "The #define Directive") and the #if series of directives.

The Macro Continuation Operator (\)

A macro usually must be contained on a single line. The macro continuation operator is used to continue a macro that is too long for a single line. When you are breaking a macro over several lines, use the macro continuation operator as the last character in the line to be continued. Here's an example of a multiline macro:

```
#define PRINTMSG(operand) \
        printf(#operand " = %d\n", operand)
```

This line is exactly equivalent to the following:

```
#define PRINTMSG(operand) printf(#operand " = %d\n", operand)
```

The macro continuation operator allows your macros to be read and formatted more easily. It doesn't affect the operation of the macro.

The Stringize Operator (#)

The stringize operator is used in creating a macro. It takes the particular operand to the macro and converts it to a string. To see how this works, look at this example:

```
#define PRINTMSG(operand) printf(#operand " = %d\n", operand)
```

When an integer variable (nCount) is being used as a counter, for example, you might use the statement to display nCount's value for debugging:

```
PRINTMSG(nCount + 1);
```

This statement then is expanded by the preprocessor to create the following source line:

```
printf("nCount + 1 " " = %d\n", nCount + 1);
```

This sample line of code shows that the variable's name has been included (using string literal concatenation) as part of the format string that printf() uses.

The stringize operator causes the particular operand to a macro to be converted to a string, by taking the literal characters of the operand and enclosing them within double quotes.

The Characterize Operator (#@)

The characterize operator, which works much like the stringize operator, is used in creating a macro. It takes a particular single character operand to the macro and converts it to a character literal, by surrounding it with single quotes. To see how this works, look at the following example:

```
#define MAKECHAR(operand) #@operand
```

When you want to create a character literal, as part of a case: statement, for example, you can use the MAKECHAR macro:

```
    switch(nCount + 1)
    {
        case MAKECHAR(A):
/*          Action for capital A */
            break;
        case MAKECHAR(B):
/*          Action for capital B */
            break;
        default:
            break;
    }
```

The first case statement then is expanded by the PP to create the following:

```
case 'A':
```

In this sample line of code, the operand has been surrounded by single quotes, yielding a character literal. This example isn't the most useful for using the characterize operator, but it gets the point across.

The characterize operator causes the particular operand to a macro to be converted to a character literal, by taking the characters of the operand and enclosing them within single quotes. This operator fails if it is given a single quote character.

The Token Paste Operator (##)

The token paste operator tells the preprocessor to paste, to the token on the other side, the operand that either precedes or follows it. For example, you might code a macro to print one of several variables that have meaningful names:

```
#define PRINTCOUNTER(variable) \
        printf("counter %d is %d", variable,  nCounter#variable)
```

This macro definition can then be used in a program such as the following:

```
int    nCounter1;
int    nCounter2;
int    nCounter3;
int    nCounter4;

    PRINTCOUNTER(1);
```

This call to the macro can be expanded to

```
printf("variable %d is %d", 1, nCounter1);
```

You decide how to use this operator. It has many uses when you create macros to help debug programs that use structures heavily.

The Defined Identifier Operator (defined())

The defined() operator is used with the #if and #elif preprocessor commands. This operator returns a logical true (nonzero) value if the identifier used as its operand is currently defined and a logical false (zero) if the operand is not defined.

The primary use for defined() is in testing two different identifiers to see whether they are defined. You can use nested #ifdef statements; using defined(), however, makes the code easier to understand.

The #define Directive

The #define command defines macros. C's macros help you create powerful functionality. Macros can be defined with substitutable parameters or as simple identifiers. The simplest macro probably is the following:

```
#define TRUE    1
```

This macro defines the identifier TRUE that always has the numeric value of 1 substituted for it. For example, the following lines have a conditional statement (and some comments):

```
#define   TRUE    1

/* Later in the program... */

    if (nOurTime == TRUE)
    {/* Process our time... */
/*      our time code is here. */
    }
```

After the preprocessor finishes, this simple bit of code then reads:

```
if (nOurTime == 1)
{

}
```

This code fragment shows that the preprocessor has substituted the number 1 for the identifier TRUE. In this example, TRUE is the simplest form of a macro—so simple that it usually is referred to as the definition of an identifier. A more complex macro might have one or more operands, which enable you to test and create different statements, such as MACROS (see Listing 15.1).

Listing 15.1. MACROS.C.

```
/* Program MACROS, written 23 June 1992 by Peter D. Hipson */
/* A program that shows macros. */

#include <stdio.h>
#include <stdlib.h>
```

continues

Listing 15.1. continued

```
/*
 * The DONOTHING identifier, although it is defined, is basically
 * a no-operation. An example of its use is shown in the body
 * of the program. Some programmers define DONOTHING as a
 * semicolon; doing so, however, can create problems and is
 * not recommended.
 */

#define DONOTHING

/*
 * Both TRUE and FALSE, below, can be considered to be macros
 * that don't have any operands. When they are included in a
 * source line, they expand to their literal contents.
 */

#define TRUE                    1
#define FALSE                   (!TRUE)

/*
 * Now define some stock macros. Both MIN() and MAX() may be
 * included (in lowercase) in stdlib.h (with many C compilers);
 * I define them in uppercase, however, to remind me that they
 * are macros, subject to side effects.
 */

#define MAX(a, b)   (((a) > (b)) ? (a) : (b))
#define MIN(a, b)   (((a) < (b)) ? (a) : (b))

/*
 * SWAP() is a neat little variable swapper that swaps the
 * contents of two variables in-place without temporary storage.
 * The only caution is that the variables must be of the same
 * size (but can be of differing types if necessary).
 *
 * Notice SWAP()'s use of braces around the expressions, in
 * case the macro is invoked as a single line after an if()
 * statement that has no braces itself. Failure to include
 * the braces can lead to some strange problems with macros
```

```
 * that have more than one statement included in them, such
 * as is the case with SWAP().
 */

#define SWAP(a, b) {a ^= b; b ^= a; a ^= b;}

/*
 * Notice that PRINTAB() uses the stringize operator to form
 * its format string. This usage enables you to have a nice
 * printf() statement without having to do a lot of typing.
 */

#define PRINTAB(a, b) printf(#a" = %d "#b" = %d  \n", a, b)


int    main()

{

int    nOurTime = FALSE;
int    nSum;

int    a = 10;
int    b = 11;


/*  The DONOTHING identifier tells you that the for()'s statement(s)
 *  have not been omitted:
 */

    for (nSum = 0; nSum == nOurTime; nSum++)
        DONOTHING;

    if (nOurTime == TRUE)
    {/* Process our time... */
/*      our time code is here. */
    }

    PRINTAB(a, b);
```

continues

Listing 15.1. continued

```
    SWAP(a, b);

    PRINTAB(a, b);

    return(FALSE);

}
```

Each of the macros in the MACROS program is useful in a real program. The MIN() and MAX() macros are the most useful to me. The SWAP() macro has been around a long time. (I came across it when I was writing assembly code for mainframe computers.) It enables two variables to be swapped without using any temporary storage—a handy tool if you are either short of memory or cannot allocate a temporary variable because of context.

The #error Directive

The #error directive typically is used as part of an #if type conditional preprocessor statement. For example, if you include in MACROS.C the #error directive as shown in the final line of this code fragment:

```
/* Program MACROS, written 23 June 1999 by Peter D. Hipson */

#include <stdio.h>
#include <stdlib.h>

#error "This is an error"
```

This directive, when encountered by the compiler, prints on the compiler's stderr stream a message similar to the following:

```
D:\ADC\SOURCE\MACROS.C(6) : error C2189: #error :   "This is an error"
```

Notice that the compiler's error message includes the source file's name and line number, and a compiler error message that includes the string included in the #error directive.

The #include Directive

The #include directive tells the compiler to include a header file at the current point in the source file. Header files generally don't contain actual executable statements, but rather contain #define identifiers, function prototypes, and so on.

When you are including a header file, delimit the operand using either double quotes or a <> pair surrounding the operand.

The directive #include "ourfile.h" causes the compiler to search for the header file first in the current directory and then in the directories specified in the include search order.

The directive #include <ourfile.h> causes the compiler to search for the header file in the directories specified in the include search order.

If the header file specified in the #include directive has a fully qualified path name, this path is used to find the header file.

The #if Directive

The #if directive is a useful part of the preprocessor's directives. It enables you to conditionally include (and exclude) parts of your source code. Unlike the other preprocessor directives usually grouped at the beginning of a source file, the #if directive may be found at any point in the source file.

The #if directive is followed by a constant expression (which the preprocessor evaluates) and has several restrictions, including the following:

- The expression must evaluate to constants. A variable cannot be used in the #if directive.

- The expression must not use sizeof(), a cast, or enum constants.

- The expression is evaluated mathematically; string compares do not work.

The #if directive enables you to compile code conditionally based on factors such as which operating system your program will run under and the compiler's memory model. When the #if directive is used, you can combine the #if directive with either the #else or the #elif directives.

The block of source code affected by the #if directive is ended with an #else, #elif, or #endif directive.

The #ifdef Directive

To test whether an identifier has been defined, you can use the #ifdef directive. The identifier to be tested can be one you create (using #define) or a predefined identifier created by the C compiler.

You might use the #ifdef directive to avoid creating problems with macro redefinitions or for specific macros being redefined with slightly different (but functionally identical) operands.

The most common use I have for the #if directive is to comment out large blocks of code that may contain embedded comments. Because you cannot use a surrounding comment with such a block of code, a simple workaround procedure is to use #if as shown in this example:

```
    for (nSum = 0; nSum == nOurTime; nSum++)
        DONOTHING;

#ifdef DONOTCOMPILE /* Never compile this code */

    if (nOurTime == TRUE)
    {/* Process our time... */
/*      our time code is here. */
    }

#endif /* DONOTCOMPILE */

    PRINTAB(a, b);
```

Notice that the if() block of code (with its comments) has been removed using an #ifdef/#endif directive pair. I make sure that the identifier DONOTCOMPILE never is defined. You can choose to use a different identifier; DONOTCOMPILE, however, is descriptive.

A second use of the #ifdef directive is to enable you to undefine an identifier if you know that you will redefine it.

```
#ifdef SWAP
#undef SWAP
#endif
#define SWAP(a, b) {a ^= b; b ^= a; a ^= b;}
```

In this code fragment, you want to define a macro called SWAP(); however, you want to avoid any problems in redefining an existing SWAP() macro. This code is necessary to avoid an error message if SWAP() already exists and then is redefined.

The #ifndef Directive

To test whether an identifier has *not* been defined, you can use the #ifndef directive. The identifier to be tested can be one you create (using #define) or a predefined identifier created by the C compiler. If the identifier has not been defined, the statements following the #ifndef directive are executed until either a #endif, #elif, or #else is encountered.

An example of the #ifndef directive is the code used to prevent a header file that is included twice from creating problems with macro redefinitions. An example of the use of #ifndef to prevent problems with multiple inclusion of a header file is shown in the following code fragment. This code fragment assumes that the header file's name is OURHEAD.H.

```
#ifndef __OURHEAD

/* The include file's lines are here... */

#define __OURHEAD
#endif /* __OURHEAD */
```

Notice that the first time the header file is included, the identifier __OURHEAD will not have been defined, and the test will succeed. The lines for the header file are processed and the final line defines the identifier __OURHEAD. If this header file is included a second time, the identifier __OURHEAD then is defined, and the test fails. The lines for the header file are ignored.

A second use of the #ifndef directive is to enable you to define an identifier if it has not been defined yet. In the following classic example, the NULL identifier (which is in a number of header files) is defined.

```
#ifndef NULL
#define NULL (int *)0
#endif
```

In this code fragment, be sure that the NULL identifier is defined. If it is defined, you accept the definition; if it is not defined, you define it. This code is necessary to avoid an error message if NULL already exists and then is redefined.

The #else Directive

Like the C language's if() statement, the preprocessor has an if/else construct. Often, you must use either one block of code or another depending on the results of a given test. You can make two separate #if tests, each having the opposite effect; this technique, however, creates code that is generally unreadable and difficult to maintain. (You might change one #if and forget to update the other.)

Typically, #else is used when you need to use one block of source code (which can include other preprocessor directives), or another, but never both. An example of the #else is shown in the following code fragment:

```
#if defined(VERSION1)
/* Lines for the first version. */
#else /* it's not VERSION1 */
/* Lines for the other versions. */
#endif /* VERSION1 testing */
```

The same code written without the #else is more complex and more difficult to understand:

```
#if defined(VERSION1)
/* Lines for the first version. */
#endif /* Not VERSION1 */

#if !defined(VERSION1)
/* Lines for the other versions. */
#endif /* Not VERSION1 */
```

Using #else when it's needed can make your preprocessor code more manageable.

The #elif Directive

To make the creation of nested testing using preprocessor directives easier, ANSI C has introduced the #elif directive. It follows an #if (or another #elif) directive, effectively ending the #if (or #elif)'s block and introducing a new conditional block.

Typically, #elif is used where you need multiple tests, for example, to test for two or more versions of a compiler. An example of the #elif is shown in the following code fragment:

```
#if defined(VERSION1)
/* Lines for the first version. */
#elif defined(VERSION2)
/* Lines for the second version. */
#elif defined(VERSION3)
/* Lines for the third version. */
#endif /* VERSION? */
```

The same code written without the #elif is more complex and more difficult to understand:

```
#if defined(VERSION1)
/* Lines for the first version. */
#else /* Not VERSION1 */
#if defined(VERSION2)
/* Lines for the second version. */
#else /* Not VERSION2 */
#if defined(VERSION3)
/* Lines for the third version. */
#endif /* VERSION3 */
#endif /* VERSION2 */
#endif /* VERSION1 */
```

Using #elif when it's needed can make your preprocessor code more manageable.

The #endif Directive

The #endif directive ends the nearest #if preceding it. Every #if requires an #endif statement; #else and #elif directives, however, do not require separate #endif statements.

633

The following code fragment shows nesting of conditional preprocessor statements and the effect of the #endif statements. Notice how the comments following the #endif directives make the code easier to read and modify. Try to get into the practice of commenting your preprocessor directives just as you would comment your regular C source code.

```
#ifdef DLL /* Creating a Dynamic Link Library */
#ifndef MT /* DLLs must be multitasking */
/* Error message for this condition! */
#error "Cannot define DLL without MT"
#else
/* whatever is required for a DLL */
#endif /* MT    */
#endif /* DLL   */
```

Using nested conditional preprocessor directives enables you to make complex decisions about what is being done with the program. Your program (commonly) might have three versions: a low-priced entry version, a higher-priced full-featured version, and a freebie demo version. Using #if directives enables you to maintain one set of source code that compiles differently depending on which version of the program is being created.

The #line Directive

By using the #line directive, you can change either the current line number (which then is successively incremented for following lines) or, optionally, the filename associated with the current source file.

When you are using an integrated debugger, which checks the error and warning messages produced by the compiler, changing the line or filename can produce results that may not be what you expect. When you are using #line, make sure that you understand what its effects will be in your environment.

The current line number is always available in the predefined identifier __LINE__, and the current filename is available in the predefined identifier __FILE__. Both of these identifiers are used with the assert() macro, and you can create error message substitutions using them. Let's look at an example of using the #line directive.

```
/* Source file is OURFILE.C */

   printf("This file is '%s' the line is '%d' \n", __FILE __,
__LINE __);

#line 10000 "DEBUGIT.C"

   printf("This file is '%s' the line is '%d' \n", __FILE __,
__LINE __);
```

Here are the results of running this program fragment:

```
This file is 'OURFILE.C' the line is '3'
This file is 'DEBUGIT.C' the line is '10002'
```

The #line directive can be useful when your source files don't have meaningful names and renaming them is not practical.

The #pragma Directive

The #pragma directive is, by ANSI standards, implementation-defined. It is used to issue special commands to the compiler, using a standardized method. Do not assume that any specific operand with #pragma is present when using a given compiler. Two pragmas are relatively common—message and pack. Your compiler probably offers several other pragmas in addition to these two.

The message Pragma

The message pragma enables you to write a message to stderr while the file is compiling. When you are debugging, check to see which identifiers are defined. The following code fragment has a message indicating which of the three versions of the program is being compiled:

```
#if defined(VERSION1)
#pragma message "The first version."
#elif defined(VERSION2)
#pragma message "The second version."
#elif defined(VERSION3)
#pragma message "The third version."
#endif /* VERSION? */
```

The pack Pragma

The pack pragma enables you to control the packing of structure members. This pragma usually is used with a parameter; used without a parameter, however, it restores the default packing value. Figure 15.1 shows an example of the effects of packing structures. This packing, called *data alignment*, affects the way each element in a structure is stored.

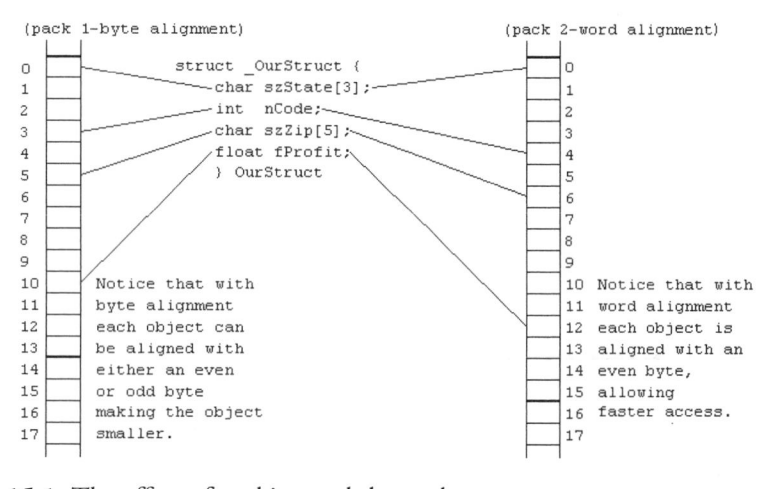

Figure 15.1. The effect of packing and the pack pragma.

All computers most efficiently access objects aligned on boundaries that are even multiples of the memory bus width. For an 80286 CPU, which accesses memory in 16-bit widths, accessing words that are aligned to even bytes is optimal. For an 80386/486—that is, a 32-bit processor that accesses memory in 32-bit widths—memory is accessed optimally using every other even address. The effects of accessing data objects that are not optimally aligned are difficult to predict. On one hand, aligning on a byte boundary makes the aggregate data objects smaller (and if they are used in arrays, the size difference can be significant), and the speed of even alignment may also be significant for an object that is accessed often.

Many programmers experiment with alignment to find the optimal compromise between size and speed. I usually use byte alignment for infrequently accessed objects and word alignment for objects that are accessed more frequently.

The #undef Directive

At times you might need to redefine a macro, often when an identifier has been defined outside your program and you are using it for a different purpose. To remove a definition of a macro, you should use the #undef directive. The following code segment shows how this directive is used:

```
#if defined(VERSION1)
#undef VERSION1
#endif
#define VERSION1 "The is Version 1.0"
```

Using #undef to remove a definition of a predefined macro is not a good idea.

Predefined Macros

ANSI C defines a number of macros. Although each one is available for your use in programming, the predefined macros should not be directly modified.

The _ _DATE_ _Macro

The _ _DATE _ _macro contains the current date as a character literal in the following format:

```
"MMM DD YYYY"
```

where MMM is the three-character month abbreviation, in mixed case; DD is the current day, padded with a blank if the day is less than 10; and YYYY is the year.

The _ _TIME_ _Macro

The _ _TIME _ _macro contains the current time as a character literal in the following format:

```
"HH:MM:SS"
```

where HH is hours, MM is minutes, and SS is seconds.

If any of the three is less than 10, the field is padded with a leading 0.

The_ _FILE_ _Macro

The _ _FILE _ _macro contains the current filename as a string literal. This macro's contents can be changed using the #line directive.

The_ _LINE_ _Macro

The _ _LINE _ _macro contains the current line number as a decimal constant. This macro's contents can be changed using the #line directive.

The_ _STDC_ _Macro

The _ _STDC _ _macro is defined as a decimal constant (value of 1) when the compiler complies with the ANSI standard.

NULL

NULL is defined as a pointer guaranteed not to point to anything valid. This pointer often is used as both an initializing value and an error return. You generally should use the NULL macro rather than 0 when you are assigning a null pointer to a pointer variable.

NULL commonly is assigned to variables of other types; you must be sure, however, that the results are what are expected. You should not assume that NULL is the equivalent to zero (which is often defined as a macro called FALSE), because this may not be the case.

The offsetof() Macro

The offsetof() macro returns the offset (in bytes) of a member of a structure from the beginning of the structure.

Summary

In this chapter, you learned about the preprocessor's directives.

- The preprocessor directives enable you to control the compilation of the program and to optionally include or exclude parts of a program based on predefined identifiers.

- Preprocessor directives can be in header files and in your source files.

- All identifiers defined with the #define directive are macros; a macro that has no parameters, however, often is referred to as simply a defined identifier.

- ANSI standard C defines a number of macros that can be used in programming to assist in debugging and development of a program.

Debugging and Efficiency

Just because a program has been written does not mean that it works correctly or is efficient. This chapter looks at debugging a program and methods for making the program more efficient.

Debugging

It is a rare program that works the first time. Many C programs are complex, containing thousands of lines of code. Even if the programmer has not made any syntax errors, the assumptions made when writing a program can create serious problems.

Debugging a program involves several steps:

1. Correct all warnings and errors that the compiler finds. Many programmers assume that the default error level is enough. This is incorrect—set the error level as high as possible. Correct all warnings and errors, or understand why you do not have to correct them.

2. After the program compiles without warnings or errors, the real debugging takes place. Use the program and make sure that it performs as you expect. This process, called *alpha testing*, may take some time. The more problems you find and correct, however, the fewer the user will find.

3. After finding and correcting problems during the alpha testing, find a few qualified users to test the program in an environment as close as possible to that which the program will be used in. This testing is called *beta testing*. Make sure that the testers really use the program. Generally, beta testers get a free copy of the product for their effort.

4. After beta testing, the product should be bug free. Any problems found by you (in alpha testing) and your test users (in beta testing) should be corrected. Beta testers often test two or three versions of the product.

5. Now that the product is finished, you ship it. Remember the first customer's name, because this is the person who finds the first bug, usually within a few minutes of using the product. Find ways to minimize the bug's effect. After the product has been used for a few months, create an updated version that corrects all the bugs the users have discovered.

The first part of debugging is finding the errors, the second part is correcting them, and the third and final part is ensuring the correction does not create new errors.

Common Bugs

Following are some of the most common errors made when programming in C:

- Using uninitialized variables
- Misusing the assignment and equality operators
- Unexpected side effects
- Misuse of global variables

- Misuse of automatic variables

- Using variables of different sizes or types together

- Incorrect operator precedence

- Not using the proper array bounds

- Misusing pointers

- Assuming the order of evaluation for function parameters

- Assuming the order of evaluation for operations where the order of evaluation is undefined

Each of these errors is discussed in this section.

Uninitialized Variables

Using a variable that has not been initialized is a problem when the variable is a floating-point variable. Almost anything can happen, such as a trashed operating system, Windows programs that create UAEs, or OS/2 programs that do not work correctly.

Misused Operators

Misusing the assignment operator (=) and the equality (==) operator is another common bug. For example, the following for() loop will never end:

```
for (i = 0;  i = 1; i++)
```

You will get a warning—*assignment within conditional expression*—but if you do not understand the warning message, you may think the compiler is referring to the initialization section (where i is initialized to 0) of the for() loop. The variable i is initialized to 0, then it is assigned the value of 1 in the test section of the for() loop, then it is incremented at the end. The next time around, i is again set to 1, and so on. If the loop is tight (no calls to I/O functions or functions that may call DOS), it's power-switch time.

In the next example, the compiler does not return a warning:

```
i == 20;
```

This line of code compares i and 20, then throws away the result. If you don't look sharply, you'll spend a lot of time wondering why i is never set to 20.

Side Effects

Most macros can cause strange side effects. Consider the following, where max() is a macro:

```
i = max(i++, j);
```

If i and j are originally 1, what is i on return? Try it, and you will find that i is still 1. The i variable is incremented after the max() macro is evaluated but before the result of the max() macro is assigned to i.

So, what is the result of the following?

```
i = max(++i, j);
```

The result is not 2, but 3. The i variable is incremented when the comparison is performed, and because the variable is then 2, it is assigned to i. But there is a prefix increment on the assignment, so the variable is incremented again!

Be careful when you use prefix and postfix increments and decrements with macros, or you may get different results than what you expect.

Global Variables

Never use a global variable as a scratch variable. Even if you know that the global variable is not used elsewhere, you may choose to use it later, and then... When you change the value assigned to a global variable, think about the effects your change will have on the other places where the variable is used.

Automatic Variables

When a variable is defined inside a block and has not been declared with the static identifier, the variable is called an automatic variable and exists only while the block is executing.

Automatic variables do not retain their value between calls to the function. Automatic variables cannot be passed back to the calling function (the compiler creates a static variable to pass back if necessary). They are not initialized and therefore may contain unpredictable values.

Mixed Variable Sizes and Types

Another common bug results when you use variables of different sizes or types together. You cannot successfully assign the unsigned int uSomething, which has a value of 45000, to the signed int iElse. The results are not right, because iElse will have a value of -20536.

The same is true if you try to assign lThing, which has a value of 2345678, to iElse. The result (-13619) is again incorrect. Unlike signed errors, size errors return a warning.

Operator Precedence

I have adopted a simple rule regarding operator precedence: When in doubt, use parentheses, lots of parentheses, because they override any other order of precedence.

In the following example:

```
int i = 3;
int j = 5;
if (i = max(i, j) == 5)
```

1 is assigned to i. This is the TRUE condition because max(i, j) is equal to 5.

When the example is changed to the following:

```
int i = 3;
int j = 5;
if ((i = max(i, j)) == 5)
```

the correct value, 5, is assigned to i. The parentheses force the assignment to occur first, even though the conditional test normally has a higher order of precedence.

When in doubt, use parentheses. Table 16.1 lists the operator precedence for C. When more than one operator belongs to the same group, they have the same precedence and are evaluated according to the rules of associativity.

Table 16.1. Operator precedence in C.

Operator	Function	Group	Associativity
( )	Function call	1	Left to right
[ ]	Array element	1	Left to right
.	Structure or union member	1	Left to right
->	Pointer to structure member	1	Left to right
++	Postfix increment	1	Left to right
— -	Postfix decrement	1	Left to right
:>	Base operator	1	Left to right
!	Logical NOT	2	Right to left
~	Bitwise complement	2	Right to left
-	Arithmetic negation	2	Right to left
+	Unary plus	2	Right to left
&	Address	2	Right to left
*	Indirection	2	Right to left
sizeof	Size in bytes	2	Right to left
++	Prefix increment	2	Right to left
— -	Prefix decrement	2	Right to left
(type)	Type cast	3	Right to left
*	Multiplication	4	Left to right
/	Division	4	Left to right
%	Remainder	4	Left to right
+	Addition	5	Left to right
-	Subtraction	5	Left to right

Operator	Function	Group	Associativity
<<	Left shift	6	Left to right
>>	Right shift	6	Left to right
<	Less than	7	Left to right
<=	Less than or equal to	7	Left to right
>	Greater than	7	Left to right
>=	Greater than or equal to	7	Left to right
==	Equality	8	Left to right
!=	Inequality	8	Left to right
&	Bitwise AND	9	Left to right
^	Bitwise exclusive OR	10	Left to right
¦	Bitwise inclusive OR	11	Left to right
&&	Logical AND*	12	Left to right
¦¦	Logical OR*	13	Left to right
e1?e2:e3	Conditional*	14	Right to left
=	Simple assignment	15	Right to left
*=	Multiplication assignment	15	Right to left
/=	Division assignment	15	Right to left
%=	Modulus assignment	15	Right to left
+=	Addition assignment	15	Right to left
-=	Subtraction assignment	15	Right to left
<<=	Left-shift assignment	15	Right to left
>>=	Right-shift assignment	15	Right to left
&=	Bitwise-AND assignment	15	Right to left

continues

Table 16.1. continued

Operator	Function	Group	Associativity
^=	Bitwise-exclusive-OR assignment	15	Right to left
¦=	Bitwise-inclusive-OR assignment	15	Right to left
,	Comma*	16	Left to right

* Everything preceding the operator is evaluated before the operator is processed

Not Using Proper Array Bounds

Arrays always start at 0. For example, if iArray is defined as

```
int    iArray[25];
```

the first element is iArray[0], and the last element is iArray[24].

The next example goes a step further:

```
for (i = 1; i <= 25; i++)
{
iArray[i] = i;
}
```

This example fails, perhaps causing one of those difficult problems that take so much time to find and correct. The example assigned something to the 26th element of an array that is defined with only 25 elements. Also, the first element is skipped because the for() loop starts at 1, not 0.

A loop that correctly assigns all the elements of iArray follows:

```
for (i = 0; i < 25; i++)
{
    iArray[i] = i;
}
```

Misused Pointers

When you understand pointers, arrays, and indirection, you know you are a real C programmer. Until that day, you will sometimes use them incorrectly. Pointers and indirection can cause major problems when functions are involved.

If you do not feel comfortable with the concepts of pointers, this is a good time to review Chapter 3, "Pointers and Indirection."

Order of Evaluation

The order of evaluation for function parameters cannot be guaranteed. The following code is unacceptable because you do not know when `YourFunc()` will be evaluated:

```
OurFunct(x = YourFunc(), x);
```

The second parameter, x, could be either the new value from `YourFunc()` or what x contained before the call to `YourFunc()`.

The order of evaluation for some other operations is also undefined. For example, in the following code:

```
int i = 0;
int nArray[10];

nArray[i] = i++;
```

you cannot determine whether `nArray[0]` or `nArray[1]` is assigned; it could be either one. To correct this, ANSI C defines sequence operators, which guarantee that the compiler has evaluated everything that must be evaluated at that point.

Rules for Debugging

When you debug a program, the following rules will help you and perhaps save a bit of time:

1. Assume nothing. Do not assume that a variable has the correct value, even if you see that the variable was assigned a value. Print the variable's value at the time of the failure. Some other part of the program may have trashed it.

2. When the value of a variable changes to something unexpected, check the logical tests to see whether you have inadvertently assigned a value rather than tested it.

3. Take a break. By working on something else for a while, more often than not you will suddenly realize the cause of the original problem.

4. If the bug is not in the section of code you originally suspected, it is somewhere else. Do not fall into the trap of thinking, "The bug can't be in this part of the code because I checked it."

5. Correct all the compiler's warnings. Set the warning level as high as possible. If you are writing Windows programs, use STRICT to assure the maximum checking.

6. Pointers cause the most problems. Array-bound overwriting causes almost as many problems. Strings are arrays. In most C compilers, nothing detects when a string's bounds are exceeded. If the string is on the stack when its bounds are exceeded (because it is an auto variable), the program will probably do some strange things.

7. Back up your disk. One of my first C programs promptly trashed my disk. The only blessing was that I did not have a backup of the program that did the dirty work—it did itself in!

8. From time to time there are compiler bugs, but they are not usually the reason your program fails.

9. Have another C programmer look at your code.

10. When all else fails, rewrite the code so that it works differently.

You are not guaranteed a perfect program just because you avoid these common errors. The most common bug is the simple program logic bug. The program doesn't work the way you think it does. The program is syntactically correct and does not have any programming bugs, but its logic is incorrect. With a lot of work, a debugger, and patience, you can trace the program's execution. Eventually, you can find the spot where the results are not what you expected, and perhaps the bug.

Using the assert() Macro

The C language provides the programmer with an important feature, the assert() macro. This macro enables you to make a conditional test, then prints an error message and ends the program if the test fails.

Listing 16.1, ASSERT.C, shows how the `assert()` macro is used. You must be careful and read the message correctly. Note that `assert()` activates when the test is FALSE (fails).

Listing 16.1. ASSERT.C.

```
/* ASSERT, written 1992 by Peter D. Hipson */
/* This program shows the assert() macro.  */

#include <limits.h>
#include <stdarg.h>
#include <stdio.h>
#include <stdlib.h>
#include <assert.h>

#define TRUE                1
#define FALSE               (!TRUE)


void    main()

{

int     nValue = 1;
char    szBuffer[256];


    while (TRUE)
    {
        printf("Enter anything but 25 to test the assert() macro: ");
        gets(szBuffer);
        sscanf(szBuffer, "%d", &nValue);

        assert(nValue == 25);
    }
}
```

Typical output from the `assert()` macro follows:

```
assert
Enter anything but 25 to test the assert() macro: 345
Assertion failed: nValue == 25, file assert.c, line 27

abnormal program termination
```

The filename and the line number are provided; both of these can be changed with the `#line` directive.

When you have finished debugging a program, it is not necessary to comment out the `assert()` calls. Instead, you should define the NDEBUG identifier and simply recompile the program. The preprocessor strips out the `assert()` calls for you. Later, if you discover that the program still has bugs, a quick recompile without defining the NDEBUG identifier will restore all your `assert()` calls.

Debug Strings and Messages

Writing lines to the screen, a communications port, the printer, or a file while a program is executing can be a powerful debugging tool. Because this technique does not require a debugger, it can be easy to implement.

You can trace the entire program's execution using such a technique, but you must carefully plan your debugging session. Listing 16.2, DBGSTRNG.C, shows the use of a debugging output function.

Listing 16.2. DBGSTRNG.C.

```
/* DBGSTRNG, written 1992 by Peter D. Hipson */
/* This program has a debug output function */

#include <limits.h>
#include <stdarg.h>
#include <stdio.h>
#include <stdlib.h>
#include <assert.h>

#define TRUE            1
#define FALSE           (!TRUE)
```

```
#undef  DebugString

#ifdef NDEBUG

#define DebugString(exp, file, msg)      ((void)0)

#else

void __cdecl _DebugString(void *, FILE *, void *, void *, unsigned);

#define DebugString(exp, file, msg) \
        ( (exp) ? _DebugString(#exp, file, msg, __FILE__, __LINE__) :
          (void) 0)

#endif /* NDEBUG */


void    main()

{

int     nValue = 1;
char    szBuffer[256];


    while (nValue)
    {
        DebugString(nValue >= 15 && nValue <= 20, stderr, szBuffer);

        printf("Enter 10 to 25 for message, 0 to end loop: ");
        gets(szBuffer);
        sscanf(szBuffer, "%d", &nValue);

        DebugString(nValue >= 10 && nValue <= 25, stderr, szBuffer);
    }
}


void __cdecl _DebugString(
    void * szTest,
    FILE * File,
```

```
    void * szMessage,
    void * szFile,
    unsigned nLine)

{

    fprintf(File,
        "\n'%s' MSG '%s' IN '%s' LINE '%d'\n",
        szTest,
        szMessage,
        szFile,
        nLine);
}
```

For example, using the _DebugString() function to debug a program run produces the following typical run of DBGSTRNG.C:

```
dbgstrng
Enter 10 to 25 for message, 0 to end loop: 10

'nValue >= 10 && nValue <= 25' MSG '10' IN 'dbgstrng.c' LINE '48'
Enter 10 to 25 for message, 0 to end loop: 1
Enter 10 to 25 for message, 0 to end loop: 14

'nValue >= 10 && nValue <= 25' MSG '14' IN 'dbgstrng.c' LINE '48'
Enter 10 to 25 for message, 0 to end loop: 15

'nValue >= 10 && nValue <= 25' MSG '15' IN 'dbgstrng.c' LINE '48'

'nValue >= 15 && nValue <= 20' MSG '15' IN 'dbgstrng.c' LINE '41'
Enter 10 to 25 for message, 0 to end loop: 19

'nValue >= 10 && nValue <= 25' MSG '19' IN 'dbgstrng.c' LINE '48'

'nValue >= 15 && nValue <= 20' MSG '19' IN 'dbgstrng.c' LINE '41'
Enter 10 to 25 for message, 0 to end loop: 0
```

When using a function such as DebugString(), you are not restricted to using stderr. Instead, you might open a communications port or the printer as the debugging file or write the output to a file. When writing to a file, be sure you flush

the file's buffer after each write. Otherwise, you could lose the most important part of the program's output if the program fails without closing the file or flushing the buffer.

When programming under Windows, you could call `OutputDebugString()` rather than `fprintf()`. The `OutputDebugString()` Windows function writes a string to the debugging terminal (or whatever destination you choose if you use the `DBWIN` program), without halting the program or destroying the contents of the Window's screen.

Debuggers

Every compiler comes with a debugger. Regardless of the environment (DOS, Windows, OS/2, or UNIX), the concept behind the use of a debugger is the same: to allow access to various commands while the program runs so that you can monitor its execution.

Typical services offered by most debuggers follow:

- Execution in an environment similar to the typical operating environment. This involves using as little memory as possible (a requirement that was difficult with DOS on a PC, but is easier with the rapid acceptance of protected-mode operating systems such as Windows and OS/2) and not interfering with the output device (the screen). To avoid interfering with the screen, the debugger generally uses a serial terminal, a second monitor (often a monochrome adapter, or MDA), or two workstations (with network-based debugging).

- Memory examination. This includes simple memory dumps, examination of external variables (by name), and examination of local variables.

- Memory modification. This generally is limited to changing variables, both global and local.

- Program breakpoints. At a program breakpoint (a specified point of interruption), the debugger is given control before the line or instruction is executed. At a breakpoint, you might examine variables, registers, or memory.

- Memory breakpoints. These are similar to program breakpoints, but the memory specified need not be an instruction. For example, the breakpoint could be at a data object. Memory breakpoints are useful if you want to determine what part of the code is modifying a variable. You could specify a value at the given location, and when the value is stored there, the breakpoint is entered.

- Program modification. Some debuggers enable you to correct minor errors, then continue program execution. This feature is useful for programs with complex setup or initialization processes.

- Execution stepping. Almost all debuggers can execute statements one line at a time. This technique, called *stepping*, enables you to trace the flow of the program (for example, the number of times the loop executed, and the functions and subroutines that were called). Some debuggers enable you to trace in both the high-level language (such as C) and assembly (or machine) language. Tracing the program's flow in C is often the fastest and most valuable option because you can see the effects of each program statement.

When using a debugger, you must balance the learning curve (that is, how long it takes you to learn to use the debugger), the amount of time needed to set up the program and the debugger, and how quickly you can find the problem.

In C programming on the PC, each compiler has its own debugger. There are also a number of stand-alone debuggers, most of which require additional hardware (plug-in cards or special switches). Soft-Ice/W, Multiscope, and Periscope are examples of debuggers that are not compiler-specific. Each offers features unavailable in compiler-supplied debuggers.

Codeview

Microsoft's Codeview debugger has been around for a long time. Its predecessors include the DOS DEBUG command (a crude and simple debugger) and the SYMDEB debugger.

You can debug most complex programs with Codeview. Codeview enables you to debug to a serial monitor or to configure two monitors for debugging. Under Windows, you can debug to a separate window. Unless you have a large screen monitor and a high-resolution video system (1024 x 768 at a minimum), however, this mode of debugging can be difficult.

QuickC for Windows

QuickC for Windows from Microsoft offers an integrated debugger. (It doesn't have its own name because it is part of QuickC's Integrated Development Environment.) This debugger can debug only at the C source level; it cannot debug in assembly. Therefore, you must have the source code for the sections of the program that you want to debug.

When using QuickC's debugger, you lose the advanced features of the Windows debugging kernel, which helps find programming errors caused by incorrect calls to Windows functions.

Turbo Debugger

Borland's Turbo Debugger enables you to debug programs compiled with Borland's compilers. This debugger offers many of the features found in Microsoft's Codeview, including dual-monitor support and the ability to use a debugging terminal.

Watcom's VIDEO Debugger

When using Watcom's 32-bit compiler (Watcom C/386), you have access to their debugger, called VIDEO. This debugger offers many interesting features. The compiler is compatible with DOS, Windows, and OS/2, so the debugger supports each of these environments, as well as QNX.

VIDEO, like many of the other debuggers, offers dual-monitor support. It also debugs using two PCs linked by serial ports, by parallel ports, or over networks.

Efficiency

Program efficiency is an important aspect of programming. It does not matter how well your program performs if it takes forever and a day to accomplish the job. Efficiency consists of many parts—you cannot use some aspects of creating an efficient program while ignoring others.

Statements that slow a program usually are in loops. For example, a typical `for()` loop that calls some functions can use a lot of time. When you write a loop, consider how many times the loop will be executed, which functions are called, and what the functions are doing. If the loop will be executed a large number of times (thousands of times or more), you should consider optimizing the loop. When efficiency is the most important objective, you can sometimes make the program run faster by coding a frequently called function inline, instead of calling the code as a function.

32-Bit Programs

Most PC programming uses the 16-bit programming model. Every time a `long int` is added, two 16-bit adds are performed. For programs that will be running only on 386 (or higher) CPUs, it might be more efficient to use the 32-bit instructions that these CPUs offer. Remember, however, that a program written for the 32-bit instruction set of the 386 cannot run on a 286 or an original PC.

Programs written using the 32-bit mode of the CPU run only in protected mode. Therefore, an interface is required between DOS (which runs only in real mode) and your application running in 32-bit mode. This interface is called DPMI (DOS Protected Mode Interface). Following is a list of common DPMI products:

- Microsoft Windows 3.1 in 386 enhanced mode provides DOS sessions with DPMI service by Windows. This interface is included with Windows 3.1 at no charge.

- DOS/4G from Rational Systems, Inc. (and DOS/4GW, which is supplied with Watcom's C/386 compiler) provides the necessary DPMI services for your programs. DOS loads DOS/4G each time a program that must use its services is loaded by the user or executed by DOS.

- Phar Lap 386/DOS-Extender from Phar Lap Software, Inc. is another DPMI interface. It is similar to DOS/4G in that it is loaded each time a program requiring its services is executed.

- OS/386 from ERGO Computing, Inc. provides DPMI services. Because OS/386 is a TSR, it must be loaded only once. The drawback is that the DPMI interface continues to occupy memory after the program that required it completes its execution.

- Intel Code Builder is another DPMI system.

- OS/2 V2 from IBM. This is not a true DPMI because it is not MS-DOS. It is, however, a competent 32-bit platform, offering one of the best 32-bit environments with some MS-DOS compatibility. Watcom's C-386 is an excellent 32-bit compiler for OS/2.

- Windows NT from Microsoft is a 32-bit operating system that is not CPU-dependent. The user interface of this OS, which was initially produced for 386/486 CPUs and the MIPS ARC CPU, resembles Windows 3.1. To write Windows NT software, you must have a special version of Microsoft C7 that produces 32-bit code.

A number of 32-bit C compilers support C++ as well as standard C programming. The more popular 32-bit C compilers include the following:

- Watcom C/386 is an excellent compiler that you can use to develop applications that execute under MS-DOS, OS/2 V2, and Windows 3.x. This compiler supports only C programming, but the C++ version should be available soon. A royalty-free copy of DOS/4GW is included with Watcom C/386, and the compiler supports all other DPMI interfaces (see the preceding list). Watcom's compiler provides the only 32-bit support for Windows 3.1. The ability to write 32-bit Windows programs is a powerful feature that should not be ignored by Windows programmers.

- Microway NDP C/C++ is an expensive compiler that offers much to programmers writing math-intensive code. This compiler has excellent support for math coprocessors but lacks a DPMI interface program, so one must be purchased separately.

- Zortech C/C++ is a compiler that can produce either 16-bit or 32-bit programs. It comes with a DPMI program (called DOSX) that you can use royalty-free, or you can use Phar Lap's DOS Extender.

- Intel's Code Builder provides a 32-bit compiler based on Microsoft's C compilers. This product is most compatible with the Microsoft compiler. Version 1.1 supports 386MAX and QEMM-386 as well.

Creating 32-bit code can improve your program's performance from several standpoints. One, you can perform math on 32-bit data objects. Two, your program can access protected-mode memory. Many DPMI programs provide access to virtual memory, allowing truly large programs. Finally, 32-bit programs are more compact (after they are loaded into memory). In summary, if you can live with applications that run only on 386 (and greater) systems, converting to a 32-bit compiler can substantially improve the performance of your programs.

Compiler Optimization

One of the easiest ways to gain more performance from your applications is to have the compiler optimize the program. Most compilers allow optimization for size (important if you are developing for a plain DOS environment with its 640K memory limit) or speed. Some compilers optimize both for size and for speed, although you cannot ensure that compromises between the two will produce code that is both small and efficient.

Typical optimizations are shown in Table 16.2. If an optimization is not offered by your compiler, another optimization might perform a similar task.

Table 16.2. Typical optimizations for compilers.

Microsoft	Borland	Watcom	Function
/G0	-1-		Generate code for 8086
/G1	-1		Generate code for 80186
/G2	-2		Generate code for 80286
/G3	-3		Generate code for 80386
/G4	N/A		Generate code for 80486
/Gc	-p		FORTRAN/Pascal calling conventions
/Gr	-pr		Register calling conventions
/Gs	-N-		Remove stack overflow checks
/Gy			Function-level linking (links only called functions)
/O, /Ot	-Ox, -G, -Ot	/ot	Minimize execution speed (default)
/Oa	-Oa, -G-	/oa	Assume no aliasing

Microsoft	Borland	Watcom	Function
/Ob*n*	-Oi		Control inline expansion (*n* is a digit from 0 through 2)
/Oc	-Oc		Enable block-level common subexpression optimization (default)
/Od	-Od	/od	Turn off all optimization
/Oe	-Oe		Ignore register keyword and allow compiler to perform global register allocation
/Of	N/A		Turn on P-code quoting (default)
/Of-	N/A		Turn off P-code quoting
/Og	-Og		Enable global-level common subexpression optimization
/Oi	-Oi	/oi	Generate intrinsic functions
/Ol	-Ol	/ol	Enable loop optimization
/On	-Ol-Om		Turn off potentially unsafe loop optimizations
/Oo			Turn on post code-generation optimizing (default)
/Oo-			Turn off post code-generation optimizing

continues

Table 16.2. continued

Microsoft	Borland	Watcom	Function
/Op			Improve float consistency
/Oq	N/A		Turn on P-code optimization
/Or	N/A		Enable single exit point from functions (useful when debugging with CodeView)
/Os	-O1, -Os	/os	Minimize executable file size
/Ov	N/A		Sort local variables by frequency of use; P-code only (default)
/Ov-	N/A		Sort local variables in the order that they occur; P-code only
/Ow			Assume aliasing across function calls
/Ox	-Ox	/oxat	Maximize optimization
/Oz			Turn on potentially unsafe loop optimizations

As you can see from Table 16.2, each compiler offers some similar optimization options. The Microsoft compiler offers more different optimizations, but some of these are specific to how the compiler works (such as the Microsoft compiler's ability to generate P-code).

Some of the more common optimizations include loop optimization, intrinsic function generation, and common subexpression optimization. These are the subjects of the following sections.

Loop Optimization

In *loop optimization*, expressions that always result in the same value are moved outside the loop. An example of this follows:

```
// Local (auto) variables:
    int i = 0;
    int x = 1;
    int y = 2;

        while(i < 250)
        {
            i += x + y;
            OurFunction(i);
        }
```

The value of the i variable is incremented by the sum of x and y. The values of x and y do not change in the loop, so their sum does not change. However, x and y are summed each time the loop is iterated. Perhaps the programmer could be more careful, but I have found it difficult to catch simple things such as invariant expressions.

When the compiler performs a loop optimization, it modifies the code to resemble the following:

```
// Local (auto) variables:
    int i = 0;
    int x = 1;
    int y = 2;

// Compiler added temporary storage:
    int __temp = x + y;

        while(i < 250)
        {
            i += __temp;
            OurFunction(i);
        }
```

Notice that the compiler has created a new temporary variable (which actually doesn't have a name). This temporary variable is assigned the sum of x and y. In the loop, i is incremented by the value of the temporary variable, so the sum does not have to be recomputed for each loop iteration.

Sometimes loop optimization can create problems during debugging. For example, suppose there is a problem in the temporary variable's computation (such as a divide-by-zero error). The line number for the error will not match a line in the program, making it difficult to determine the location of the error. As well, when tracing the program's execution, the machine instructions will not have a linear correspondence to the source code lines, making it more difficult to debug the program. For these reasons, you might want to turn off loop optimization when you initially debug your program.

Generating Intrinsic Functions

The library functions are defined as separate, callable functions. Some compilers, however, can generate inline code for many library functions. Inline code generation for these functions saves the overhead of a function call, which can be important when the function is called from a loop that has many iterations.

The functions in Table 16.3 have intrinsic forms. Only the ANSI functions are listed. Each compiler, however, offers a number of other intrinsic functions that are compiler-specific.

Table 16.3. ANSI-supported intrinsic functions.

Function	Microsoft	Borland	Watcom C/386
abs()	√		√
acos()	√		
asin()	√		
atan()	√		
atan2()	√		
ceil()	√		
cos()	√		
cosh()	√		
div()			√
exp()	√		
fabs()	√	√	√

Function	Microsoft	Borland	Watcom C/386
floor()	√		
fmod()	√		
inp()			√
inpw()			√
labs()			√
labs()	√		
ldiv()			√
log()	√		
log10()	√		
memchr()		√	√
memcmp()	√	√	√
memcpy()	√	√	√
memset()	√	√	√
movedata()			√
outp()			√
outpw()			√
pow()	√		
rotl()		√	
rotr()		√	
sin()	√		
sinh()	√		
sqrt()	√		
stpcpy()	√	√	
strcat()	√	√	√
strchr()		√	√

continues

Table 16.3. continued

Function	Microsoft	Borland	Watcom C/386
strcmp()	√	√	
strcpy()	√	√	√
strlen()	√	√	√
strncat()		√	
strncmp()		√	
strncpy()		√	
strnset()		√	
strrchr()		√	
tan()	√		
tanh()	√		

The only disadvantage to using intrinsic functions is that they increase the size of the compiled code. For example, if `strlen()` is called 50 times in a program, an intrinsic function will generate 50 copies of the code that does the string copy, whereas the library function would generate one copy.

Common Subexpression Optimization

When performing common subexpression optimization, the compiler replaces redundant expressions with a single common subexpression. This process is similar to loop optimization. An example of a common subexpression follows:

```
k = 20;
i = k + 10;
j = k + 10;
```

The compiler optimizes this code as

```
k = 20;
int __temp = k + 10;
i = __temp;
j = __temp;
```

As in loop optimization, the compiler creates a temporary variable that holds an interim value. Often, the compiler can store the result of the computation in a register, so no memory is used. However, the statement's location in the code (including the presence of intervening statements), dictates how the compiler processes the source code.

Common subexpression optimization is subject to the same problems as loop optimization (see the "Loop Optimization" section).

Direct Video I/O

At one time, almost all programs did direct video I/O because the original PC video systems (such as the CGA) were not designed for speed. To update the video quickly, programs had to write directly to the video's memory.

You should consider several factors when deciding whether your program should support direct video. First, the display adapters in use today (some are EGA, but most are VGA) are better performers than the old CGA standard of 10 years ago.

Second, to support direct video I/O, your program must support a number of standards. Each system (CGA, MDA, EGA, and VGA) manages its display memory differently, with different buffer locations and arrangements in memory.

Do you access video memory directly? For most applications, there are better ways. For example, if you write a Windows or OS/2 application, accessing video memory directly is unacceptable because Windows manages the video. In addition, the efficiency of VGA video systems makes direct I/O unnecessary.

Some programmers assume that you must use direct video I/O to perform random writes to the screen (perhaps to place a message box in the center of the screen). This is untrue. On the PC, you can use the ANSI.SYS device driver for many screen operations, such as color changes and direct cursor addressing.

Floating-Point Optimization

You can significantly improve a program that relies on floating-point math (that is, a program that has data types of `float`, `double`, or `long double`) by using the proper floating-point compile and link options.

Microsoft C has five options (and various suboptions) for floating-point support. You can choose from three libraries when linking floating-point programs. These libraries control calls to floating-point routines:

- The Alternate Math Package Library (mLIBCA.LIB) generates calls to floating-point math routines. There are both the true floating-point functions and routines to emulate the math coprocessor. If a coprocessor is installed, this package simply ignores it. This library produces the smallest executable program, but it does not support `long double` data types.

- The Emulator Library (mLIBCE.LIB) generates calls to a library of functions that emulate the 80x87 math coprocessors. Floating-point functions are contained in the library; these functions also call the emulation routines rather than use a floating-point coprocessor.

- The Coprocessor Library (mLIBC7.LIB) is not a library for support of floating-point operations because all floating-point operations are coded inline and are performed using an installed math coprocessor, which is required. Floating-point functions are contained in the library, and these functions also use the floating-point coprocessor directly. A math coprocessor is required to execute a program linked with this library.

These libraries are used with the floating-point compiler options, which are as follows:

/FPa	Your code generates calls to a library. You can select which library is linked: mLIBCA (the default), mLIBCE, or mLIBC7. (mLIBC7 does not take advantage of inline instructions to the math coprocessor).
/FPc	Your code is similar to that generated with /FPa, except the default library supports `long double`. You can select which library is linked: mLIBCA, mLIBCE (the default), or mLIBC7. (mLIBC7 does not take advantage of inline instructions to the math coprocessor).
/FPc87	Your code requires a math coprocessor. This option is a good choice if you know that the target computer has a math coprocessor. The code is similar to that generated using /FPc. You can select which library is linked: mLIBCA, mLIBCE, or mLIBC7 (the default).

/FPi   Your code is generated using interrupts for floating-point operations rather than inline floating-point instructions. The software interrupt handler then checks whether a coprocessor is installed. If a coprocessor is installed, the handler patches the code to support the coprocessor. A problem with some compilers is that this technique creates self-modifying code, something that does not work well under protected mode, in which code segments can be read only. You can select which library is linked: mLIBCA, mLIBCE (the default), or mLIBC7.

/FPi87   Your code is generated using interrupts for floating-point operations. The software interrupt handler then checks to see if a coprocessor is installed. If one is installed, the handler patches the code to support the coprocessor. One problem with some compiler versions is that this technique creates self-modifying code, something that doesn't work well under protected mode where code segments may be read only. You can select which library is linked: mLIBCA, mLIBCE, or mLIBC7 (the default).

The default option is /FPi, which works for most applications.

Inline Assembly

There is no argument about it—well-written assembly creates the fastest and smallest programs. However, many programmers are uncomfortable writing even small programs in assembly, let alone a major project. Writing an assembly program can take five times as long as writing a C program, and there may be five times as many lines in an assembly program, and five times as many chances to make a mistake.

One quick and not too difficult solution is to use inline assembly. In this technique, you use C to develop the underlying foundation for a function, then write the critical code in assembly. One useful feature of this technique is that you could write the entire function in C, then after determining that the program is functioning correctly, rewrite the function's critical parts using inline assembly.

Inline assembly comes with a price, however. One problem is that the compiler cannot perform many of the optimizations it can do for a normal C function. This is not too critical if most of the function is written using inline assembly. If the function is written primarily in C with only a small part using inline assembly, the lack of full optimization may be a problem.

Another problem is that any function that relies on inline assembly is not very portable. If you plan to run your application on different computer systems, you may want to avoid inline assembly.

Linking for Performance

Some linker options affect the application's performance. These options can create problems if you do not understand what they do.

One important factor in creating an efficient executable program is to be sure that the linker is not including any debugging information (such as line-number tables) in the executable program. We often remember to compile the final versions of our programs with the correct compiler options, then forget to change the link options.

Many link programs have options that pack the executable program. These options are categorized as follows:

- Packing redundant bytes. Using a simple compression technique, the link program can pack multiple occurrences of bytes with the same value. Most linkers pack only bytes that are zero (because multiple bytes of a nonzero value are rare). When the program is loaded, the loader expands these bytes to their original count. This process reduces the size of the executable file and may shorten the load time.

- Packing CODE segments. When a program is created on the PC using the Large or Medium compiler option, each source file has its own code segment. Often, several of these segments can be combined, and then calls to functions in the combined segment can be converted to NEAR calls (which are faster than FAR calls).

- Packing DATA segments. When a program is created on the PC using the Large or Compact compiler option, each source file has its own data segment (assuming that the segment has sufficient data). Often, several of these segments can be combined into one.

One way to make an application more efficient is to write it as an overlay program. The main advantage is that RAM does not have to be permanently allocated for infrequently called functions. This leaves more memory for data storage (perhaps eliminating the creation of temporary work files). A disadvantage of overlays is that

many linkers require you to determine which functions are part of which overlays. In addition, overhead is incurred when functions not currently in memory must be loaded.

Pascal and cdecl Calling Conventions

Calling conventions are the rules on how parameters are passed to a function being called, and whether the caller or the function being called is responsible for removing the parameters from the stack when the function is finished.

For many functions, using the Pascal calling method is slightly more efficient than the native C calling conventions. The degree of performance improvement depends on the number of parameters and how often the function is called. Note that the Pascal calling conventions cannot be used with a function that has a variable number of arguments.

Precompiled Headers

Using a precompiled header increases the performance of the compiler when it is compiling the program but does not affect the performance of the application while it is executing. If you are spending too much time compiling your programs, look into the benefits of precompiled headers. Borland compilers and Microsoft compilers support precompiled headers.

Using 80286/80386/80486 Instruction Sets

The use of the 80286 (or 80386 or 80486) instruction set is an overlooked but important way to improve program performance. An 80486 executes all instructions that an 80286 executes, but the reverse is not true. After a program is compiled using a specific CPU's instruction set, it will not run on a CPU that is less than the target CPU.

Windows supports only the 80286 instruction set and above, so you should always compile Windows applications using the 80286 options.

Most of the power of the 80386/80486 cannot be utilized unless your application supports the CPU's 32-bit mode. Because this requires a 32-bit compiler, you must plan ahead for 32-bit programs, ensuring that you have access to the necessary compiler.

Using a Source Profiler

One way to make an application more efficient is to determine which functions take the most time, then optimize them. Guesswork will not work—you cannot look at a function and determine that it is using a lot of CPU resources. You must use a *source code profiler* to determine where the most CPU time is being spent in your program.

Most source code profilers work by setting a very fast clock interrupt. Each time an interrupt occurs, the profiler records the name and address of the function that is executing. A second program then correlates the function and address information, and creates a source file/function table that shows where most of the time was used.

Using Intrinsic Functions

When your application calls a library function (such as `strlen()`), overhead is incurred: the function's arguments are placed on the stack, registers are saved, and the function is called. When the function returns, the arguments must be removed from the stack and the registers must be restored.

Many modern C compilers enable you to substitute inline code for common C library functions. This eliminates much of the overhead for a function call, but at the expense of having more than one copy (usually many more copies) of the code that performs the function.

When you use an intrinsic function in a loop and the function is called many times, you can boost the loop's performance substantially. (See Table 16.3 for a list of which functions are available as intrinsic functions.)

Using Memory Models

When programming for a computer that uses segmented memory architecture, such as the PC, you can choose which memory model the compiler uses. For small programs, any memory model usually works. The issue is to use the most efficient memory model for the task at hand. Each memory model has both benefits and drawbacks, as shown in Table 16.4.

Table 16.4. Memory models.

Model	Description	Attributes
Tiny	One segment for both data and code	Fast and small, usable only with .COM files. The total size of the data and the code cannot exceed 64K.
Small	One segment for data, and one for code	Fast and small, usable only with .EXE files. Neither the code nor the data can exceed 64K each.
Medium	One segment for data, and separate code segments for each source module	Calls are slower, but data can be accessed quickly because it is always in the default data segment. The code may be as large as necessary (to the limits imposed by the system RAM), but the data cannot exceed 64K.
Compact	Separate data segments for each module, and one segment for code	Calls are faster, but data accesses are generally performed using FAR pointers, which slow data access. The program's

continues

673

Table 16.4. continued

Model	Description	Attributes
		code cannot exceed 64K. The data is limited only by the amount of available RAM. Individual data objects cannot exceed 64K in size.
Large	Separate data segments for each module, and separate code segments for each source module	Calls are slow and data accesses are generally performed using FAR pointers, which slow data access. The program's code and data are limited only by the amount of available RAM. Individual data objects cannot exceed 64K in size.
Huge	Separate data segments for each module, and separate code segments for each source module	Calls are slow and data accesses are generally performed using FAR pointers, which slow data access. The program's code and data are limited only by the amount of available RAM. Individual data objects can be larger than 64K.

Most programs can be written using the Small model. Programs with a large amount of code or data often need the Large (or Huge) model.

Summary

In this chapter, you learned how to debug a program and improve a program's performance.

- There are a number of common bugs. Checking your code for these common bugs first can save debugging time.

- The C assert() macro assists in debugging. It enables you to test a condition. If the condition fails, the program ends with a diagnostic message.

- If a debugger is unavailable, writing a debug output function can save time in determining the flow of a program.

- Most compilers come with a debugger.

- Most debuggers require a substantial setup and learning curve.

- A debugger is the only effective way to find some problems.

- When programming for efficiency, you can program in the 80386/80486 32-bit mode if your compiler supports such a mode.

- Using the compiler's optimization can make your program run faster. Generally, you should develop the application with optimization turned off. When the application is finished, turn on optimization and retest the application. Sometimes, the compiler's optimization will cause a program to fail that worked with optimization turned off.

- Inline assembly can be useful for creating fast functions without resorting to full assembly code.

- A source profiler can determine which parts of your program are executed most frequently. By combining these routines, you get the maximum benefit from hand optimization.

- Intrinsic functions allow the function's code to be placed inline rather than being called. Although intrinsic functions increase the program's size, they can greatly enhance the program's efficiency.

- The memory model you choose for a program affects its performance. Choose the Small model for small, simple programs.

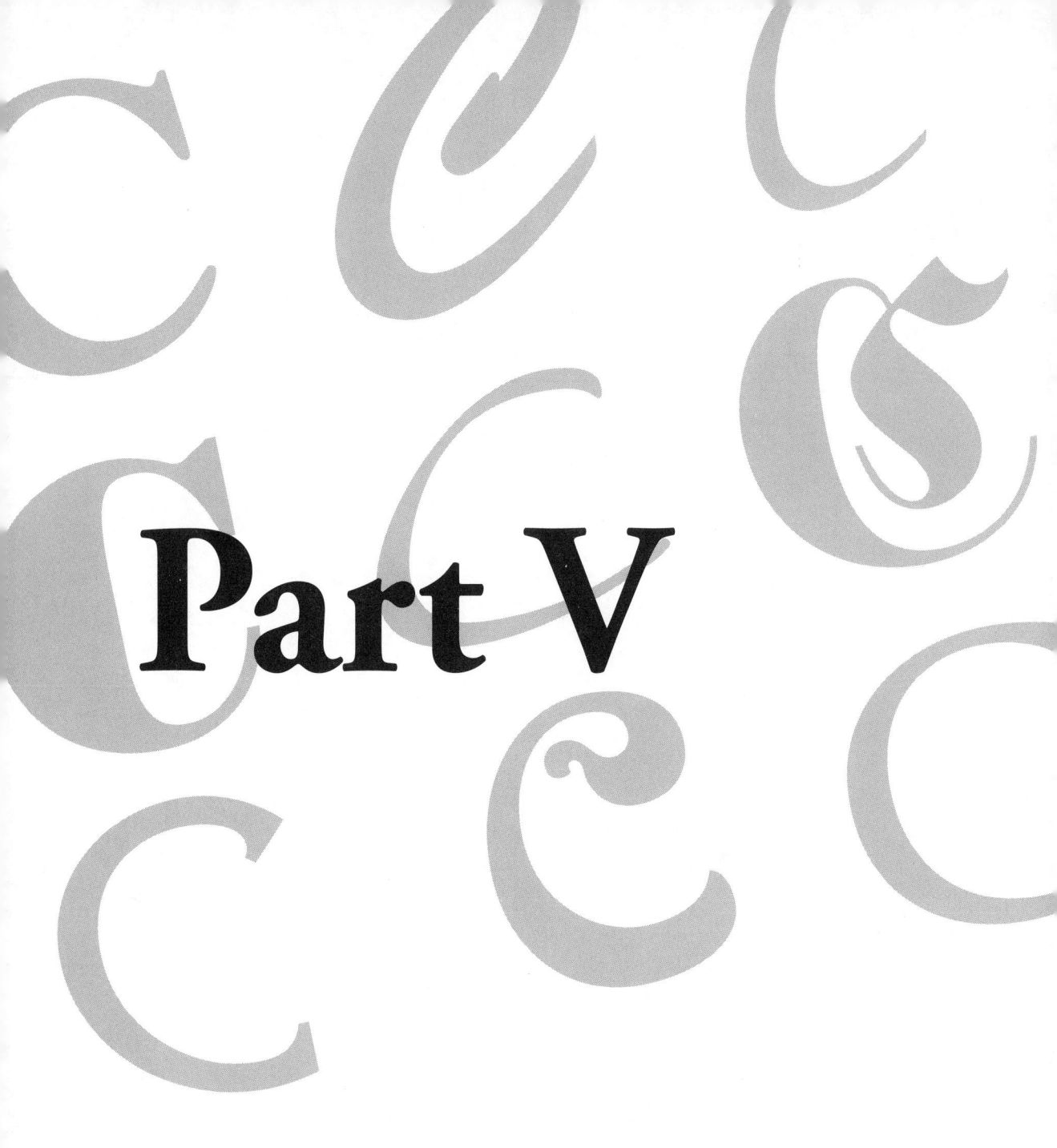

Part V

Appendixes

The ASCII
Character Set

Table A.1. The ASCII Character Set

	0	1	2	3	4	5	6	7	8	9	A	B	C	D	E	F
0																
1																
2		!	"	#	$	%	&	'	(	)	*	+	,	-	.	/
3	0	1	2	3	4	5	6	7	8	9	:	;	<	=	>	?
4	@	A	B	C	D	E	F	G	H	I	J	K	L	M	N	O
5	P	Q	R	S	T	U	V	W	X	Y	Z	[	\	]	^	_
6		a	b	c	d	e	f	g	h	i	j	k	l	m	n	o
7	p	q	r	s	t	u	v	w	x	y	z	{	|	}	~	
8																
9																
A		¡	¢	£	¤	¥	¦	§	¨	©	ª	«	¬	-	®	¯
B	°	±	²	³	´	µ	¶	·		¹	º	»	¼	½	¾	¿
C	À	Á	Â	Ã	Ä	Å	Æ	Ç	È	É	Ê	Ë	Ì	Í	Î	Ï
D	Ð	Ñ	Ò	Ó	Ô	Õ	Ö	×	Ø	Ù	Ú	Û	Ü	Ý	Þ	ß
E	à	á	â	ã	ä	å	æ	ç	è	é	ê	ë	ì	í	î	ï
F	ð	ñ	ò	ó	ô	õ	ö	÷	ø	ù	ú	û	ü	ý	þ	ÿ

680

Compiler Variations

This appendix reviews four popular C compilers for the PC. Each compiler enables you to compile ANSI C programs, and each offers enhancements as well. Though all share a number of common enhancements, no one compiler offers everything.

These products are covered in alphabetical order by their supplier. This is not a critical review of these compilers; my intent is to simply discuss the features and possible shortcomings of each product.

I use all four of these products; however, it is impossible for me to be fully conversant on all features and parts of these products. All are versatile products, providing many features and utility programs. If I've not covered something regarding any of the compilers, I apologize.

Borland also offers entry-level Windows-based development systems in Turbo C++ for Windows and Turbo C++ for DOS. I do not have these products, so I cannot comment on them, but both products have received good reviews in magazines and should serve you well.

Borland's C++ 3.1

It's big! This compiler requires about 50M hard disk space and a reinforced bookshelf to hold the documentation. Borland, in creating its premiere C++ compiler, made one of its nicest products yet.

This product fully supports both DOS and Windows development environments. Generally, you can develop applications for the same environment in which the IDE (integrated development environment) is running; I'd recommend using the Windows version—it's a slick, easy to use IDE.

With its EasyWin program, Borland C++ can migrate a character-based DOS application to Windows by creating a single window that serves for the screen. This window displays both STDOUT and STDERR, while the STDIN input comes from the keyboard. The appearance of these applications is good; however, the application does not have a menu bar. Borland C++ determines the type of application by analyzing the main() function—if it has a main() function, the application is a DOS application and will be built as an EasyWin program; if it has a WinMain() function, it is a Windows program.

You can reduce disk storage requirements by installing only the system parts you plan to use and leaving out some components, such as sample code, library source, and Windows specific components. Not everyone wants to develop Windows programs. However, Windows is becoming a popular environment for programmers who want to create applications with slick user interfaces.

Some of the most significant features of the Borland C++ 3.1 compiler include:

- Powerful and slick Windows IDE for programmers who develop Windows software.

- Competent DOS-based IDE, offering many features the Windows IDE offers (although you can't cut and paste from other applications, as you can with Windows).

- For Windows developers, Borland offers the Workshop. This program enables you to modify the resources of existing applications, such as dialog boxes, menus, icons, cursors, and bitmaps. The Workshop is powerful: you don't need the source code for the program you are modifying. You can change applications you didn't write—modifying that menu you don't like or that awkward dialog box because it works on an .EXE file. You can, of course,

develop your own application's resources using Workshop. This one program replaces Microsoft's DIALOG and IMAGEDIT programs, while adding many new features.

- For Windows developers, Borland offers a powerful window-monitoring facility. It lists, in a listbox, all existing windows and their relationships. This feature is much more flexible than Microsoft's SPY (which requires you to hunt for a given window). After you select a window, you can monitor the messages passed to and from it.

- For Windows developers, Borland offers an import library generation tool. This program works much like Microsoft's IMPLIB program, but runs under Windows. You use an import library tool to develop .DLL (dynamic link library) files.

- For Windows developers, Borland offers Turbo Debugger for Windows. This debugger has many powerful features such as remote debugging, dual monitor use, and network-based debugging.

- For Windows developers, Borland offers a source code profiler. This profiler is useful for determining which parts of an application consume the most CPU resources. It is tuned for Windows applications.

- For Windows developers, Borland offers a UAE monitor (much like Microsoft's Dr. Watson). This program, which runs constantly, traps hardware exceptions generated by some types of programming errors and creates a log file of information you can use to help debug the application.

- For Windows developers, Borland offers a file conversion utility to convert OEM characters to ANSI. This program helps make files created under DOS that have special characters Windows compatible, without a long conversion edit session.

- For Windows developers, Borland offers a hot spot editor. This utility is from Microsoft and is the standard Windows SDK hot spot editor.

- Borland's C++ 3.1 offers precompiled headers. A flexible implementation, precompiled headers help speed up the creation (compilation) of large, multi-source file projects.

- Besides the various programs, an extensive online help system is provided. Online help is becoming increasingly important because the documentation for many compilers (including Borland's) often exceeds 10,000 pages.

When managing large projects, a make facility is necessary. Borland's compiler offers both the IDE's make facility and a stand-alone make that you can run under DOS.

When used under Windows, Borland C++ creates a program group like the one shown in Figure B.1. This group gives you access to each of the features Borland's C++ offers to the Windows programmer.

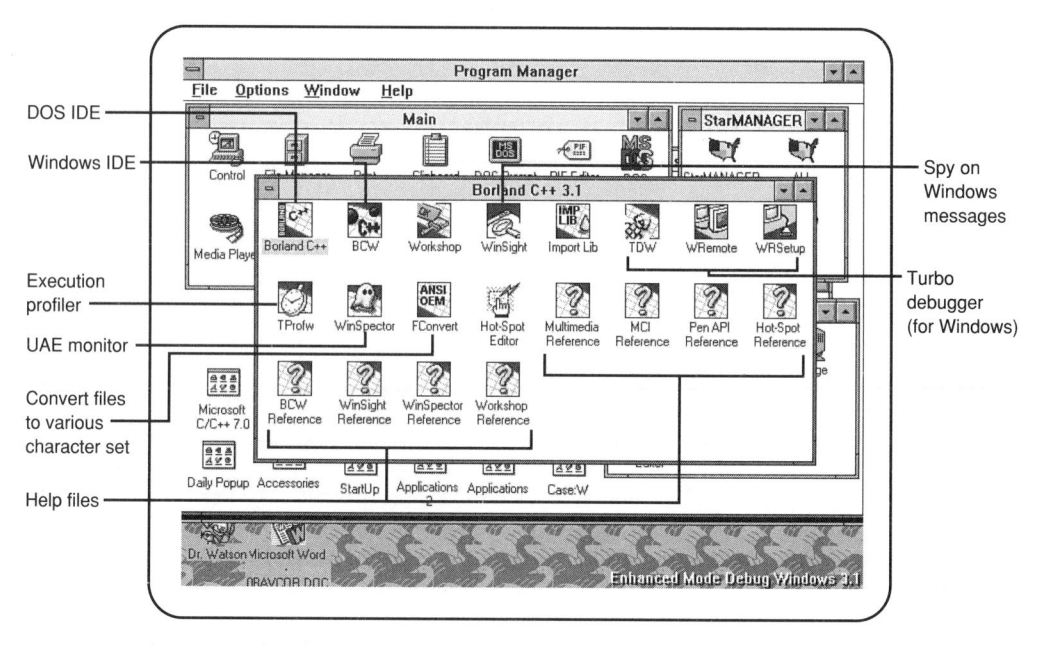

Figure B.1. Borland's C++ Group under Windows.

When you start the IDE under Windows, you get an attractive application that enables you to do the following:

- Define what files make up the application.
- Define the application's attributes (for example, whether it is a Windows application or a DLL).
- Edit the application's files.
- Compile and link the application.
- Debug and run the application.

Various configuration options control the environment, compiler and linker options, and project options. Borland's C++ IDE (under Windows) is shown in Figure B.2. Borland's C++ IDE under DOS is shown in Figure B.3.

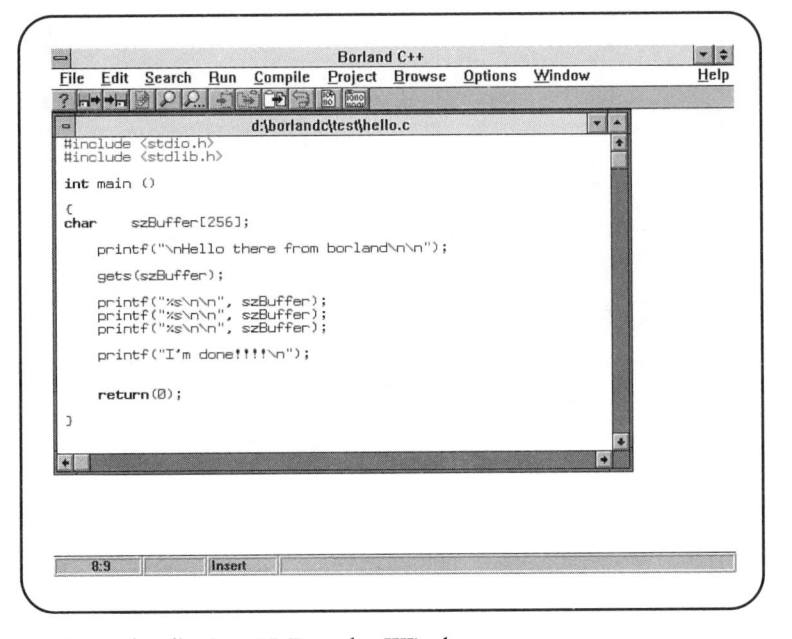

Figure B.2. Borland's C++ IDE under Windows.

Notice the similarity between the IDE under DOS and the IDE under Windows. The main difference is the lack of the push-button toolbar under DOS. In the Windows IDE, it is found just under the menu structure. Under the DOS IDE, the lack of this toolbar isn't a major problem for most programmers because the functions in the toolbar are available as menu functions.

A shortcoming of the Borland products is they produce only 16-bit code. Hopefully, Borland will soon make a 32-bit code-generating compiler.

Generally, Borland's C++ compilers are well designed and are a pleasure to use, especially under Windows.

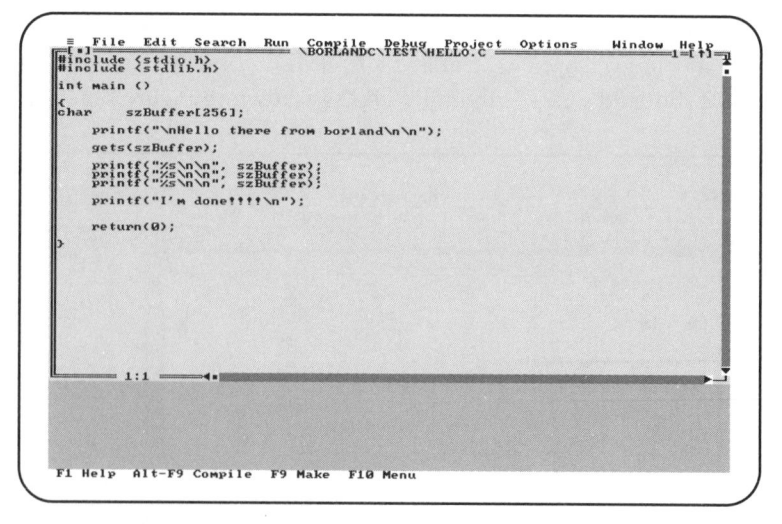

```
  ≡   File   Edit   Search   Run   Compile   Debug   Project   Options   Window   Help
┌─[■]───────────────────────\BORLANDC\TEST\HELLO.C═══════════════════1─[↑]─┐
#include <stdio.h>
#include <stdlib.h>
int main ()
{
char    szBuffer[256];
        printf("\nHello there from borland\n\n");
        gets(szBuffer);
        printf("%s\n\n", szBuffer);
        printf("%s\n\n", szBuffer);
        printf("%s\n\n", szBuffer);
        printf("I'm done!!!!\n");
        return(0);
}
└──── 1:1 ◀─────────────────────────────────────────────────────────▶─┘

F1 Help  Alt-F9 Compile  F9 Make  F10 Menu
```

Figure B.3. Borland's C++ IDE under DOS.

Microsoft

Microsoft currently markets two C compilers. Their main product, C/C++ V7.0, is massive. It has documentation for C, C++, and Windows, and requires a large amount of disk space.

Microsoft's entry-level compiler, QuickC for Windows, is similar to Microsoft C 6.00. QuickC for Windows currently supports only Windows 3.0.

C/C++ 7.0

Microsoft's mainline C compiler supports C++ and has a number of new features including incorporation of the Windows SDK with Version 7.0. This compiler is certainly technically competent, but some of its features lag behind the competition.

For one thing, although Microsoft's compiler probably produces the best compiled code—having extensive optimizations and a long track record as a trustworthy compiler—it offers only a DOS-based IDE. The creators of Windows still haven't created a true, top-of-the-line Windows development system, which could be viewed as a serious omission.

Some of the notable features of Microsoft's C/C++ 7.0 include the following:

- Competent DOS-based IDE with many of the same features that are offered by QuickC for Windows IDE. You must still use a DOS window to create and compile your Windows applications.

- For Windows developers, Microsoft offers a series of programs to develop a Windows program's resources. These programs enable you to modify the resources (objects such as dialog boxes, menus, icons, cursors, and bitmaps) of applications you're developing. These programs include Microsoft's DIALOG and IMAGEDIT.

- For Windows developers, Microsoft offers a window-monitoring facility called SPY. After selecting a window, you can monitor the messages passed to and from it, sending the output from SPY to either a window, a file, or the debugging terminal if one is attached to COM1.

- For Windows developers, Microsoft offers an import library generation tool. You use an import library tool to develop .DLL files.

- For Windows developers, Microsoft offers CodeView 4.0, a competent debugger for Windows. This debugger has many powerful debugging services, such as remote debugging and dual monitor use.

- For Windows developers, Microsoft offers a source code profiler, a useful tool in determining which parts of an application consume the most CPU resources. This profiler is tuned for Windows applications.

- For Windows developers, Microsoft uses Dr. Watson (which is part of Windows 3.1) as a UAE monitor. This program runs constantly in the background. It traps hardware exceptions generated by some types of programming errors and creates a log file that you can use to help debug the application.

- For Windows developers, Microsoft offers a hot spot editor, the standard Windows SDK hot spot editor.

- Microsoft's C/C++ 7.0 offers precompiled headers. Less flexible than Borland's implementation, they are still helpful to speed up the creation of large, multi-source file projects.

- Besides the various programs, an extensive online help system is provided. Online help is important because the documentation for many compilers (including Microsoft's) often exceeds 10,000 pages.

One downside is this compiler requires at least an 80386 CPU or faster. It cannot run on an 80286 or slower CPU. For professional developers, this may not be an issue, but for those of you who program as a hobby, it's important to check whether the compiler runs under your hardware.

When managing large projects, a make facility is necessary. Microsoft's compiler offers both the IDE's make facility and a stand-alone make (NMAKE), both of which you can run under the DOS prompt. NMAKE accepts standard .MAK files (which can be written by hand); however, the IDE requires a make file it has created (because of its rather strict contents rules). You can take the IDE's make file and use it with NMAKE without modifications.

When used under Windows, Microsoft C/C++ creates a program group like the one shown in Figure B.4. This group gives you access to each of the features that Microsoft's C/C++ product offers to the Windows programmer.

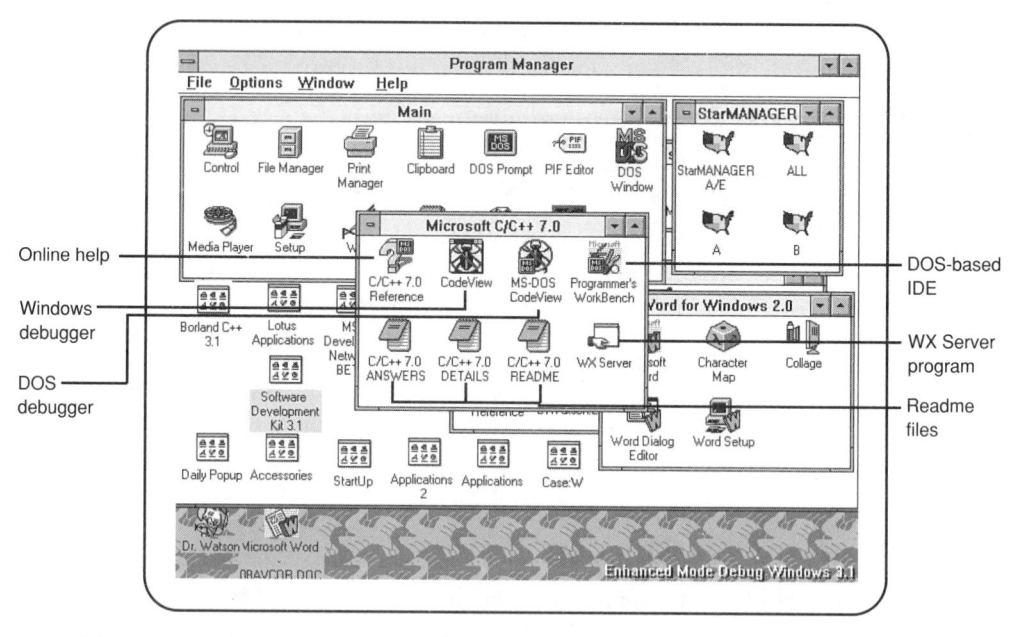

Figure B.4. Microsoft's C/C++ Group under Windows.

When the IDE starts under Windows, you are presented with a character-based DOS application. This application enables you to do the following:

- Define the files that make up the application.

- Define the application's attributes (such as whether it is a Windows or DOS application).

- Edit the application's files.

- Compile and link the application.

- Debug and run the application.

Various configuration options control the environment, compiler and linker options, and project options. Microsoft's C/C++ IDE (under Windows) is shown in Figure B.5. Other powerful features include the extensive customizing ability of the IDE, including the ability to create functions and complex macros, which Borland's IDE doesn't enable you to do.

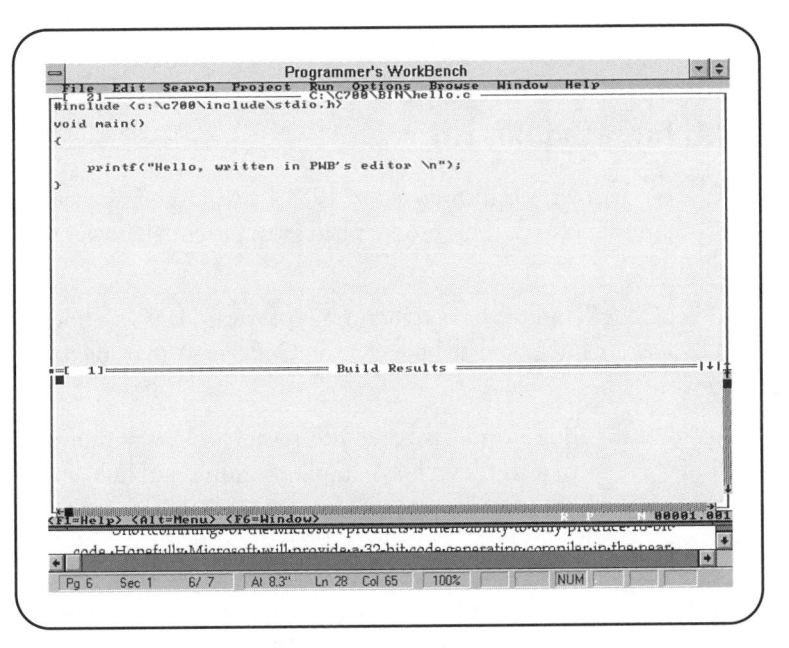

Figure B.5. Microsoft's C/C++ IDE (in a Windows DOS Box).

Notice the similarity between the IDE under DOS and Borland's IDE under DOS.

With a DOS-based IDE, the loss of a toolbar is still the main difference. Perhaps making up for this is the fact that for some computers, the DOS-based IDE is faster when the computer is running in a character video mode. Lack of a toolbar doesn't present a major problem for most programmers because the functions in the toolbar are available as menu functions.

Like the Borland compilers, a shortcoming of the Microsoft compilers is they produce only 16-bit code. I hope Microsoft soon provides the 32-bit code generating version of this product because many C programmers will be developing 32-bit code in the near future.

Microsoft's C/C++ compiler generally produces better and faster programs than many of its competitors, mostly because of Microsoft's extensive compiler development experience. This program is a good choice if you don't need a Windows-based IDE and you can live with the requirement for an 80386 or better operating environment.

QuickC for Windows 1.0

QuickC for Windows was introduced in 1991 by Microsoft as their first Windows-hosted IDE product for C. This product had great potential; however, it has not kept its popularity.

QuickC for Windows has a rather straightforward IDE, as shown in Figure B.6. This IDE has an integrated debugger (not Codeview) that allows C source level debugging.

Again, as for other Windows-based IDEs, QuickC for Windows offers a toolbar to give quick access to features such as compile, compile and link, and access to some debugger functions.

This product has several advantages.

- I've noticed (but others who have benchmarked QuickC for Windows don't agree with my results) that QuickC for Windows is a fast compiler.

- It is easy to use, with its projects easy to create and build.

- It offers the ability to create DOS applications under Windows, something no other Windows-based IDE does.

- It does optimizations (but not to the level that C/C++ 7.0 does). Because this compiler is similar to C 6, it probably could be effectively compared to C 6.

• It offers, for an attractive price, an entry into Windows programming. It includes many of the features of the Windows SDK; most notably missing are the help compiler and the debugging version of Windows, though both can be purchased separately.

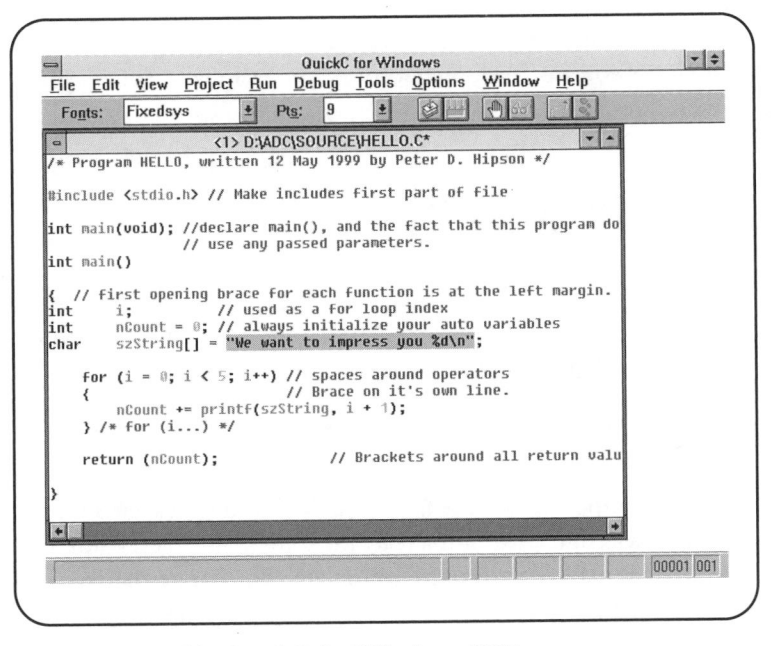

Figure B.6. Microsoft's QuickC for Windows IDE.

The following section outlines some disadvantages of QuickC for Windows:

This product doesn't interact well with Windows error trapping and debugging. QuickC for Windows can trap UAE's, but it doesn't provide any information to enable you to locate the error. It's generally easier to bypass the QuickC for Windows IDE and run the errant program directly under Windows, let it UAE, and check the DrWatson log file to determine where the failure occurred.

Again, when using the debugging version of Windows (an option with QuickC for Windows), many of the usual errors Windows traps and makes known to the programmer sometimes go unreported. Also, OutputDebugString() doesn't function when a program runs under QuickC for Windows IDE, making it difficult to write debugging information to the debugging terminal.

A final and most serious defect of QuickC for Windows is that it supports only Windows 3.0, but not the later versions such as Windows 3.1. Many QuickC for Windows users hope Microsoft will correct this problem, but Microsoft has not indicated it will upgrade this product soon. However, you can purchase the Windows SDK, which is compatible with QuickC for Windows.

In all, QuickC for Windows is a good way to get started writing Windows programs, but if you are developing software professionally, you may find QuickC for Windows too restricted.

Watcom C/386 9.01

If Microsoft's QuickC for Windows and Borland's Turbo C++ for Windows are cars...and Microsoft's C/C++ 7.0 and Borland's C++ 3.1 are pickup trucks...then Watcom's C/386 9.01 compiler is a dump truck—a big dump truck.

Give this compiler a job and it does it. Watcom's C/386 might easily be described as "for professional use only."

The most important feature missing in Watcom's package is the IDE. You must provide your own source editor to create the source code files. With so many capable source editors available, this is not a problem. You create the make files by hand. Watcom includes an effective make facility for larger programs.

The most important aspect of Watcom C/386 is that it is a 32-bit compiler, unlike the other compilers I've discussed. This means you can create true 32-bit applications (which then require an 80386 or better to run) that take full advantage of the more powerful 32-bit CPUs.

This product produces DOS applications (32-bit protected mode), Windows programs (again, 32-bit, with a special library of 32-bit Windows functions), and OS/2 V2.0 programs. It also produces AutoCAD ADS and ADI compatible code.

Watcom C/386 offers options that take advantage of some of the 80486's better instructions. Contrary to popular belief, the 80486 is not an 80386 with a built-in math coprocessor, but an improved CPU, offering better instruction timings, a built-in cache, and other features that the compiler can use.

Some of the Watcom C/386's advantages include:

- Generates highly optimized 32-bit 80386/80486 code. This code allows an application to support a "flat" model program up to 4,000M (4 gigabytes).

- Is both ANSI C and IBM SAA compatible. Its compatibility with Microsoft C makes it easy to port applications written with Microsoft C.

- Supports Windows 3.x, DOS, OS/2 V2.0, and AutoCAD ADS and ADI.

- Gives optimizations for the 80486 processor.

- Watcom C/386 includes a 32-bit protected mode DOS Extender. This product, from Rational Systems, has a royalty-free license. It also supports up to 32M of virtual memory.

- The debugger works within large 32-bit applications, using a number of different techniques.

- The compiler comes with a high performance 32-bit linker.

- The compiler executes under both DOS and OS/2.

- The compiler supports inline assembly.

- Source code profiler assists in code optimization.

- Graphics library supports EGA, VGA, and Super VGA modes.

- Includes support for PenPoint.

- Under OS/2, Watcom C/386 integrates with WorkFrame/2 to provide a solid development environment.

- OS/2 applications can access up to 512M virtual memory.

- Windows programs can be fully 32-bit. You don't need to develop part of the program as a 16-bit application and part as a 32-bit.

- Watcom C/386 includes the Microsoft Windows SDK components.

- Creates 32-bit DLLs with Watcom C/386. These DLLs are easier to create because you don't need to consider the issues of segments.

- Watcom C/386 offers probably the most extensive optimization possible.

693

- Watcom C/386 provides excellent error checking, including checks for questionable type matches, uninitialized variables, unreferenced variables, questionable operations, and potentially incorrect statements.

Additionally, the Watcom C/386 includes the following utilities:

- A linker that supports 32-bit executable programs; this linker runs interactively or in a command-line mode. The linker supports debugging symbolic information (such as line numbers and variable names). There is also a protected mode linker that enables you to link large programs.

- A make utility that is basically compatible with UNIX-type make programs, such as Microsoft's NMAKE program.

- A source profiler program that helps determine which parts of the program consume the most CPU time.

- An object code librarian that creates .LIB files.

- A bind utility that creates 32-bit Windows programs.

- A disassembler that can disassemble .OBJ files. This disassembler works with software created with Watcom C/386 and many other compilers and assemblers. This tool can be invaluable when debugging software at the machine-code level.

- An object (.OBJ) file converter that converts .OBJ files to other (standard) formats, such as Microsoft format.

- A comprehensive graphics library that is compatible with Microsoft's graphics functions.

The full Windows SDK is not included. Programmers who wish to develop Windows programs will want the SDK for its tools and documentation. Acquisition of the SDK solves the problem of a lack of Windows development documentation. This situation is also true for OS/2 V2.0 software. You will want to use IBM's development tools with Watcom C/386 when developing OS/2 applications, something for which this compiler is well suited.

Overall, Watcom C/386 is an advanced optimizing compiler that offers many tools, but has no IDE interface. The programmer must set up the project by hand, invoke the source editor directly, and compile (or build) and correct bugs, as programmers have done for years.

I hope Watcom soon offers an IDE for this compiler and thus effectively eliminates the C/386's only shortcoming.

Introduction to C++

What is C++?

C++ was created as a preprocessor for C and was originally called *C with classes.* This name proved to be too long and was shortened to C++. The relationship between C and C++ is easy to understand: C++ is a superset of the C language. This association makes it easier for a C programmer to become proficient in C++ programming; however, if you are not yet proficient in C, jumping into C++ would be difficult.

The most commonly used basic reference for C++ is *The Annotated C++ Reference Manual* by Margaret A. Ellis and Bjarne Stroustrup (Addison-Wesley, 1990).

The C++ ANSI standards committee, X3J16, has not yet defined an ANSI standard, but AT&T is setting the dominant standard. AT&T's version 2.1 is the most commonly followed implementation of C++. Only a few compiler producers still use version 2.0. AT&T's later standard, version 3.0, is beginning to be accepted and will soon be the most commonly implemented C++ standard.

Object-Oriented Programming (OOP)

C++ was designed from the outset to support object-oriented programming (OOP). To better understand OOP, you need to understand the concepts of *abstraction, encapsulation,* and *hierarchies.*

Abstraction

Abstraction is the capacity to ignore the details of an object. In this case, the object can be either a data object or a function.

When you write in a low-level language, you spend a lot of time working out the details (at the machine level) of a process or the exact representation (the ordering of bits and bytes) of data objects. With a higher-level language, you gain the advantage of fewer details for which the programmer is responsible. For example, a function written in assembly language might require thousands of lines of code to perform a simple task, while a function written in C might do the same task using only hundreds of lines. An even higher-level language might do the task with less than one hundred lines of code.

Data abstraction might enable a programmer to look at a floating-point data object that contains the value 3.1415926 without considering the likely hexadecimal or binary representations.

Encapsulation

Encapsulation is the process of making a class's internal data parts invisible to the actual program. The only way to access or modify a class's data is to use one of the class's functions.

Limiting access to data offers two important benefits.

- First, you don't need to consider the internal representation of the data when accessing it. If the data is part of an array, you don't need to question whether the access exceeds the bounds because the encapsulation functions can check for you.

- Second, the program is much sturdier because only a limited number of functions actually modify the data, and all are located within a single, defined part of the program. If the data is modified incorrectly, the encapsulation layer must be improved with better error checking and correction.

If possible, encapsulate a class's data. Doing so makes the application more reliable, and easier to modify and improve as the application grows.

Hierarchies

Our lives are categorized by hierarchies: our houses are organized in blocks; those blocks are in neighborhoods; those neighborhoods are in towns; those towns are in counties; those counties are in states; and so on.

In programming, organizing objects into a hierarchy simplifies management of the objects. For example, your database might have fields for a dozen variables. It is easier to write these variables to a disk file as a single object rather than as a dozen separate writes, one for each field.

Learning C++

The best way to learn C++ is to first learn C, and then write a C++ program with most of the program in C and only a few lines in C++. Listing C.1, HELLOCPP.CPP, is written this way. Also notice the new filename extension, *.CPP*—shorthand for C++. .C++ isn't a valid filename extension on many computer systems.

Listing C.1. HELLOCPP.CPP—A first C++ program.

```
#include <iostream.h>
// Stock C++ hello program
void main()

{

    cout << "Hello world, this is C++\n";

}
```

Only two lines in HELLOCPP.CPP are different from a standard C program. The first line differs because the include file is a new concept to C programmers. The header file `iostream.h` accesses C++'s standard I/O functions. These functions are similar to C's `printf()` and `scanf()`, and the header file is much like `stdio.h`, which most C programs include.

The line that prints the message to the screen is the other difference:

```
cout << "Hello world, this is C++\n";
```

This line may seem strange to the C programmer. It doesn't appear to take the form of a function call, yet it gets the message to the screen, as if by magic! To the C programmer, using the right shift operator seems to be wrong as well.

C++ has slightly different I/O facilities. Known as *streams* (the same as in C), these facilities have descriptive names, as shown in Table C.1.

Table C.1. C++ Standard streams.

stream	Description
cout	Output to the standard screen or console, as in C's `stdout`.
cin	Input from the standard keyboard or console, as in C's `stdin`.
cerr	Output to the error screen or console, as in C's `stderr`. Characters sent to the error screen cannot be redirected using I/O redirection.

Also in the preceding example line, you use the << operator differently from how it is defined in C, because with C++ you can redefine an operator's function. This redefinition is contextually significant: the meaning of the << operator when used with the stream functions is different from how it's used in some other context. With stream functions, the >> and << operators are *insertion operators* that tell C++ what is being sent to the screen or received from the keyboard.

In C, the comment delimiter is the characters /* and */. C++ has introduced a new type of comment, in which all characters following // until the end of the line are treated as a comment. This type of comment doesn't require an ending comment marker.

This can create a problem if you're not careful how you use blanks in statements that are part of mathematical equations. The following lines of code (i = j+k/l) will be improperly parsed by a C/C++ compiler that allows the // comment:

```
i = j+k//* divide by l */l;
+l;
```

The intent of this code is that the comment runs to just before the /* delimiter and the variable l, but what happens is the compiler produces:

```
i = j + k + l;
```

because the // characters started a C++ single line comment that continues to the end of the line. This isn't what the programmer wants, however. Because the code is syntactically correct, no warning or error is generated, and the mistake probably won't be found for some time—probably several hours after the product has been shipped.

To avoid this sort of problem, *always use spaces* around all operators, including comment operators, as in:

```
i = j + k / /* divide by l */ l;
+l;
```

With the spaces, the above fragment compiles correctly, and the spaces make the source easier to read.

Simply stated, C++ accepts // as a delimiter for a single comment line, but it is easy to create the // comment operator in error if you are not careful. C++ also accepts /* */ for opening and closing comment lines.

Unlike C, C++ is a more strongly typed language. C++ also requires you to fully use function prototypes. Function prototypes allow the compiler to check and ensure that all the types match.

Listing C.2 is a slightly more complex program, EXAMP1.CPP. It shows input, output, and a for() loop. With your understanding of cout and cin, this program is self-explanatory.

Listing C.2. EXAMP1.CPP—A C++ program with both input and output.

```
#include <iostream.h>

void main()

{
int     nCount = 0;
int     nStart = 0;

    cout << "Enter a starting point:";

    cin >> nStart;

    cout << "nCount \nHex  Decimal   Octal \n";

    for (nCount = nStart; nCount < nStart + 16; nCount++)
    {
        cout << hex << nCount << '\t'
             << dec << nCount << '\t'
             << oct << nCount << '\n';
    }
}
```

The output of this program, where the starting point was 0, is shown in Figure C.1.

This program shows more of the C++ stream functions, including the method to change the output from decimal to hexadecimal and octal. With cout you can actually do formatted output, but doing so isn't a trivial matter.

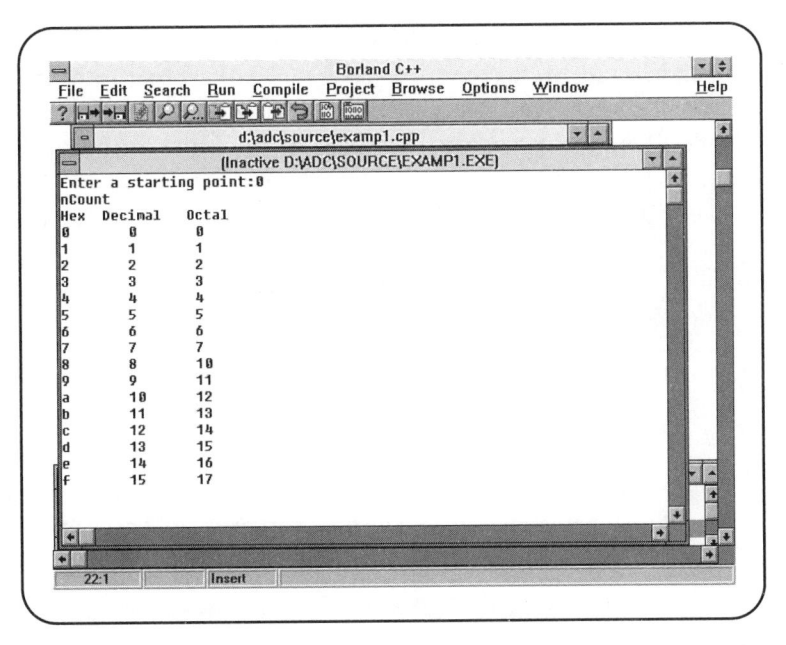

Figure C.1. Output from EXAMP1.CPP.

> **Quick & Dirty:** If you can't figure out how to program something in C++,
> simply do it in C. Then later, when you understand how to write the applica-
> tion in C++, you can convert it. Reverting to C is acceptable when you are
> first learning how to program in C++, but first try it in C++ before going
> back to C.

The rest of this chapter covers some of C++'s main features.

Overloading Functions

When you overload something, you expect it to break. C++, however, enables you to
overload functions without much risk of breakage.

What is overloading? Many articles written about overloaded functions assume the reader understands overloading. But many readers don't because it isn't an obvious concept. For example, you have a program written in C that has floating-point variables (doubles), short int variables, and long (32-bit) integer variables. You can assume that in various places in your program you need to determine the maximum of each data type. With C, you must write a function for each data type, and when writing the code, be sure you call the correct function. If in error you call the integer function to determine maximums and inadvertently pass double parameters, things won't work well!

Wouldn't it be nice to have one generic, maximum function that handles all three types? That simply isn't possible. The function must know the data type when you write it, not when it is called.

C++ gives you an alternative: you can have three functions, all with the same name, but different parameter types. The C++ compiler looks at the parameters and selects the correct function for the data type.

Listing C.3, EXAMP2.CPP, is a program that uses overloaded functions. It shows a maximum function; however, you could choose any function that might use different parameter types with different calls.

Listing C.3. EXAMP2.CPP—Program showing C++ function overloading.

```
// Program EXAMP2.CPP, written 27 July 1992 by Peter D. Hipson
// Shows the use of overloaded functions.

#include <iostream.h>

// A double, long, and an int max() function are defined. You can
// also have others, such as char, float, and so on.

double   max(double a, double b);
int      max(int    a, int    b);
long     max(long   a, long   b);

void main()

{

int      nValue1 = 0;
```

```cpp
int     nValue2 = 0;
long    lValue1 = 0;
long    lValue2 = 0;
double  dValue1 = 0.0;
double  dValue2 = 0.0;

    cout << "Enter two integer values: ";

    cin >> nValue1 >> nValue2;

    cout << "The max of " << nValue1 << " and " << nValue2
        << " is " << max(nValue1, nValue2) << "\n";

    cout << "Enter two long integer values: ";

    cin >> lValue1 >> lValue2;

    cout << "The max of " << lValue1 << " and " << lValue2
        << " is " << max(lValue1, lValue2) << "\n";

    cout << "Enter two floating point values: ";

    cin >> dValue1 >> dValue2;

    cout << "The max of " << dValue1 << " and " << dValue2
        << " is " << max(dValue1, dValue2) << "\n";
}

double  max(
    double a,
    double b)
{
    if (a < b)
    {
        return (b);
    }
    else
    {
        return(a);
    }
}
```

continues

Listing C.3. continued

```
int     max(
    int     a,
    int     b)
{
    if (a < b)
    {
        return (b);
    }
    else
    {
        return(a);
    }
}

long    max(
    long    a,
    long    b)
{
    if (a < b)
    {
        return (b);
    }
    else
    {
        return(a);
    }
}
```

This program enables you to call max() without considering whether you need to call the floating-point, integer, or long version of the function.

Declaring Variables When Needed

With C, you can declare a variable only at the beginning of a block. Your programs often end up declaring variables far from where they are used, making correlation between a variable and its usage difficult.

One C++ feature enables you to declare a variable wherever it is needed. In the program EXAMP3.CPP (in Listing C.4), an index that will be used in a `for()` loop is declared in the `for()` statement.

Listing C.4. EXAMP3.CPP—Program showing variable declaration in a statement.

```
// Program EXAMP3.CPP, written 27 July 1992 by Peter D. Hipson
// Shows the use of variable declarations when needed.

#include <iostream.h>


void main()

{

int    nStart = 0;

    cout << "Enter a starting point:";

    cin >> nStart;

    cout << "nCount \nHex  Decimal   Octal \n";

//  Here, you declare an integer, nCount, which is used as the
//  for() statement's loop counter. The variable is actually
//  declared in the for() loop statement.

    for (int nCount = nStart; nCount < nStart + 16; nCount++)
    {
        cout << hex << nCount << '\t'
             << dec << nCount << '\t'
             << oct << nCount << '\n';
    }
}
```

In the program, the nCount variable is actually declared in the for() statement, where it is first used:

```
for (int nCount = nStart; nCount < nStart + 16; nCount++)
```

This sequence makes it easier to construct loops and other blocks without placing the block's variables in the program where they are obviously not used.

Default Function Argument Values

When writing functions, you may often create a function that requires many of its parameters for some purposes, yet other calls need only the first few parameters.

You also sometimes need functions that seem to have a variable number of arguments, and you don't want to code a parameter describing the number of arguments.

Finally, some functions often use default values for some parameters. It is then up to the programmer to code these default values for each call of the function. Heaven forbid should one of the defaults change: you'll be changing each of the call by hand— a long and tedious process.

C++ provides a solution: specify default values for parameters. This process is simple, being done in the function's prototype. Listing C.5 is the EXAMP4.CPP program, which demonstrates how to implement default arguments to a function.

Listing C.5. EXAMP4.CPP—Program showing default values for arguments.

```
// Program EXAMP4.CPP, written 27 July 1992 by Peter D. Hipson
// Shows the use of default values for functions arguments.

#include <limits.h>
#include <float.h>
#include <iostream.h>

// Defined are a double, long, and an int max() function. You can
// also have others, such as char, float, and so on.
//
// In this version, you have four parameters and find the max of
// the four. Because the minimum number of arguments is two, the final
```

```
// two arguments must default to a value that doesn't cause
// error values.

double    max(double a, double b, double c =  DBL_MIN, double d =
             DBL_MIN);
int       max(int    a, int    b, int    c =  INT_MIN, int    d =
             INT_MIN);
long      max(long   a, long   b, long   c = LONG_MIN, long   d =
             LONG_MIN);

void main()

{

int    nValue1 = 0;
int    nValue2 = 0;
int    nValue3 = 0;
long   lValue1 = 0;
long   lValue2 = 0;
long   lValue3 = 0;
long   lValue4 = 0;
double dValue1 = 0.0;
double dValue2 = 0.0;

    cout << "Enter three integer values: ";

    cin >> nValue1 >> nValue2 >> nValue3;

    cout << "The max of " << nValue1 <<
        " and " << nValue2 <<
        " and " << nValue3 <<
        " is " << max(nValue1, nValue2, nValue3) << "\n";

    cout << "Enter four long integer values: ";

    cin >> lValue1 >> lValue2 >> lValue3 >> lValue4;

    cout << "The max of " << lValue1 <<
        " and " << lValue2 <<
        " and " << lValue3 <<
        " and " << lValue4 <<
```

continues

Listing C.5. continued

```
            " is " <<
                max(lValue1, lValue2, lValue3, lValue4) << "\n";
        cout << "Enter two floating point values: ";

        cin >> dValue1 >> dValue2;

        cout << "The max of " << dValue1 << " and " << dValue2
            << " is " << max(dValue1, dValue2) << "\n";
}

double    max(
        double a,
        double b,
        double c,
        double d)
{
        if (a > b && a > c && a > d)
        {
            return (a);
        }
        if (b > a && b > c && b > d)
        {
            return (b);
        }
        if (c > a && c > b && c > d)
        {
            return (c);
        }

        return (d);
}

int        max(
        int    a,
        int    b,
        int    c,
        int    d)
{
        if (a > b && a > c && a > d)
        {
```

```
        return (a);
    }
    if (b > a && b > c && b > d)
    {
        return (b);
    }
    if (c > a && c > b && c > d)
    {
        return (c);
    }

    return (d);
}

long     max(
    long    a,
    long    b,
    long    c,
    long    d)
{
    if (a > b && a > c && a > d)
    {
        return (a);
    }
    if (b > a && b > c && b > d)
    {
        return (b);
    }
    if (c > a && c > b && c > d)
    {
        return (c);
    }

    return (d);
}
```

Notice this program incorporates function overloading as well. As shown, none of these C++ features are mutually exclusive. Any unused parameters default to the minimum value the data type can hold, which enables your maximum function to work correctly. That way, you'll never select an unused argument as the maximum—nothing can be smaller than the default values.

References

In C, you can use a pointer to access a variable. Using a pointer allows a program to use a variable in two different ways, using different names. Pointers have their downside—they are often misunderstood, have the wrong value stored in them, and are awkward because you must try to remember whether you are dealing with a pointer, the object it is pointing to, or an object's address.

C++ has a method that allows a variable to have more than one name. The second name isn't a pointer (once defined, it can access only the variable by which it was defined), but is another way to access the variable's storage.

EXAMP5.CPP, Listing C.6 is a program that shows the use of a reference variable in a C++ program.

Listing C.6. EXAMP5.CPP—Program showing a reference variable.

```
// Program EXAMP5.CPP, written 27 July 1992 by Peter D. Hipson
// Shows the use of reference variable, externally used as a
// function's return value...

#include <iostream.h>

// function max() returns a reference variable...

int      max(int    a, int    b);

void main()

{

int     nValue1 = 0;
int     nValue2 = 0;
// Create a reference variable, which is not quite the same as a
// pointer to the original variable, because there is no actual
// pointer. A reference variable is more like a second name for
// a variable.
int     &nRef1 = nValue1;

    cout << "Enter two integer values: ";
```

```
    cin >> nValue1 >> nValue2;

    cout << "The max of " << nValue1 << " and " << nValue2
        << " is " << max(nRef1, nValue2) << "\n";

}

int     max(
    int     a,
    int     b)
{
    if (a < b)
    {
        return (b);
    }
    else
    {
        return(a);
    }
}
```

Notice in the cout statement

```
    cout << "The max of " << nValue1 << " and " << nValue2
        << " is " << max(nRef1, nValue2) << "\n";
```

that it refers to the variable nValue1 using the reference variable nRef1. The effect is the same as you would get by using the name nValue1.

References as Return Values

Using a reference variable as a return value creates an interesting situation. In this case, you can use the function's name on the left side (as an lvalue) of an assignment operator.

The EXAMP6.CPP program in Listing C.7 shows the effect of using a reference variable as a return value.

Listing C.7. EXAMP6.CPP—Program showing a reference variable.

```
// Program EXAMP6.CPP, written 27 July 1992 by Peter D. Hipson
// Shows the use of reference variable, externally used as a
// function's return value...

#include <iostream.h>

// Defined is an int max() function.

int      nLimit = 0;

// function max() returns a reference variable...

int      &max(int    a, int    b);

void main()

{

int     nValue1 = 0;
int     nValue2 = 0;
// Create a reference variable, which is not quite the same as a
// pointer to the original variable, because there is no actual
// pointer. A reference variable is more like a second name for
// a variable.
int     &nRef1 = nValue1;

    cout << "Enter two integer values: ";

    cin >> nValue1 >> nValue2;

    cout << "The max of " << nValue1 << " and " << nValue2
        << " is " << max(nRef1, nValue2) << "\n";

    cout << "The value of nLimit is " << nLimit << "\n";

    max(0, 0) = 99;

    cout << "The value of nLimit is " << nLimit << "\n";
```

```
}

int     & max(
    int    a,
    int    b)
{
    if (a < b)
    {
        nLimit = b;
        return (nLimit);
    }
    else
    {
        nLimit = a;
        return(nLimit);
    }
}
```

To better understand the effects of running this program, take a look at its output, shown in Figure C.2.

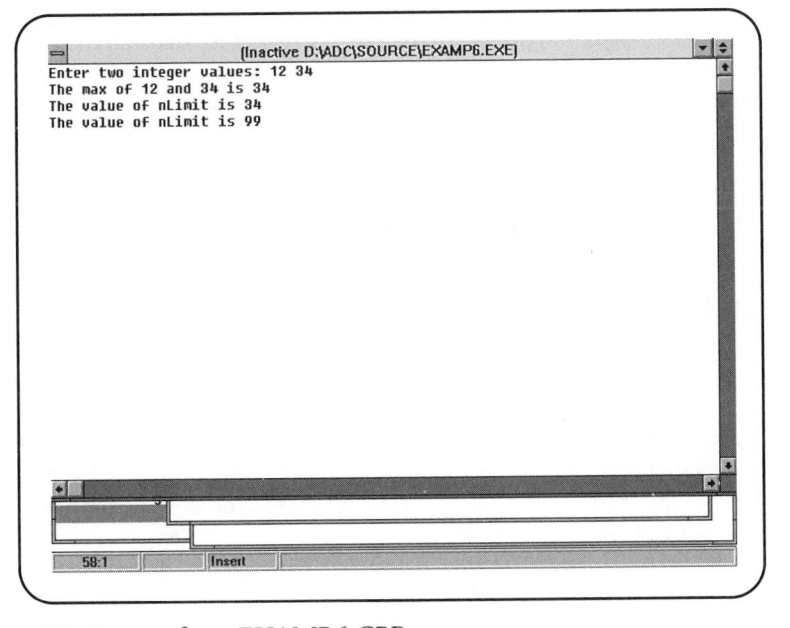

Figure C.2. Output from EXAMP6.CPP.

Notice after the statement

```
max(0, 0) = 99;
```

was executed the value of nLimit changed to 99. Only your creativity limits how you use this ability of C++.

Classes

Classes are one of the most important elements of C++. They enable you to use one of the most powerful features of the language—data object management. You might think of classes as an extension to C's user-defined types. In C, when defining a type (using typedef), you can include only actual data objects in that type. No checking takes place to find if correct values have been assigned to a C user-defined type.

Using C++ classes gives you many advantages. These advantages, described in the following section, are valuable in maintaining your application's data integrity.

A class can have all the allowed data types within it, including other classes. Nesting classes is done much the same as you would nest typedef'd objects in C.

A class has a *constructor*, a function called whenever a data object of that class is created. You may have more than one constructor, each of which must have a different number of parameters. The constructor is responsible for ensuring that each member of the class is properly initialized and that any initialization values passed to the constructor are valid.

A class has a number of manipulation functions that you can use to store values in the class's members, retrieve member values, print, output, input, or otherwise manipulate its members.

A class also has a *destructor*, a function called whenever the class object is about to be destroyed. This function can take care of housekeeping, such as freeing any allocated memory.

Using a class requires you to determine, as well as you possibly can, what you will use for members in the class. You never have a problem adding members as needed or writing class functions to access new members; however, planning ahead helps prevent unchecked changes that can cause problems.

Listing C.8, EXAMP7.CPP, is a program that creates a class based on the database example program CREATEDB.C in Chapter 7, "C Structures." The CREATEDB.C program makes a database record for either a customer or a supplier.

Listing C.8. EXAMP7.CPP—Program showing C++ classes.

```
// Program EXAMP7.CPP, written 27 July 1992 by Peter D. Hipson
// Shows C++ classes, initialization, and so on.

#include <string.h>    // Used for strcpy(), str...(), etc.
#include <iostream.h>  // C++'s stream I/O header.

// Define your class structure, similar to those
// created in earlier chapters showing database techniques.

#define CUSTOMER_RECORD 1
#define SUPPLIER_RECORD 2

/* Define your structure for the customer database. */

class   Customer
{
public:
    Customer();              // The default constructor
    Customer(int nRecType,   // The class constructor
        char * szCustName,
        char * szAddr,
        double dSales);

    void GetCustomer();
    void PrintCustomer();    // Print a customer's information

    ~Customer();             // Destructor

private:

    int    nRecordType;
    char   szCustomerName[120];
    char   szAddress[120];
    double dCurrentSales;
```

continues

Listing C.8. continued

```
};

Customer::Customer()    // The class constructor, default values.
{
    nRecordType = CUSTOMER_RECORD;
    strcpy(szCustomerName, "-NONE-");
    strcpy(szAddress, "-NONE");
    dCurrentSales = 0.0;
}

Customer::Customer(int nRecType,    // The class constructor, explicit
                                    // values
        char * szCustName,
        char * szAddr,
        double dSales)
{
    nRecordType = nRecType;
    strcpy(szCustomerName, szCustName);
    strcpy(szAddress, szAddr);
    dCurrentSales = dSales;
}

void Customer::GetCustomer()
{
char szLine[2]; // Used to store a NEWLINE for cin.getline

// You get, from the console, the object's data values, using a simple
// multiline format:

    cout << "Enter '" << CUSTOMER_RECORD << "' for a Customer '" <<
        SUPPLIER_RECORD << "' for a supplier: ";
    cin  >> nRecordType;

// Below you don't use cin, but cin.getline, which gets all
// characters until the delimiting character (the optional third
// character). If the delimiting character is omitted, a
// newline is assumed. When getting input, cin.getline() does not
// retrieve more characters than the second parameter specifies,
// taking into consideration the ending NULL for the string.
```

```
        cin.getline(szLine, sizeof(szLine)); // discard NEWLINE from last
                                              // input.
        cout << "Enter the name: ";
        cin.getline(szCustomerName, sizeof(szCustomerName));

        cout << "Enter the address: ";
        cin.getline(szAddress, sizeof(szAddress));

        cout << "Enter the sales: ";
        cin  >> dCurrentSales;
    }


void Customer::PrintCustomer()
{
// You print the object's data values, using a simple
// multiline format:

        cout << "Type\t" << nRecordType << "\n" <<
            "Name\t" << szCustomerName << "\n" <<
            "Address\t" << szAddress << "\n" <<
            "Sales:\t" << dCurrentSales << "\n";
}


Customer::~Customer()
{
// Nothing done here. You don't have anything to do when the
// object is destroyed.
}


void    main()


{


// The first object is initialized with the default values.
Customer Customer1;

// The second object is initialized with explicit values.
Customer Customer2(CUSTOMER_RECORD, "John Smith", "New York, NY 10000",
                   1234.5);
```

continues

Listing C.8. continued

```
        Customer1.PrintCustomer();

        cout << "\n";

        Customer2.PrintCustomer();

        cout << "\n";

        Customer2.GetCustomer();

        cout << "\n";

        Customer2.PrintCustomer();

        cout << "\n";
}
```

In this program, you first create a class. Then you tell the compiler the class name and describe the class:

```
class  Customer
{
```

Following specification of the class name, describe those members in the class that are to be public. If a member is public, you can access it from the actual program; if a member is private, you can access it only from a function of the class.

```
public:
```

In the public section, declare two class constructors by overloading the class constructor function. This way, you create a default constructor with no parameters and a constructor that initializes the class to specified values. Then declare a function to get, from the keyboard, the class's data. You declare a function to print that data to the screen. You also create a class destructor.

Both the constructor and the destructor are required in creating a class. If you don't need these functions, you still must create a function that does nothing. A class constructor always has the same name as the class. The destructor also has the same name as the class, but is preceded by a ~ character.

```
Customer();              // The default constructor
Customer(int nRecType,   // The class constructor
    char * szCustName,
    char * szAddr,
    double dSales);

void GetCustomer();
void PrintCustomer();    // Print a customer's information
~Customer();             // Destructor
```

Well hidden from your actual program, in the private section, are the actual data objects for this class. You keep them hidden (by making them private) so the program cannot modify them directly, but instead can modify them only through a function of the class.

You define each variable just as you define a structure in C. Any data type is permissible, including other classes.

```
private:

    int     nRecordType;
    char    szCustomerName[120];
    char    szAddress[120];
    double  dCurrentSales;


};
```

Once the class is defined, you must provide the functions that are part of the class. You must define these functions after the definition of the class itself.

The first function you create is the class constructor that initializes the class's members to default values. These default values can be any that are appropriate for both the data's type and the application. Like a class destructor, a class constructor has neither a return value type nor a return statement.

```
Customer::Customer()    // The class constructor, default values.
{
    nRecordType = CUSTOMER_RECORD;
    strcpy(szCustomerName, "-NONE-");
    strcpy(szAddress, "-NONE");
    dCurrentSales = 0.0;
}
```

The next function is also a constructor (done by overloading the constructor function) that allows your program to specify the values to assign to the class's members.

```
Customer::Customer(int nRecType,    // The class constructor, explicit
                                    // values
        char * szCustName,
        char * szAddr,
        double dSales)
{
    nRecordType = nRecType;
    strcpy(szCustomerName, szCustName);
    strcpy(szAddress, szAddr);
    dCurrentSales = dSales;
}
```

You next define the class function that gets, from the keyboard, new values for the class's members. This function uses C++'s cin and cin.getline classes. Using cin for numeric values is fine; however for character string values, cin.getline is better because it limits the number of characters assigned and ignores any white-space characters in the input string. Class functions, other than constructors and destructors, can have return values. You can use these return values to indicate either success or failure of the function, or to return a class member's value.

```
void Customer::GetCustomer()
{
char szLine[2]; // Used to store a NEWLINE for cin.getline

// You get, from the console, the object's data values, using a simple
// multiline format:

    cout << "Enter '" << CUSTOMER_RECORD << "' for a Customer '" <<
        SUPPLIER_RECORD << "' for a supplier: ";
    cin  >> nRecordType;

// Below you don't use cin, but cin.getline, which gets all
// characters until the delimiting character (the optional third
// character). If the delimiting character is omitted, assume a
// newline. When getting input, cin.getline() does not
// retrieve more characters than the second parameter specifies,
// taking into account the ending NULL for the string.
```

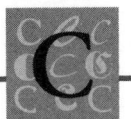

```
        cin.getline(szLine, sizeof(szLine)); // discard NEWLINE from last
                                             // input.
        cout << "Enter the name: ";
        cin.getline(szCustomerName, sizeof(szCustomerName));

        cout << "Enter the address: ";
        cin.getline(szAddress, sizeof(szAddress));

        cout << "Enter the sales: ";
        cin  >> dCurrentSales;
}
```

The next function prints the class's contents to the screen. You can also send the contents to a file, a communications port, and so on. This function is simple, using only cout to print.

```
void Customer::PrintCustomer()
{
// You print the object's data values, using a simple
// multiline format:

        cout << "Type\t" << nRecordType << "\n" <<
            "Name\t" << szCustomerName << "\n" <<
            "Address\t" << szAddress << "\n" <<
            "Sales:\t" << dCurrentSales << "\n";
}
```

The final function is the class destructor (which, like the constructor, is required). Because nothing must be done when the class object is destroyed, you simply return. Like a class constructor, a class destructor has neither a return value type nor a return statement.

```
Customer::~Customer()
{
// Nothing done here. You don't have anything to do when the
// object is destroyed.
}
```

Once you are skilled at using classes, you will find these features helpful. Proper use of class objects limits the potential for program errors by requiring accessing and modifying class members by using an interface layer of functions that perform error checks.

Function/Header File Cross Reference

The prototype for each function is in one or more header files. The following table lists the header file(s), whether the function is ANSI, and the function's prototype.

If the column labeled ANSI has no entry, the function is not part of the ANSI standard. Many compilers may offer this function; however, you must carefully check whether a given compiler supports the function as you expect.

Table D.1. Header/Function Cross Reference.

Header file(s)	ANSI	Function prototype
process.h & stdlib.h	ANSI	abort( )
math.h & stdlib.h	ANSI	abs( )

continues

Table D.1. continued

Header file(s)	ANSI	Function prototype
io.h		access( )
math.h	ANSI	acos( )
math.h		acosl( )
malloc.h		alloca( )
time.h	ANSI	asctime( )
math.h	ANSI	asin( )
math.h		asinl( )
assert.h	ANSI	assert( )
math.h	ANSI	atan( )
math.h	ANSI	atan2( )
math.h		atan2l( )
math.h		atanl( )
stdlib.h	ANSI	atexit( )
math.h & stdlib.h	ANSI	atof( )
stdlib.h	ANSI	atoi( )
stdlib.h	ANSI	atol( )
math.h & stdlib.h		atold( )
malloc.h		bcalloc( )
malloc.h		bexpand( )
malloc.h		bmalloc( )
malloc.h		brealloc( )
malloc.h		bfree( )
malloc.h		bfreeseg( )
malloc.h		bheapadd( )

Header file(s)	ANSI	Function prototype
malloc.h		bheapchk( )
malloc.h		bheapmin( )
malloc.h		bheapseg( )
malloc.h		bheapset( )
malloc.h		bheapwalk( )
malloc.h		bmsize( )
search.h & stdlib.h	ANSI	bsearch( )
math.h		cabs( )
math.h		cabsl( )
malloc.h & stdlib.h	ANSI	calloc( )
math.h	ANSI	ceil( )
math.h		ceill( )
process.h		cexit( )
conio.h		cgets( )
conio.h		cgets( )
direct.h		chdir( )
direct.h		chdrive( )
io.h		chmod( )
io.h		chsize( )
float.h		clear87( )
stdio.h	ANSI	clearerr( )
time.h	ANSI	clock( )
io.h		close( )
io.h		commit( )
float.h		control87( )

continues

725

Table D.1. continued

Header file(s)	ANSI	Function prototype
math.h	ANSI	`cos( )`
math.h	ANSI	`cosh( )`
math.h		`coshl( )`
math.h		`cosl( )`
conio.h		`cprintf( )`
conio.h		`cputs( )`
io.h		`creat( )`
conio.h		`cscanf( )`
time.h	ANSI	`ctime( )`
math.h		`dieeetomsbin( )`
time.h	ANSI	`difftime( )`
stdlib.h	ANSI	`div( )`
math.h		`dmsbintoieee( )`
io.h		`dup( )`
io.h		`dup2( )`
stdlib.h		`ecvt( )`
io.h		`eof( )`
process.h		`execl( )`
process.h		`execle( )`
process.h		`execlp( )`
process.h		`execlpe( )`
process.h		`execv( )`
process.h		`execve( )`
process.h		`execvp( )`

Header file(s)	ANSI	Function prototype
process.h		execvpe( )
process.h & stdlib.h	ANSI	exit( )
math.h	ANSI	exp( )
malloc.h		expand( )
math.h		expl( )
math.h	ANSI	fabs( )
math.h		fabsl( )
stdlib.h		fatexit( )
malloc.h		fcalloc( )
stdio.h	ANSI	fclose( )
stdio.h	ANSI	fcloseall( )
stdlib.h		fcvt( )
stdio.h		fdopen( )
stdio.h	ANSI	feof( )
stdio.h	ANSI	ferror( )
malloc.h		fexpand( )
stdio.h	ANSI	fflush( )
malloc.h		ffree( )
stdio.h	ANSI	fgetc( )
stdio.h		fgetchar( )
stdio.h	ANSI	fgetpos( )
stdio.h	ANSI	fgets( )
malloc.h		fheapchk( )
malloc.h		fheapmin( )
malloc.h		fheapset( )

continues

Table D.1. continued

Header file(s)	ANSI	Function prototype
malloc.h		fheapwalk( )
math.h		fieeetomsbin( )
stdio.h		filbuf( )
io.h		filelength( )
stdio.h		fileno( )
math.h	ANSI	floor( )
math.h		floorl( )
stdio.h		flsbuf( )
stdio.h		flushall( )
malloc.h		fmalloc( )
stdlib.h		fmblen( )
stdlib.h		fmbstowcs( )
stdlib.h		fmbtowc( )
memory.h & string.h		fmemccpy( )
memory.h & string.h		fmemchr( )
memory.h & string.h		fmemcmp( )
memory.h & string.h		fmemcpy( )
memory.h & string.h		fmemicmp( )
string.h		fmemmove( )
memory.h & string.h		fmemset( )
math.h	ANSI	fmod( )
math.h		fmodl( )
math.h		fmsbintoieee( )
malloc.h		fmsize( )

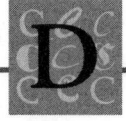

Header file(s)	ANSI	Function prototype
stdlib.h		fonexit( )
stdio.h	ANSI	fopen( )
float.h		fpreset( )
stdio.h	ANSI	fprintf( )
stdio.h	ANSI	fputc( )
stdio.h		fputchar( )
stdio.h	ANSI	fputs( )
stdio.h	ANSI	fread( )
malloc.h		frealloc( )
malloc.h & stdlib.h	ANSI	free( )
malloc.h		freect( )
stdio.h	ANSI	freopen( )
math.h	ANSI	frexp( )
math.h		frexpl( )
stdio.h	ANSI	fscanf( )
stdio.h	ANSI	fseek( )
stdio.h	ANSI	fsetpos( )
stdio.h		fsopen( )
string.h		fstrcat( )
string.h		fstrchr( )
string.h		fstrcmp( )
string.h		fstrcpy( )
string.h		fstrcspn( )
string.h		fstrdup( )
string.h		fstricmp( )

continues

Table D.1. continued

Header file(s)	ANSI	Function prototype
string.h		`fstrlen( )`
string.h		`fstrlwr( )`
string.h		`fstrncat( )`
string.h		`fstrncmp( )`
string.h		`fstrncpy( )`
string.h		`fstrnicmp( )`
string.h		`fstrnset( )`
string.h		`fstrpbrk( )`
string.h		`fstrrchr( )`
string.h		`fstrrev( )`
string.h		`fstrset( )`
string.h		`fstrspn( )`
string.h		`fstrstr( )`
string.h		`fstrtok( )`
string.h		`fstrupr( )`
stdio.h	ANSI	`ftell( )`
stdlib.h		`fullpath( )`
stdlib.h		`fwcstombs( )`
stdlib.h		`fwctomb( )`
stdio.h		`fwopen( )`
stdio.h	ANSI	`fwrite( )`
stdlib.h		`gcvt( )`
stdlib.h		`gcvt( )`
stdio.h	ANSI	`getc( )`

Header file(s)	ANSI	Function prototype
conio.h		getch( )
stdio.h	ANSI	getchar( )
conio.h		getche( )
direct.h		getcwd( )
direct.h		getdcwd( )
direct.h		getdrive( )
stdlib.h		getenv( )
process.h		getpid( )
stdio.h	ANSI	gets( )
stdio.h		getw( )
time.h	ANSI	gmtime( )
malloc.h		hugehalloc( )
malloc.h		heapadd( )
malloc.h		heapchk( )
malloc.h		heapmin( )
malloc.h		heapset( )
malloc.h		heapwalk( )
malloc.h		hfree( )
math.h		hypot( )
math.h		hypotl( )
conio.h		inp( )
conio.h		inpw( )
ctype.h	ANSI	isalnum( )
ctype.h	ANSI	isalpha( )
ctype.h		isascii( )

continues

Table D.1. continued

Header file(s)	ANSI	Function prototype
io.h		isatty( )
ctype.h	ANSI	iscntrl( )
ctype.h		iscsym( )
ctype.h		iscsymf( )
ctype.h	ANSI	isdigit( )
ctype.h	ANSI	isgraph( )
ctype.h	ANSI	islower( )
ctype.h	ANSI	isprint( )
ctype.h	ANSI	ispunct( )
ctype.h	ANSI	isspace( )
ctype.h	ANSI	isupper( )
ctype.h	ANSI	isxdigit( )
stdlib.h		itoa( )
math.h		j0( )
math.h		j0l( )
math.h		j1( )
math.h		j1l( )
math.h		jn( )
math.h		jnl( )
conio.h		kbhit( )
math.h & stdlib.h	ANSI	labs( )
math.h	ANSI	ldexp( )
math.h		ldexpl( )
stdlib.h	ANSI	ldiv( )

Header file(s)	ANSI	Function prototype
search.h		lfind( )
locale.h	ANSI	localeconv( )
time.h	ANSI	localtime( )
io.h		locking( )
math.h	ANSI	log( )
math.h	ANSI	log10( )
math.h		log10l( )
math.h		logl( )
setjmp.h	ANSI	longjmp( )
stdlib.h		lrotl( )
stdlib.h		lrotr( )
search.h		lsearch( )
io.h		lseek( )
stdlib.h		ltoa( )
stdlib.h		makepath( )
malloc.h & stdlib.h	ANSI	malloc( )
math.h		matherr( )
stdlib.h	ANSI	mblen( )
stdlib.h	ANSI	mbstowcs( )
stdlib.h	ANSI	mbtowc( )
malloc.h		memavl( )
memory.h & string.h		memccpy( )
memory.h & string.h	ANSI	memchr( )
memory.h & string.h	ANSI	memcmp( )
memory.h & string.h	ANSI	memcpy( )

continues

Table D.1. continued

Header file(s)	ANSI	Function prototype
memory.h & string.h		memicmp( )
malloc.h		memmax( )
string.h	ANSI	memmove( )
memory.h & string.h	ANSI	memset( )
direct.h		mkdir( )
direct.h		mkdir( )
io.h		mktemp( )
time.h	ANSI	mktime( )
math.h	ANSI	modf( )
math.h		modfl( )
memory.h & string.h		movedata( )
malloc.h		msize( )
malloc.h		ncalloc( )
malloc.h		nexpand( )
malloc.h		nfree( )
malloc.h		nheapchk( )
malloc.h		nheapmin( )
malloc.h		nheapset( )
malloc.h		nheapwalk( )
malloc.h		nmalloc( )
malloc.h		nmsize( )
malloc.h		nrealloc( )
string.h		nstrdup( )
stddef.h	ANSI	offsetof( )

Header file(s)	ANSI	Function prototype
stdlib.h		onexit( )
io.h		open( )
conio.h		outp( )
conio.h		outpw( )
stdio.h & stdlib.h	ANSI	perror( )
math.h	ANSI	pow( )
math.h		powl( )
stdio.h	ANSI	printf( )
stdio.h	ANSI	putc( )
conio.h		putch( )
stdio.h	ANSI	putchar( )
stdlib.h		putenv( )
stdio.h	ANSI	puts( )
stdio.h		putw( )
search.h & stdlib.h	ANSI	qsort( )
signal.h	ANSI	raise( )
stdlib.h	ANSI	rand( )
io.h		read( )
malloc.h & stdlib.h	ANSI	realloc( )
io.h & stdio.h	ANSI	remove( )
io.h & stdio.h	ANSI	rename( )
stdio.h	ANSI	rewind( )
direct.h		rmdir( )
stdio.h		rmtmp( )
stdlib.h		rotl( )

continues

Table D.1. continued

Header file(s)	ANSI	Function prototype
stdio.h	ANSI	scanf( )
stdlib.h		searchenv( )
stdio.h	ANSI	setbuf( )
setjmp.h	ANSI	setjmp( )
locale.h	ANSI	setlocale( )
io.h		setmode( )
stdio.h	ANSI	setvbuf( )
signal.h	ANSI	signal( )
math.h	ANSI	sin( )
math.h	ANSI	sinh( )
math.h		sinhl( )
math.h		sinl( )
stdio.h		snprintf( )
io.h		sopen( )
process.h		spawnl( )
process.h		spawnle( )
process.h		spawnlp( )
process.h		spawnlpe( )
process.h		spawnv( )
process.h		spawnve( )
process.h		spawnvp( )
process.h		spawnvpe( )
stdlib.h		splitpath( )
stdio.h	ANSI	sprintf( )

Header file(s)	ANSI	Function prototype
math.h	ANSI	sqrt( )
math.h		sqrtl( )
stdlib.h	ANSI	srand( )
stdio.h	ANSI	sscanf( )
malloc.h		stackavail( )
float.h		status87( )
string.h	ANSI	strcat( )
string.h	ANSI	strchr( )
string.h	ANSI	strcmp( )
string.h		strcmpi( )
string.h	ANSI	strcoll( )
string.h	ANSI	strcpy( )
string.h	ANSI	strcspn( )
time.h		strdate( )
string.h		strdup( )
string.h	ANSI	strerror( )
time.h	ANSI	strftime( )
string.h		stricmp( )
string.h	ANSI	strlen( )
string.h		strlwr( )
string.h	ANSI	strncat( )
string.h	ANSI	strncmp( )
string.h	ANSI	strncpy( )
string.h		strnicmp( )
string.h		strnset( )

continues

Table D.1. continued

Header file(s)	ANSI	Function prototype
string.h	ANSI	strpbrk( )
string.h	ANSI	strrchr( )
string.h		strrev( )
string.h		strset( )
string.h	ANSI	strspn( )
string.h	ANSI	strstr( )
time.h		strtime( )
stdlib.h	ANSI	strtod( )
string.h	ANSI	strtok( )
stdlib.h	ANSI	strtol( )
stdlib.h	ANSI	strtold( )
stdlib.h	ANSI	strtoul( )
string.h		strupr( )
string.h	ANSI	strxfrm( )
stdlib.h		swab( )
process.h & stdlib.h	ANSI	system( )
math.h	ANSI	tan( )
math.h	ANSI	tanh( )
math.h		tanhl( )
math.h		tanl( )
io.h		tell( )
stdio.h		tempnam( )

Header file(s)	ANSI	Function prototype
time.h	ANSI	`time( )`
stdio.h	ANSI	`tmpfile( )`
stdio.h	ANSI	`tmpnam( )`
ctype.h		`toascii( )`
ctype.h & stdlib.h	ANSI	`tolower( )`
ctype.h & stdlib.h	ANSI	`toupper( )`
time.h		`tzset( )`
stdlib.h		`ultoa( )`
io.h		`umask( )`
stdio.h	ANSI	`ungetc( )`
conio.h		`ungetch( )`
io.h & stdio.h		`unlink( )`
stdarg.h	ANSI	`va_arg( )`
stdarg.h	ANSI	`va_end( )`
stdarg.h	ANSI	`va_start( )`
stdio.h	ANSI	`vfprintf( )`
stdio.h	ANSI	`vprintf( )`
stdio.h		`vsnprintf( )`
stdio.h	ANSI	`vsprintf( )`
stdlib.h	ANSI	`wcstombs( )`
stdlib.h	ANSI	`wctomb( )`
io.h		`write( )`
math.h		`y0( )`

continues

739

Table D.1. continued

Header file(s)	ANSI	Function prototype
math.h		`y0l( )`
math.h		`y1( )`
math.h		`y1l( )`
math.h		`yn( )`
math.h		`ynl( )`

Index

A

F

lists, linked, 344-345
    disk-based, 346
    double, 346-347
    dynamic memory, 345
    linear searches, 367
literals, character, 623
lNumberRecords variable, 471
local
    memory, 247
    scope, 31
Locale parameter, 571
locale.h header file, 509-510
localeconv() function, 510, 553
localtime() function, 553
lOffset parameter, 542
log() function, 554
log10() function, 554
LOGICAL_FIELD identifier, 472
long double-floating-point constants, 27
long int constants, 26
long keyword, 9
long modifier, 20

LONG_MAX identifier, 22, 509
LONG_MIN identifier, 22, 509
longjmp() function, 512, 554
loop optimization, 663-664
low-level I/O, 278-280
_LOWER identifier, 502
LSB (baud rate divisor register), 300
lseek() function, 279
lValue parameter, 552

M

machines, state, 135-136
macro continuation operator (\), 622
macros
    _ _DATE _ _, 637
    _ _FILE _ _, 638
    _ _isascii(_c), 504
    _ _LINE _ _, 638
    _ _STDC _ _, 638
    _ _TIME _ _, 637
    _ _toascii(_c), 504
    _tolower(_c), 504
    _toupper(_c), 504
    assert(), 501, 650-652
    converting to strings, 622
    defining, 625
    isalnum(_c), 503
    isalpha(_c), 503
    iscntrl(_c), 503
    isdigit(_c), 503
    isgraph(_c), 503
    islower(_c), 503
    isprint(_c), 503
    ispunct(_c), 503
    isspace(_c), 503
    isupper(_c), 503
    isxdigit(_c), 503

O

T

W

X—Z

Installing the Disk

Advanced C comes with a disk that includes all the source code listings from the book plus additional utilities from the C Users' Group. To install the disk, follow these steps:

1. Create a DOS subdirectory named ADC to hold these files.

2. Copy all the files into C:\ADC.

3. Read the *read.me* file for the chapter breakdown of all the files. A separate subdirectory named TWOFILE contains the TWOFILE program, which is a multisource file program from Chapter 6.

4. The C Users' Group utilities are in a separate subdirectory called CUG236.

What's on the Disk?

Applications from the book including:

- A menu program that implements pulldown menus
- A dump program that dumps files providing a hexidecimal and ASCII listing of the file's content
- An arcade program that shows a simple arcade game
- A B-tree program that arranges data in a structure format

33 separate utilities, such as:

- Diagnostic helper
- C source code formatter
- Cross-reference generation utility
- Search and replace utility

The utilities on this disk are from the CUG236 disk provided by The C Users' Group Library. These utilities are a collection of very portable programs that compile and run with minimal hassle. William Colley III took these programs from other CUG library volumes, then edited, rewrote, and tested them to make them even more portable.